Clerical Ideology
in a Revolutionary Age

Latin American and Caribbean Series

Waking the Dictator
Veracruz, the Struggle for Federalism, and the Mexican Revolution, 1870–1927
Karl B. Koth

The Spirit of Hidalgo
The Mexican Revolution in Coahuila
Suzanne B. Pasztor
Co-published with Michigan State University Press

Clerical Ideology in a Revolutionary Age
The Guadalajara Church and the Idea of the Mexican Nation, 1788–1853
Brian F. Connaughton, translated by Mark Alan Healey
Co-published with University of Colorado Press

Monuments of Progress
Modernization and Public Health in Mexico City, 1876–1910
Claudia Agostoni
Co-published with University Press of Colorado
and Instituto de Investigaciones Históricas, UNAM

Latin American and Caribbean
Christon L. Archer, general editor

University of Calgary Press is pleased to be the publisher of a series that sheds light on historical and cultural topics in Latin America and the Caribbean. Works that challenge the canon in history, literature, and postcolonial studies in this area of the world make this series the only one of its kind in Canada. This series brings to print cutting-edge studies and research that redefine our understanding of historical and current issues in Latin America and the Caribbean.

CLERICAL IDEOLOGY
IN A REVOLUTIONARY AGE

The Guadalajara Church and the Idea of the Mexican Nation, 1788–1853

Brian F. Connaughton
Translated by Mark Alan Healey

University of
Calgary Press

University Press
of Colorado

University of Calgary Press
2500 University Drive NW
Calgary, Alberta
Canada T2N 1N4
www.uofcpress.com

University Press of Colorado
5589 Arapahoe Ave.
Boulder, CO 80303
U.S.A.
www.upcolorado.com

National Library of Canada Cataloguing in Publication Data

Connaughton Hanley, Brian Francis
  Clerical ideology in a revolutionary age: the Guadalajara church and the
  idea of the Mexican nation, 1788-1853 / Brian F. Connaughton; translated
  by Mark Alan Healey

(Latin American and Caribbean series 1498-2366 3)
Translation of: Ideologia y sociedad en Guadalajara (1788-1853)
Includes bibliographical references and index.

ISBN 1-55238-108-0 (bound) University of Calgary Press
ISBN 1-55238-083-1 (pbk.) University of Calgary Press
ISBN 0-87081-718-3 (bound) University Press of Colorado
ISBN 0-87081-732-9 (pbk.) University Press of Colorado

1. Church and state—Mexico—Guadalajara—History—19th century.
2. Catholic Church—Mexico—Guadalajara—History—19th century
3. Guadalajara (Mexico)—Church history.
4. Mexico—Politics and government—19th century.
I. Healey, Mark Alan, 1968-   II. Title.   III. Series.

BX1428.2.C5813 2002   322'.1'097235   C2002-911378-4

The Universidad Autónoma Metropolitana-Iztapalapa
graciously financed the translation of this book.

Canada 🍁

We acknowledge the financial support of the Government of Canada
through the Book Publishing Industry Development Program (BPIDP)
for our publishing activities.

The Canada Council for the Arts
Le Conseil des Arts du Canada

Printed and bound in Canada by AGMV Marquis.
∞ This book is printed on acid-free paper.

Page, cover design, and typesetting by Kristina Schuring.

The present book is a much-revised translation of *Ideología y sociedad en Guadalajara
(1788–1853)*, Mexico City: Consejo Nacional para la Cultura y las Artes, 1992.

Contents

Acknowledgments

I have become much more conscious of how interdependent we all are after writing this book. Roughly sixteen years ago, I told Dr. Enrique Florescano of my interest in the ideological life of nineteenth-century Mexico. With his encouragement, I began a journey which has become progressively more captivating and endless. I do not wish to blame him, but rather to offer my thanks.

Dr. Florescano sent me off to Guadalajara, to the Fondo de Misceláneas of the Biblioteca Pública del Estado de Jalisco. I had the opportunity there, and in the Archivo de Jalisco, to meet Dr. Carmen Castañeda, of whom Dr. Florescano had spoken so highly. I had long known that the directors of research archives are key people, indispensable for the development of any project. Here I confirmed this. It is impossible to say just how important Dr. Castañeda and her assistants have been for this study.

In similar fashion, my colleague Luis Humberto Olivera introduced me to the Colección Lafragua of Biblioteca Nacional in Mexico City. He gave me considerable advice and led me to Liborio Villagómez and Roberto Beristain, who also helped me with their knowledge and expertise.

On the long road between my entrance into these document collections and my decision to write down the results of my research, I received a great deal of help from a large number of people. I consulted Dr. Andrés Lira constantly on all aspects of the interpretation of the documents I was finding. Professor Lira guided this research as a dissertation director in order to fulfill the doctoral requirements of the program in Latin American Studies at the Universidad Nacional Autónoma de México. He and his wife Cecilia offered me a home on many trips I made to the Colegio de Michoacán, in Zamora, to receive guidance, constructive criticism, and in general a sympathetic hearing. Due to his formidable critical capacity, Dr. Lira forced me to strive for a higher level of analysis than I otherwise would have.

I had the good fortune to meet William Taylor in Guadalajara while he was researching topics similar to my own. During lunches, in various conversations, and later through correspondence, Professor Taylor offered me valuable suggestions on how to handle the material I was discovering. He freely and extensively shared with me the results of the research he was carrying out on the Mexican Church. Dr. Taylor critiqued this book chapter by chapter, contributing to the difficult task of evaluating documentary discoveries. This helped to prepare me more fully for the revisions of each chapter with Dr. Andrés Lira.

Special recognition is reserved for Dr. Álvaro Matute, then director of the Center for Foreign Students at UNAM. He gave me singular support, as well as understanding, to the point of giving me full institutional and personal backing and significant financial, moral, and professional assistance. The employees there were also always supportive of my research.

My colleagues in the Center for Foreign Students, in the Facultad de Filosofía y Letras of the UNAM, and in the Universidad Autónoma Metropolitana – Iztapalapa, as well as my students and immediate superiors, all had to deal with the highs and lows of this research. I was fortunate to experience their solidarity. In the Facultad de Filosofía y Letras, Dr. Norma de los Ríos, then coordinator of Latin American Studies, and her academic secretary, Dra. Carolina Ibarra, gave me continuous support. At the Universidad Autónoma Metropolitana – Iztapalapa, I received intellectual stimulation and indispensable administrative support from colleagues like Maestro Daniel Toledo and Maestra Norma Zubirán. Their help and understanding is sincerely appreciated.

Conversations I had at different points with Charles Hale, Richard Morse, Rosa de Lourdes Camelo Arredondo, Sergio Ortega Noriega, Luis Ramos, José María Muriá, the late Heriberto Moreno, Guillermo de la Peña and Jaime Olveda were crucial to broadening my perspective and resolving specific problems. When it seemed like this project would have to come to a stop

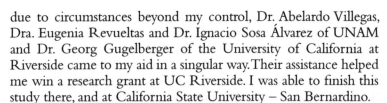

due to circumstances beyond my control, Dr. Abelardo Villegas, Dra. Eugenia Revueltas and Dr. Ignacio Sosa Álvarez of UNAM and Dr. Georg Gugelberger of the University of California at Riverside came to my aid in a singular way. Their assistance helped me win a research grant at UC Riverside. I was able to finish this study there, and at California State University – San Bernardino.

I owe a special debt to Dr. Leopoldo Zea, founder of Latin American Studies in the Facultad de Filosofía y Letras, UNAM. The constant support he and his wife, María Elena Rodríguez, have given me has been useful and stimulating. The Centro Coordinador y Difusor de Estudios Latinoamericanos, previously directed by Dr. Zea, has provided me with a forum for exploring my ideas. There Dr. Juan Manuel de la Serna and his wife Zoila granted me unlimited assistance. Other colleagues in the Center, especially Dr. Elsa Cecilia Frost, gave me their priceless friendship and understanding. Appreciable traces of all these good people are present here.

The educational and research institutions of Mexico City, Zamora, and Guadalajara, with their dynamism and cultural commitment, have provided me with a favorable setting for carrying out this study. By meeting with many Mexican and foreign colleagues, I was able to constantly enrich my own outlook. In the United States, the University of California and California State University systems also provided considerable help. The scholars and general libraries at several campuses, and the Bancroft and Sutro research collections at UC Berkeley and San Francisco State University, have been a constant stimulus. In addition to those already mentioned, I have also received friendly assistance from Dr. Eric Van Young, Dr. David Sweet, Dr. John Borrego, and Dr. Carlos Cortés, all colleagues at different campuses of the UC system. Their contributions are sincerely appreciated.

For the publication of this study in English I owe special thanks to Dr. Jaime E. Rodríguez, at the University of California – Irvine, and to Dr. Eric Van Young, at the University of California San Diego. Dr. Christon Archer and Dr. Walter Hildebrandt of the University of Calgary have given me crucial assistance in this regard. At the Universidad Autónoma Metropolitana – Iztapalapa I received enthusiastic support from the campus president Dr. Luis Mier y Terán Casanueva, and from other colleagues such as Dr. José Lema Labadie, Dr. Carlos Illades, Dr. Gustavo Leyva Martínez and Dr. Luz María Uhthoff López. I would also like to thank Dr. Gilbert Joseph of Yale University for suggesting a translator and Dr. Mark Alan Healey of New York University for his thoughtful and creative work in translating this book into English.

I want to express my deepest gratitude to my children Erik, Tania, and Marisa. They have been able to stoically put up with many difficulties during the long years of my research. I appreciate the constant understanding and love I have received from them. My brother Michael also gave me much needed help on several occasions, for which I would like to express my thanks here.

Finally, I would like to thank the late Marcos and Celia Mauss for the public recognition they gave this work, awarding it the prize as the best history dissertation presented to the Facultad de Filosofía y Letras of the UNAM in 1988, and to the Universidad Autónoma Metropolitana, which awarded the Spanish-language edition of this study the 1994 research prize.

Introduction

I t is well known that the periods of Mexican history least subject to the scrutiny of historians have been the seventeenth
century (roughly speaking, from 1630 to 1750) and the first
half of the nineteenth century (except for Independence).[1] Yet
there is a widespread sense that these periods might be key
to understanding the long-term structures and development of
Mexico. Far from the din of the century of conquests, the seventeenth century, with international trade fallen into a lull,
long seemed terrain unworthy of the heroic efforts of a serious
historian. Similarly, the nineteenth century had been trapped
between the fervor of the Enlightenment and Independence and
the fury of the War of Reform. The study of the first half-century of independent life – taken as a whole – seemed appropriate
only to intrepid souls wanting to lose themselves in a historio-
graphical maze.

Such intrepid historians have of course existed, and the success
of their efforts has underscored the possibilities of forging useful
knowledge from the studies of both periods. This study comes
out of the admiration inspired by reading several of these works.[2]
Since I began this research, numerous valuable works have been
published on the period stretching from the second half of the
eighteenth century to the first half of the nineteenth. William B.
Taylor has produced a magisterial study of the parish priests of
Indian villages covering the Bourbon Reforms and the beginnings of Independence.[3] An excellent collection of his essays
on the same period is about to be published.[4] Virginia Guedea,

Manuel Chust, Jaime Rodríguez and Josefina Vázquez have enor-
mously broadened our understanding of the transition from
the late colonial era to Independence.[5] François-Xavier Guerra,
Annick Lempérière and other have suggestively problematized
the ideological leanings of the regime being born then.[6] The
range of historical subjects worthy of analysis has been extended:
Peter Guardino, Florencia Mallon, Guy Thomson and Dorothy
Tanck have studied the centrality of peasants, and even of their
political discourse, to the period of transition and new life under
the republic.[7] Christon Archer, Antonio Serrano Ortega and Juan
Ortiz Escamilla have delved deeper into the world of soldiers and
militiamen.[8] Donald Stevens, Michael Costeloe, Richard Warren,
Eric Van Young, Antonio Annino, Marcello Carmagnani, Pedro
Pérez Herrero, Reynaldo Sordo and others have contributed to
clarifying the answers to questions about the first half of the
nineteenth century, and especially about the very nature of the
political regime.[9] It is also necessary to mention several sug-
gestive works, in addition to those of Taylor, recently published
about the Church in Mexico between the Bourbon Reforms and
Independence.[10] I trust that within a growing field of such distinguished authors, this book may still provide a fresh view of the
role the Mexican clergy played in that period, above all the high
clergy whose hegemony was subjected to singular stress by the
rise of new values and doctrines such as "popular sovereignty."

Some have suggested a new historical periodization for the
nineteenth century, positing the years between 1750 and 1850 as
a distinct period. This question of the appropriate time frames for
Mexican history has drawn my attention. It has strengthened my
desire to explore a period long and varied enough to be able to
test a traditional historical dividing line, in this case Independence.
Perhaps, for the study of the Church's role in Mexican history,
Independence may not be the definitive watershed it is usually
thought to be. At the same time, by including in a single study
what we frequently think of as the most and least heroic periods
of Mexican history (heroic Independence and the less-than-
heroic eras before and after), we may illuminate more sharply the
most enduring structures in the country's historical experience.[11]

Charles Hale has suggested that the best way to overcome
preconceptions – whether economic or cultural – about the
nineteenth century may be the direct "reconstruction of nineteenth-century politics." He adds that "this can be done most
effectively through the systematic and critical study of ideas."[12]

Hale warns historians against adopting the partisanship inherent to the period by making imprecise use of the political labels used at the time. He also insists that historians resist a deceptive sociologizing of the history of ideas which presumes to know the authors and the interests of the proponents of various ideas, without having analyzed those ideas in depth and examined their internal cohesiveness.

This in no way rules out referring to specific evidence about the socio-political behavior of the authors and groups responsible for ideas. But it does not assume such behavior without rigorous prior analysis. Hale insists that we must study ideology without prior partisanship, if we want to advance our knowledge of the period.[13]

The study of ideas does not mean adopting an idealist perspective in which ideas are equivalent to the totality – or the determining portion – of a historical reality. But it does mean that we still must study governance and formal institutions of social power, even in the nineteenth century when they have generally been seen as less important, in order to produce a historically rigorous analysis of the composition and social meaning of political ideas. Hale suggests that "the rationale or logic of central government policy and the assumptions of the governing elite are still so insufficiently understood as to warrant searching examination." He underlines the usefulness of the printed writings of intellectuals close to government circles, of statements in newspapers and official and semi-official pamphlets, and of laws and parliamentary debates, while not excluding unpublished manuscripts, although not considering them "intrinsically superior." He rejects the priority some wish to give to supposedly unique sources, instead emphasizing the absolute need to "grasp the intractable and often elusive nature of the assumptions" of the documents under study.[14]

To paraphrase Hale, we could say that we need to pay attention not only to the ideas being expressed but to how they are embedded in an implicit culture or historical situation, where ideas themselves are to some extent predetermined by sociocultural values or understandings which need to be specified. From another standpoint, Hale adds, this is the study of ideology, especially to the degree that "the *political* objective and *polemical* function of ideas ... make them ideological. Ideology ... presupposes conflict in society or the existence of conflicting interpretations of the social order." Insofar as a political program is associated with a rhetoric and program of its own, these are ideological, even when they draw on unifying or supposedly non-partisan traditions or myths. Hale suggests that handling ideological statements in a non-Manichean way requires a willingness to address the contradictory aspects and internal dialectics of each line of thinking.[15]

If we conceive of ideas in their social context as another dimension of the political action of individuals and groups, we cannot escape some reflection, however brief, on the nature of all human society. Richard Burks has stressed Alfred North Whitehead's idea that "no civilization can endure without transcendental goals."[16] Both religious and secular ideologies have a unifying function for their followers within society, giving them a global interpretation of history, a concrete theory of the social order, means for perpetuating themselves through education and self-promotion, significant popular support, and identification with a center of power, be it a party or the state. Although one could well assume the existence of illusory or deceptive elements in such ideologies, or of interests which could be "unmasked," such elements are not the only factors in explaining an ideology's success. In addition, the specific elements involved in a given ideology may well change over time, interacting with other constitutive elements.[17]

Stressing this last point, Georges Duby has stated that "all ideologies are 'practical' and therefore contribute to the movement of history. But by the very fact of this movement, they are themselves transformed."[18] He insists that there is enough correspondence between ideology and reality that a change in reality affects the transformation of ideology. In the struggle between the different groups existing in any society, or as an effect of demographic and economic changes and their political effects,

> Ideologies must adapt if they are to survive or win. In their struggle with opposing ideologies, they become more or less aggressive, affirm themselves more openly, or else take refuge behind some new facade. When they are in a dominant position, they partially absorb the images or models which threatened them, taming them and turning them to their own advantage.[19]

In Duby's words, "the stuff of the history of ideologies" is made up of "processes of struggle, revolt, incorporation and integration." Of particular importance for this study is the French historian's assurance that certain ideological systems are transformed

[w]hen the culture of which they are part is subjected to the influence of neighboring foreign cultures. This cultural penetration is frequently the result of an unequal balance of power between the civilisations in question.... [Frequently] it proceeds insidiously, through the distant attraction of foreign beliefs, ideas and ways of life. It can also be the result of deliberate borrowing, since ideologies will seek reinforcements from any quarter.[20]

In any case, the objective of studying ideology for Duby would be to trace its survival in the long term, to define not only "successive adaptations" but also "its influence on the overall development of social relations."[21]

The principal interest of this study will be to closely follow what one Spanish author has called the Church's struggle – from the late eighteenth to the mid-nineteenth century – to win "a public place after the eighteenth century revolutionary upheaval which threw the religious foundations of civil society into question, affirming the independence of civil society from the ecclesiastical institution." This was the "battle of a corporation to find new ways of establishing its social reach."[22]

This author rightly states that "the influence of the Church does not end with its own religious actions but extends to the furthest lay ideas, because of how Church actions have suffused the most diverse ideologies." By freeing the study of the Church from the framework of critique or apologetics, we can delve into the Church's internal organization and external influence as an organization or corporation within larger society. One crucial aspect of the study of this organization, although not the only one, is the activity of the ecclesiastical hierarchy commonly known as the high clergy.[23] Speaking specifically of the Spanish Church, this historian points out that one way the clergy kept much of its influence in the midst of a society undergoing secularization was by adopting strong nationalism:

> Nationalist ideology with its spiritualization of the concept of the *people* [not opposed to the religious meaning] was able to offer clerics the possibility of strengthening their pastoral ministry by means of priestly dedication to the human salvation of that people who appeared, as a people, to be threatened by the dominating drive of another cultural or ethnic community.[24]

Scholars need to go beyond tracking the Church's nuanced shifts of position on matters of divine absolutism, liberalism, traditionalism, and conservatism. They must reflect on the production of a clerical space which, interacting with the spheres just mentioned in a more creative way than is usually recognized, also managed to undergo its own version of the modern transition towards the dominion of the "people" over matters of state.[25] Furthermore, one could argue it could hardly have been otherwise. Considering that the task of the Church in the nineteenth century was to produce a space of its own within secularizing changes, it could not ultimately place itself at the margins of the emergence of popular sovereignty.

The people came to be "the obligatory reference, the source and standard for all politics after the 'ideals' ... of the glorious French Revolution resounded in Europe and across the world."[26]

The nation, conceived as "a single and homogeneous body [which receives and exercises sovereignty] ... by means of elected representatives," is the instrument by which the people assume sovereignty.[27] Thus the state became the only vehicle for sovereignty, and all owed it unquestionable loyalty, since it derived from the people and the nation.[28] Yet if the Church could dispute, in one particular case, whether national legislative representation effectively expressed the national will, then could that not be the basis for a broader challenge to the hegemony of the rising liberal state?

Since the eighteenth century, the Bourbon state in Mexico had been much less concerned than its Hapsburg predecessor with keeping the moral support of the Church. During the same period, regionalism and a clearer identification with local interests in the New World were on the rise.[29] With the advance of liberalism in the nineteenth century, a lay elite fought the Church for its hegemonic role, and the Church had many reasons to grow uncomfortable. If the Church could argue that the majority of the people, and national interests, were harmed by the measures of the liberal state, would that not lay the groundwork for arguing that the liberal state was an illegitimate spokesman for the nation? And if that were the case, the Church could well suggest that for a Catholic people, the Church was a more sure navigator than a handful of men smitten with the idea of making private interest into the ethical standard and goal for national political activity. Reaching that point meant the Church had implicitly and explicitly negated what one author has called the "general political anthropology" of liberalism, underscoring the crisis of the Church's adaptations to the new era.[30] Yet while this study will show that the Church reached this point, that does not negate what we have been arguing, namely, that the play of ideologies in the struggle for political hegemony always involves changes, even if at a certain moment those changes come to an end, or prove unable to go beyond certain limits without betraying their own origins.

In independent Mexico, just as in the Spanish Empire, the Church and the state were united in law and social practice. This obviously affected the structure of power, and limited "the impulses toward pluralism ... [and] subsystem autonomy." Thus, "aspirations for new types of prestige and status remained tied to pre-independence frameworks." We might say that the very internal weakness of the Church forced it to insist on continued union with the state because of its fear of not being able to maintain a viable position in society without state support. Because of its privileged role in the Ancien Regime, the Church had not developed full internal solidarity, nor did it enjoy widespread and well-informed support among parishioners, beyond ritual observance and routine orientations. "Consequently, when basic changes occurred in the political sphere, the Church did not possess bases of autonomous religious strength." Only legal assurances and alliance with political elites could compensate for this weakness.[31]

The Church proved adaptable to the new situation, but could never be dissuaded from looking for traditional political guarantees. It allied itself with those social forces willing to guarantee its existence as a corporation with a monopoly on religious and moral matters. Turned toward this struggle, it had difficulties in properly attending to the internal dynamics of its own integration. When the traditionalists and conservatives lost in the political arena, the Church found itself facing a difficult choice whose solution unfortunately falls outside of this study. But this does not counter Vallier's claim that "the Church is actually one of the most innovative and experimental of large-scale organizations, being continuously engaged in the process of sociological construction."[32]

Is there some way to measure the extent of these changes – and their impact on national life – in the nineteenth century Latin American Church, and specifically in the Mexican Church? Frederick Pike has concluded that the Latin American Church often joined in the liberal New World optimism which argued that the New World could avoid the ills of the Old, and even the rise of class conflict.[33] E. Bradford Burns has observed the confluence of liberal and conservative opinion in Latin America, including the Church in his observation that the essentially urban elites of Latin America were obliged to follow the course of European liberalism in order to guarantee their own survival. The speed of change was open to debate, but not the overall direction.[34] A closed conservatism like that attempted in some parts of Europe was simply unviable. While this argued for greater flexibility in the Mexican Church's adaptation to the changes during the period, Pike himself fundamentally agrees with Ivan Vallier. He determined that the Latin American Church ultimately followed the course of Spanish Catholicism, commenting that in the latter case:

> Theological pluralism, the give-and-take competition between religious ideas, became inescapably associated with social pluralism, the unregulated competition among different social classes and functional interest groups in which the right of a permanent elitist directing group to exercise a never-to-be questioned moderating power was not recognized. This association between theological and social pluralism helped doom the cause of religious diversity....[35]

Howard Wiarda has interpreted such limitations on the Church's ability to adapt as a Latin American inheritance of Spanish corporatist tradition. He sums up this tradition's implications as follows, looking forward to the twentieth century:

> Along with the rejection of liberalism went the rejection of its institutional accoutrements. The need for unity and authority was at cross purposes with checks and balances and a coequal parliament. Divisive political parties would be replaced by a single movement. Since society's interests were to be represented functionally, competitive elections were no longer necessary. Civil liberties would be respected, but they could also be limited for the common good. While these changes would likely serve to expand the power of the central state, the creation of corporate intermediary structures and the revitalization of society's natural associations (family, community, guilds, etc.) would provide for decentralization and limits on state power.[36]

But however much corporatist tradition the Church had, after Independence it found itself openly competing for the loyalties of its fellow Mexicans. Speaking of Mexican Independence, Hugh

Hamill discovered that after 1808 even the propagandists most opposed to changes along the lines of the French Revolution proved to be "fearful of radical change, yet inventive in communicating traditional values."[37] The character Hamill studied was capable of ferocious and radically traditionalist rhetoric, but even in the midst of the anti-Independence counterrevolution he made use of a wide range of arguments, diverse sources – including even modern experts – and he did not refuse to speak of the "wise Benedictine Feijóo."[38] His thinking was even able to respond to the socio-racial worries of Mexicans, going so far on one occasion as to state:

> There is no dignity or honor, however high it may be, which cannot be had and enjoyed by a loyal Indian, and even the child of an Indian man and a Spanish woman, or of a Spanish man and an Indian woman.[39]

One might say that it is by combining ideology with the desire to preserve the status quo, while admitting the fewest possible changes, that the phenomenon of traditionalism or conservatism in the broadest sense emerges. More than one author has cited Count Metternich's statement that "la stabilité n'est pas l'immobilité."[40] Mayer argues that

> In ordinary times conservatives can afford to be purely practical and empirical in defense of the established order, while claiming special credit for being antidoctrinaire and above partisan politics. In times of crisis, however, the logic of their position forces them into joining, condoning, or supporting those advocating an antirevolutionary prophylaxis that is both ideological and aggressive.[41]

According to Mayer, while a distinction can be made between ideological conservatives – who tend towards reaction and counterrevolution – and pragmatic ones, at times of crisis there are often attempts to fuse these different currents. Given the complexity of the matter, only increased by the variety of possible concrete settings, the relative shortage of works on this theme is unfortunate. Mayer recognizes, by the way, that once a revolutionary change has taken place somewhere, "the mere existence of a model is enough to stimulate political actors to locate themselves in relation to it by positive, qualified, or negative imitation."[42]

Until now, the most impressive effort to study conservatism in Mexico was that of Gastón García Cantú. García Cantú confesses, however, in a note preceding the text of his book, that "I am far from having fulfilled my objective. This is only an attempt."[43] If one gives any credit to the idea that there was opposition to the liberal transformation of nineteenth-century Mexico, then undertaking a new attempt would seem appropriate. In so doing, it might seem most appropriate to draw close to the corporation that has been most accused of leading reaction, traditionalism, conservatism or counterrevolution in Mexico at the time. Bourbon absolutism contained a good portion of anti-clericalism and secularization of political power. Liberalism took the same tendencies much further. Thus it would be only natural for an institution under siege, at first partly, and later completely, to be inclined to try to block the changes threatening it. Yet it is imperative, returning to the point made by Hale, that we not assume beforehand what research into the historical phenomenon seeks to discover and reveal. Or to put it in the words of a theorist: "no subject is constituted outside of the [historical] process."[44]

If the Mexican Church was indeed at the center of effort to hold back a historical change raising the secular state and the earthly ends of man to new importance, and if the Mexican Church was indeed opposed to a more plural and atomized vision of civil society in relation with the national state, than that is precisely what must be proven, taking the broadest possible view of the historical forces of the time.[45] However much the Church represents a key organization in Mexican society, and however much it does have a certain accumulated ideological tradition, we must think of it within the setting of a specific time and place if our analysis is to remain historical. The Church is part of a larger whole, and we should observe not only the internal variety and evolution of its actions, but also its efforts to reach out to elements which did not necessarily share its social interests. One scholar has put it well:

> Hegemonic action would be that constellation of political and cultural practices carried out by a fundamental class by means of which that class manages to articulate other social groups beneath its control through the construction of a collective will which translates its corporatist interests into universal ones, partially sacrificing them along the way. This implies a process of political constitution of classes which cannot be seen outside an analysis of the balance of forces and the history of social practices expressed on an organizational level.[46]

In the Mexican case, we could well claim that the structure of the concrete "historical bloc" presumably articulated by the Church still remains to be clearly determined. Insofar as the overall analytical structures for studying colonial Mexican and Latin American society have become uncertain, we must discard any possibility of resolving this question easily. While this is unsettling, it also may impel us to drawing closer to the specific characteristics of the concrete historical structures of Mexican society.[47] This may yield very positive results for historiography.

Some time ago, Karl Mannheim wrote:

> [The modern researcher] will no longer be inclined to raise the question as to which of the contending parties has truth on its side, but rather he will direct his attention to discovering the approximate truth as it emerges in the course of historical development out of the complex social process. The modern investigator can answer, if he is accused of evading the problem of what is truth, that the indirect approach to truth through social history will in the end be more fruitful than a direct logical attack. Even though he does not discover 'truth itself', he will discover the cultural setting and many hitherto unknown 'circumstances' which are relevant to the discovery of truth. As a matter of fact, if we believe that we already have the truth, we will lose interest in obtaining those very insights which might lead us to an approximate understanding of the situation. It is precisely our uncertainty which brings us a good deal closer to reality than was possible in former periods which had faith in the absolute.
>
> The study of intellectual history can and must be pursued in a manner which will see in the sequence and co-existence of phenomena more than mere accidental relationships, and will seek to discover in the totality of the historical complex the role, significance, and meaning of each component element.[48]

The goal of the analysis that follows is to study the struggle of the Mexican Catholic Church, particularly the high clergy of the Guadalajara diocese, to maintain its hegemony against the waves of Bourbon secularization, to sustain order in the midst of social upheaval, and to preserve ecclesiastical privilege as the theory of popular sovereignty redefined the nation. In so doing, Guadalajara clergymen transformed a respectable tradition of regional patriotism into a transcendent vision of Mexico's destiny as a nation. The critical element that they developed was that of Providence as the motor of Mexican history.

How did the divine will come to play this complex political role? David Brading, in particular, has enriched the study of the seventeenth and eighteenth centuries with his important contribution to the understanding of how the notion of God-given destiny worked its way into the intimate fibers of a nascent sense of Mexico's uniqueness within the Spanish Empire and indeed within the divine plan for human salvation.[49] His analysis has centered on the Virgin of Guadalupe and the rise of a precocious search for identity among key clerical thinkers that clearly anticipates national consciousness in Mexico. In so doing he has deepened our knowledge of the once-forgotten seventeenth century and linked its events to the formation of a burgeoning Creole group awareness that prefigured a growing Mexican national identity through the eighteenth and into the early nineteenth century.

My own study has led me to believe that understandings of the meaning of Providence in Mexican history were by no means tied exclusively to the Guadalupe tradition. Moreover, for many years after 1810 the notion of providential destiny was in dispute and far from fully woven into the political fabric of the nation. Although it is well known that Father Miguel Hidalgo made a significant statement in bringing the banner of the Virgin of Guadalupe to the fore in his cry to end bad government and improve Mexico's collective destiny, the political content of his movement was by no means fully worked out. Bishop-elect Manuel Abad y Queipo of the Diocese of Michoacán believed, by contrast, that providence was tied to his own grand project of a bicontinental Spanish nation.[50] After 1815 the popular insurrection in Mexico would be violently repressed, allowing for its remnants to be swept along by a much more politically conservative, elite-led independence movement under Agustín de Iturbide in 1821. Certainly a strong notion of Mexico's God-given role in Christian civilization was present in the movement of 1821 and the years following. But the Virgin of Guadalupe does not appear, in my study, to displace a broader Marian devotion and concern with God's plan, the precise political significance of which was still being decided in the decades under analysis in this book.

A free press and a wider public debate after independence allowed for the challenging of fundamental political and social beliefs in the decades after 1821. Churchmen in Mexico often perceived that Christian norms, as they understood them, were coming under increasing attack. They felt compelled to define the relationship between divine transcendence and national destiny and to exercise a key role in debating the goals of the nation and their legal expression. In their opposition to the secularization of the state and of social mores, clerical writers grappled with the introduction of an individualistic, opinionated liberalism which on the basis of resounding abstract principles would re-order society with little respect for the past. In fact, speaking with growing assurance that they represented the best interests of a sovereign people, Jacobin liberals advocated ecclesiastical and religious, as well as civil, reform. Faced with a challenge to their authority as churchmen and social spokesmen, clerics tended to strike back by appealing to the liberal notion of constitution and law as bulwarks against arbitrary attacks on Church interests, and increasingly to a sense of the free will and the purportedly Catholic views of a Mexican nation. As they built the sense of a providential Catholic nation into this political discourse by the 1830s and 1840s, clerics did not consistently or exclusively have recourse to the Virgin of Guadalupe. In the 1840s, a Christ-centered notion of providentiality in Mexico's history was emphasized by some to counter conservative Christian leanings and promote the idea of an intimate connection between Christian liberation from sin and the political renewal promoted by liberalism. More research has to be done on both Marianism and Christo-centric thought in Mexican Catholicism.[51]

As this research develops, it is necessary to re-open the whole question of the formation of Mexican nationalism and the role played therein by providential Christianity as developed by clerical or even non-clerical thinkers. The divine dispensation may have been contemplated differently in different regions and by different groups in Mexico. For example, in a recent study on Puebla I have shown how not only providential thinking but also holistic religious thought permeated civic discourse there and was promoted by it. It has seemed to me that a region such as Puebla was more susceptible than others to an organic metaphor – such as the "body," the "family," or the "mystical body of Christ" – for social life because of long-standing ethnic conflict and economic decline which threatened the coherence and the peace of local society.[52] Guadalajara, by contrast, was a relatively more uniform Creole-mestizo society, with strong individualistic qualities and a generalized sense of economic and social improvement as well within the grasp of the immediate future. Regional outlook seemed to gravitate towards optimism rather than border on despair.[53] Guadalajara churchmen seemed to connect to this climate of optimism even in their attacks on secularization and "Jacobin" liberalism. The holistic approach, while not absent, seems less developed there. Contrary to imagining the national community as a secular experience, however, as Benedict Anderson would have us expect,[54] these clerics conceived of a commonwealth whose progress was a Christian pageant most faithfully reflecting the deep-felt beliefs and desires of the people. This was not a simple story of Mexico having been chosen once and for all above other nations; it was rather a pact in which Mexico must merit its place in the divine scheme: Mexico must stand out by standing up for certain Christian goals. Clerics clearly developed the idea that this was fully compatible with representational government; after all, the people of Mexico were seen as steadfast in their Christian commitment, even while a handful of politicians might be pushing a vastly different agenda. If only the nation's desires were represented transparently by its politicians! Guadalajara optimism brought forth a peculiar synthesis of liberal and providential thinking, here. The national community was imagined in religious and civic terms simultaneously.

Churchmen in Mexico after Independence coupled, in Anderson's terms, an anachronistic "Messianic time, a simultaneity of past and future in an instantaneous present" to the modern "homogeneous, empty time" of the clock and calendar which allowed them to compare Mexico with developments in the United States and Europe.[55] The providential pact between the Mexican people and God was seen as ethically and religiously undergirding Mexico's desire to progress and stand out in the international sphere. Mexican churchmen and their allies wrote in ways that appealed to a broad audience with whom participation in national values could be shared through satire and laughter, not just through high-minded goals. Mexican nationalism of the 1830s and 1840s in many ways looked like Anderson's "last wave" Third World nationalism after World War Two – still uncertain, still inheriting colonial modes of conduct and views, enjoying at best a troubled hegemony, still lacking public institutions and a school system to disseminate a national project which was still too Creole in a largely mestizo and Indian population.[56] But both Churchmen and Catholic laymen in Guadalajara were actively involved in responding to the calls of nationhood and citizenship, now understandable only within the liberal-leaning climate of the Cádiz Constitution of 1812 and then the Mexican Constitution of 1824. However, even in Guadalajara there were moments in which ecclesiastical nationalism looked strangely like the "official nationalism" which Anderson studies in nineteenth-century Europe: a response by privileged pressure groups to current political and nationalist demands to avoid exclusion or marginalization.[57]

While such a preemptive corporate ethos was present, focus on it alone does not do justice to a larger process of Catholic adjustment to change. Even the early national awareness promoted by the insurgency under Hidalgo and Morelos borrowed from a long-standing Spanish Catholic identity, setting it on its ear by determining that Spain had fumbled this identity under French influence.[58] The insurgent newspaper during Father Hidalgo's stay in Guadalajara, *El Despertador Americano*, referred to the French threat in religious terms, crying out against Americans who had been deceived by Napoleon's overtures toward the New World:

> What hurts the most is that, when all is said and done, in the bitterness and chains of your oppression you will not have the solace of the Catholic religion, which [even] in the loss of your freedom and other temporal belongings would have encouraged you with the hope of eternity. Do not be deceived, oh perverted Americans, all countries dominated by the monsters aborted by the Corcegan will sooner or later be touched by the contagion of atheism which they profess, and which those Despots have spread.[59]

El Despertador Americano went back to this topic again and again. In its second issue it reminded readers that "we count on the declared patronage of Holy Mother of Guadalupe, Protective Guide of this Empire, and Sworn Captain of our legions."[60] In its fourth issue it chided Spanish policy for having succumbed to French materialism and dared to attack the Church. The rejection of secular oppression was followed by bitter comment against taxes on Bulls granting indulgences and the loosening of Lenten observance. The newspaper added:

> "Have not even the goods of brotherhoods, [as well as] the funds of Wills, Chaplaincies and Pious Works of all sorts been placed on public auction, to ship their earnings back to the Metropolis? Have not the precious jewels of our Churches been despoiled only to disappear for ever from our sight?"[61]

Such ideas opened the way for the advance of a providential notion of Mexico's national role, already prefigured in the Guadalupe tradition, which the independence under Iturbide could not pass over lightly. Yet the use of Guadalupe to divide Mexican society between Creole and peninsular Spaniards in the insurgency may have impeded her use as an exclusive symbol of providential destiny after 1821. As Lucas Alamán would later suggest, caste war was much feared in Mexico down to the 1850s, and the appropriation of the banner of the Virgin of Guadalupe had been associated with a bloody civil war in which Spaniards were mercilessly pursued.[62]

By elaborating on a providential notion of the Mexican nation, then, churchmen were responding to, as much as leading, the quest for Mexican national identity. In Mexico, clerical nationalism was not tied to dynastic or even governmental interests. In fact it represented a growing breach within the Creole establishment wherein Church-related intellectuals argued that government and society were drifting toward secularism and menacing both Church wealth and Church spiritual leadership in a Catholic Mexican society. Nationalism as promoted by clergymen thus aimed at re-sacralizing Mexican bonds of community and elevating common destiny to a sense of mission. While this was grounded in clerical conviction regarding the non-Jacobin character of the Mexican people, and thus hoped to ensure ecclesiastical presence in society and constitutional guarantees for the clergy in the polity, this nationalism contributed to an imagining of the Mexican nation as a community under law, bound by a territorial – if not ethnic – past and destined for a sovereign, national future of increasing social and economic improvement. In this view, accountability of elected authority was a primary topic, and thus all public representatives were responsible to the nation.

In this way, Mexican clerics helped form a composite nationalism which is as much a response to the legacy of the French Revolution as it is a manipulative or hide-bound reaction by a vested interest. Clerical nationalism assuredly benefited from the past of bureaucratic pilgrimage and the viceregal print culture in Spanish – as Anderson would suggest – since they contributed to bonds of identity related to what was to become, approximately, the Mexican national territory. But it dug deeply into the history of providentialism that David Brading has studied through the Virgin of Guadalupe tradition and which William Taylor has persuasively shown to be growing dynamically through the eighteenth century in the mestizo center-north and north of the country.[63] Clergymen and their allies were continuing the process of imagining begun long before in quite different circumstances. They chose, or chose not, to emphasize the Virgin of Guadalupe, but their notion of a national destiny under an accountable, lawful government was not simply manipulation, although it indeed was developed in response to a need to protect Christian and ecclesiastical interests.

It may be that Guadalajara played a particularly relevant role in this process because of the active political participation in Cádiz and the Constituent Congess of 1823 by prominent local clergymen, and their often outspoken identification with the goals of federated states (for example, Jalisco and Zacatecas) and the independent nation. Canons José Miguel Gordoa, Diego Aranda, José Miguel Ramírez and José Domingo Sánchez Reza had significant experience within this political tradition. Gordoa and Aranda would become bishops of Guadalajara. The wording of their published documents can be read as a complex response to the dual demand of loyalty both to a cherished political tradition and to Church interests as they saw them. They can also be read as reflecting a more self-confident regional attitude that emphasized the present and the future. Dutifully respectful of the past, many Guadalajara churchmen were not slaves to it.

In this sense, the Guadalajara Church must be seen within the polemics of Mediterranean Catholic society over internal reform of the Church and the place of the papacy and the state within this process, not only within the turbulence of Bourbon reforms and Mexican independence. Since the Church Council in Pistoia, Italy, in 1786, political reformers and religious reformers had tended to be very closely associated in Spain itself,[64] and there is a complex history of how this thinking made its way into Mexico over the next few decades, a history largely still to be written.[65] Despite massive Mexican rejection of secularization or impiety as French in origin, the Pistoia tradition is clearly present in Mexico by the 1820s. The Church's response to this threat in Guadalajara brought it into the public forum to protect its values and interests in a way which led it to imagine and promote nationalism. It did so, as Lomnitz has said in his remarks on Anderson's view of nationalism, "not as an ideology, but rather as a hegemonic, commonsensical, and tacitly shared cultural construct."[66]

Clerical nationalism in Guadalajara is not unparalleled and there is a global context; Adrian Hastings has tellingly found the role of religion to be integral to the history of "ethnicity and construction of nations."[67] Central to Hastings view of nationhood is the development of a "self-conscious community" which is creating "a horizontally bonded society to whom the state in a sense belongs," all within a community characterized by "an extensively used vernacular literature."[68] A sense of threat to the "proper character" of the community can be part of this. Beyond any definitive secular–religious divide, Hastings sees "Biblical Christianity" providing a model for the development of a sense of nationhood, emphasizing "a unity of people, language, religion, territory and government."[69] In his view, whereas a state can be instrumental in creating it, a nation "is not a nation until it senses its primacy over and against the state."[70] In fact, Hastings sees religion as potentially crucial in this regard, observing as he does the "defiant power of a nationalism grounded in religious identity."[71]

In the Mexican case, William Taylor has shown how eighteenth-century parish priests helped to weld Indian parishioners into a body politic that transcended Mexico City.[72] And in independent Mexico, parish priests were considered such bellwethers of popular opinion as to have their conduct carefully monitored by government authorities.[73] Priests, including Fathers Hidalgo and Morelos, were very much at the center of Mexicans' imaginings of themselves as a people. Indeed, not only priests but bishops and canons were at the heart of determining the sense of national "holiness and special destiny," to use Hastings' words again.[74] Although later historical events profoundly transformed and secularized this identity, it would be safe to follow Hastings' caution that "one must not be deceived into thinking … that modernised, secularized forms of nationalism in any way represent its beginning." In the eyes of this English historian, the enduring strength of a nationalism to transport the nation through thick and thin is related to this "religious rock" on which nationalism is generally founded.[75]

Although later to be partially superseded by a more secular legal and nationalist development during and after the Mexican Reforma starting in the 1850s, the promotion of early Mexican nationhood is very much a part of events related to the commonsense perception of the Mexican community as eminently Catholic. Catholic nationalism in Guadalajara was an attempt to shore up Mexican national identity on one side of the divide represented by the Council of Pistoia. Diocesan churchmen claimed popular support for Church autonomy, exclusively Church-led

– not state-directed – ecclesiastical reforms and the defense of Church interests as corresponding to the constitutional rights of citizens and to Mexico as a Catholic nation. In so doing, they were juggling contrary traditions. While ultimately not triumphant, bowed by the deepening and popularizing of liberal reformism, this nationalist Church discourse built off and contributed to an ongoing sense of Mexican identity as distinct from the state, tied to constitutional guarantees, embracing a broad territory and competing in a complex but distinctive way with cultural, social, economic and political models in Europe and in the United States. Although it is generally assumed that modern Mexican nationalism is a secular product of nineteenth-century liberalism, it may be more appropriate to see it as forged by these contrary forces of Christian fulfillment and secular liberal commitments, and perched on the horns of its own dilemmas.

As José Gutiérrez Estrada made clear, the war with the United States would bring national survival to the fore in all political debate.[76] Even liberals would be faced with the need to reckon with the nation's complex past, which made the implant of liberal institutions extremely difficult or impossible. Church opposition to anti-clerical liberalism in the press and in government had in fact promoted the forum of public opinion, with writers on one side and the other aiming their discourse at a national audience. Down to the time of the war with the United States, liberal authors seemed more concerned to catch up with progressive countries in Europe and the United States; they rarely if ever developed the national question as a distinctive issue. From the mid-Forties they would have to modify their outlook and show that liberalism was indeed more conducive to Mexico's social fiber and future well-being than anything social conservatism or monarchy could offer. The question they never could fully address was Catholicism and its role in Mexican nationhood. Ultimately, this would become a moot question after the Constitution of 1857 eliminated any reference to an official religion.

Understandably, however, many Mexican liberals and conservatives were moving in the direction of a pragmatic political culture in which survival of the nation was a preoccupation. Erika Pani may be right to argue that it is a fallacy to think that the convergence of such thinking around the Second Empire, followed by its defeat, was the end of such an orientation.[77] Not only would triumphant liberals become more conservative, as Charles Hale has argued,[78] and more authoritarian, as Pani and Laurens Perry[79] have suggested, but they would be noticeably concerned with the survival and celebration of the nation.[80] But it may have only been in the twentieth century that public nationalism truly displaced Church-led collective identity. According to Claudio Lomnitz,

> In the Porfirian arrangement, schools and patriotic festivals were mainly organized by and for regional elites, and the church still provided the broadest arena for the political assertion of collective force in its fiestas. It is only after the revolution, with the decline in the coercive power of local politicians and the introduction of competitive sports, that the civic fiesta became a forum in any way comparable to the church fiesta, and, interestingly, it is only at this point that rural schoolteachers mustered the local support they need to really expand the school system with the tight budgets that they have always had.[81]

It remains to be seen whether Mexican religious nationalism has been superseded by its secular successor, or whether indeed there still is a complex mix within Mexican nationhood of two distinctive projections of what it means to be Mexican. Do the strengths of Mexican nationalism come from the "religious rock" of its origins, or do they proceed from the liberal and libertarian tradition so clearly identified with the figure of Benito Juárez? More telling, are these two traditions separable in any attempt to explain the composition and the internal tensions of Mexican livelihood as a national experience? Are they always antagonistic? Did Mexican Catholic nationalism cease to stoke the fires of national imaginings of the nation after the liberal Reforma triumphed over the Second Empire in 1867? Has it done so now? Are we dealing with leftovers, or with live coals within a living tradition?

1

A Framework for Studying Clerical Ideology in Guadalajara

Clerical Ideology in a Time of Change

Clerical ideology played an important role in the complex cultural transition Mexico underwent from the late eighteenth to early nineteenth centuries. This study aims to accurately situate clerical ideology in relation to the social, economic and political transformation promoted by both the Enlightened absolutism of the late colonial regime and the new, independent state born in 1821. The first step is setting out an overall framework.

This period was marked by deep changes and the transformation or reformation of the ruling groups of society. Therefore, we should think about clerical ideology in the context of the changes produced in ideological hegemony. What new interests were effectively expressed in the ideological sphere? How much did inherited ideological patterns change? How much room was there to re-accommodate the interests emerging from new ideological forms?[1]

In the pre-Bourbon status quo, the union of secular and religious power was laid down as the foundation of society. The effective exercise of royal patronage kept these two forces in delicate balance. The Church kept its autonomy on matters of faith; the state took up its authority by guiding suitable appointments. The Catholic state based its legitimacy on the support provided by the Church. Nearly a co-ruler, the Church watched over

the state in many ways, and was directly entrusted with preserving orthodoxy in morals and doctrine. The relationship between
Church and state was rightly symbolized by repeated declarations
of the union of "throne and altar."[2]

Beginning with the eighteenth-century Bourbon reforms,
Spanish-American society underwent increasing secularization in
the standards and assumptions of collective behavior. Considered
"decadent" by many inside and outside the Iberian peninsula,
Spain responded to its international marginalization with a progressively more ambitious and systematic program of changes and
transformations. The bourgeoisie, long subordinated within the
structure of imperial power, became a valued and protected element of society. The strength of rival foreign powers was seen as
a product of their potent bourgeoisies and their efficient systems
of production and distribution. To become their equal, absolutist
Spain set out to alter the internal make-up of imperial power. This
sparked – among other things – a process of secularization of the
core institutions and values of society.[3] When independence was
achieved in 1821, the declaration of popular sovereignty caused
the ideological make-up of Mexican society – already undergoing
secularization – to be subjected to intense and open questioning
of unprecedented depth and frankness. The ideological unmaking
and remaking of the state, of state power in its most basic sense,
was accompanied by a period of singular critiques proposing radical transformations.[4]

For the purposes of this study, the ideological production of
this period (from the late eighteenth to the mid nineteenth
century) should be seen as part of the complex linkage of the
Hispanic world to the most "advanced" northern parts of Western
Europe. Overcoming "decadence" and developing untapped or
neglected resources set the tenor for the period. Equally important was the new and unprecedented phenomenon of a growing
number of lay people, inside government and out, asking questions and offering answers about the basic make-up of society.[5]
This was not just a matter of minor or technical proposals, but
of wide-ranging and deep examinations which began with the
ills that afflicted and weakened Hispanic society – as opposed to
foreign powers. The crumbling of the Hapsburg Empire made
critiques of its failings come to be prized. Independent Mexico
would inherit this crisis of remaking state power from the late
Spanish Empire.

The Bourbon monarchy had harvested this growing unease, and attempted to guide it to new ends. Clerics and statesmen in particular, from Feijóo to Campomanes, had subjected everything to questioning. They had proposed – with some differences of opinion – that the future of the Hispanic world had to significantly break with its past, lest the misfortunes of that past be repeated, which would be intolerable. This questioning was broadened, popularized and extended by political crisis, and its result, in nineteenth-century Mexico, was the shattering of any comfortable and triumphalist traditionalism – like that which might have characterized the prideful and buoyant Spain and Hispanic America of the Renaissance.[6] The weakness of the Spanish state was seen as rooted in the nature of Spanish society and its economic and cultural practices. The overall make-up of society was inevitably problematized. Giving priority to the role of the bourgeoisie, secularizing the state, downgrading the corporations in favor of a single citizenship status, consolidating mechanisms for popular representation and promoting practical and general education became tasks for social development from the eighteenth century forward. Their place in independent Mexico is the logical, although conflicted, sequel to the crisis of the Spanish Empire.[7]

The Church was at the center of the debate, both as a participant and as a subject. Its role in the dialectic of change between society and the state should not be underestimated. This was a crisis of assumptions about the social life of man, an ideological and cultural crisis which affected the foundations of the social edifice and its possible state organization. Should the social achievements of man be governed by reason and free will inspired by self-interest, or should they be subject to a collective ideal which effectively overruled individual or group experience? In the latter case, a special body should be entrusted with spreading the vision of a collective life and setting and enforcing standards for socially acceptable behavior. The traditional Western response to this problem had been religion preserved by a jealous hierarchy. This avoided many problems concerning the relationship between society and the state. As an English thinker put it as late as the end of the eighteenth century: "He who worships God in spirit and truth will love the government and laws which protect him without asking by whom they are administered."[8] From this viewpoint, the laws governing collective life reflect and protect that life. Particular interests cannot be imposed, but must first be debated and incorporated by a government which acts as arbiter over the supposedly harmonious whole of society. The Hispanic variant of this vision took the form of a society ordered into bodies and estates, within a supposedly organic whole, governed by accepted laws and customs under an absolutist monarchy.[9]

Orienting the society of the eighteenth and nineteenth-century Hispanic world towards a more open approach to worldly life meant fundamentally changing the core standards and assumptions of societal behavior.[10] This step was taken on behalf of the bourgeoisie, rather than directed by it. Naturally, it also affected any ideas of the state pertaining to worldly existence. No longer to be seen as a passing means to an other-worldly end, worldly pursuits would now be seen as ends in themselves. Instead of representing and adjusting an organic whole made up of corporate bodies and estates, the state would become the instrument for remaking society. By changing the legal and moral codes of society, the state would come to represent the collective interests of citizen-individuals. The conservation of the organic whole would give way to the promotion of individual interests as the assumed guide for state conduct.[11]

Scholars have too often assumed that clerical ideology foolishly opposed this historical moment. Yet the survival of clerical ideology would seem to challenge this interpretation. The documents analyzed for this period in this study do not suggest any stuffy narrowness of thinking, or any retreat by clerical ideology, either intellectually or emotionally, as an *overall response* by the Church to the winds of change. In addition, it is singularly important to note that during the entire period under study – and until 1856 – the standards and legal framework keeping the Church joined to the state remained in force. Clerical discourse had the advantage of being able to take for granted the survival of a legal framework which favored it. So long as the Church did not fight for complete reaction, the established order reserved a privileged space for it at the core of society, despite the growing rise of ideologies calling for social change and the making of a single, anti-corporatist citizenship. The Church could employ this privileged space to influence changes, to moderate them, and sometimes even to eliminate them.[12]

Regional Pressures as Ideological Factors

As the center of an emerging but still peripheral region, Guadalajara could hardly aspire to merely keep the cultural and social structures of the past alive. The well-being of the city and its region depended on present and future gains. The past could be a starting point, but never a fixed goal. That is why it is important to examine the role of traditionalism in Mexican life in a region in an open process of transformation and consolidation. Clerical ideology, generally identified with traditionalism, was in particular tension on this point. Traditionalism, in this sense, was not only associated with keeping the Church bound to the state, but also with a vision of society as an organic and harmonious whole whose structure and hierarchy were protected by inherited cultural values. Traditionalism was characterized by emphasis on otherworldly religious themes and eternal values, rather than worldly social behavior and the pursuit of "progress."[13]

Guadalajara was a recently formed region where the Bourbon reforms had driven notable economic growth. It is likely that the anti-corporatist spirit of the reforms benefited the region rather than harming it. The attack on the interests of the merchant guild in Mexico City redounded to the benefit of commerce in Guadalajara. There was no solid guild tradition in Guadalajara and its industries accelerated around 1770 without resorting to that corporatist system.[14]

Far from the Atlantic and the threat of the English, and therefore a less vulnerable center of the Spanish Empire, Guadalajara seems to have experienced relatively little of the Bourbon reforms' component of anti-Creole suspicion. Creoles had achieved a level of political participation in the *audiencia* of Guadalajara far above what was customary in the capital of the viceroyalty. Even though this participation declined in this period, it spurred notable social and economic ties between Spaniards and Creoles.[15] Regional energies were fueled by transformations and did not experience the weakening produced by a strong division between Creoles and Spaniards. If an entrepreneurial spirit was going to be more prized than before, that was a good sign for the region.

The traditional corporation with the deepest roots in Guadalajara was the Church. Within this institution, at the end of the colonial period, Spaniards and Creoles commonly associated with each other. The outstanding personalities of the Church, without distinction, gave the warmest of welcomes to the implementation of Bourbon reforms in Guadalajara, *explicitly* because of what they promised in terms of regional development. In this way, Guadalajara became a singularly favored zone of America on the verge of Independence. It was a region where the firmest institutional base of the old order – the Church – aimed to identify itself with the forces of change. This began during the period of Bourbon absolutism and, although it underwent major changes after 1810, continued afterwards. The Church did not give up on its attempts to connect to social change, even after Independence and the proclamation of popular sovereignty as the political basis of the country.[16]

Forging the Region

Just as the *audiencia* of Guadalajara was originally created subject to the authority of the viceroy in the capital, so the regional economy was subjected to the ups and downs of the hegemonic center in Mexico. New Galicia was born dependent, economically and politically, on the controlling forces of Mexico City. The capital gave Guadalajara political orders and economic goods, receiving and distributing its major product, different kinds of livestock (cattle, mules and horses).[17]

During the sixteenth and seventeenth centuries, the Guadalajara region had no possibility of forming its own economic space, or a semi-autonomous territory, within the great internal market of the Viceroyalty presided over by the merchant guild [*consulado*] of Mexico, formed in 1592. It is even doubtful whether we can speak organically of a region, since centrifugal forces wrested from Guadalajara whatever hegemony it may have coveted.

Yet by contrast, the course of the eighteenth century was shaped by the growing consolidation of a regional internal market based on the expanding population of the capital of Guadalajara. Between 1700 and 1800, city residents increased six times in number, reaching 28,000 in 1793, 35,000 in 1803 and 40,000 in 1821. Guadalajara came to be the third city in the Viceroyalty, and the population of its hinterland supported this prominence. Very important processes took place, especially in the fifty years before Independence. While available data do not allow definitive conclusions, it seems that the intendancy of Guadalajara came to occupy first place, or close behind, in economic growth.

Extensive cattle raising was set up on the coast, while the eastern reaches of the territory consolidated a specialization in mule and horse raising. A transition towards intensive agriculture took place in a wide zone bordering Guadalajara, due to the city's growing demands.

In the midst of so many changes, all of society underwent a deep shift. With the mobilization of productive resources, disputes over borders between towns, or between towns and haciendas, became common. The demographic growth of the area outran the possibilities of labor absorption due to agricultural growth. As available land became scarce, the excess rural population faced a difficult situation. Peasants suffered from a more unequal distribution of natural resources within their own communities. Social difficulties aided in increasing artesanal production, a compensating activity at this critical socioeconomic moment. Similarly, crime, banditry and vagrancy also increased, clear indices of a hardly promising sociological outlook. With their subsistence threatened, more peasants hired themselves out for work on the haciendas. At the same time, the haciendas consolidated their control over the supply of food to the city. New investments and the expansion of areas cultivated directly by landowners pushed sharecroppers aside.

Yet while the most unprotected sectors of society went through difficult times, businessmen saw their luck improve. Hacienda activity was stabilized by the economic strengthening due to the nearby urban market. The commercial groups providing credit for agricultural activity and local distribution of goods prospered. Their political star shone ever brighter as they increased their presence in the municipal government of Guadalajara and achieved the establishment of a merchant guild there in 1795. No longer a mere stopping point for supplying California and Sonora, the port of San Blas was cleared for international commerce in 1796, which also favored the commercial groups. Mining in the intendancy was now in open decline, but despite that it did not cease to contribute to the making of great fortunes. The booming mining centers outside the region continued to be a powerful drive to local production of cattle, certain manufactured goods, and even agricultural products, all of which were to the benefit of commercial interests.

Ideology and Society

Ideological reactions to the changes in Guadalajara society were varied. City life required an economic and political regulation which was qualitatively different from earlier eras. Regional culture was promoted by the founding of a university, a printing press, and a theater towards the end of the eighteenth century. Problems of excess population and urban crowding were addressed by the creation of a new hospice and hospital and the building of housing under the bishop's auspices. In 1812 a mint was built to ease commerce, and in 1821 a patriotic society was created to contribute to "progress." Even before Independence, there were attempts at industrial development with capital and technical innovations. Civil and ecclesiastical authorities looked favorably on the spread of manufacturing, seen as providing useful work and creating jobs. Attempts at manufacturing would reappear during the national period.[18]

The Church still represented a key channel in the ideological continuity of Mexican society at the time. The critical thinking of *prominent clerics* in Guadalajara society did not only represent the interests of a privileged group.[19] The clergy identified with the groups responsible for key transformations of the heart of society in order to influence political, economic and social change. We could say that what the Church in Guadalajara went through between 1790 and 1853 represented the crisis of its hegemony over a changing world. Clerical discourse, eminently social at every moment, was transformed by an ideological trend which only became clear at the end. The objective of clerical discourse was to overcome the swift fragmentation of society, the product of both economic growth and the greater prominence of lay critics in public affairs, by reaffirming an organic vision of social order as one and indivisible. Within this order, the clergy would maintain a vitally important role.

Such a reformulation was something to be won, not an automatic result. It had to respond to the growing complexity of a region subject to growth and consolidation which, for that very reason, was undergoing processes of social breakdown.

Secular ideologies – especially those of foreign inspiration – presented important challenges to the Church's struggle for social hegemony. As a result, it should not surprise us that in the midst of these internal ideological reformulations carried out by the members of the clergy, important schisms appeared within the ecclesiastical hierarchy itself. The lack of a homogenous clerical response to the crisis became more serious and evident as the need to reorient the sociopolitical setting became crucial. It is worth stressing that because royal absolutism had begun the change, later losing out to the political and economic forces of Mexico, the Church never had the opportunity to present a clear or totally opposed alternative to the change underway.

Since the beginning of the last decade of the eighteenth century, the ecclesiastical hierarchy of Guadalajara had taken full part in the regionalist drive that promoted and reflected the social and economic restructuring of the area. It solidly supported the creation of the local university and the formation of the merchant guild. The high clergy debuted a new language for both, making allusions to natural rights and civil society based on property rights. They did not fail to speak of clerical abuses and of superstition as being opposed to true religion. Yet at the same time, they showed reticence towards the drive to restructure the Church along more modern and politically submissive lines which had originated in royal circles, and not directly with the clergy itself. Even so, the Enlightened clerics of the 1790s were ready to put up with the frustrations that went along with bringing their country up to date. Modernization was identified with a prosperity that both Church and society needed. In addition, Christianity would expand into new territory and reformulate the relationship between the temporal and the spiritual, between science and theology. All this was seen as a worthwhile gain.[20]

In this period, the Church was still sure of itself in social life and the ideological sphere. Its discourse was optimistic and frankly positive. It mediated between the government and the governed with the assurance of being listened to. In keeping with the royalist tone of the 1753 Concordat and the 1771 Fourth Mexican Council, the Church obviously conceived of itself as a participant in an important change of direction for the Empire and for its region.[21] Prosperity and greater competitiveness were fundamental for all of the Spanish Empire: the King, the Church and the people. The new businessmen, assertive regional interests and new knowledge were all allies in religious and imperial development. They were thought of as complementary, rather than opposed.

In the years after 1810, the ideological discourse of the prominent clergy of Guadalajara indicated a notable change towards the spirit of progress of the time. To be sure, the sociopolitical context had already changed. The introduction of Bourbon reforms in the intendancy in those twenty years had not only promoted greater economic prosperity, but it had also intensified the materialism and scientific pretensions of the well-off. On the other hand, it had also sharpened certain social antagonisms. The ecclesiastical hierarchy had changed after the deaths of Bishop Alcalde and his immediate successor in the mid-1790s. Now the hierarchy raised new questions, or raised old doubts formerly silenced, about the possibilities of social progress. By then, the French Revolution was a menacing backdrop. Napoleon's invasion of the Iberian Peninsula in 1808 intensified the dilemmas of the Guadalajara clergy, and the consolidation of Independence would only continue to deepen them.[22]

Throughout the period under study, however, the Church in Guadalajara refused to take a passive attitude towards the changes generated at the heart of society. It always demonstrated a certain ability to find points of contact between opposing social outlooks. Certainly this was something of a historical necessity if it wanted to preserve the vital role of the clergy as an intermediary in social conflicts and as the bond ensuring the coexistence of opposing interests. The difficulty of achieving this increased as royal absolutism was beaten back, and the doctrine of popular sovereignty managed to replace it, from Independence forward. In this sense, the period between 1810 and 1821 is a watershed in the clerical discourse of Guadalajara. Even between 1825 and 1831, when it lacked a bishop, the Guadalajara Church continued to struggle to adapt to the changes taking place. By first carefully marking religious terrain off from political terrain, then insisting on the organic whole that the "nation" represented, the Church attempted to demonstrate both its steadfastness and the vitality of its message for the social well-being of the country.[23]

The Ecclesiastical Body
From the Ideology of Accommodation
to Concrete Historical Change

This study looks at the clergy as an ecclesiastical institution, a "body" endowed with an ideological power initially intertwined with absolutist royal power. Immersed in the crisis of the Imperial state, it found itself implicated in the remaking of the power and therefore the international viability of the Spanish Empire. The intendancy of Guadalajara stood out as a thriving new region, and therefore offered an ideal site to test the reformist drive of the clergy. Beyond this local factor, another factor was no less important. Throughout this process, the effective exercise of royal patronage influenced the advancement of appropriate clerical figures, because appointments to positions in the clerical hierarchy implied a recognition of political loyalty. The struggles after Independence over the effective exercise of this patronage by the newborn Mexican state aimed to preserve this balance of power.[24] The Mexican state was destined to lose this struggle, it is true, but the clergy would not cease to grapple with new directions in society and the state, despite this conflict. Indeed, the clergy would persist in its drive to coordinate and reflect the hegemonic interests of regionalism and nationalism, as well as to dominate the more narrowly political–ideological field.[25]

Yet certain aspects of this should not be overlooked. From the beginning, regionalism in the intendancy of Guadalajara opened up the possibility of going beyond a mere renewal within the Empire. It was associated with the emergence of new groups and a new awareness of identity. Although this would not clash directly with Bourbon reformism before 1810, it would do so afterwards. In fact, regionalism and the Mexican nationalism that historically went along with it would end up giving abstract liberal individualism a geographic and horizontal expression. Gradually connecting up with doctrines like popular sovereignty and the individual pursuit of self-interest, regionalism and nationalism threatened to break apart the organic unity of Mexican society, which until then had been a mere segment of Hispanic Imperial unity. Even without the effective exercise of patronage by the new Mexican state, the clergy could not dodge the complexity of this societal change. It found itself obliged to offer a view that went beyond the mere negation of new trends. From the end of the eighteenth century until 1853, its efforts were neither insignificant nor unimportant to the future history of Mexico, and they await detailed study.

We could associate liberalism with a certain break with the values of the past. By contrast, clerical ideology was always distinguished by its spirit of order, discipline and reverence towards the memory of things past. It did not deny change, but it required change to more clearly pass through mediations.[26] It explicitly supported the state as the preferred authority for this task of directing change. It strove to avoid religious or civil questioning which might threaten to destabilize the harmony of the social collective. When disputes arose between social sectors or even between the civil and ecclesiastical bureaucracy, these were to be treated as administrative or perhaps jurisdictional matters, but never as deep disagreements. By contrast, both Enlightened absolutism and liberalism promoted a greater split between the secular and the spiritual and a weakening of traditional social arrangements. They shared an openly critical attitude towards the past.[27]

As long as the traditional alliance of Church and state lasted, civil non-conformity was accepted and tolerated. But open civil dissent was not, as its spread might have threatened the peculiar unity of political and spiritual society. The difference may appear minimal, but it was crucial. The organic social whole still took precedence over the individual. Nevertheless, one should not lose sight of the decreasing naturalness of this over the course of the seventeenth and eighteenth centuries due to the multiplication of spontaneous or deliberate changes. This is when the long-delayed dispute between the Church and the state comes to the fore. Non-aristocratic social forces strove to fortify their position in the state at the expense of the status quo and the syncretic regime which until then had been the peculiar response of Spain and New Spain to the emergence of new forces within society. The Mexican Church was not ready to accept a radical liberal and individualist redefinition of the state, nor was it prepared to separate civil and religious society, sundering political and religious unity. It fought to impose metaphysical ideals on society, reinforcing the old alliance between Church and state, between Church and society, and between various social sectors and the state. From the viewpoint the Church repeatedly expressed, the civil government may have been supreme in secular matters, but the Church continued to set the ultimate goals of all of society on a transcendent plane. Together, the state and the Church would promote the unity of society.[28]

According to its way of thinking, the Church was the moral and intellectual leader of state and society. Yet it would see its successes become progressively more fleeting and partial. The eighteenth century and the Bourbon reforms placed the status quo under tension and in question. The decline of the metropolitan economy spurred attempts to achieve a swift, guided change. The result was a dangerous balancing game, taking place within a new and stimulating tension. The half-measures came to an end when Napoleonic France decided to advance on Spain in 1808 and completely subdue the Spanish Empire. From this historical circumstance, there emerged an archipelago of nations – and regions – of Latin America. And each fragment of the worn-out Spanish Empire would face the same challenge as the discarded metropolis: change or repeat? To adopt popular sovereignty, or to remain faithful to a sovereignty which was colonial, metropolitan, and – in the final instance – divine and distant from human view? Adopting popular sovereignty meant facing a threatening situation in which the multiple voices of a heterogeneous people were pulling social unity apart and questioning the authority of not only the royal sovereign, but also his historical ally, the Church. The importance of work in society could later be framed in terms of a human "progress" hardly oriented towards clerical consecration. In the face of such unknowns, the Mexican Church had to take a stand.[29]

The nineteenth century in Mexico was marked by economic recession, open or latent civil war, and a tenacious dispute at the top of society to set the ideological framework to find a path out of the crisis. Society was opened up by the force of the blows dealt by groups and individuals demanding a voice and a vote. This itself was a sign of the breakdown of the status quo. But at the same time, the majority of the population could not fully take part in social debates, even though they did suffer from the experience of society's failures and reshaping. The majority of the people were still poor, ignorant and far from the effective exercise of political power. Although overall social discontent seems to have intensified, those who could channel it effectively were part of a privileged minority whose social models were divided between periodically updated traditionalism and some adaptation of Northern European liberalism. Thus the crisis of breaking colonial ties and definitively forming a new nation was an extension of the crisis of the Catholic Hispanic world. The rupture of colonialism cracked and partly broke up the corporatist society of castes centered around royal absolutism. But Mexico was still far from being able to genuinely remake society as a collection of individualized citizens, with effectively equal rights, each one openly pursuing his sovereign personal interest.[30]

What this implied for the possible structure of the new society would only emerge over time, and after bitter struggles.

Of course, Mexican society was only nominally aristocratic-monarchical in the European sense.[31] Following the fleeting empire of Iturbide, the republican form of government was generally accepted, and it only lost its absolute hegemony after the debacle of the war with the United States.[32] Yet throughout this period, the clergy and the Church were granted a privileged space in society. Calling into question the role of religion and the Church in society seemed to threaten a nationality which was still weak and could hardly withstand more surgery than it had already undergone – or was undergoing – and still remain strong and unified against outside threats. But there was a great ambivalence. If priority was given to the surviving legal, administrative and cultural ties vital to linking society and the state, then only unavoidable changes should be undertaken, and even these should only be done slowly and cautiously. But if, on the other hand, priority was given to the need to bring up to date the representativeness of government and the distribution of wealth, in order to promote a new individualist and classist basis for society, then national sovereignty in the form of *popular* sovereignty should be given substance as quickly as possible. In that case, the aim would be a unity of compromise and convenience based on the notion of an explicit and reformable social contract.[33]

The first approach underscored the social role of the Church in national life, pointing towards an organic, indissoluble unity, forged in a past that was still partly sacrosanct. That unity was perpetuated more through tradition, cultural norms, and bureaucratic authority than through open acceptance or interest, strictly speaking. In practice, the rejection of past Spanish rule was mitigated by administrative routine and by the real hegemony of the Church in interpreting past and present social life for most of the population. The danger was that this vision might not offer a swift and predictable resolution of national problems, and that it might sacrifice the strengthening of citizen participation and republican virtues for a passing strength forged from the dangerous denial of unsatisfied interests. The opposing vision also held its dangers. Based on an optimism that trusted in the national ability to quickly and deeply heal three centuries of difficult colonial history, it could hardly guarantee avoiding the socially divisive tendencies of rational individualism among a supremely heterogeneous people. Thus it is hardly strange that the initial period of self-government should be based on a fragile and perhaps desperate attempt at compromise. In this transition, popular sovereignty was checked first by monarchical principles, and later by a republicanism closely tied to the Church.[34]

In any case, whatever their ideological preferences, the old corporatist bodies of the Army and the Church were not all that had survived within society. The old confraternities of artisans and peasants also endured, the rural townships were intact despite some changes, the universities still sheltered those privileged by erudition, and the land owners and urban businessmen – who had never required a noble title to exercise their hegemony – continued to hold a status unreachable by the great majority. Society was still structured by behavior which required something more than mere liberal individualism to reasonably coordinate the interests of the whole. This is surely what guaranteed that ideological projects were always, whatever their premises, accompanied by a certain pragmatism designed to ensure their effectiveness in historically specific ways. The ideology of change, first absolutist and later liberal, never overcame the dilemma this implied.[35] Moreover, it made headway among governing sectors – statesmen, lawyers, those aspiring to popularly elected posts – but it left most of society intact. The autonomy and ideological viability of ecclesiastical institutions remained safe for a long time. Social discourse reflected this compromise with reality, and helped prevent a definitive reformulation of society and the state.

Clerical Pamphleteering
A Measure of the Continuities and New Possibilities of an Era

Drawing closer to actual society leads us to study the formation of the Mexican nation and the forging of Mexican nationalism as specific historical processes. Symptomatically, the clergy was very much present in both processes. Under Spanish colonial power, the formation of the nation was as an underlying and undesired process, and of course nationalism was officially ruled out. Following the national declaration of Independence in 1821, the tradition of submission to Spain, the presence of many Iberians in Mexico, and the Holy Alliance's support for Spanish recovery of its American colonies all underscored the dangers threatening the Mexican nation during the 1820s and 1830s. With the fading of the Spanish threat at the end of the 1830s, the specter of United States expansionism emerged with the breaking away of Texas in 1836. Foreign diplomatic challenges were evident throughout the period, accompanied each time by threats of internal breakup produced by the form of state organization and the ideological make-up of the nation. Although optimism was the dominant national attitude after the declaration of Independence, disillusion rapidly set in and the frustration and

perplexity produced by multiple failures was followed by bitter
and dark pessimism after the war with the United States in 1847.
These were not the adequate circumstances, externally or inter-
nally, for effective cohesion of the forces of change.[36]

Nevertheless, with Mexican Independence and the strengthening of liberalism, there began a period suddenly based on a
single clear set of ideological perspectives. Institutions and values
should be based on singular principles guided by the rights and
duties of an egalitarian citizen. In an incipient way, this society
was becoming more plural so that social actors might become the
representatives and agents of change. But the 1824 Constitution
was only moderately liberal. It perpetuated the alliance of Church
and state which, rooted in the Hapsburg past, had managed to
survive the reformist absolutism of the Bourbons. Could such
an agreement withstand the popular movement the most radical
wing of liberal constitutionalism would lead in later years? Clerical
ideology was more accustomed to social discussions about the
speed and opportune moment of change than to debates about
basic principles whose living embodiment was the historic alliance between Church and state. Thus, it was only partly ready
for the new direction of public debates. But it would prove to
be much more prepared than one might think, as available documentation from Guadalajara shows.

The aim of this study is to allow the ideological moments
of social discourse to be defined by the thrusts and parries of
the pamphlets of the time. This points us towards those sectors
of the population who were able to read and write, and who
were closely tied to political power. They could intervene in the
processes which clearly defined the place of politics in society,
publishing ideas and refuting those of their opponents. While this
is a minuscule segment of the social whole, we must not forget
that this is precisely the segment which set society's guidelines in
terms of culture, politics, and social and economic standards, and
set them all the more strongly the less effective democracy
there was. This is the segment which exercised the intellectual
control of structures hegemonic over the rest of the population
and made checkered claims to reflecting and representing the
interests of the whole. Spokesmen for the ruling institutions, or
self-appointed spokesmen for transforming or preserving them,
they were knights in a battle aimed to shape the destiny of all.

The clerical propagandists treated here are a particular portion
of these elites. Close reading will allow us to more clearly identify

many of the authors of the pamphlets analyzed here. Further bio-bibliographic research would undoubtedly reveal their positions high in the clerical ranks, or their aspiration to such positions. But that is not the path I have chosen to follow here, out of a conviction that it is more important to place emphasis on discourse than on men. For the analytical aims pursued here, it is more useful to stress the plasticity and adaptability of polemics than the supposedly unchanging nature of interests. This "decentering of the subject" of history allows us to follow how discourse itself "constitutes individuals as subjects." Such subjectivities "do not refer back to ... a substance, but rather to a position which can be occupied by different individuals." From this standpoint, what is in dispute is not only goods, posts, or specific influences, but how such goods, such posts, and such influences are seen and understood by members of society. There is no greater or better guardian of order than the consensus of public opinion.[37]

One should very much keep in mind that freedom of the press was only established in 1812. From that year, it followed an erratic course until the declaration of the republic in 1824. With the coming of the republic, freedom of the press came to an entirely new legal and effective fullness. Even though censorship on religious matters had not yet been lifted, the point where politics ended and religion began could never be specified. That is why there was such effective freedom of the press that accusations of licentiousness were frequent and widespread. Since this was a "popular government," a "government of the people," the Mexican civil authorities did not generally dare to control the free expression of ideas. So there flourished everywhere the varied attitudes and opinions of a people becoming sovereign through the exercise of an authority whose existence required no more justification than the mere fact of being Mexican. In addition, Mexicanness was felt to be fully universal, without any barriers to hold it back or reduce it to the level of a provincial or minor experience. It is precisely in pamphlets where one can clearly sense that national independence included a popular revolt in Mexicans' perceptions of themselves. These sharp dynamics of the period give it a moving vitality which even today impresses anyone interested in the constitution and reconstitution of the country.[38]

Prior to full freedom of the press, the hegemony of conservative pamphlets over material published in Guadalajara was indisputable – except for the decrees and a newspaper issued during the brief government Hidalgo formed there(late November 1810 to mid-January 1811). A wide range of publications appeared, but sermons and pastoral letters made up the key pamphlets of the period for the purposes of this study. It is worth pointing out that the counterinsurgency launched a newspaper – albeit a short-lived one – which during the brief constitutionalist period tried to form an alliance between localist forces striving for rapid provincial expansion and the larger forces of Iberian colonialism.[39]

After 1821, the very same ideological writings associated with the exercise of political sovereignty produced an expansion of the genres in print. In these pamphlets, the roles of the central and regional governments were discussed, and all kinds of constitutional debates took place between the various pamphlets and newspapers. Clerical publications continued to include sermons, pastoral letters and ecclesiastical edicts, with updated themes and outlooks, except for a lapse due to a lack of a bishop between 1825 and 1831. Clerical thought was also clearly expressed in polemical pamphlets since this was a time when there were attempts to found sovereignty on specific constitutional and organizational acts that were subject to debate. This was likely accentuated precisely by the absence of a bishop. In addition, the establishment of local presses increased the number of publications and the production of publishers.[40]

This marked an impressive break with the days when things were published only in Spain or in Mexico City, without any need for a local press. With its interest in economic and social development, Bourbon Enlightened absolutism had already brought about a change in this situation by supporting a press and other institutions representative of potentially dynamic local interests. But the press still spoke from the top of a pyramid of power, and pamphleteers adopted the tone of authorities setting directives for a people not yet able to speak for itself. When they wished to, these documents could capture and reflect reigning local feeling. But they selectively gave voice to interests who could demand rights within the frame of governing imperial institutions. It is also significant that certain fundamental documents from the period – some of which are examined here – were not printed, despite their great importance in shaping public life.[41] Public life was clearly still governed by mediating groups which were far from popular and which, despite the changes, continued to do without an open, public forum.

The sovereignty theoretically exercised by the people required turning that pyramid upside down. Everything constituting sovereignty had to be the product of a more direct popular voice. That is what was theoretically achieved by the nearly unrestrained freedom of the press. With a pen, paper, and some connection with a printer, any Mexican could be a true sovereign, exercising the sovereignty shared by all the people. Political institutions should therefore be shaped to take forms appropriate to a differentiated and heterogeneous public. This assumption was inherent in the idea of freedom of the press as it appeared in Mexico at the time. Yet it was in deep conflict with the usual proceedings of the bureaucracy and the Church, as well as with the social groups nurtured under the colonial order who had become the pillars of society. Writers at the time could hardly avoid referring directly or indirectly to these contradictions, whether to reconcile those institutions and groups to the new national situation, or to wage an assault upon them.[42]

Since popular sovereignty could only be exercised by the people, the nature and character of this group had to be defined. Popular sovereignty and its exercise represented a problem and an opportunity which could not be separated from the messy issue of sorting out the nation-state. This question not only involved the problem of constituting "public affairs," but went further, because it included the idea of sovereignty within the concept of "national being." Prior to Independence, no debate on such a theme could have officially taken place.[43] There were Peninsular Spaniards and American Spaniards, peoples of mixed origin, and indigenous peoples. All were included, even at the level of their group interests, within an idea of empire which, despite its clearly Spanish origin, did not yet establish a full nation-state identity. In this sense, the Hapsburg accommodation to the coexistence of different types of peoples or communities was still in effect throughout the entire Bourbon period up to the eve of Mexican Independence.[44] Sovereignty had a dynastic origin which claimed a universal basis. There was no need to define a united people in order to give it a fixed, civic meaning. The universality of the empire was eaten away by the implications of the conquest itself, the resulting regime of discrimination against castes and Indians, and the Bourbon tendency to attack American Creoles and subordinate them in various ways. But the premise of universality would radically change only with the spread of theories of popular sovereignty.[45]

Harvesting the fruits of seventeenth- and eighteenth-century European thought, nineteenth-century Mexico would face the question of how to exercise popular sovereignty within the territorial and demographic confines of a nationality in the making. This problem included the need for social coexistence beyond the level of principles and general standards of idealist thinking about sovereignty. That is why the groups contending in this period for a dominant role in defining the Mexican nation and nationality should be seen in the fullness of their contradictions and their historical presence. That is to say, the presence of tensions and the resulting contradictions at the core of their ideologies should be understood as a product of the efforts of their ideologues, in the midst of the struggle, to play a vital and effective role in defining the future course of the nation. For example, liberalism would repeatedly evince a need to observe certain conventions in order to help overcome a constantly unmanageable present. To preserve the liberal state that emerged from the 1824 Constitution, its supporters prized order and the respect for governing authorities, whether based on liberalism or some other ideology. In this context, clerical ideology offered a potentially important support, since it underscored the obligation of all Catholics to obey the established authorities. In the face of such circumstances, liberalism's drive towards the effective exercise of popular sovereignty could weaken. On the opposing side, it was only by means of a double movement, looking to the past but also to the future, that the traditionalist ideology of the clergy could hold back the destructive outburst of new events and opinions. These threatened to overthrow clerical ideology, with the priority it gave harmony and the social whole over dissension and the individual. In any case, the architectural richness of the historical moment clearly appears, in both cases, as a specific interweaving of competing hegemonies.[46]

Pamphlets are an ideal place to study the fractures within ideological positions in their contemporary political dimensions. It is in pamphlets that we can capture the elaboration of shared hegemonies in which opposing positions weave new points of effective agreement. It is the best place to analyze the points of continuity.[47] The needs of the state and the bureaucracy as well as the traditionalist opposition represented a burden difficult to cast off in Independent Mexico. The exigencies of internal order and international peace were tasks worth consideration. The recognition of the new national state by foreign powers, even the Papacy in the religious-diplomatic sphere, became a problem of state as much as a liberal dilemma. The state could hardly emphasize its liberalism with complete disregard for other practical considerations. The Mexican state was subject to the inertia of its bureaucratic past and to a need to endure even at the expense of sacrificing its liberal character. Besides, there was no single or homogeneous interpretation of liberalism, and there were always debates among its supporters.[48]

What has been said about the problems of the liberal state is no less true for the study of the clergy and its traditionalist ideology. They, too, can be studied more subtly through pamphlets. The clergy did not enjoy full ideological hegemony, as was already clear from the emergence of Bourbon reformism during the crisis of the Spanish Empire. The clergy could hardly have such hegemony after the declaration of Mexican Independence and the emergence of popular sovereignty. The clergy had taken part in the crisis of the Hispanic world from the eighteenth century, and under Bourbon reformism, they had participated in some of the solutions to this crisis. Thus the clergy had some reformist and enlightened credentials in their theoretical positions and practical actions.[49] Pamphlets enable us to take the measure of this reformism, both during the Bourbon period and after Independence. Similarly, pamphlets can help us understand how the Church, just like the state, faced a situation where it could not exercise complete hegemony over ideological domains, and thus made its own adjustments between past ideological orientation and the irreducible present. The Church underwent renewal in Independent Mexico, but at the same time managed to perpetuate a traditionalist organic understanding by employing certain aspects of liberal ideology itself and important facets of the nationalism of the newly independent country.

Clerical pamphlets were guided by three basic premises: doctrinal orthodoxy, the organic character of society as a whole, and the indispensable role of the ecclesiastical body in watching over both. This gave clerical discourse a deep anchoring in past doctrine and practice. But it did not obviate the need for creative updating with an eye to the dilemmas of the moment. Clerical discourse did not predetermine the specifics of the material and civil life of man. It only presupposed general guidance, whose specific outline was subject to debate. The specific responses to new moments always recovered the ideological inheritance of the Church, but also adjusted to the new social setting of which the clergy themselves formed a part. The desire for shared hegemony with the state even rewarded a certain flexibility towards changes in national ideology.[50]

The clergy made an appreciable effort to adapt advantageously to the new course of the country. The clerical modus operandi demanded that the individuals with the right to speak about the moment be selected according to the standards of the ecclesiastical body. In Jalisco, except for the period immediately following the death of Bishop Cabañas in late 1824, there is a recognizable shaping of clerical ideology by the bishop and his cathedral chapter (college of canons of the diocese). Even anonymous clerical pamphlets, since they generally did not spark rejection by the church authorities, can be presumed to have been published with their tolerance or tacit support. While their positions certainly varied, they were clearly instruments in the Church's search for a sure path as an institution. Once an officially proclaimed position had been set, all other parts of the Church owed obedience. In the meantime, the coexistence of different and heterogeneous elements within the ecclesiastical body was assured, although there was an attempt to keep certain common assumptions about doctrinal orthodoxy, the vital role of the clergy in national life, and the organic integration of the whole of society. That is why the pamphlets can be read as an expression of the tensions between inherited ideology and the demands of the moment. We can measure the efforts of the Church to position itself vis-à-vis the dominant social groups of the period by examining the discourse Church spokesmen, official or self-proclaimed, produced at different political moments to achieve that clear objective, and even by examining the inconsistencies, contradictions, and variability of that discourse. This suggests that the official positions of the Church itself were to a significant degree reached by debate between the potentially different opinions of the various clerical leaders.[51]

In summary, during this period clerical ideology proved itself as shifting in its expression and formulation as liberal ideology. Therefore the reconstitution or transformation of clerical ideology is best viewed in terms of ideological hegemony. The parameters of social domination changed constantly and profoundly throughout the period under study. The union of government power with the Church was constitutional until 1856, but even so, as an ideological foundation of the state, it suffered significant blows. Society allowed for more people to express their views, since liberalism exalted individual rights. That in itself reflected a change in the status quo. Independence gave voice to an increasingly more plural society, where social actors became the representatives and agents of change by appealing to the central and unquestionable principle of the basic freedom of man. Independence was connected to a new concept of sovereignty. Now sovereignty should be a product of freedom directly exercised by the people, which, as already suggested, implied turning the traditional pyramid of power upside down. In fact, the nearly unrestricted freedom of the press would exert pressure on the structures of political power. There was an aspiration to shaping the country so as to include a collection of groups with equal rights in social and political life. But, meanwhile, in the midst of the change towards popular sovereignty, the interests of the bureaucracy and the Church continued to exercise a power which is still not adequately understood. To put it differently, the state bureaucracy and the Church bureaucracy would have to redefine themselves with regard to popular sovereignty, even while still entertaining doubts about it. In turn, sovereignty was vulnerable on questions of internal order and foreign threats. The following chapters will explore some aspects of this dynamic, placing special emphasis on the central role of the Church in Guadalajara.

2

Imperial Spokesmen for Regional Interests

The Clergy and Government of Guadalajara in the Colonial Period

Imperial Plans and Regional Energies

Over the course of the eighteenth century, New Spain experienced the growing regionalization of "economic spaces" in the hands of local elites. Alejandra Moreno Toscano and Enrique Florescano have described the regional consolidation of Guadalajara within this larger setting. Regional competitors grew stronger in the face of Mexico City, which attempted with mixed success to rule over the whole territorial economic space of New Spain. Guadalajara exercised progressively larger influence over an important portion of western Mexico. As the seat of an *audiencia* and an extensive diocese, Guadalajara was already a legal and administrative center, and now it expanded its economic and cultural role.[1]

New dynamics in Spain favored the strengthening of Mexico's regions. In fact, the goal was to break them away from their old colonial center, Mexico City. In general terms, the objective was to produce a commercial renewal of Spain based on the promotion of Spanish agriculture and industry. Manufactures in particular were to be destined for the American market, which itself would grow due to the greater prosperity produced by the development of regional resources. To this end, the idea was to encourage in the Americas the mining of precious minerals and large-scale agriculture for domestic and export markets. Even subsistence agriculture was to expand, through the redistribution of excess lands to indigenous communities and higher-ranking casta groups. The desire to effectively carry out this great transformation led Spanish authorities to consider how regional government in America could be made more effective. As a result, the interests of the affected regions would have to be promoted.[2]

The new drive was set within a larger, clearly military effort at imperial defense. Since the 1760s, there had been interest in fortifying regional interests in northern New Spain. This meant defending them from foreign attacks by building a stronger socio-economic basis for military power. This turned out to be a difficult task. But it involved the Guadalajara region from the beginning, with the outfitting of the port of San Blas for supplying the population of California and Sonora. Shortly afterwards, artisan industry began to grow. The causes were the war in the Atlantic and its interruption of overseas commercial flows, along with the growing regional population. Both commerce within the region and exports outside the region expanded. The traditional linking of regional growth to the livestock market of the center of the country – and to the power of Mexico City – weakened. The agricultural market of Guadalajara grew stronger along with the population increase, and local manufactures expanded dynamically.[3]

The policies of Charles III produced hopes that this expansion, in good measure spontaneous and without state direction, might continue. The death of the monarch in 1788 led to a certain ideological reading of the situation on the part of the Guadalajara elite, encouraged by new Intendant Jacobo Ugarte y Loyola and members of the traditional high clergy. To understand this, we should stress that, by this time, New Spain had been administratively reorganized, with the creation of the system of intendancies and a centralized military command on the northern frontier [*comandania general de las provincias internas*].[4]

The new situation also brought territorial adjustments to Guadalajara. The intendant of Guadalajara assumed clear military functions and proceeded to organize militias at strategic points across his territory. The new intendancy of Guadalajara gave clearer administrative definition to the territory under the economic sway of the city market. Nonetheless, the financial interests of the capital reached beyond these new limits. The founding of a merchant guild in 1795, six years after the effective organization of the intendancy, officially reasserted the supraregional role of Guadalajara by establishing its control over the entire territory of New Galicia. Similarly, the Royal and Literary University of Guadalajara, created in 1792, exercised effective power over the enormous hinterland of New Galicia, and not merely over the immediately neighboring territory of the intendancy. The *audiencia* consolidated its broad jurisdiction, and the creation of the mint in 1812 should be seen as an additional sign that the scope of Guadalajara's influence was more New Galicia than Jalisco proper.[5]

There was already talk of a new viceroyalty in the north of New Spain, and Guadalajara figured among the proposed capitals. The region was on the road to consolidation, but its exact future course was not yet clear. Invoking the legal framework of a viceroyalty for social life meant looking to the past, since this was a Hapsburg administrative form, not a Bourbon one. But this call was sparked by what was in many respects a radically new situation for New Galicia. In addition, the creation of a viceroyalty need not eliminate the system of intendancies as a mode of political organization subordinated to the new Viceroy. It could well be an instrument to make the future government of the new entity more viable. If so, the new regional force of Guadalajara would draw most of northern Mexico towards it, creating a parallel with the traditional reach of the viceroyalty of New Spain.[6]

The Elaboration of a
Regionalist Ideological Discourse

No single movement proposed a political platform and socioeconomic project for the future of Guadalajara, its immediate surroundings and larger hinterland. The elements that, bit by bit, would make up the vision of local interests and their project for the future became clearer over the course of the period under study. Before 1821, the clergy played a noteworthy role in the ideological formulation of this growing regionalism. The clergy had a forum for their ideas in the pulpit and the printing press and were subject to almost obligatory consultation in forging new directions for the political and socioeconomic development of the area.[7]

There was not yet any insuperable opposition between the clergy and the state, much less between the clergy and society. The ecclesiastical corporation, an entity inherited from the Hapsburg era, attempted to adjust itself to demands for change and saw an effective means of contributing to that change in the new

Bourbon approach to reform and transformation. For the regionalism that was taking shape, Bourbon efforts to shake up the
Hapsburg regime seemed to augur a brighter future. It was not
immediately evident that the prosperity foreseen would put the
ecclesiastical corporation in check. Enlightened absolutism promised to carry out the necessary change without meddling in thorny
questions of political power. Growth promised greater incomes –
not only for individuals and the state, but also for the Church itself.
With greater rents, the corporation could set its course for the
future, increasing its presence in education and other activities of
public benefit, as well as broadening its missionary efforts in the
far north. Trimming away what was worthless about local tradition, and speeding up the flowering of what was best about it,
seemed to constitute a clear mandate in Guadalajara. Here, love of
the land was linked to support for its growth and regional consolidation. Reformulations did not seem to imply annihilating the old
regime, but rather gradually improving it. Since there was no clear
boundary between promoting local interests and new Bourbon
measures, tradition was not opposed to modern ideas about the
state, or to the architects of its transformation.

Thus, it is not surprising that leading figures of the Guadalajara
priesthood fervently lined up behind eighteenth-century reformist policies. While these policies reached their peak during the
reign of Charles III, they only produced powerful effects in the
intendancy during the reign of his successor. After the change of
the guard, examples of this kind of ecclesiastical thinking abound.
In 1789, Doctor Gaspar González de Cándamo, canon of the
cathedral, saw an opportunity to preach on the Bourbon reforms
in his sermon honoring the recently deceased Charles III. He
took advantage of the moment to favorably sum up the policies
of Charles III and suggest that similar reforms be applied to New
Galicia. The printing of the sermon, which ran to forty-six pages
and a one-page errata, preserved for posterity the force of hopes
for change and for political, intellectual and economic progress
awakened by the government whose future was now uncertain
due to the change of the throne. In the first six pages of his
sermon, González de Cándamo found a way to remind his parishioners that they had received great benefits from the monarch,
who had concerned himself with the well-being of his vassals and
had always been guided by the recognition that "the love and
trust of subjects are the only solid foundation for the duration and
prosperity of empires."[8]

In his speech, which was called a sermon although it did not touch deeply on any religious theme, the vigorous priest made clear that Charles III always strove for peace in order to "attend in its midst to the sole, solid, and true prosperity of his dominions, which he saw as his first obligation." This was necessary in order to straighten the erroneous ways of Spain over the past two centuries, since the death of Charles V. Because it had erred so tremendously in its government policies, this country

> ... which from the times of that Charles, who made himself obeyed and respected by the entire world, to those of his great-great-great-grandson Charles II, had fallen from the summit of power and opulence to the depths of weakness and misery, had fought in continuous and extremely costly wars in the days of Philip V, and had barely begun in the brief years of Ferdinand VI to lay down the foundations of its true happiness, when Charles III took in his hands the reigns of government.[9]

Canon González de Cándamo was now coming to his point. He immediately painted a portrait of a desolate Spain whose decline Charles III had come to conjure away:

> Agriculture decayed, the countryside half-depopulated, industry fully lost, commerce in the hands of foreigners, the arts of all kinds ignored, and the sciences treated mostly in uncultured style, and nearly reduced to stubborn and useless disputes: witness the state of the Crown of Spain when it was placed on the head of Charles III.[10]

What was behind the agricultural misery of Spain? González de Cándamo pointed to the price control on grains and the defense of extensive grazing lands for the ranchers of the Mesta. These made agriculture expensive and stagnant. He declared that it was the wisdom of the statesman king which had overcome these difficulties, and along with them, those which had blocked the profitable exporting of grains. Old canals were widened and new ones were opened. At the same time, the difficult colonization of the Sierra Morena was carried out, leaving the area in the hands of "the simple worker, the industrious artisan, the man of honor and integrity, *agreeable to the eyes of God and useful to the King and the Fatherland*."[11]

Charles III brought industry and commerce, those "two foundations of true riches," back to life in Spain. With this, he proved that Spanish character was not made up of "laziness, idleness and slackness." The "danger of the utter ruin of the Fatherland" and the dependence of Spanish consumption on imports were conjured away by the new monarch along with the mistaken system of government which Spain had followed for more than two centuries. Appropriate care was give to "the mechanical arts," and this encouragement revived them. Textile factories managed to recover the markets of the peninsula and the Americas, and "all branches of industry grew greatly in [just a] few years. The means of subsistence increased, and with that, the population, which is the principal foundation on which the prosperity or misfortune of states is built."[12] The canon declared:

> Neither can commerce flourish without agriculture and industry providing material for its flows, nor can agriculture and industry endure, if they are not animated and enlivened by commerce, which for that reason is rightly called the soul of the republic and the life of states.[13]

To promote commercial interchange, Charles had opened new roads, pursued bandits, managed "to reduce and correct the coin to a single minting," increasing the circulation of money with the founding of the National Bank of San Carlos, upheld the value of royal debts, facilitated and cheapened mercantile exchange, and impeded the clandestine flight of precious metals. He pushed for the improvement of old guilds and founded new ones in many places, while more effectively uniting Spain and the Americas by establishing maritime mail service. Even more importantly for the Americas, González de Cándamo argued, Charles had broken Cádiz' monopoly over commerce with the dominions of the New World, a measure accompanied by the suppression of some taxes and the reduction of others. There was a strong push for overseas navigation: more goods were carried and the cost of sending them dropped. "The Royal Tribunal of Mining was created in these domains, and the price of mercury had previously been lowered, all towards the goal that a greater abundance of fruits and metals give a rapid push to commerce to the common utility of Spain and the Americas."[14] In addition, a greater human freedom was added to the free flow of goods:

> Shortly afterwards, he removed from the necks of the unhappy inhabitants of the New World the heavy yoke under which they had

groaned in exhaustion, the barbarous and tyrannical custom which – in opposition to the liberty nature itself gives – had demanded of the miserable Indian that he sell the sweat of his brow to those who held the authority to value it as they pleased.[15]

Looking on the reaction that Charles III's reforms had drawn from monopoly interests and their allies as "worry and ignorance," the cathedral Canon comforted himself and assured his parishioners that "justice will prevail over cunning, and the son of Charles III will confirm and even extend the providences of his August Father." Undaunted, he turned immediately to the accomplishments of the King in avoiding war in Africa and Europe which, along with his creation of the Royal Philippines Company, had advanced commerce on all three continents. He quickly reviewed the King's promotion of the fine arts, including the creation of the San Carlos Academy in New Spain, from where "lights will reach these far-off provinces."[16]

As for the sciences, he asserted:

> Charles opened the doors which *worry and ignorance dressed up in the cape of religion* had kept under double lock. Light came in, and shadows melted away immediately. The universities were reformed. Those endless disputes which had been virtually our only occupation, in which entire centuries had been wasted without advancing a single step, began to be looked upon with disdain, and the straight path that leads to truth was taken.[17]

Modern philosophy was cultivated. Theology was renewed by direct consultation with primary sources. The study of canon law was based on the history and "discipline of the Church." Public and national law replaced the preoccupation with Roman tradition. Oriental languages were positively valued, and natural history, chemistry, minerology and metallurgy were introduced, "sciences which were more important than any others, not to say indispensable, for the prosperity of the state." Similarly, botanists and naturalists were sent to the Americas to learn of "its mostly unknown wonders."[18]

As González de Cándamo drew nearer to American shores, near the middle of his speech, he apologized to his parishioners for going on at such length. Then the fearless Canon continued with his summary of what was most important about the regime of the deceased King. He celebrated the attack on vagrants, beggars and the idle, the good government and cleanliness of cities, and the increase and enlightenment of the army and navy which had been achieved "without damaging agriculture or industry." Among the new administrative arrangements, the King had "increased the number and staff of all the ministries of every judicial court in the Americas." But more than all these wise and prudent measures – and many more similar ones – Charles had known how to fulfill the role of a monarch. He had shown this by declaring that "all the earthly tragedies that could befall me would affect my heart less than the unhappiness of my subjects whom God has entrusted to me." The Canon's voice boomed: "O words worthy of being etched in marble for the instruction of sovereigns! Come, Kings, understand your obligation, you who rule this earth; learn the charge the crown brings with it."[19]

Again and again he came back to this same question of the political direction of the reforms, which ultimately was a reflection of the exhaustion of the Hapsburg hierarchy and the new attention to producers and merchants. This new direction promised to bear great fruit. Charles' convictions had smoothed the response to complaints, reforming abuses and dictating

> ... such enlightened policies. A new light seemed to illuminate Spain. A new sun seemed to have been born. And since we have made use of this comparison, allow me to make use of one more. Just as in the regions situated on the other side of the Tropics, the rays of the spring sun bring to life a nature half-dead from the rigors of winter, or *as in these lands where we live, the summer rains bring lushness and greenness to fields scored by long drought,* so the deceased King Charles gave new life and made his dominions flourish again, after they had been reduced to nearly the lowest state of listlessness and misery.[20]

Before finishing, González de Cándamo would find a way to praise economic societies, to recall the royal foundation of hospices, hospitals, and colleges of surgeons, to take advantage of the suppression of the branding of slaves to mention again "the laws you are given by nature," to claim once more that the government of Charles had been in keeping with "the sacred right of property, foundation of civil society," to praise the personal virtues of the King, and to demonstrate that the monarch's reforms of clerical abuses were due to his matchless zeal for true religion, including his establishment of the dioceses of Linares and Sonora.[21]

This very kingdom we dwell in can testify to the large sums spent on its shores, and to the difficult and most costly voyages that were made in order to extend ... [the Catholic faith] to the furthest reaches of new California.[22]

All that remained for the Canon was the required closing prayer, which he fulfilled with half a page on behalf of "a King at last, who fulfilled exactly the obligations of his crown, searching by all means to exalt his peoples."[23]

The banner of Enlightenment don Gaspar González de Cándamo raised up in Guadalajara would have a worthy sequel. When Bishop Friar Antonio Alcalde was consulted, on 25 August 1791, about the viability of establishing a merchant guild in Guadalajara, he entrusted the matter to the doctoral canon of the cathedral. He was to write a response representing the opinions of the highest ranks of the Church, including the dean and the cathedral chapter. The terms of the response he produced are interesting. It supported the idea of a guild, not only to resolve disputes between merchants but also to duly help its members to avoid personal bankruptcies and extend commerce. Guadalajara's role was seen not only in terms of its remoteness from Mexico City, but also in terms of the even greater distance from Mexico City of many other towns in New Galicia (that is to say, places within the authority of the audencia, and not only the intendancy, of Guadalajara). On this basis, it explicitly supported the petition for establishing a guild that merchants had made to the intendant of Guadalajara.[24]

The document stressed the last part of this proposal:

The intendancy of Guadalajara, which other parts are subject to, has twenty-seven subdelegations, twelve mines, and taking into account the jurisdiction of the Royal Audiencia, no fewer than sixty-seven mines. This Diocese includes seventy-four positions for parish priests, seventeen *doctrinas* [mission parishes] and six *encomiendas* [Indian jurisdictions under the rule of individual Spaniards or Creoles], totalling ninety-seven.[25]

The sales taxes from the city of Guadalajara and its dependent areas exceeded 200,000 pesos, considered a substantial sum. The functions of the new guild, the document continued, would encompass the promotion of commerce in New Galicia, which the guild of Mexico was incapable of adequately advancing due to its greater commitment to "the vast territory of the archdiocese of Mexico and the dioceses of Puebla, Valladolid, and Antequera."[26]

> With the guild of Guadalajara established, commerce will flourish in the interior provinces, the population increase recommended by the Sovereign will be achieved, many abandoned mines will be worked, many uncultivated lands will be sown, tithing will multiply, and the worship of the true God and the Catholic religion will be able to spread more easily among the barbarous Indians, all of which would be *useful to individuals and to the state, to the Church and to the King, which are the objectives that should be aimed for.*[27]

The ecclesiastical hierarchy proposed that the guild dedicate itself to "promptly providing for the grave urgent public necessities of this city," such as the introduction of water. This would also contribute to improving surrounding agriculture and reducing the harmful dust of the area, which was a health problem. The dust would also be reduced by the swift paving of the streets, which the new guild would undertake. Another problem peculiar to Guadalajara which the guild would fight against was the constant erosion by rain and deepening of ravines "which are nearly at the edges of this city." New roads would be made and the existing ones would be repaired. Meanwhile, under the authority of the guild of Mexico, the indispensable bridges to ease coming and going from Lagos and San Juan had not been built, even though that town celebrated nothing less than the "most famous fair in all of this America."[28]

The natural industries of the region would be spurred by the establishment of the merchant guild of Guadalajara. According to the cathedral chapter, these industries included silver and gold mining, the production of dyes and paint, "curing of all kinds of leather," and cotton and wool textiles. The idea of promoting the spread of these enterprises fit into a broader vision of the social question in the area:

> As a result of these establishments, Indians of little wisdom will be instilled with taste and civility and will seek employment in work useful to themselves and the state. This will uproot from among the remaining people vagabond begging, the object of indignation, *in order to aid true poverty, the object of charity* ... because experience has proven in this city that when there are public works such as the royal palace, the hospital, the cigar factory and other private works

employing many workers, if those works cease for lack of materials, then beggars abound and from this comes much vagrancy which, even if it doesn't cause any harm, at least causes alarm. Factories also lead to population, because having something with which to support a family multiplies marriages.[29]

The document closed with a mention of how the founding of the port of San Blas had spurred agriculture, industry, population and commerce. It also mentioned the increased contribution of Guadalajara merchants to the well-being of the local and viceregal public coffers and to the development of mining, agriculture and other economic transactions "regularly carried out only by merchants, doing without the support of ordinary *alcaldes* [magistrates], *regidores* [councilmen] and other officials employed in public works." Bishop Friar Antonio dispatched it to Intendant Ugarte with a separate note recommending that he trust in the "solid thinking" of the cathedral chapter. The Bishop added that the example of Mexico City should be taken into account, along with "the feelings of enlightened reason and policy, which recommend the distribution of utilities derived from any source among those places and peoples aiding in their collection." The Bishop explicitly stated that his support for the measure in question – the establishment of the merchant guild – derived from his love for his diocese.[30]

Not all the manifestations of clerical support for the spirit and practice of Bourbon reforms were made with such zeal for delving into detail. Yet fitting occasions for expressing sentiments like the above were not lacking. One appropriate moment, for example, was on 10 November 1792, at the funeral for Bishop Friar Antonio de Alcalde, who had been in charge of the diocese since 1770 with the exceptional support of Charles III himself, as expressed in a 1788 message. Don Juan Joseph Moreno, the distinguished treasurer of the Guadalajara cathedral, was entrusted with preaching the sermon. In opposition to the defamations of those who had accused the late Bishop of greed and avarice, Moreno turned to detailing his work on behalf of convents, the poor and education in general, whose colleges and schools would show "the Christian and political benefits of such useful establishments."[31] Moreno could not help but mention

[t]hat hospital [San Miguel] as ample and open as his heart, and so many other buildings in which sums have been spent from alms

distributed wisely, since they were directed to uproot idleness and larceny and to promote the arts, so that money might circulate among all the city's inhabitants by means of the close ties and dependence among them, and in this way the poor would have a means to aid those who were poorer.[32]

According to Moreno, the Bishop had lived in dignified Christian retreat. But he had not lived in an "Anchorite retreat," since he rightly thought that "the day is for the public, and the night is for me".[33] Moreno reproduced Alcalde's own words again in explaining the emphasis placed on detailing the Bishop's charitable gifts – made, we might add, with a certain touch of modern philanthropy. It was necessary, the Bishop had said, "to avoid after my passing the malice which can emerge from one or more men who dislike the light but zealously love the darkness, and take to be true whatever their passion or imagination tells them."[34]

It is significant and symptomatic that, despite the Enlightened current evident throughout these documents, the sermons leave room for some doubt about the support Bourbon reforms enjoyed on religious matters. Who was it who was tempted to associate new ideas and the eradication of clerical abuses with irreligion, in González de Cándamo's words, or to denounce Alcalde with calumnies, according to Moreno?

Locating the resistance to committed reformers without falling into their own polarized reading of the ideological situation is always a delicate business. Fortunately, we know of another sermon Moreno preached earlier, on the occasion of the two hundredth anniversary of Santa María de Gracia. Moreno celebrated then the "negative benefits" this convent had received, in contrast to the natural disasters that had affected so many other religious houses.[35] Then he asked, with emotional rhetoric:

> How many monasteries of the religious orders have we seen suppressed in our own days? How many of the religious orders have we seen extinguished, abolished even in the memory of men, in these two hundred years? O God, unchanging and eternal in your Being! How great is the goodness with which you transmit a fragment of your sovereign attributes to living creatures who, by their very being, are walking headlong towards not being? Four are the religious orders confirmed by the Apostolic See which have been extinguished in these two centuries.[36]

And the magisterial Canon of the Guadalajara cathedral enumerated the four orders in a side note: "That of the Jesuatos, that of Saint George *in alga*, that of the Jerónimos of Fiesoli, and that of the Jesuits." He immediately turned to how the convent of Santa María de Gracia had fortunately been founded as "a workshop of customs" and so the nuns had become "distinguished in human society." Here he balanced, then, the fear of the strong hand of reform with the implicit assertion that the Church and its various institutions could make useful contributions to human society.[37]

To be sure, not all of the Church was ready to walk the tightrope between reformist demands and its own corporatist interests. If we look forward, the ideas expressed in Spain by Friar Fernando Cevallos in 1812 and reprinted in Puebla in 1820 were kept alive in Guadalajara. Cevallos denied secular authorities the right to reform the clergy and invoked both Protestants and Rousseau to show that such attempts by the state lacked any foundation.[38] He defended the clergy's right to "inherit or receive inheritance," but he opposed clerical conscription in militias. He asserted that there was a large but not excessive number of priests in Spain, that the Inquisition was feared only "by those ready to sin," and that reform and discipline of the clergy could only be achieved by "provincial, or national, councils." Cevallos held the reformers of the state really to be traitors to the throne. For him, their gazes were primarily directed at usurping the Church's goods and jurisdiction. Yet clerical riches, which the Church held as "rigorous property," in reality propelled the economy.[39] The illustrious Bishop-elect of Michoacán, recipient of a doctorate from the Royal and Literary University of Guadalajara and well known in the area, had expressed more moderate ideas along similar lines on the matters of Church property and jurisdiction.[40]

In between Moreno's insinuations and Cevallos' strong pronouncements, the Church had gone through difficult times. It had been forced to stretch itself in order to link its loyalty to absolute monarchy and reform to the defense of its own institutional and corporatist integrity. With the passing of time, the easy accommodation between old and new guidelines wore thin. Differences of opinion appeared, along with frictions between the representatives of old interests and the aims of the new royal bureaucracy and its spokesmen.

These tensions are barely evident in the pastoral letters and edicts of Bishop Alcalde, compiled and published by Alberto

Santoscoy.[41] His first writings in this genre were dedicated to putting in order questions of chaplaincies, annual confessions by Indians and castas, and the observance due in towns and haciendas on religious feast days. One edict from 1773 dealt with a Bull by Pope Clement X, duly authorized by Charles III, which dealt with strictly religious questions of indulgences and confession.[42]

Several of the later communications, from 1774, clearly did reflect the shared and delicate relationship between Church and state, as well as its particular complexity in this period of pronounced absolutism. Discussions of matters such as "lessening asylum" for prisoners who fled to churches, the Papal extinction of the already expelled Jesuit order, and the prohibition of clerical interference in the marriage of soldiers without a royal license, suggested strict adherence to state decrees. The renewed stress on the prompt fulfillment of religious obligations and the immediate suggestion of a state jealous of its authority, however noteworthy, did not yet seem to indicate a crisis. The overall emphasis on the throne and altar as social pillars supporting each other did not change radically.[43]

Other writings appearing shortly afterward took up the subjects of the correct administration of confraternities, parish altars, incest in marriage and a general tour of part of the diocese. Clearly the extra-religious aspects of these missives pointed towards the Church's strong ties with civil society. And perhaps there was some indication of relaxed conduct by the latter, and reestablishment of effective Church control. For example, a 1775 edict condemned those who, in trying to marry close relatives, attempted to pressure the Church by means of "carnal mixing with their projected spouses."[44]

Only after 1778 do certain themes become more notable in the Bishop's writings, and perhaps the beginnings of a slight change of tone can be detected. A 1778 edict transmitted the Royal Edict against recurring to the Roman Curia without first passing through the diplomatic channels of the Spanish Crown. Another message from 1779 detailed a dispute with "*alcaldes ordinarios* [magistrates], *alcaldes mayores* [superior magistrates], *corregidores* [governors], their lieutenants and other secular justices" over their right to consult parochial records. With the support of the Viceroy of New Spain, the Bishop managed to severely limit that right.[45]

There was friction between the civil and ecclesiastical administrations. In 1778 the Bishop resorted to the King to change customary protocol regarding religious practice on Maundy Thursday and Good Friday. He considered the exposure of the "Most Holy Sacrament to the Vice-Patron" [the provincial governor] to be an unacceptable irreverence, which the King accepted. These frictions must have seemed like a sign of the growing uncertainty about the roles of the two bureaucracies. But the union of throne and altar was still in effect. Although it was especially careful and precise in citing the intentions of the civil authorities, a 1781 missive about the Church's cooperation in tax collection written on the occasion of a patriotic campaign clearly reproduced the long-standing cooperation between both hierarchies.[46]

More noteworthy are the pastoral writings of 1782, which address apparent problems relating to "disorders in the administering of sacraments" and "the notable diversion and decline of tithing income in recent years." On the first point, interestingly, Alcalde indicated the high clergy's lack of control over a wide range of activities carried out by lower-ranking priests.[47] He wrote:

> Having seen, with great suffering for us, how certain ministers … who do not wish to expose themselves to the work of administering [sacraments and related activities] to which they are subject by force of the vows by which they were promoted to the holy orders, voluntarily separate themselves from administering [sacraments], with false pretexts of illness, or what is even more worthy of reproach, to demand greater earthly gains they move to other parishes, under their own authority, abandoning the parish priests they were employed with.[48]

On the matter of tithes, the Bishop asserted that the problem "is mostly attributable to the carelessness [!] of many contributors, who refuse to pay what is appropriate on the crops produced on their haciendas, or at least hide part of their harvest, in order to decrease their contribution." The remaining writings from later years, however, returned to strictly religious questions, or were devoted to other instances of effective collaboration between the government of the Church and the government of His Majesty. In 1785, for example, the Bishop addressed the shortage of food and how to aid in relief.[49]

Interestingly, some sermons from this period place particular emphasis on the mysteries of the faith, and show notable leanings towards Marian devotion. This gives the impression that the Church was looking for a space of its own, over which it could exercise unquestioned power. Similarly, this suggests that the Church was aware of its own institutional weaknesses in terms of providing moral guidance for society. A greater emphasis on the purity of religious practice thus offered the Church possibilities of renewal. A greater integrity would prepare it for the changes in society.

One of these sermons deals with the "Eucharistic mystery." Incidentally, it is dedicated to "the Indian nation, so enlightened as to be able to compete with all nations presently existing."[50] The sermon promises to "mathematically" develop three points, in order "*to provide the clearest of ideas about the darkest of mysteries.*" This was the "sacrament of sacraments": "God could give us nothing more, or nothing greater."[51]

In the first point, the glories of transubstantiation – "the greatest of all the miracles divine omnipotence has worked" – were contrasted with its inability to yet win "from human liberty a perfect and rational obedience."[52] In the face of the invitation to men to renew themselves in Christ, that is to truly live as Christians, results were meager:

> And what efforts have the sons of Adam made to destroy the old man, and to transform themselves into the new man, so that they could truly say, I live, but I am no longer myself, it is Jesus Christ who lives in me? On the contrary, they prefer instead to exert themselves by usurping from His Majesty what is so rightly his.[53]

The second point emphasized the miraculous and absolute surrender of Christ to man. Yet man in his "indolence" had turned away from the fervor of ancient Christians, going so far as to not even voluntarily comply with the minimal demand of receiving the Eucharist once a year at Easter. Sadly, the priest indicated

> [w]e unfortunately have come to a worn-out world in the depths of corrupted times, when it is not enough for ministers to go forth down streets and plazas, or to take every path and route across the fields, or even to climb up to a lookout post on the walls, to rise up and lift their voice from the fortress or the pulpit.[54]

Faced with such a situation,

> [i]t has become necessary for the Church, coming to terms with the average worshipper, to restrict such a strict obligation to only one occasion during the entire year. For this observance, the Church, even though it is a dove without bitterness, has found it necessary to use the strength of the secular arm [of the state], to wield the rigor of its censure, and to employ the loud racket of its outside jurisdiction *compelle intrare.*[55]

In the third point, the symbolic functions taken up by the Eucharist can be seen even more clearly. These functions reasserted Christian thinking's objective of sacralizing and making transcendent man's social life, in addition to the question of individual salvation.

> O sacrament of piety! O banner of unity! O bond of charity! The members [of the body] can hardly be united with the head, if they do not remain united themselves.
>
> Why do you think that among such a variety of foods Christ chose nothing more than bread and wine as material for this sacrament? It is only because, as Saint Augustine and [Saint John] Chrysostom noted, bread is made of many grains of wheat, and wine is formed from the juice of many grapes, but they are so united and mixed that later on, no one could separate them. O symbol of charity! It is right that of all the mysteries of the Catholic religion, only the Eucharist rises up with the glorious name of Communion, that is, of *Common Union.* This is not so much because infants and magnates, the ignorant, the wise, the poor and the rich, the good and the bad, the weak, the blind, the lame, the crippled, the paralyzed, the leprous, all sit at this table without distinction, perhaps not even excluding lovers and madmen, as because, as the Apostle explained, all of us who partake of a single bread form a single body, without ceasing to be many: *multi unum corpus sanum.* That is why Eucharist in Greek is called *syntaxis*, that is, congregation, confraternity, or joining.[56]

Proposing a way of thinking or living outside the framework of Christian tradition was not a step forward, but a step back. Directing himself "to the people," this clerical thinker stated:

> And you, Christian, recognize your dignity, and as a partner in divine nature do not try with crude actions to slip back into your ancient baseness and villainy. At all times keep in mind which Head and which Body you are a member of.... Let us expend all our possibilities, all our judgment and goods, to dedicate all our words, works and thoughts to the service of the Holy Eucharist. I don't know why all Christians do not become living flames which, fed continuously by the oil of all virtues, burn day and night waiting for this Sanctuary![57]

And all of this was a function of the sacrament whose memory should serve "so that we can never forget that immortal benefit which overcomes time."[58]

Seven years later, this same preacher gave another sermon (published only in 1798).[59] He began with a verse that beckoned to the public: "Do not then conform yourselves to the ideals of this age." On the occasion of a young woman's profession as a Dominican nun, the preacher was able to take potshots at this "windstorm of an age," and make a point of the uncertainties of salvation. In his eyes, the profession of the young woman left her "forever bound to Christian perfection."[60]

> Oh, how many are the advantages you have over [those in] common states! Since they have no method to base their conduct on, nor daily distributions except those subject only to their judgment, they regularly fail to stand up for their virtuous actions, they easily give up on them, they pursue novelties, they shift shapes more than Proteus, and they are satisfied with nothing. Even among the exercises they do practice, they nearly always prefer the ones which conform to their complexion and humor to those which repel them. Even in the most hidden parts of the Sanctuary, they consult their personality, their ease and their very nature, which they would do better to mortify with actions more useful, or less fitting their natural leanings under such circumstances.[61]

The preacher pointed out that religious life, with all of the struggle it implied between Christian transcendence and the temptations of a more sensual existence, was no more nor less than what the novice would face "in any other state or situation of life." What the preacher found most terrible was that some, in their desire to surrender to the sensuality of earthly living and elevate it to an ideal, now attacked religious life precisely because of what it represented in terms of this ancient struggle of Christianity against immanence, and because of what it suggested about the difficulties of virtue outside of religious life.[62]

> Here are the sophistries with which the sons of the age, fascinated by the terrible aspect glimpsed in Christian conduct and religious perfection, use logic to discredit them. Not happy to fool their own indolence, they aim to delude others with their same vanity. Could this be believed among Catholics?[63]

Finally, this was a matter of avoiding that "the torch of the good example be doused by a gust of any vanity" and of achieving "the consummation of the perpetual holocaust of the entire earthly man, which renews you for another, purely spiritual, life." The preacher reminded them that if "each of those present fulfilled the obligations of their respective state," all were invited to eternal bliss.[64]

Three other sermons before 1810 were dedicated to the Virgin Mary in her avocations as "the Most Pure Conception," "Our Lady of Guadalupe," and "Our Lady of Refuge." It seems significant that only the first of these sermons was published around the time it was presented to the public; the other two were not published until 1852. Their powerful invocation of the image of the Virgin Mary on behalf on the Mexican people may have seemed excessive.[65] The first, printed by the Zacatecan miners "as a testimony to their cordial devotion and with the greatest desire that this be spread as much as possible among all the faithful," was the least likely to attack undesired tendencies in society or the state, since the miners' devotion was evidently a tribute to the Church and its spiritual message. Even so, a few teachings could be underlined. Thus the knowledge of Mary's miraculous exemption from "the ugliness and crude rub of guilt" of original sin was intended to move the public. It would be very bad "if after all this your spirit remained sterile." The Christian purity of Mary should inspire other Christians to "purify our souls." As for the miners, the abundance they had been blessed with in mining should be directed "as a gift to you, to the worship of God and the aid of the needy [so that] we might deserve the priceless prize of eternal bliss."[66]

Although the first sermon did not markedly advance its message of renewal, despite its focus on a mystery of the faith, specifically Marian devotion, the other two sermons – which were not published immediately – were able to go further. The sermon in honor of the Virgin of Guadalupe began by citing the Psalm that "no other nation has received so much good." Right away the preacher declared that the issue to be addressed was "the most stupendous of the wonders on behalf of the American nation." Through this apparition, the Mother of God had declared herself "your protector" and "come at last to declare herself in these countries as a doctor of the faith, as an apostolic teacher of the Gospel, as a strong column and unbreakable foundation of our holy religion."[67]

In this case, this was a "great mystery of clemency." The preacher referred negatively to the pre-Hispanic and pre-Christian era, comparing it to a "contagious and pestilent poison with which the ancient serpent infected the provinces of this vast country." But this was contrasted with the new protection Mary offered to Americans: "Rejoice! For you will soon be the chosen portion, the favored ones, the ransomed people, and the sole object of the caresses, attentions, and care of the Mother of the God of Mercies."[68]

America would defeat the temptation of sin, just as it had received the Gospel during evangelization, with special assistance from the Virgin Mary:

> Who could doubt Most Holy Mary's having spread in these countries faith in Jesus Christ, if he meditates seriously upon how observance of this very religion for more than three centuries has kept it beautiful, flowering, and always free of the malign attacks of dissent and heresy?[69]

But things had to be taken further still. It was necessary to sacralize, to see the life of northern America sacralized, by the force of Marian intervention. This was coming soon:

> How fortunate the natives or inhabitants of this happy soil, who Most Holy Mary did not disdain to visit, descending from the heights of heaven down to those whom she declared to be her children, enlightening them in the maxims and foundations of Christian religion, down to those whom she promised her favor and support near the shadow of that image of hers with which she

wished to bless us, down to those whom she filled at last with her gifts and graces, until she awakened the imitation and the envy of all other nations. To you it has been given for these and many other reasons to bear the glorious name of sons of Mary, and to reciprocate by fulfilling the corresponding obligations justly and faithfully. To you it has been given to serve as a model and example for all true devotees of this Great Mother and to prove, with your conduct and behavior, to be a living replica of the virtues she bequeathed to us in this image of her original eminence.[70]

And lest anyone think otherwise, he drove home the point that this was no superficial matter. No, "she will throw [frivolous actions] away like stinking excrement, being in her judgment nothing more than an ingenious artifice of self-love." What was wanted was a purified religiosity, far removed from "corrupted customs" and in keeping "with the practice and exercise the Gospel prescribed for us."[71]

The invocation of a transcendence based on surrender to the Virgin in no way suggests that all was well in Mexican religiosity. Instead, it seemed aimed both at countering the lack of popular devotion to systematic and constant religiosity, and at avoiding the spreading of foreign influences closer to the secularizing thinking of Western Europe. The references to the latter kind of thinking indicate a fear that a new set of human values was being created. At the same time, the lack of religious devotion or observance by Mexicans was denounced as "indolence." The promotion of Marian devotion now offered to the practitioners of that imperfect religiosity a new, hardly intellectually demanding direction which was dependent on clerical guidance. The success of this orientation would cement an organic relationship between the clergy and other members of society, independent of the government and of new secularizing tendencies. Morality was based more on a well-directed will than on flawless conduct.

The third Marian sermon closed stressing that last aspect. It offered Mexicans the consolation of the Virgin as a "refuge for sinners":

Does the tyranny of bad habits, the violence of the passions, the ugliness of sins, and finally all the weight of inveterate vices, of bad inclinations, of ungratefulness and infidelity under which you have been so long groaning, not leave you any breath for raising your eyes to the heavens and looking there for your remedy? Then know, says

Saint Bernard, and never let it be erased from your memory, that the
great quality of Mary is especially being the Mother of sinners.[72]

It is worth noting that by the time of these last sermons, even
Canon González de Cándamo, well known from his sermon
praising Charles III, was showing certain signs of disenchant-
ment with his earlier Enlightened positions. In 1800, in his
new post as magisterial canon of the metropolitan cathedral in
Mexico, he gave another sermon, in honor of the late Archbishop
Alonso Núñez de Haro y Peralta. In apparent contradiction to
his vision in 1789, now the priest saw noteworthy barriers to the
harmonious development of secular and religious life. He cautiously declared that only science united with Christian charity
could reach "true wisdom, whose source is the fear of God."
Similarly, he asserted that only Christianity could be the basis of
human coexistence, rather than "all that much-vaunted humanity of philosophy," because it offered "that peace of the soul
which the world cannot give, which is only proper to the
spirit of God." Gónzalez de Cándamo emphasized that the late
Archbishop had been a man known for his understanding and
clemency, but that he "never gave anyone the least motive to
offend the lofty dignity of the high priesthood." The Canon
counseled the prelates of Mexico to guide their parishioners
with love, not with fear. This did not mean they should act with
irresponsible tolerance. To the faithful, the priest had to "make
easy the yoke of His [God's] divine law, and lighten his precepts,
without profaning his holiness with a new looseness repugnant
to the spirit of the Gospel." Haro y Peralta was a singular example, for he "settled disagreements, reconciled spirits, and amiably
resolved the differences which so harm religion and the state."[73]
    After mentioning the "countless benefits Mexico received"
from the deceased archbishop, González de Cándamo specified
something which further underscores our point:

> If the temporal needs of his flock were worthy of so much attention,
> even more worthy were their spiritual needs. The most pressing spiri-
> tual objective was driving his sheep away from the harmful pastures
> they were frequenting, and nourishing them in the healthy pastures of
> true Christian morality, not yet fully cleansed at the time of the black
> stains with which casuistic polemicists of recent times had disfigured
> its candor. The Vatican and the Throne, the Priesthood and the Empire
> worked together to restore its pristine purity as quickly as possible.[74]

Church and state supported each other, he claimed, but "their cries, although they did not fail to make an impression on the spirits of lovers of truth and justice, still found much resistance from laxity, bias, and ignorance."[75]

Haro y Peralta had understood that Christianity could only be based on "the sole and solid foundation of good study," as he had shown by intervening in the seminary program.[76] The Canon exhorted the young in particular to

[d]isdain the voices of the foolish who, confusing enlightenment with impiety and religion with ignorance, and disguising themselves with the cloak of piety, never cease to try to draw you away from the path your wise Father placed you upon. No, do not abandon the only road by which you may come to be worthy pastors of Jesus Christ's flock, and useful workers in his vineyard.[77]

Before finishing his sermon, the fiery Canon praised the Archbishop for one more achievement: his use of the College of Tepotzotlán, abandoned by the Jesuits, as a place of "instruction, voluntary retreat, and correction for the clergy of his diocese." He added,

Who can fail to see how important this place was for the reform of the clergy and for the spiritual good of the faithful? We can rightly call it a safe port where the priesthood turned from the storms of the world, and a life raft where the unfortunate victims of shipwreck found life.[78]

The problems between Church and state, and Church and society, would become even clearer and more evident in the pastoral letters of Doctor Juan Cruz Ruiz de Cabañas y Crespo, Bishop Alcalde's successor in the Guadalajara diocese and the one responsible for presiding over the difficult period that followed. Cabañas was bishop of Guadalajara for a lengthy period, from 1796 to November 28, 1824. He should be understood within the context presented here. This man was the promoter both of the house of charity, which proposed to teach trades to the underprivileged, and of the clerical seminary, which sowed the hope of an enlightened and disciplined clergy for Guadalajara.[79]

As his actions and ideas indicated, Cabañas was not insensitive to the winds of change in society and the Church. What largely ended up defining him historically was the need to take a stand against the 1810 insurgency led by Father Hidalgo and its occupation of Guadalajara. After being installed as bishop of Guadalajara, Cabañas continued Alcalde's work, and much of his public discourse directed toward cooperating with the government on social and religious matters. He wanted economic and social progress and ecclesiastical reform.[80] Nonetheless, even before Hidalgo's uprising he had grown disenchanted with some of the social changes he helped produce. Months before the outbreak of the insurgency, he had already declared that "the days are so evil that there is no one who does good, and human acts know no other motive but sensual pleasure and sordid interest, following the erroneous principles of the evil and dominant philosophy of the last century."[81]

In the midst of "the dark reign of self-love," the good Bishop would ask the faithful "to give at least the leftovers of your rents, entails or patrimonies, and also of your mines, industries, and profitable commerce" for the defense of the Spanish dominions.[82] He would ask,

> Is it not luxury that ruins families, brings continuous quarrels, promotes competitions and odious imitations, confuses all classes, strikes against our manufactures, holds back agriculture and arts, impoverishes the richest provinces, and does away with the most opulent and abundant Kingdoms? Is it not luxury that enriches the foreigner, and that necessarily produces the shortage of coin that you so bitterly complain of?[83]

But Doctor Cabañas was not certain he could count on his parishioners' support, because "luxury has been ruling us for some time, now." Nevertheless, not being an easy man to defeat, the Bishop appealed to "science, or the mania for calculation that has become so common in our times," asking those so inclined to "calculate the exorbitant sums spent on luxury and gaming and other disorders" in order to show that their suppression "would provide enough to meet the needs of the budget." Cabañas reminded the faithful that the legitimate King of Spain counted on God's blessing. But if that was not enough, he predicted: "You know the infinite importance of holy brotherhood and mutual love − or social ties, as it is called now − and the baneful consequences of discord and division in every realm, province or town."[84]

By 1812, now facing the revolutionary forces unleashed by Hidalgo, Cabañas would phrase his good shepherd's language more effectively. The forces unleashed by the insurgency, he explained, wished to overturn even the foundations of the great and still glorious edifice of our religious, political and moral society, the Holy Sanctuary of Laws, of Justice, of Truth and Majesty, overthrowing or plunging these precious Countries into the dark and deep abyss of the anarchy of the most execrable immorality and impiety, of that monster with as many heads as there are furies of Hell and capital sins, and attempting to seize, devour and annihilate everything that was necessary, useful or delicious among us, in Towns, Villages, and Cities as well as in the Fields, Haciendas, and Mines, which for the good of all were greatly prospering, and still aspire honestly and importantly to greater increase, richness and perfection.[85]

The Church had an obvious function at this moment when piety and prosperity had to be jointly re-established. Moreover, it had to extend to all the people the knowledge that

> [t]he overabounding grace of amnesty is nothing more than a shining testimony to humanity and charity properly understood, and a most evident sign of a great and generous political government, which, deeply penetrated by the supreme Law of any state, [strives for] nothing other than public health and happiness, and uses all means to achieve it, increase it, and secure it in all its dominions.[86]

While the situation stabilized, priests should provide broad information to the Bishop of suspicious movements on the part of presumed "enemies of the throne and the altar."[87]

To be sure, the support Bishop Cabañas offered to the alliance of the Crown, the Church and the largest economic and social interests of the intendancy of Guadalajara was not given lightly, nor did it lack a solid foundation prior to the immediate crisis of insurrection. We have already seen many examples of clerical discourse in earlier years. In addition, the Church had helped to overcome the dangerous famine of 1785/1786 and to spread the smallpox vaccine at the beginning of the century.[88] In 1813, it was the pillar of the effort to contain the advance of "the terrible plague which currently afflicts some of the towns in New Spain," and in 1814, in keeping with the attack on the plague, it supported both ending burials inside churches and creating cemeteries outside towns.[89] But in these years, new emphasis was given to defending "that eternal and universal law of subordination to the head, and unity of the parts and of the whole of the body and society we are members of" since "our civil and religious existence" was threatened by "the scathing and impious insolence of libertine philosophers" and their disciples.[90] The latter, finally meeting in a "so-called Mexican congress," set out to draw up a constitution and arrange the Church's matters in the territory under its control. Doctor Cabañas specifically exhorted the clergy to close ranks with "the civil, military and ecclesiastical corporations which speak for the whole of its inhabitants" to form "a powerful and great nation," "ruled by a government as ancient, respectable, rational, equitable and just as the sovereign himself is domestic and paternal." Cabañas did not cease promoting certain leading aspects of the clergy's alliance with Enlightened Guadalajara regionalism, but met with the challenge of the insurgency, he ended up explicitly invoking the framework of Hapsburg patrimonialism.[91]

In this context, it seems opportune to mention another singular document from this period. This is the memorial petition in which the municipal council of Guadalajara and the cathedral chapter joined forces, in 1816 and 1817, to ask the King "that granting their just and submissive requests, he establish in this Capital a General Captaincy totally separated from the Viceroyalty of Mexico, investing it with all the authority, faculties and privileges with which all the other superior heads of other realms are invested."[92]

Clearly, this petition was not framed in exclusively civilian terms. The union of Church and state seemed to the municipal council and cathedral chapter to imply that raising the civic status of Guadalajara and its rulers would also spur a raised status for the diocese of Guadalajara and its ecclesiastical authorities. And so, apparently speaking from a civil perspective, they stated:

> Similarly, [the province] expects that with its Capital elevated in this way, what would be most appropriate for the ancient discipline of the Church would be for Ecclesiastical power to follow civil power in every way. This is why, wanting to draw ever closer the bonds of union and perfect harmony between the Priesthood and the Empire ... in accord with these canonical dispositions, and considering that the Mitre of Guadalajara, with its two hundred seventy years of age, and with a greater extension and increase in the faithful than Tolosa (already elevated to an Archdiocese with assigned subordinates), has already been dismembered three times with the establishment of the dioceses of Durango, Monterrey and

Sonora, whose churches are truly and legitimately daughters of this one, as well as being notably less distant from this Church compared with Mexico, this [the establishment of an Archdiocese in Guadalajara] will save it from immense difficulties, many harms, and excessive expenditures.[93]

The bulk of the document, which closed with this call on behalf of an archdiocese in Guadalajara, was dedicated to retelling the great potential and achievements of the realm of New Galicia,

[w]hich, overcoming the narrow limits of smallness and subjection in which it has not been able to survive without suffering the most violent and back-breaking, disfiguring oppression, justly and necessarily demands not only greater distinction and freedom, but also persuades and promises this will bring the greatest of advantages to Crown and state, which the current system of subjection has denied them until now.[94]

The memorial petition specifically applauded the Bourbon reforms on the matter of subdividing provinces and archdioceses, creating intendancies and establishing new dioceses. The situation in South America, it stated, was now more balanced. What was missing was a similar adjustment for Mexico so that New Galicia might serve the interests of the King even better.[95]

The clumsiness of administration from Mexico City, lamentable in civil and ecclesiastical matters and disastrous in economic and fiscal terms, held back the growth of the realm. By causing discord, it exposed Guadalajara to the envy of foreign powers. "And so we must proceed with the necessary and immediate dependence of these colonies on Guadalajara which, invested with all authority, will be able to firmly preserve these dominions and make their inviolability respected, with fewer barriers and greater promptness and correctness." Indicating how useful the existence of several independent governments had proven to the Crown in South America, as it had thus always preserved a base of support, even in full insurgency, the memorial petition underlined the usefulness of the changes requested. Needless to say, it did not mention that in South America only the oldest viceroyalty, not the new ones, showed signs of unyielding loyalty to the Crown. More recent independent governments were precisely the centers of rebellion.[96]

Conclusions

One cannot help but see the Guadalajara Church as taking part in, and benefiting from, the regionalization of life in New Spain. The Church, above all in the person of the Bishop, was behind the creation of the Royal and Literary University of Guadalajara, helping to found it in collaboration with other social sectors.[97] In keeping with the times, it duly compiled its statistics, supported the establishment of the merchant guild of Guadalajara, and contributed to other improvements in social, economic and public health affairs. By means of the merchant guild, it awarded money prizes to innovative growers, and in 1812 it participated in the high-level consultations in which agreement was reached to legally recognize the improvised and controversial international commerce run out of San Blas as a response to the interruption of normal commerce by the insurgents. Time and again, the clerics found themselves, by their own volition, within the reformist line of the Bourbons and their "enlightened policies."[98]

Nonetheless, it would be naïve to think that this meant that the clergy were not clearly distinguished from other social sectors in some way. Signs of this have already been seen in clerical discourse itself, but there are other indications. Of the first ninety-one graduates of the university between 1792 and 1821 for whom we have information, only about thirty-six percent took government posts, while more than seventy-five percent ended up as priests, monks, members of ecclesiastical councils, or some kind of church official. Similarly, of the first 119 graduates, more than three-quarters opted for a degree in theology or canon law.[99]

The Church was not a monolithic group. It is noteworthy that during the insurgency, Bishop Cabañas called on the village priests for help, the same priests he had created a clerical seminary to aggressively correct and he had antagonized with a reform of parochial fees. It is evident that the same split between high and low clergy that took place in other parts of the country also took place here.[100] But the Church spokesmen had a record of promoting change. It would seem contradictory, at the very least, for Cabañas to lament that this was an age of materialism and pretentious calculations. The Church's interests were tied to the new economy; after all, didn't he himself raise funds against Napoleon – and against the insurgents – from the new businesses, and didn't he propose to advance them in various ways in his campaign against vagrancy? His predecessor, Alcalde, had already set a course in this direction.

It is important to grasp that the Church did not face a united and opposed civil society. In 1792, the municipal council of Guadalajara was indignant because it was only belatedly consulted about the establishment of the merchant guild.[101] And this happened despite the fact that, by this time, merchants already controlled the council.[102] The government had preferred consulting the Church on the matter. In no way do we see here a lay society profoundly disenchanted with its Church. Among the first graduates of the university, many opted for a degree in theology or canon law, supported by prominent members of commerce and government. There were graduates in other studies supported by clerics. Maldonado, a priest, was scandalized because Hidalgo had broken social concord, an eminently secular concept from a certain perspective. Other clerics ended up appealing to the King's civic responsibility to his people to halt the radical change in the status of the clergy. Commerce in Guadalajara had maintained the Virgin of Guadalupe as its holy patronness since 1746, and its zeal would even deepen at the end of the nineteenth century.[103]

Yet it is evident that there was a certain social division between the clergy and lay society. While Tutino and Powell have pointed out cases of priests who sometimes acted as merchants in central Mexico, no priests have been found among the notables of commerce in Guadalajara, although there certainly were a few *hacendados*. At the very least, the near monopoly sectors of commercial and landowning wealthy were not even remotely dominated by the clergy. Similarly, although the holders of Church offices in the area included some individuals who were neither priests nor members of the relígous orders, the Church itself did not carry out any extensive business directly, except for renting its urban properties.[104]

With the creation of the clerical seminary and the University of Guadalajara, the highest ranks of the Church reached new cultural heights. The merchants of the city, however, were eminently practical men, perhaps fascinated by high culture and clerical education but not necessarily a product of them. In fact, Lindley has suggested that many of the merchants were the classic Bourbon-era Spaniards who came to America to make their fortune. On the other hand, the most important hacendados were directly involved in reorganizing their lands and increasing their output, while the clergy only applauded them from its theoretical heights.

Certainly the tenor of the lives of these merchants and land-owners must have been very different from those of the high clergy. As already seen, Cabañas showed his distaste for materialism and calculation, but even the youngest clerics who were most filled with the thirst for change must have been distant from the activities that forged these values. Although one could cite the inventions and commercial interest of at least one outstanding priest of the period, this was an exception and not the rule.[105]

The strongest indications of the split between lay society and clerical society only emerge in the 1820s, and even then they are a decidedly minority trend. The terms of the ideological discourse analyzed until now show how members of the Church were forced to bring themselves up to date with Bourbon reforms without losing their validity as a corporate institution. The drive of Enlightenment thought was profoundly anti-corporatist, as shown by its attacks against corporate bodies, guilds and various religious groups. The new University of Guadalajara was not "Royal and Pontifical" but "Royal and Literary," and life statistics had begun to be collected by royal bureaucrats and members of the local merchant guild. The Church nevertheless still found much room to maneuver and to adjust its corporatist policies to changes in society and the state.[106]

The composition of society could not yet be imagined without an ideological discourse which in some way overcame different interests and reunited them in an idealized whole. Similarly, the Church's preoccupation for the well-being of the population thought of as a whole stood out again and again. The Church promoted government measures at the same time as faith and charity. It supported various aspects of commercial activity and favored the participation of the masses in the works and culture that the civil and clerical authorities considered useful and socially acceptable. The Church still played an important ideological role here, characterizing the Spanish government by its Christian and wise character, and not by its recourse to power and armed subjection of the people. These were days in which popular sovereignty barely showed its head, and the divine legitimation of a power that was as impartial and rational as possible – in the words of Bishop Cabañas – still convinced many. This was good for the gradual change that both the government and certainly the lay authorities preferred.

The rupture of this arrangement after 1810 would have grave consequences. It would not be until the second half of the nineteenth century that Mexico would briefly return to the mutual accommodation that the Church and the absolutist monarchy had managed for so long. In the meantime, society was subject to progressively more bitter internal conflicts. But it is significant that up to this point, the principal representatives of the new economic forces who would benefit from change did not often manifest their ideological positions in convincing political actions.[107] Could it be that in these moments of transition, the most powerful bourgeois elements of the population were characterized by a divided, politically accommodationist way of thinking that contrasted sharply with the high flights of totalizing theory characteristic of ecclesiastical theologians and their immediate successors? In the end, indecision and pragmatic syncretism are also a kind of politics, and the Church's continued efforts to link up with a gradual change, as well as to guide it, would open up more alternatives than is usually suspected.

3

Tensions at the Heart of Clerical Ideology in a Revolutionary Era, 1810–20

From Confidence to Caution

Perhaps the clergy of Guadalajara experienced the late eighteenth-century questioning of the dominant ideology of New Spain more forcefully than clergy elsewhere in the country. Nonetheless, the high clergy were ready to accept Bourbon Enlightenment and, especially, its material benefits. Those benefits were identified with greater Church income and the propagation of Christianity into new lands, in keeping with regional interests. The clergy was not averse to reformulating the relationship between the temporal and the spiritual, and between science and theology, along modernizing lines. Despite their misgivings, the high clergy of Guadalajara publicly and enthusiastically accepted the new social orientation coming from Spain. The clergy do not seem to have carefully weighed all the theoretical and practical implications of this movement. Neither did they fully take into account the possibility that certain local forces might appropriate this shift, taking it further and more radically calling into question those who had made up the established order under the Spanish monarchy.[1]

Uneasy with the Bourbon reforms, the high clergy of Guadalajara had opted nonetheless for a relatively confident attitude towards reformism. They elaborated a discourse in which the ecclesiastical reform measures put forward by the Bourbon regime were considered issues open to negotiation between Church and state. The goodness and religiousness of the ruler were the final guarantee that everything would turn out well in the end. The Church had a considerable ability to adapt itself to new circumstances, and if a single Church policy could be identified, it would be moderation between extremes. A confident and self-assured clergy could consider themselves part of an imperial crusade for modernization. Didn't the acts of the clergy even mean a certain religious and imperial advocacy of the value of things Spanish? Feijóo had clearly seen the purification of the faith and the modernization of Spain as compatible and related matters. Both aimed to recover the ancient grandeur of the country. Wasn't there some influence of this kind in the clergy of Guadalajara?[2] Clearly, Guadalajara's location between the north and the center-south of the country contributed to its ideological posture. Long-standing economic dependence on Mexico City was locally resented. This matter of regional advocacy undoubtedly added an element of self-interest to the clergy's actions.[3]

But the local element could complicate the region's linkage to the new imperial project as well as easing it. Evidently, this gradually became clear to the high clergy of Guadalajara. Encouraging change did not ensure being able to shape or direct it. The new movements at the core of society could still distance themselves from the guidance of Church and state, and thereby threaten to go beyond the limits they imposed. If such movements managed to challenge the authority of the King, they could place the union of throne and altar in danger. If the Church did not always have sure recourse to a religious monarch, the moderate and ultimately trusting strategy of the clergy would be placed in check. There is a certain element of inevitability to the clergy's conduct, here. As far as sovereignty was concerned, the status quo beneath a strong monarchy was the best guarantee that no change would radically alter clerical hegemony.[4]

The welcome given to the Enlightenment gradually turned cautious and circumspect. The basis for this shift by the high clergy had already been evident at the close of the eighteenth century. The outbreak of the insurrection lead by Miguel Hidalgo y Costilla in 1810 gave it greater force, but the political and social movements that motivated the public stances taken by the clergy after 1810 were swift and unforeseeable. Ecclesiastical interventions were, for their part, so opportune and intentional that their assumptions had obviously already been worked out (as argued in the last chapter).

The year 1810 does represent a watershed for the clergy of Guadalajara, but this is only because their misgivings towards change crystallized in the face of its social implications. Those misgivings themselves could no longer be held in check by confidence in the good will of the monarch. Since he was jailed in France, he offered no guarantees whatsoever. The headless Spanish state, handed over to liberals, did not steer a clear course. In such an uncertain situation, clerical uneasiness deepened and turned towards more open critique and moral condemnation. Clerical enlightenment had run into new social motives, and it quickly turned to freely questioning the basis of political liberalism. It worried about the difficult situation of the monarchy, now leaning towards secularization. The changes the monarchy had made were ultimately unable to overcome imperial decadence and internal social division.

The deepening of ecclesiastical reservations towards change did not mean a radical rupture with earlier thinking. The clergy continued to struggle to overcome the increasing crisis of the dominant ideology and to find points of agreement between opposing orientations. Regional clergy persisted in their complex political stance. They maintained their deep sense that they not only belonged to and represented local interests, but they were also the cornerstone for any social alliance, indispensable for present and future well-being. The clergy's declarations of support for absolutism were sincere, but the passing of time would show that the clergy could do without it. What did prove essential was its gradualist strategy for reaching out to social sectors benefiting from change, so long as it did not go beyond certain social limits.[5]

This chapter will try to go deeper into the ideological transformation of the clergy of the intendancy of Guadalajara. Looking over the independence period, we note a shift. Our analysis will emphasize sermons published between 1811 and 1820 in particular, although we will also draw on additional materials. More often than not, these sermons were the product of members of the cathedral chapter of the diocese. Printing such sermons, like those already seen, required the authorization of the highest local church authorities. Therefore, the scrutiny of ecclesiastical authorities suggested that the sermons had a trustworthy basis in dogma and that there had been consideration of the political repercussions that publicly taking a position in a printed sermon might have.[6]

Only one of our major sources for this period comes from outside the high clergy. This is the newspaper *El Telegráfo de Guadalajara*, published between 1811 and 1813 by the priest Francisco Severo Maldonado. Is this a case, as suggested in Chapter One, of the high clergy's extending beyond the limited circle of the bishop, the cathedral chapter and others of similar authority? Was a unique education especially valued in an era when freedom of the press was already under debate? Could a lone clerical voice assume an important role, authorized only by the power of his arguments, even without holding a position among the traditional high clergy? One could argue that his prestige and influence had given Maldonado a voice in a society that was now more ready to listen to those who were not members of the elite. The Enlightenment era was a particularly propitious moment to begin to redefine power and authority. Now criticism of the past and the invocation of reason enjoyed new legitimacy. In this context, we should view *El Telégrafo de Guadalajara* as a first indicator of the cracking of the traditional limits of the high clergy, and of their broadening in the atmosphere of a new era, reformist at first, and later revolutionary in inspiration.[7]

Not only did the ecclesiastical authorities readjust their own values; they also found themselves obliged to tolerate and even condone the ideological activities of notable members of the lower clergy. Their weight in lay society allowed the lower clergy to forge values and concepts along lines parallel to those of the traditional high clergy's. They could range beyond the pulpit, as in the case of Maldonado, and place themselves in the field of royalist-constitutionalist journalism. This broadening and reorienting of the high clergy to give voice to new elements can also be seen in the case of the priest ultimately called to preach a sermon on behalf of independence under Iturbide.[8] Later on, in the 1820s, this tendency was in some ways accentuated by the absence of a bishop due to the lack of resolution of the state patronage problem.[9] The high clergy was undergoing an ideological transition in two dimensions, both in terms of its ideological discourse and in terms of the shifting makeup and autonomy of the group of priests who spoke publicly.

We have already suggested some of the traditionalist and corporatist aspects of the social discourse of the high clergy of Guadalajara. These aspects hardened with the arrival in 1796 of the new bishop, Juan Cruz Ruiz de Cabañas y Crespo. Inspired by a desire for spirituality and social peace which doubtless was intensified by the French Revolution, Cabañas expressed conservative ideas and acted accordingly, within the larger context of the Bourbon reforms. After 1810, the Mexican counterrevolution deepened this tendency. The counterrevolution demanded an ideological mobilization of the discursive resources and social network of the Church. Thus the Church made use of its role as legitimator of established society and its future development. At this moment, traditionalism was renewed, to the disadvantage of more progressive ideological reformulations.

The high clergy's uneasiness with new social causes, its partial retreat from progressive political theory, its renewed devotion to spirituality and other-worldliness, as well as its sudden rediscovery of social hierarchy and the limits to man's social improvement, all reached their fullest expression after 1810. However, more attention should be paid to how careful the clergy was not to give up the ideological discourse supporting societal change. For all its growing misgivings, the Church was inevitably committed to an attenuated modernization.

The documents discussed here are not treatises aimed at the erudite, but rhetorical pieces that aim to convince. In this sense, clerical speakers prudently attempted to ground their positions in the most deep-rooted convictions of their external and heterogeneous audience. Therefore, this discourse is not strictly religious or ecclesiastic, but eminently social in nature. The course of Church history in Guadalajara suggests that there was more behind the discourse of the high clergy of Guadalajara than the pure calculation of oratorical effects.

Even so, there is a change of degree from the period before 1810. Before the insurrection, authority was more firmly established and secure. It is true that some clerical misgivings had been evident even in Bishop Alcalde's pastoral letters and sermons after 1788. Then the French Revolution, the invasion of Spain, and the overthrow of the King in 1808 had made the situation much more difficult. But with the 1810 insurrection, clerical ideology had to directly assume its old role as the foundation of social unity. It had to promote the overcoming of the differences at society's core, so that the whole of society might take priority over the fragmentation of its parts. The Church insisted that they come together in harmony, as a single, indivisible whole.

Above all, the greatest difference from the ideological statements analyzed earlier is the speaker's clear sense of being on the defensive, fighting against imminent peril. This contrasted significantly with the earlier period, in which the clergy, invested with greater optimism, allied itself to the modernizing drive directed by the civil authorities. The discourse, then, and not just society itself, had in fact traveled from enlightened absolutism to this difficult struggle between different parts of the great social edifice over reconstruction. The civil war represented by the insurrection was set against the other war, no lesser in scope, of minds. At the heart of the ideological counterrevolution lay the seeds of the forced transition towards a society with an axis of its own and a greater diversity of members given voice and vote. Clerical discourse was cautious to recognize this process, but it did not deny it either, and this dynamic is constantly evident.

Bishop Cabañas was an interesting example of this. In his sermons, he had not attacked non-aristocratic property or riches; he had implicitly accepted them. But he had asked that they be distinguished from luxury, vanity, and prohibited games of chance. In April 1810, he solicited funds for the counterrevolution.[10] He declared then that "I am not asking you to take solemn vows of poverty, or to place all you have and possess at the feet of the first ministers of God ... but I exhort you in the name of the Lord to give whatever you have left over." Growing riches and the morality related to encouraging and keeping them undoubtedly worried the prelate. In the end, he could not completely disassociate it from political calculation and thus from an orientation that threatened to undermine social life by emphasizing self-interest. It seemed to be negating the existence of God and making idols "of sensual pleasure and sordid interest, following the erroneous principles of the evil and dominant philosophy of the last century" as the only motives for social man. Ultimately, he suggested, leaving material concerns behind was more noble and honorable. So he stated that "I can tell you with confidence: prideful luxury and intolerable vanity ... have never provided nobility and honor."[11]

Similarly, intellectual modernization had been a given in Cabañas' thinking. What he seemed to deplore was that science should descend to a simple "mania for [crude] calculation." In the same way, while it was not worthy of condemnation to speak "of social ties, as they are now called," it may have seemed more astute to shore up the social edifice by invoking "the infinite importance of holy brotherhood and mutual love," more recognizably traditional and Christian concepts.[12]

Two years later, in the 1812 document, Cabañas had offered thanks for the support given to the counterrevolution.[13] At that moment, he could contrast "the great and still glorious edifice of our religious, political and moral society, the Holy Sanctuary of Laws, of Justice, of Truth and Majesty" with "the dark and deep abyss of the anarchy of the most loathsome immorality and impiety." But once again he assumed material progress as an integral part of this society suddenly redrawn along traditional lines. Therefore he made immediate mention of "the Fields, Haciendas, and Mines, which for the good of all were greatly prospering, and still aspire with honest and interesting aims to greater increase, richness and perfection." Clearly, this material well-being and its development were in contrast with the destruction of the insurrection, but it was established that the status quo was now a guardian of such progress, and never its opponent, nor a disinterested observer. However, on this occasion, civic participation was only seen in connection with "the essential and public virtue of subordination," the same virtue that members of the priesthood should promote without any other concerns.[14]

Cabañas would speak again in 1815, before the convincing triumph of the royalist forces brought a prolonged silence on these dilemmas. Due to the publication of the Constitution of Apatzingán, he once more expressed the outlines of his social ideology.[15] Just as in 1810, the prelate was worried by the arrogance of a thinking which located the development of society in mere self-interest. This time, he pointed out that this meant attributing "to chance the most perfect works and the economy and conduct of always adorable Providence." Popular sovereignty did not allow for men to form "any society but that which they themselves were willing and able to form under the tumultuous impulse of the crowds."[16]

But Cabañas pointed out that opposition to popular sovereignty need not exclude civic participation. On the contrary, one of the worst aspects of the Constitution of Apatzingán was that it claimed to speak for all the inhabitants of New Spain, but it was not true that all of them had united "their voices with those of the rebels." In any case, what he was looking for was the peace and well-being of the "goods and lives of the law-abiding, and the just, the industrious, the hard-working, and the peaceful, who *should place themselves within the civil, military and ecclesiastical corporations formed by the whole populace.*" The building of a "great and powerful nation" was not at all in conflict with a "rational, equitable, and just" government. But those characteristics were viewed as inherent characteristics of the government, and not responses to popular outcry.[17]

However, the Bishop did not clear up doubts on this point. He was more inclined to moralizing than towards conceptual clarity.[18] The faithful should oppose every "internal division of the Church" and concern themselves only for "liberty rightly understood." This equilibrium should be achieved without "the audacity of believing ourselves judges of iniquity or justice, or good or evil, of truth or falsity." Navigating without a clear conceptual direction, under the aegis of a tradition that had only been partly renewed from top down, Mexicans should "postpone our whims, passions and personal interests *in favor of the inviolable rights of the community.*" Cabañas was losing his intellectual clarity, here, and giving himself over to a confused and defensive all-inclusiveness. He also intended to lead his flock down the same path. The political possibilities of a mediated discourse of this kind should not be underestimated.[19] Brian Hamnett has pointed out the delicate balance of the feelings of the New Spain Creoles, who were no less alienated from an authoritarian and fiscally burdensome monarchy than from the masses they looked upon with condescension and fear.[20]

In the frame of mind set out in Cabaña's discourse, we can glimpse the general tendency evident in the other documents under analysis from 1810 to 1815, with the partial exception of Maldonado's newspaper. An "elegiac song" from 1811 found that the insurrection had set the horde against "all sensible and enlightened souls."[21] "Machiavellianism" and "materialism" were like a contagion, a "malign plague" spread by Hidalgo. Once again, arrogance and anarchy were presented as enemies of civil society. Only the rabble questioned "the legitimate powers," but the priest contradicted himself by recognizing the general appeal of Hidalgo's anti-European ideas of a better future. He had to resort to the specter of a government of the masses, enemy of the Church, to dissipate the possibility that fascination with things new might lead the people down the wrong path.[22]

A similar fear was expressed in other documents from the same year. One of these spoke openly of the civil war and attack on the material basis of society that the insurrection represented:

Now no one respects a compatriot, and being honorable, or having goods, is a crime.... No property is secure. The towns are sacked and their inhabitants reduced to misery. Commerce is blocked, and the most-needed articles are missing. Mining has been made impossible, as well as reaping any of its fruits. Agriculture, the perennial source of public prosperity, has decayed and laborers are lacking.[23]

The world was returning to "the primitive chaos it came from" without improving the basis of society. Yet the priest denied that "the present war is a war of religion" – instead, it led to anarchy and the loosening of ties between men. It only indirectly implied their distancing from God. What was worrisome, in addition, was that the heads of the insurrection should claim leadership without enjoying "the vote and consent of the nation." Only laws and subordination to the authority of the ruler – which he affirmed came from God – could be the basis of public happiness. Curiously, the relationship between popular votes, laws, and sovereignty was not specified; perhaps he felt that the connection was clear or inevitable, and there was no need to belabor the obvious.[24]

Nonetheless, four years later the same priest struck against the apparently resilient doubts of his parishioners.[25] Pride and ambition were not the basis for anything, but the product of original sin.[26] Human well-being was based on otherworldly virtue and not on a socio-political structure or its transformation:

Whatever state you find yourselves in, being solidly and truly great depends on you, understanding that true greatness has no other basis but humility, regardless of differences of class or condition. Neither nobility of descent nor inherited honors, neither luxury nor wealth, none of these makes you great except in the eyes of the world.[27]

But the role of laws and the popular vote were left out of consideration, here, while sovereignty seemed to be equated with submission and conformity, since all recourse to self-interest was denied. On the other hand, the priest's dismissal did away with all social pretensions, even of the noble, and not merely that of the rising bourgeois.

The traditional high clergy thus found itself close to an irresolvable dilemma in its discourse between 1810 and 1815. Yet

this cannot be said of a new and potent voice whose lesser clerical standing and clear ties to Spanish constitutionalism perhaps
allowed him to resolve the problem more expeditiously. This was
Francisco Severo Maldonado, the insurrectionary priest and ally
of Hidalgo who, taking advantage of the offer of amnesty, dedicated himself to counterrevolutionary journalism for a period of
two years after 1811.[28]

Breaking Ranks:
Maldonado and Renewed Reformism

Like those priests of twenty or more years before, Maldonado
began with the idea of "the flawed and complicated system that
has ruled over the monarchy for a period of two centuries." The
reforms begun by Charles III and Charles IV were once more
presented as the cornerstone upon which to construct considerations of social, political and economic questions. Meanness of
thought, for Maldonado, was the product not of popular sovereignty but of old corporatism, represented by the fleets and mercantile monopoly of Cádiz, the monstrous offspring of "sordid
interest and incompetence."[29]

Maldonado contrasted the "defects and vices of our ancient
Spanish constitution" with the enlightened and enthusiastic
reforms to be expected from the Spanish Cortes re-established
in 1810, where Americans were active participants in sovereignty.
The new political situation meant the possibility of bringing the
work of Charles III and Charles IV to culmination without violating the natural, that is to say gradual, course of things. The
reformist path offered greater security in the international setting of the war-torn Atlantic. It also promoted peace among
the distinct and ultimately opposing segments of the American
population. Every war for American independence would turn
into a civil war, disastrous to longed-for progress. Besides,
viewed as a whole and in comparative perspective, Spanish colonialism was not so terrible, especially at that felicitous political
moment, which offered all the benefits but none of the risks
of independence.[30]The ex-insurgent's choice of terms is quite
revealing. In the fourth issue of the newspaper, published on 17
June 1811, Father Maldonado had gone on about the broad distribution of civil and ecclesiastical posts to Creoles within the
Spanish empire, refuting an opposing passage from *El Despertador
Americano,* which he himself had directed.[31] Similarly, he insisted

that the Creoles called to serve the state and the Church under the Empire had included men of exceptional abilities. But those raised up by Hidalgo had been "some scoundrels of obscure extraction, without education or principles, who didn't know how to read or write."[32] Maldonado admitted that there had been problems with equality between Spaniards and Americans under the Spanish regime. But he summed the situation up thus:

> The barriers to commerce and industry cause no more delays and damages to men of Europe than to men of the Indies. We all reciprocally suffer from the defects and flaws of our ancient economic constitution. And we all find ourselves more needful everyday of the reform and improvements which we should so justly promise ourselves from the enlightenment and zeal of our representatives meeting in the august assembly of the National Magistrature [the Spanish Cortes].[33]

The editorial for this issue ended with a reference to the sorrows Ireland suffered under British government, in comparison with the "singular and enviable benefits" Spain always granted America.

In issues five and six of his newspaper, Maldonado had called upon the Indians of the region who had been charmed by Hidalgo's promises to free them of Spaniards and return them their lands.[34] In issue seven he again took up the theme of imperial decadence. He contrasted the "the flawed and complicated system that has ruled over the monarchy for a period of two centuries," causing economic backwardness, with the healthy Colbertism promoted by Campillo and Ward. Under the government of Charles III in particular, Indians were freed from coercion in their work. Some taxes were suppressed, while others were lowered, along with the price of mercury. The government then proceeded to abolish the fleets, a measure "only resisted by sordid interest and ignorance." This allowed the flowering of agriculture and industry in America, which earlier had not been profitable. Despite Godoy, his private favorite, the government of Charles IV had continued to contribute to "the good fortune of Americans [by permitting] … the free distillation of *aguardiente* from sugar cane, an article important due to its great consumption." It also freed certain products from paying *alcabalas* [sales taxes] and gave license to form "the university, and the merchant guild, establishments which are as healthy as they were longed for, and which have contributed so much to spread light across all of the province [of New Galicia]." Finally, in the face of the French invasion, the Spanish government "made us participants in sovereignty, associating us with the august body of the Supreme Magistrature, and placed the improvement of our future fate in our very hands." The greatest barrier to all this achievement was none other than the "monster Hidalgo." Father Maldonado closed his commentary: "Americans, when will you see the light?"[35]

Maldonado dedicated himself to helping them see that light. In the next three issues of his newspaper, he first published Hidalgo's retraction, signed on 18 May in the Royal Hospital of Chihuahua. Then, he briefly and summarily reviewed the "conduct of foreigners in their colonies compared with that of the Spanish government," basically finding that Spain had established its dominion "not by force of arms, but only by virtue of the peaceful insinuation of the Gospel." Finally, he rendered severe and astute judgment on "Friar Bartolomé de las Casas' slanders against the conduct of Spaniards in America." The following issue, number eleven, was dedicated to demonstrating the "failed calculations of Hidalgo about the fate of Mother Spain," an error the insurgent made because he spoke without "fully knowing Spanish character."[36]

But the journalist priest sensed that he had moved away from his reading public. Issue twelve of *El Telégrafo de Guadalajara* begins:

> Every journalist in Spain without exception openly and frankly confesses to the hard oppression Americans have suffered in past centuries. Meanwhile, the seductive printed words in the *Telégrafo* herald only the softness, generosity, Enlightenment and principles of wise and healthy politics constantly followed by the last Spanish government.[37]

Maldonado had the valor and astuteness to publish "the cry that has risen up against the author of this newspaper," but only in order to refute it. He declared it unjust because it failed to take into account the "noble frankness" and "ardor for restoring the Cortes" which motivated Spaniards. Public outcry suffered from exaggeration. What was missing was reflection:

> It is necessary not to lose sight of the great existing difference between political government and economic government. The first leaves absolutely no room for complaint, since we have been made

equal to the vassals of the metropolis, and since the same laws that govern Spain also govern, with minor differences, the Indies.

If we turn our gaze to economic government, we will find it defective and prejudicial to industry in more than a few of the branches it addresses. But on this same point we should make one observation, namely that this erroneous system has been proportionately more damaging to the metropolis than to the colonies themselves. Hence Spain has collapsed at the same time America has progressed to reach the flowering state we see it in now, which makes it the object of foreigners' envy.[38]

Thus, in opposition to the revolution Hidalgo promoted, Maldonando turned to the protection of the constitutional framework of the Cortes. He promoted the idea that America was already achieving progress within a reformist setting. The editor of *El Telégrafo de Guadalajara* had evidently come to the conclusion that the economic, social and political costs of independence under Hidalgo would have been too great. The rise of reform in Spain assured the impulse that Americans needed to achieve prosperity by means of gradualism. He immediately dedicated various issues to demonstrating progress in agriculture, manufactures and the domestic and foreign commerce of America, utterly denying that public agencies or Spanish "free trade" policies were responsible for paralyzing the economy of New Spain because they exported money overseas. He insisted on the liberal reformism of Spaniards in Spain and America, pointing out how the Spanish and their fortunes were Americanized in the New World. He praised the multiplication of merchants, artisans, and small producers since 1778.[39]

Maldonado stressed again and again the need for a union of Americans, as opposed to the disunity promoted by Hidalgo:

Entirely occupied in disuniting Americans from each other and in sowing the seeds of enmity and mutual persecution between classes in every way, the apostate [Hidalgo] never attempted, or even pretended, to organize anything. He remained in this unfortunate capital for two months, and in that long period it was nothing more than a theater for all kinds of theft, looting, murders, evils and assaults. Nothing of reforms or improvements. It is true that he furiously declaimed a few times against the system of government our Spaniards had set up in this and the other [i.e., South] America. But it is also true that he entirely conformed to that system, without any difference beyond replacing the well-deserving and capable officials appointed by the legitimate authorities with the most vile, inept and despicable subjects from the lowest of the rabble.[40]

Maldonado had become convinced that the independence of Mexico was impossible because it went against the natural course of things. He expressed the opinion that Mexico was still a very backward nation. He claimed that because of this it did not have, on its own, the means to promote the union of its children; only the tie to the motherland could give Mexico true social peace. Without it, Mexico would tear itself apart. In this, he asserted, there was no comparison with the United States. That country had enjoyed the support of three European powers in its independence, had been forged out of the mutual tolerance of its inhabitants, and was fully dedicated to true economic development, not "the extraction of factitious [*sic*] and conventional wealth." The fate of Mexico did not fit into that happy picture.[41] Maldonado had already judged that:

> … we find ourselves facing the unavoidable choice between being an integral part of the magnanimous and generous nation which tries to treat all our ills, or of being victims of a foreign despot who imprisons us by regaling us with promises of friendship and protection. Only our union can save us.[42]

Later on he would add: "every war for independence launched in America will necessarily degenerate into a civil war which will destroy the realm rather than separating it from the metropolis."[43]

Free of the growing ambiguities of the Church authorities and equipped with erudition and a voice supported by the civil government, Maldonado valiantly returned to faith in reforms and modernization.[44] A similar faith had originally characterized González de Cándamo and the cathedral chapter of Bishop Alcalde in supporting the creation of the merchant guild, but subsequent complications, and now the fleeting quality of this constitutionalist moment, underscored the difficulty of the transition. Even so, another attempt would be made in the 1820s, proving temporary and less than fully successful. The path was treacherous, particularly because the high clergy could not allow themselves to forget their corporatist role, and this implied not merely a set of material interests, but a whole conception of social and political life.

Yet the clergy could not ignore changes in Mexico or abroad. That is why the exact connection between reformism, sovereignty and the growing plurality of popular interests, a burning issue throughout the Independence period and subject to even greater debate in the 1820s, continued to elude clerical thinkers. It is worth stressing that Maldonado's fragile solution, based on how Mexicans would share sovereignty in the Cortes with Peninsular Spaniards, would not prove viable after 1814.[45]

Grappling with Politics and New Values:
The Debate Intensifies

Clerical discourse did not stand still between 1815 and the 1820s. Sermons would continue their uncertain and frequently contradictory casting about for solutions. Another sermon, now in 1816, celebrated the surrender of the forts of Mezcala and Cuiristarán (San Miguel) to the royal forces.[46] Preached by a priest from the diocese of Valladolid, it was nonetheless printed in Guadalajara in 1817. Manuel Tiburcio Orozco found that "the prideful leader of the rebellion" had overturned the temporal and spiritual order as well as "the glory of the Lord, the rights of the throne, and the reciprocal rights of man, which were violated, offended and trampled upon by the horrific system of the insurrection." Both the Faith and the state had been endangered by the winds of an insurrection which, under the appearance of a mere political reform, had managed to "completely delude the lesser ranks." But the real question went deeper, as became clear later on. The heart of the question was "that a popular commotion, promoted by a corrupted priest, should deform customs in a moment, alter the faith, confuse reason, and cause the most ominous damages in the moral as well as the political order."[47]

Having taking the side of good in this struggle, the Church had been accused by rebels of being "despotic, when it was all sweetness," and of being "infected, when it was all purity and holiness." "Should, then, the Church in its rulings accommodate the whims, the ideas and the disorderly aims of its proscribed children, in order to weaken the faith and destroy the precepts of Christian morality?" The philosopher's Enlightenment had unacceptably come to be framed as an alternative to religion that only required the prior suppression of the state, the "first and principal support" of religion, in order to prosper. The return of Ferdinand VII in 1814 had shown that the argument based on the issue of sovereignty was a farce. According to that argument, which always bypassed Peninsular resistance to foreign invasion, sovereignty had been usurped by Napoleon and was therefore returned to the people for its own protection. Just as ridiculous as this was "the whole gaggle of brilliant and resounding phrases" about liberty, equality, reforms, citizen's rights and liberal principles.[48] Therefore it followed that

> [t]he unjust system of insurrection, based on the subversive maxims of Diderot, Helvetius, Bayle and all their converts, does not lead to anything more than anarchy, disorder, impiety, the demolition of the throne. It leads unlucky America, choking on the cursed bait of the Enlightenment, to fall into the clumsy trap laid by its immoral regenerator [Hidalgo].[49]

Yet it seemed that those lofty-sounding Enlightenment words had found a public avid to hear them in Guadalajara and its hinterland, because the speaker immediately moved to accept them, giving each of them a new significance. The "wise" had to transmit this new content to "their ungrateful children." Significantly, the priest concluded by admitting that the true struggle was emerging among the people themselves. To the portion of the people which still stood in favor of the established order, the preacher exclaimed:

> Encourage them, therefore, make them understand that true *liberty* consists in subjecting oneself to that divine order which commands us to fear God, to honor all, to obey the King, and to order our aims by fixing them on peace; that true equality is not found in that foolishness which libertines give the specious name of patriotic independence, but in living united in the faith as the branch is to the vine, and as the sun's rays spread and gather in complete accord with the ardent dispositions of their center; that *reform* was never the work of a proud and voluptuous spirit, and that for its practice useful methods abound which subjects can propose without in any way justifying and exalting insolence and rebellion. Finally, exhort them, tell them that we are fully convinced that this so-called Enlightenment is the monstrous offspring of Machiavellianism, while on the other hand we perfectly understand that enlighten-ment aimed at the public order has such high and elevated ends as can never be achieved or reached except by Christian policies; that the honorable subordination the Gospel authorizes and commands

is not *servility*, nor can it be called so without great crime, by those who preach deceit, fraud, complacency, pleasure, wildness and all the excesses of execrable insolence and abominable pride under the wretched cloak of liberalism, who *could* indeed be called unfortunate slaves of ignominy; that the rights, the aims, the duties, and the effective obligations of man as citizen are not composed of opulence or the heavy burden of popular titles and representation, but of the keeping by each – scrupulously watching over this precious gift – of their conformity with the destiny to which God, for their happiness, has called each.[50]

This sermon made explicit the semantic redefinition of the terms of political discourse current since the times of Charles III which had more or less implicitly underlain many of the clerical efforts since then. Concerned about Bourbon reforms, the clergy had opted to accept them, while the practical and theoretical conditioning of the clergy shaped their specific understanding of the reforms. Clerical conduct and discourse would continue to reflect this compromise. Even the clergy's insistence on otherworldly themes and the insufficiency of exclusively human efforts to understand and act on the world was a way of accepting the search for ideological, social, and economic transformations, while making that search subordinate to certain crucial portions of the Old Regime. The restoration of the hierarchical sense of life was at the heart of the Church's efforts. Originally, this effort was turned towards both the political and spiritual regime. Little by little, emphasis would shift towards the spiritual dimension, and towards the transcendental mission of the entire nation. An interesting example of this, from before Mexican independence, came from the ongoing debacle of the Spanish monarchy in those years. The immediate cause was the death of Queen Isabel de Braganza y Borbón.[51] The cleric duly preaching the appropriate sermon in Guadalajara, José Simeón de Uría, took advantage of the moment to point out that

[m]iserable mortals clumsily wander, dragging themselves across the earth in search of an illusory and elusive happiness which they can never find, because [the earth is] sown with flowers and with thorns, alternating just like days and nights, joys and sorrows, fortune and misfortune.[52]

Proof of this was precisely the fatal alternation of good and evil, glories and failures, which "characterizes the epoch of our current rule" and which Isabel had to live through. It had been Isabel's fate to "see the most pathetic contrasts between exaltation and collapse, until she was completely disillusioned with the inconstancy of Earthly glories and greatness...."[53]

The tragedy of Ferdinand VII and his followers after the French invasion in 1808, like the offenses the Spanish nation suffered at the hand of France, had served to disillusion Isabel with this life.

> The King, the throne that makes her great, and the nation that raises her up, were the shining instruments used by the Lord to make her [Queen Isabel] understand from very close up how weak and fragile is the axis on which the pompous and complacent machinery of the most enviable fortunes turn.
>
> Renowned nation, illustrious nation, never praised and magnified enough for the glory of your religion and your valor: you, you are the one whose horrible metamorphosis has given the most pathetic testimony of the fatal upheavals to which everything the world praises and magnifies is subject! Ah, Princess of the Nations, you who have ruled by stepping over the decadence or utter ruin of other, once cultured and religious, nations where a bracing, fiery wind has slashed the precious vine of the faith, while Catholic Spain has preserved it in all its beauty....
>
> For more than seven years, afflicted Spain offered the most lamentable and bloody catastrophe to the world's gaze. As you well know, ... religion, state and nation were the miserable victims sacrificed in the sacrilegious and bloody pursuit of the blindest fury and the most unheard-of perfidy....[54]

Here was a notable shift. A González de Cándamo had seen the Spanish nation as benefiting from the transformations carried out by Charles III, without any clash with religiosity properly understood. The cathedral chapter of Guadalajara in 1794 had held a similar opinion about the region under its charge. Facing insurrection years later, Bishop Cabañas and other priests had suggested that no one benefited from destruction carried out on behalf of independence. But Uría took things a step further. One could sense that the Spanish nation had been entrusted with the special mission of uniting the Enlightenment to Catholic religion, and of binding both to national destiny. This discourse had gone from an abstract semantic redefinition to a complete reinterpretation of the social objectives of the nation in a revolutionary era. The idea that destruction was a leveler sweeping away progress was retained, along with the idea that the sovereign should support progress, but a new element of mission had been added, even as Guadalajara and New Spain were still considered within the horizon of Spanish sovereignty and a greater Spanish nationhood.[55]

The following year, 1820, opened with a sermon by José Miguel Ramírez y Torres, a funeral oration delivered on the death of Lady María Luisa de Borbón.[56] This occasion allowed the preacher to clarify some things urgently demanding clarification at a moment when, as the priest put it, the world found itself "in the storms of the tempestuous sea of this life on which we are swept back and forth without ceasing." The roles of Kings and people in this difficult life had to be defined. He found that only religion could give meaning to things, "because without true religion, man is nothing more than a theatrical figure who plays his role and disappears." Once again the theme of other-worldly transcendence appears, but this time more forcefully. No longer was it a matter of nobility and honor opposed to material wealth, or of all three contrasted with simple Christian humility. The split was more radical. Transcendence only came on the basis of religion, and not in relation with civic life. Yet who was knowledgeable about religion?[57]

> Ah! I know all too well, that not even the perfidious heretic or resister, the fascinated philosopher, the simple but poorly taught faithful follower, the superficial and vain wise man, the careless or dreamy devotee, the firm and exalted pious believer – and to put it simply, as I feel it – I know all too well that all Christians who are novices or inexperienced in science and virtue confuse or forget the genuine and essential idea of the religion of Jesus Christ, tacitly thinking themselves better and more Catholic than others, when in reality they are only less practical and trained.[58]

But on spiritual matters, outside of the priesthood and the Vatican, "that unmoving and divine center of religion," everything else was deceit. Under the Vatican's direction, faith must once more be placed at the center of all human activity:

> Morality, politics, customs, and reason must be rectified and guided by what the Church alone communicates, by the divine rules She alone

teaches and prescribes, which are the sole means for judging whether man is truly great, happy, a hero, or the most vile and despicable thing, a mere ghost, a nothing who plays its role, and disappears.[59]

Outside of religion, everything else in life was fleeting and open to question. No longer was monarchy or any other facet of the public life of man invested with a drive or value of its own. Disillusion was complete, and palpable reality was all too clear:

> Empires and the periods of their political lives are nothing more than the fatal cycle of value, conquest, luxury and anarchy … The throne, Majesty, the most legitimate and well-founded independence and sovereignty are nothing more than an elegant edifice built on the crumbling foundations of any old thing, a shiny vapor which clears and dissipates just after it appears.[60]

When properly understood, religion "did not depend on the scepter of any monarch." If religion supported kings, it was "only out of grace, to ennoble their authority and consecrate their power; if they sustain and protect it [religion], then God defends them, and is the most robust and immovable refuge and support of their throne."[61]

If the Spanish monarchy, fallen to the blows of the era, had managed to re-establish itself, that was due not to the praiseworthy enlightenment of the members of the ruling house, but to the providence of God, who "joined together the scepter and the priesthood according to the goal of his mission, the plan drawn out for eternity." Enlightenment and society itself depended on religion. Fortunately, the Bourbons knew how to defend it, as Lady María Luisa had shown with her "exemplary and rare veneration of the priesthood." And so, in this way, the high clergy in early 1820 underscored the theme they had already sketched out. They also pointed out to kings and to the people what should be understood as "true virtue, prudence and wisdom," defined as ever by the Catholic religion and the clergy.[62]

On the next day, another sermon was offered in praise of Charles IV, with the preacher another member of the cathedral chapter of Guadalajara. While there are echoes of both the heavenly strain of clerical discourse and of the domesticated Enlightenment in this new speech, it is worth emphasizing that the relationship between the two had changed.[63] The author of the sermon aimed to combine the idea that a king should be "kind to his people" with the conviction that only God could be the judge of his efforts. This should give due warning to kings, but security to the people. He proclaimed sententiously the moral conclusion: "What shame for criminal kings! What satisfaction and happiness for just kings! And what consolation on this day for us all!" Even royalty was exposed to the temptations of the nefarious thinking that had come out of revolutionary France.[64] Not everyone understood that

> [t]he throne and the altar were always the libertine's pitfall, since they are precisely the barrier to his dissolution and arrogance. Both were objects of the hatred and anger of the impious, who have promoted the same ideas under different names, down to the philosophers of the Age of Enlightenment. Possessed by pride and impiety, those unruly men filled the atmosphere of France with their pestilent doctrine, artfully spread their poison, and managed to draw *persons of the highest rank* to their cause.[65]

Nonetheless, the cleric managed to console himself with the "solid piety of Charles IV," which had been based on a firm agreement with Rome in all his proceedings.

> His deference and consideration of the Apostolic See were as well known as the religiosity out of which they flowed. He always went to the Highest Pontiff, as to a source of light and truth. He loved him as his own father, he listened to him as an oracle, and he venerated him as the first dispenser of the graces of Heaven.[66]

Even more, while still in mourning for the death of his father, he went against "the ceremony of his court" to speak with the Chief Inquisitor "and with the most energetic expression entrusted and recommended to him the Catholic religion, which was to be the heart of his entire reign." In this context, the priest celebrated the impulse that the now-deceased monarch gave to "the printing of the Holy Bible in our national tongue," since the sacred book "gives everyone abundant nourishment according to his situation and obligations … and teaches subordination and proper discipline."[67]

This canon of the Guadalajara cathedral had constructed a framework in which the ideas of a monarch who serves his people and an Enlightenment which promotes progress were invested before our very eyes with clerically authorized traits:

The titles of dignitaries and of the powerful dazzle and intimidate. Yet they do not move anything or drive anything, and the heart of man can only be won and surrendered without violence, when virtue is presented in all its beauty and splendor, or when the tender feeling of sincere gratitude sweetly obliges his spirit.[68]

Charles IV had won the love his subjects owed him because his "generous charity" was concerned with measures

> to spread in his dominions the knowledge that religion and culture demand of a Catholic vassal, to promote the arts, to put into practice theories of known usefulness, and in conclusion to advance the sciences.
>
> He knew that Enlightenment properly understood, without the mysteries of impiety which corrupt and deform it, is a rich river which flowing between distant fields carries fertility and abundance all over. He knew that it produces holy and instructed priests who teach the people doctrine and morality, magistrates zealous in the observance of the laws and the distribution of justice, fearless sailors who bring the riches of all nations into contact, striving agricultural workers who provide the basis for the state and raw materials for all the arts, hard-working artisans and, in sum, all the trades and professions necessary, useful or extravagant in the present state of weakness of nations.[69]

In America, the orator continued, Charles IV had extirpated smallpox with "the admirable pus of the vaccine." On an economic order, "agriculture and commerce, the true wealth of all nations, constituted the object that drew all his attention, and that he tried to protect with his fullest efforts." He made fall "a sweet rain of benefits and graces, which enlivened, encouraged, and made flourish these provinces of the Mexican realm, to a degree not seen since the days of their conquest [by Spain]."[70]

Then what justification might the rebellion that had shaken New Spain after 1810 have?

> You are the witnesses of the many millions that were coined annually, of the rapid perfection that weaving achieved, of the progress of many other branches of industry, and of the general abundance that held sway in America: all due to the loving zeal and charity of our tender Father [Charles IV].[71]

The priest immediately went on to review other improvements, like the port of San Blas, the Royal Tribunal of the merchant guild (whose creation was "as useful as it was necessary for this province"), the Royal College of San Juan, and "the singular grace of the foundation of our university." All these gifts had been granted or consolidated during the reign of the late King. Other signs of the benevolence of the government of the recently deceased monarch were the House of Charity and the Clerical Seminary – forge of "exemplary ecclesiastics" – which under the guidance of Bishop Cabañas had earned a "manifestation of the royal gratitude of His Majesty, Charles."[72]

A reproach to the cultural prominence of new men, who were sometimes prone to question the established order, could be glimpsed, here, but on the other hand, the priest asserted that "the heart of man can only be won and surrendered without violence." Contrary to the royalist and exclusive bent of the previous day's sermon, this one praised Charles IV for having "spread across his dominions the knowledge that religion and culture demand of a Catholic vassal," without making any distinctions of rank. Attention was centered on the deceased King's reforms, but there were also echoes of growing unease about "Enlightenment properly understood, without the mysteries of impiety which corrupt and deform it." Only that kind of reform would yield the necessary fruits of prosperity, productivity, ecclesiastical renewal, religious development, respect for the law, and strengthening of the state "in the present state of weakness of nations." The region of Guadalajara in particular had received numerous benefits from the hands of the late monarch, and the enumeration of them was the strongest proof of how unjustified the 1810 rebellion was. The unity of throne and altar, founded on the solid piety of the monarch and his firm agreement with Rome, was presented here as the "libertine's pitfall," the bulwark against social dissolution, arrogance, and restless men full of pride and impiety. Overall, the work of Charles IV had represented "a sweet rain of benefits and graces, which enlivened, encouraged, and made flourish these provinces of the Mexican realm to a degree not seen since the days of their conquest." The references to secular life and worldly reasoning were very evident in this sermon, along with powerful echoes of the general tenor of the clerical thinking developed since Hidalgo's 1810 insurrection.

The high clergy's ideas did not develop in a linear way. Neither was there full intellectual or conceptual coherence among their parts. A little more than a month after this last sermon, another was preached which can be more easily ascribed to the frightened, defensive, otherworldly tendency clearly dominant since 1810. It began with the conviction that the passions of "these calamitous times have tried to undermine the foundations of religion, and to sack the edifice of the Church."[73] Since antiquity, a line of thinking worthy of condemnation had emerged making human reason, the reason of "insolent man," the measure of all things, governed "by the appetites of the heart and the lights of a curious and rebellious intellect." This current culminated with the present wish to see religion as "a purely human invention, ridiculous and superstitious,… denying that its mysteries were beyond the reach of human reason," and seeing it as exercising only "limited authority." The representatives of this deistic and materialist orientation proposed to overthrow the throne and the altar, the priesthood and the empire, in search of an "imaginary liberty." They saw a combination of natural causes at the origins of everything, and were blind to the invisible hand and wisdom of divine providence. The result was a persecution of the Church only comparable to the first centuries after Christ.[74]

Even worse than this was the fact that evil had spread beyond the sectarians who were openly anti-religious, or transparently mistaken or corrupt, to reach those who claimed to be "children of a holy, pious and faithful nation." But even though they

> knew divine providence, and confessed it with their lips, they denied it with their works and conduct, looking with cold indifference and apathetic insensitivity upon the most common works of that very same providence, and counting solely on the resources of human providence – riches, power, authority, talent and valor – in their endeavors.[75]

Significantly, in "these times of dissolution and licentiousness," in the face of "the universal flood of iniquity," this priest recalled the career of the Jesuits, seen as so unjustly expelled from Spanish dominions and such "strong columns of the justice of kings, light of nations, storehouse of science and fathers of public virtues." He had not forgotten knowledge and society, but rather had placed both in their supposedly proper place within a world undergoing swift and dangerous change. In "this unhappy and unfortunate

age," the "restless spirit of innovators" could bring about anything save the very collapse of the Church. Its constitution and
government were a divine work, "the beginning of the stability
which will see centuries and monarchies come and go without
experiencing the least alteration of its component parts."

And so the otherworldly strand of clerical thinking had reached
the inevitable end of its ideological development. Faced with the
dangers of the moment and of men whose motives were dis-
connected from religion, it discovered once again that "eternal
divorce from the world" was one of the essential and fundamental elements of the Catholic religion. The identification of throne
and altar was still present, but in the end, it simply became unnecessary. The only essential matter, to which Providence itself was
utterly committed, was saving the integrity of the Church – there
was nothing more. And just as the modernizing strand of clerical
thinking had not yet worn thin, so this otherworldly strand would
not vanish in the years ahead.[76]

4

Towards a
Reordered Church

Sermons as Discursive Testimony, 1821–53

The Clergy Maintains its Presence

From 1810 to 1820 the clerical hierarchy generally rejected Independence, although a vociferous minority of rebel clerics supported it by military actions or in the press. By contrast, after 1821, all the Spanish and Mexican clergy of the country – except for a handful of Spanish ecclesiastics who went home in repudiation of Independence – accepted and supported separation from the metropolis and the political constitution of a new nation.[1]

But our vision of the clergy should not be restricted to their acceptance or rejection of national independence. The constant presence of the clergy in Mexican society at this time demands a richer and more careful treatment. Transformations of society placed pressures on the clergy. They had to respond to these pressures, lest they lose the loyalty and even the attention of the faithful.

Traditionally, the Mexican clergy had been both an arm of state and a state within the state. They had been entrusted with important aspects of the material and spiritual life of the country, a trust which largely endured even considering the noticeable secularization under the Bourbons. Independence did not produce immediate change in this respect. So the tradition of participation in and responsibility for matters of state was not easily pushed aside. Even the danger of a growing liberalism drove the Church to maintain an active political presence. We should also recall

that not only under the Empire of Iturbide but also in the 1824
Constitution, both the state and society of Mexico remained formally tied to the Catholic religion and to the Church. Thus, the
clergy's adjustments to the new times were no less important than
their explicit political stance, even their stance on such important
matters as Independence.[2]

On the other hand, the fact that the majority of the clergy was
born and raised in Mexico, in Mexican families, is of considerable importance, even if it appears insignificant. It is clear that
the prosperity and well-being of Mexico could not be alien to
the clergy. Neither their economic livelihood nor their family or
social ties would support such a stance. Their patriotic feelings and
fulfillment of their role as acting enforcers of state decisions could
at times even lead them to implement modernizing policies. The
Church and its parishes were key agents in the campaign for inoculation against smallpox. When new norms of hygiene dictated
moving cemeteries outside city limits, the Church, responsible
for cemeteries, carried out the new policy. In these cases, the
Church helped execute state decisions on behalf of the populace. Of course, in these cases the political implications of the
modernization policies were not particularly radical, yet popular
acceptance of inoculation and cemeteries outside town – measures which went against custom and aroused understandable
suspicions – depended on the support of the high clergy to
a greater degree than our secular minds can easily grasp. The
Church's support for reform of the clergy and for the consolidation of regional interests was not a matter of minor importance.
The regionalist enthusiasm of the high clergy, in particular, must
have reflected more general feelings among local clerics.[3]

More problematic, perhaps, was the fact that the Church was
under a statute making its legal regime autonomous from the
state. Although this legal autonomy had been trimmed back
since the beginning of the Bourbon reforms, it had not yet
completely disappeared. On the other hand, royal patronage
had always enabled the state to exercise influence over ecclesiastical appointments. Even after the appearance of Bourbon
reformism, accommodating state interests does not seem to have
been excessively onerous. Nonetheless, it is true that the lack of
papal approval of the excessively royalist decisions of the Fourth
Provincial Church Council of 1771 in New Spain seemed to
indicate that there were definite limits to ecclesiastical flexibility.
Farriss indicates that the royalism the Crown insisted upon was

extreme, leading to the noteworthy outcome that neither the Crown nor the Papacy passed the Fourth Council. Besides insisting that royalism became a matter of debate among Spanish clerics, C. C. Noel has stressed that the Hispanic clergy's definite preference was for material or practical renewal (for example, economic or educational), and that the clergy did not identify with intellectual freedom per se as a principle. This is similar to what we see in the Mexican case; the greatest difference is due to the importance of the emergence of regionalism, and later of nationalism, in Mexico.[4]

We must recognize that the Church still enjoyed great power and self-determination. The consecration of new members of the clergy always remained under the direct authority of the ecclesiastical hierarchy itself. In its legal status, including inherited privileges, the Church enjoyed virtual autonomy within the state. This certainly helped the Church survive Bourbon reformism. Perhaps it was unsettled and bothered, but the Church did not lose all flexibility towards the state and towards social pressures. It found itself in a much more serious situation with the arrival of liberalism, because of the latter's principles of individualism and natural rights and its anti-traditionalist and dogmatically anti-corporatist bent. Yet there are strong indications that the other-worldly and ultimately theocratic orientation developed by the clergy in Mexico did not lead to such a dramatic dead end as it did in Spain.[5]

Both Bourbon reformism and liberalism clearly bound man's destiny to his secular future. If reformism questioned the value of important aspects of the Hispano-Mexican past, liberalism exacerbated this tendency. The legal status of the Church was inherited from the same past that was being questioned. Its privileged position was due to the understanding that it would watch over the spiritual goals of society. It is true that its support for the organic unity of society was a basic premise of royal absolutism and even turned out to be useful for moderate liberalism, but there was a difficulty: the setting of precise limits between Church and state could never be done with complete precision. In a time of changes directed by the state, this was undoubtedly a serious problem.[6]

In actual practice, the roles of Church and state overlapped along a necessarily blurry boundary. In addition to the examples already given of Church participation in activities socially important to the state, we should not forget that the clergy even handled the vital statistics of Spain and of Mexico both before and after Independence.

Virtually all of the formal education of the populace took place in Church-affiliated institutions and under the authority of mostly ecclesiastical instructors. The clergy, depending on taxes and other resources provided by the national populace, profitably channeled funds to various economic sectors through property loans. In small towns, where a functionary of the national government rarely if ever came by, some member of the clergy was always a resident, or a regular visitor. He would be the only link to extra-local authorities and the prevailing political culture of the country. On the other hand, if there was debate about some new measure, like cemeteries outside towns, it was not clear whether it was appropriate to appeal to religious principles, or secular principles, or both, to resolve the matter.[7]

In this light, and recognizing the prestige and general acceptance of the Church and its doctrine by the Mexican populace during the Independence period, we should reconsider the overall transformation of the relationship between society and ecclesiastical thought. The key question here is: how did the Church support its rejection of Independence at first, and its acceptance of Independence thereafter? The immediate interests of the Church were certainly decisive in both cases, since Spain was still an absolutist monarchy in 1810, and in 1821 it was a constitutional monarchy under growing liberal influence.[8] What were the discursive changes through which the clergy was able to guide the population to first oppose and later support Independence? The clergy had to speak the language which had the greatest chance of securing the loyalty of the population. In this sense, ecclesiastical thought produced a social and political discourse whose effectiveness could be measured by the results achieved. To exercise effective hegemony over popular loyalties, the clergy could not present its particular viewpoint without interweaving it with other legitimate values of the populace. Only by combining the particular with the general and presenting it as a coherent whole was it possible to orient public opinion on these specific questions. Declaring things anathema, or issuing excommunications, were weapons to be used only when all other means had failed.[9]

Chapters Two and Three have emphasized the ambivalent character of the discourse produced by the high clergy of Guadalajara. The objective of remaining present and viable within politics of progress or modernization was manifest, but the growing tension was no less so. This was produced by the opposition between certain corporatist interests and values the Church defended, and some of the new social interests that were taking shape. The Church was unable and unwilling to reconcile itself to all the changes taking place in society, yet it accepted a number of them and was itself party to several major changes. It even willingly promoted significant changes. Cautious and circumspect when it was convenient, the high clergy kept a prudent distance from certain changes or their implications, especially when it could not guide them or influence their direction. There was an overall air of tact, diplomacy and flexibility, as well as of a disciplined thinking and behavior, to the actions of the high clergy of Guadalajara.[10]

The Sermon

If edicts and pastoral letters were a blunt reflection of overall directives at the highest level of the diocese, sermons opened up a more speculative and debatable space. They usually interpreted Church teaching on some point of doctrine or discipline, making more or less direct references, as appropriate, to relevant matters of social life. If the missive from the Bishop was an ecclesiastical ruling that was binding over the flock, the sermon became – without any force of discipline at all – a means of forging a religious framework for everyday affairs.[11] Sermons were the responsibility of individuals of varying ranks and influence within the Church, although the role of some members of the cathedral chapter is very evident, especially before 1820. In any case, it is significant that sermons required a special Church license to be published. Even after 1820, the majority of published sermons – those which must have set the general standards for the genre – came from distinguished members of the cathedral chapter or from other institutions of lofty heritage in the major cities. Even though such documents did not represent the whole of ecclesiastical thinking, it can be said that they laid out a range of opinions of widely recognized prestige at the highest levels of the Church. In general, they can be assumed to have guided the clergy and the flock in keeping with the feelings of the Church hierarchy. Some of the characteristics and even the evolution of clerical thought during this period can be traced by examining such documents, whatever the contradictions between individual orators.

Sermons are extraordinarily useful for tracing the course of this thought after 1821. It is worth stressing that despite the general agreement on Independence from then on, the future of the country remained to be spelled out in detail. Sermons could suggest ways of perceiving reality, could at times admonish the wayward, and could offer perfect vehicles for praising political figures and behavior worthy of praise in the eyes of the Church. Sermons did not impose obligatory commitments and they did not bear the weight and the implications of a pastoral letter or edict. For those very reasons, they represented an especially flexible discursive tool. The principles of doctrine and discipline underlying the sermon also granted immeasurable authority to the clergy, and established a basis for communication among initiates. In sermons, the establishment of a counter-discourse or a meta-discourse about secular reasoning was implicit when not explicit. While this did not give perfect internal cohesion to ecclesiastical expression, it did give overall unity to the clerical attempt to provide moral and final guidance of secular discourse and events. It is significant that only one sermon published in Guadalajara could be found from the period between late 1825 and early 1831, when Jalisco lacked a bishop.

A Crucial Discursive Turn

Up until 1820, sermons were produced within a context that still assumed the basic viability of the Ancien Regime. Because that regime was unquestionably undergoing reform, this committed the Church to change. Despite the growing unease of the clergy, the tone of the sermons primarily revealed efforts to moderate the speed and secularizing implications of that change, but not to block it completely. True, their published sermons in 1819 and 1820 show the Mexican clergy faced an increasing dilemma. But if the Church seems to have moved significantly away from its union with the royal state immediately prior to 1821, after this date it found itself once again committed, now to an independent Mexican state. At least part of this change in events would become the subject of debate in sermons. Since the Church's orientation was not pre-set, the speculative and tentative aspects of such proposals grew stronger. The delicacy of the moment was heightened by events such as the initial resistance of Bishop Cabañas, a Peninsular Spaniard, to accept the new regime. Yet the deeper questions between the Church and state were more serious. The tension within the Church resulting from possible contradictions between social change and corporatist needs were a fundamental source of ecclesiastical anxiety.[12]

An exceptional example of this was the sermon José de San Martín delivered in the Guadalajara cathedral on 23 June 1821, when independence was sworn under the protection of the Army of the Three Guarantees.[13] It is worth stressing that the preacher was a long-standing insurgent and not a recent convert to the cause of independence. His sermon is an important document largely due to its own internal contradictions. These contradictions seem to be at least partly intentional; they surely reflect the momentary confusion everyone was experiencing, and perhaps uncertainty among the clergy themselves. The thinking of various social sectors had certainly not yet solidified. The main point of the sermon was an attempt to connect the Independence of Mexico with Saint Peter's admonition to love our brothers, fear God and give honor to the King. The doctrinal point and the political moment had to match. For his part, San Martín saw no difficulties: the Three Guarantees promised religion, union and independence with Ferdinand VII or another member of the royal family. Rather than dwelling on the conquest, San Martín held that the Spanish had no right whatsoever over America because it was absurd that "in the nineteenth century they still claim their rights of conquest and pontifical concessions." Spain was seen as an aggressor nation, which entered into Mexico by means of the unjustified conquest of a peaceful people. Americans only wanted to exercise their legitimate sovereignty, just as Spaniards themselves were then doing in Spain.[14]

By now, the priest was warmed up; he then turned to attack the nature of Spanish domination in terms of laws, principles and rulers. Matters of sovereignty, laws and popular participation were about to receive a radically different treatment than in previous sermons. Embracing the reasoning of Friar Bartolomé de las Casas, San Martín went back to the old argument by disciples of Saint Thomas Aquinas on behalf of the original inhabitants of the Americas. Within an overall framework of incipient popular nationalism, he downplayed the problems of opposing ethnic groups and social hierarchy in the country. He conceived of Americans as a unified people, opposed to the Peninsulars. He admitted that the latter were victims of misgovernment, although Americans had suffered from it as well, and had rebelled against it:

What comparison, what correlation can there be between their oppression and ours? From the beginning of the conquest we have been subject to barbarous laws, laws incongruous to our country, damaging to our interests, crippling arts and industry, suffocating the production of our lands, and oppressing merit and talents. We have been under orders which expressly prohibited us from knowing the rights of man, which aimed at and attempted to promote ignorance, which have degraded us even from being rational, which have attributed to us every vice, and which have discredited us before all nations. Let us speak fully, with sincerity. Some of our laws have been useful and brilliant, but they have been overshadowed by those enforcing them. Their energy has been tripped up by the greed of some and the pride and haughtiness of others, and their precise observance has been frustrated by the multitude of contradictory rulings which interpreted them. In short, whatever Spain has done to America has had as its sole object the utility and exaltation of Spain, and our ruin and destruction. Can it be fearlessly argued that the social contract dictated by nature itself has not been destroyed? Can it be stated that all the links between a subject and his government have not been broken? Every contract is null and void when the tacitly or expressly stipulated conditions are not met. Every government is formed for the good and the happiness of the people, and therefore when that is missing....[15]

San Martín paused at this point, as if to suggest he realized his rhetorical excess from the pulpit was inappropriate; he apologized, only to attack once more. He immediately insinuated a dramatic parallel: Mexicans and Spaniards were brothers in many things, but the latter had behaved like true enemies. Yet our love for our brothers was demanded not only towards those who were good, but even more rightly towards those who were bad. He declaimed:

Thus let the wall of separation that has ominously been raised by our place of birth, by passions, or by the laws of the age, be knocked down forever. American and European Spaniards: work without ceasing to destroy that infamous massive work; make these be the felicitous days in which the wolf and the lamb, the panther and the goat, the calf, the lion, and the sheep live together under one roof. Let us all work of one accord so that the Spanish Lion not bloody his claws in the breast of the Mexican Eagle, and so that the Eagle not devour the Lion and tear him to pieces with his sharp and strong talons.[16]

So Mexican love for the Spanish under the guarantee of unity came armed with a terrible vision of the Spanish and an explicit threat of violent reprisal if the Spanish did not change their behavior. San Martín dedicated the rest of the sermon to demonstrating how the Three Guarantees fulfilled the other duties specified by Saint Peter – protection of religion and loyalty to the King – and he made no further use of the intentional ambiguity just described.

For this cleric, we should stress, the guarantee of religion was of particular importance. This was much more crucial than loyalty to the Spanish Crown. Loyalty to the King was simply achieved by offering the Spanish King the Mexican throne should he choose to move here. There was no need to go further; time would decide the exact result. Religion, however, could not be treated in the same way. San Martín set the defense of religion in Mexico against the opposing liberal tendencies in Spain. He even went so far as to state that "the war for our Independence is a war of religion."[17]

In the same year, another cleric would go even further than San Martín by joining freedom for Mexicans to the consecration of Independence. He referred to Iturbide as "a new Moses" who freed Mexico from slavery and led it "towards the beautiful and fertile land of Canaan."[18] The enslavement of Mexico under colonial rule had been general, he said, but religious oppression by Spanish liberalism had been the spark that aroused the Mexican people:

O Holy Independence! Without you, efforts to achieve the spreading of the Gospel were vain; possessing you, they are and will be the easiest and simplest thing. Possessing you, we will keep the apostolic colleges, whose principal institute is dedicated to spreading the Gospel, and without you, they would have succumbed to tyranny. Possessing you, the ministers of the Church will be respected, their character will be venerated, and their rights will be defended; without you, we would have been stepped upon, imprisoned and even condemned to a shameful begging due to whatever calumny was imputed to us. Because of you, customs will be reformed, and without you they would be even more corrupted by the many libertines who, frankly came from the Peninsula in these last days truly filled with the spirit of impiety. Because of you, our faith will be kept pure, and without you, it is open to being lost because of the many unfitting writings that come from that country of darkness, and circulate everywhere causing irreparable harm to souls. Finally, possessing you, we will remain united to the Vicar of Jesus Christ, we will respect his determinations, we will obey his counsels, *since our marker is piety and religion, which will give us the glorious name of the Most Catholic Mexican Empire.*[19]

Guided by leaders moved by God and the Virgin of Guadalupe, Mexico – in the vision of this cleric – was on the verge of becoming the new people definitively chosen by God. The role of the Church in this new Mexico, triumphant and liberated, was clear. The Church would be the soul of independent Mexico.[20]

In fact, Independence under Iturbide offered the country the possibility of closing the breach the civil war had opened in 1810. Guerrero joined Iturbide; the insurgent mestizo of humble origin joined the royalist Creole accustomed to luxury. Both were united in their Catholicism. Both recognized the many problems that Spanish rule had caused the country, though this did not bring their opinions into agreement on a deeper level.[21] In 1821 and 1822 the Mexican Church tried to achieve the impossible and to bring the critical vision of colonial rule, developed first by Bourbon reformers and later by insurgents and constitutionalists, into line with a theocratic vision of national destiny. It is certainly true that flashes of a sacralizing approach towards Mexican reality had appeared since the beginning of the century,[22] but we have to recognize that this posture's open approach to social criticism in 1821 and 1822 represented a mighty step in national development.

This move in clerical discourse aimed to heal the aftermath of civil war between Mexicans, a war carried out in physical combat and discursive struggle. Another sermon said:

> No longer are there dissenters or faithful [to the King]; there are no patriots or rebels; party distinctions no longer exist; even the names of insurgents and royalists are forgotten; each are children of the same fatherland, born and destined to form a single family; and the three guarantees, *that heavenly invention,* is the great secret [behind this].[23]

The Church's discursive ability to invoke a consensus view of history should not be underestimated. Suddenly, Independence could be treated not as a subversive act but as a goal always longed for and finally needed. The author of this sermon went on to say:

It is not easy to give in a few words a full detailing of the setbacks and disgraces which, over the course of eleven years, alternated with the fleeting success that our longed-for Independence achieved from time to time. But I cannot omit the noteworthy circumstance that when we least expected to shake off the yoke which tied us to the train of despotism, just then God wished to visit us in his mercy, like he did with the Israelites, raising up from among us strong and clear-minded caudillos who freed us from the oppressive hands that had reduced us to devastation and extermination....

In this way, O great God!, you wished to force us, so to speak, to recognize the true source from whence the freedom we looked for was to come. You opened our eyes to the insufficiency of our own strength to achieve a good which seemed to mock our fervent longing, retreating from us all the more as we ran to reach it.[24]

In this synthetic vision, the ups and downs of the movement for Mexican Independence had been the product of divine plans for Mexicans. When the Treaties of Córdoba were rejected shortly afterwards, sharpening the country's deep internal divisions, another sermon would reinforce Mexicans' duties towards this providential God:

Is this the great Mexican nation that proclaims itself religious? Is this the famous city proud of its perfect beauty, its adherence to the Catholic, Apostolic, and Roman faith? Are these the illustrious sons of Zion, dressed in finest gold, who boast of dwelling in the courts of Catholicism? Then where is the concord that should rule over them, as their religion declares? Where is the love for each other so called for by the one they say is the God and Savior?[25]

Christian charity had to be the mortar that united the populace; otherwise, there was nothing distinctive or glorious about the independent nation. So the cleric declared.

With some differences of opinion, another sermon a year before had claimed that Mexico had justly suffered from three centuries of colonial rule.[26] This situation had been appropriate punishment for the human sacrifices earlier practiced by Americans. Yet the author of the sermon allowed himself to support Independence under Iturbide because it preserved nobility and the rights of the corporatist bodies (including the Church) and maintained the unity of the Throne and Altar. In this context full of contradictions and demanding some clarifications, the Church took active part in the consummation of Mexican independence. In fact, it attempted to forge what another clerical speaker in 1821 had called the unity of "religion and the fatherland," a proper successor to what had been the ancient union of Throne and Altar.[27] And the efforts of the Church, while undoubtedly more comfortable with a Bourbon or an Iturbide, would prove capable of outlasting them easily.

The Theocratic Option

It is interesting that at this moment an integral idea of independence prevailed. This can be seen as a transcendent and holistic idea, not subject to partial interpretations. That is, one was in favor of Independence, or not. Whatever had been said of Hidalgo in the past no longer mattered. For those in favor of Independence, he was a historical predecessor; there was no attempt yet to deny him that honor.[28] With the elevation of Hidalgo to the level of a pioneer of Independence, there was a need to give a new importance to the anti-colonial complaints that had inspired him. This could be done invoking two different facts: on the one hand, Ferdinand VII − the legitimate monarch − was no longer the undisputed ruler of the Peninsula in 1821, and on the other, Independence separated Mexicans from Spaniards, but not from the monarch per se. Spaniards could therefore be thought of as a conquering people turned libertine and anti-religious. Mexico had turned its back on that disoriented people, to offer the Crown to Ferdinand all the same. In this way, the notion of (royal) legitimacy was saved, along with the hierarchical meaning of existence it embodied. To the conquest seen as divine punishment, a new idea was counterposed, that of Mexico as a new Israel. It was a chosen people; having purified itself by means of the true religion, it was now ready to become its fortress, and to carry its banner. Independent Mexico would thus be a Holy Mexico with a divine mission in the world. For some, the Virgin of Guadalupe clearly symbolized this mission, because she had acted as intercessor in the redemption of the Mexican people.

As already suggested, the coherence of ecclesiastical discourse throughout the period under study is not to be found in its adherence to one political formula or another. In the ecclesiastical vision documented in the sources, any political formula was subject to otherworldly goals whose fulfillment must be governed by the values promoted by the Church. Any given political formula was evaluated in terms of its service to this ideal. Thus, neither Independence nor continued ties with Spain could be an end in itself, but only a means towards more transcendent ends. Once Independence had shaken its complacency, the Church offered a theocratic response, in keeping with its earlier concerns about the important changes taking place for decades in Hispano-Mexican society. In addition, an insistence on guiding society towards transcendental goals was the best guarantee of its other corporate interests. From this perspective, all the Church had in terms of goods and privileges was in the service of undeniably valuable goals.[29]

Since the Enlightenment, there had emerged a growing tendency to convert the political life of man in itself into something transcendent and close to a self-fulfilling goal. Clearly, the Church had not participated significantly in this shift in political ideas; that is why a bitter polemic about the fundamental values of man arose during the troubled period from 1810 to 1821. For some, Independence should have been at the epicenter of the determination of appropriate values for the Mexican people. For others, especially the Church, no political question could be more than a means to carry out an essentially extra-political and other-worldly task.[30] As long as the Independence of Mexico was interpreted as an end in itself, as long as its drive and consolidation came out of popular revolt and ignored the explicit accords between the ecclesiastical body and the new state, the Church opposed it. Only after baptizing Mexican Independence and assigning it a transcendent spiritual end and meaning, thereby re-establishing a clear hierarchical meaning for the whole process, only then – driven by its repudiation of Spanish liberalism – did the Church identify itself with Independence, giving it massive support and the full force of its capacity for legitimization. In so doing, the Church regained its role as the social guide and midwife of national transformation, a role emerging liberalism fundamentally questioned. Despite this, as the sermons indicate, the Church was able to open significant dialogue with social and political criticism.

The Church, Constitutionality and Dissent

It should be clear that the larger context of this clerical creativity underwent far more shifts than a simple change from before Independence to after Independence might suggest. Following Independence, this complexity grows even greater. After the brief reconciliation under Iturbide (unity, religion, independence), there followed the fiscally sound and politically evenhanded republic of Guadalupe Victoria. Yet politics degenerated into open conflict and growing instability in the years afterwards. The role of the Church in Mexican society, as assured in the Plan de Iguala and secured in the 1824 Constitution, began to be publicly questioned. At the same time, the political struggle unleashed would call into question not only that aspect of the status quo, but a wide range of additional matters.[31]

It should be stressed that the things combated often enjoyed the protection of the Constitution. This gave those elements under attack the character of legal validity, which was the basis of the Church's identification with the state. The brief rupture of the alliance between the two in 1833/1834 would be counteracted by an even stronger reaffirmation of it from 1835 on.[32] In fact, this alliance only declined again after the war with the United States, in connection with the rise of the liberal project of rapid colonization and its insistence on religious tolerance as a promotional measure.[33] In this way, up until the Reforma – although with ups and downs – the implicit or explicit basis of clerical discourse was its identification with the constitutional order, and this was the legal side of its struggle to forge an overall alternative for Mexican historical life. The polemic definition of the nation, therefore, required it to take on both eminently abstract matters and their practical and legal consequences. Protecting the corporatist interests of the clergy could be seen as the unavoidable condition for being able to carry out in practice what was proposed in theory.

A central question was who could debate the matter. In this period, the Mexican Church moved along two very different levels. Proclaiming that it alone was able to opine on matters of faith, it only opened up to dialogue on secular issues. It challenged each secular resolution to fulfill a religious role, but reserved for itself the exclusive right to legitimately evaluate how well it did so. In this way, a good portion of its polemical intervention in social discourse revolved around its own extraordinary role within the social body.[34]

The Church allowed itself to attack others, openly or subtly, while denying them an equivalent moral status in responding. This was done by constantly referring to ideas of eternity, which outweighed Earthly worries and relegated them to secondary importance. From this standpoint, absolute values were not defined by Earthly matters but by eternal and spiritual affairs, which only the Church could legitimately speak of or debate. In this respect, it is significant that throughout the period before the Reforma, the Church attempted to repair public perception of its moral decay. Sermons emphasized its embodiment of the values of generosity, unselfish knowledge, social charity, political loyalty, sacrifice and self-denial. Even more strongly than in earlier years, the virtues of religious life were proclaimed, along with its exemplary quality for all Christians, and the shoddiness and cheapness of contrary values. It was insinuated, or openly and simply declared, that Christian values were the fulfillment and consummation of the natural values of social man. Thus, the importance of civil life was confined to its adaptation to a providential plan. Civil life was subject to a set of concerns which were not so much alien as superior to it, and about which lay persons were not expected to speak authoritatively. The weakening and later abolition of the Inquisition, like the transition first to a constitutional monarchy and then to a republic, increased the Church's need to be assertive in all social debates. Before, the superiority of the Church's voice had been assumed; now, the Church had to persuade public opinion that it was the mandatory starting point.[35]

As long as the Church could seize a privileged position in public debate, it did not have to take on a vulgar role in polemics. On the contrary, it could resort to its pre-Independence role as the arbiter of social disputes. In this way, practice could confirm the theoretical assertion that the Church only watched over society to assure the fulfillment of the best natural values of man in pursuit of the kingdom of God, which only the Church could legitimately represent on Earth. A fundamental aspect of the Church's participation in debate was that it denied it was participating in and claimed it was above polemics, guiding society towards ends beyond those of social man.

By postulating its superiority over social discourse, the Church gained extraordinary flexibility for discursive interventions in the debates of the time. No longer as a mere participant, but as a supreme judge, it could in fact sanction or censure — as it saw fit — every tendency emerging in the life of the young nation. Thus it reaffirmed the duality of civil life which ultimately went back, not only to the situation under the Catholic monarchy, but even further, to the days when the Church consecrated the Empire of Constantine. Scarred by the long series of material wounds and ideological blows it had received since the days of Charles III, the Church set out, when it took part in Mexican Independence, to renounce its confidence in the political powers, without ignoring the need and possibility of allying with them.[36]

The Foundations of
Heavenly Life after Independence

In this context, it is not so strange that in 1820 a cleric should affirm that faith had to be placed at the center of all human life and that the Church's teaching were the underpinnings of social existence, reason itself, and man's happiness.[37] Monarchies were no guarantee of human well-being.[38]. Religion, in fact, supported political power and was in no way dependent on it. Rather it lent vitality and durability to temporal authority.[39]

In 1821, as already seen, the Church made important efforts to bring critical perspectives on colonial rule into line with its theocratic vision of national destiny. If one sermon from this time spoke of the Spanish "yoke" or the "train of despotism," another held forth on "Holy Independence."[40] In the years following, efforts to consecrate Mexican Independence and set out the exact path for its transcendence did not diminish. The clergy attacked hedonism and an excessively worldly vision of the life of man. This exposed society to "the tyranny of a world which can only produce unhappiness."[41]

O worldly ones! Do you wish to live happily on Earth? Piety is useful in all things, an innocent heart is the source of true pleasure: look all around, and you will find there is no peace for the impious. Enjoy every pleasure, and you will see that they cannot cure that source of sadness that stays with you everywhere.[42]

The search for virtue was natural to man, "but in nothing else is he more open to error, due to the illusion of his passions and the vices of our societies."[43]

The lovely theories the philosophers have left us, and the brilliant descriptions their blazing works have transmitted, make virtue lovable in all situations, and the strange beauty of this respectable matron, tears veneration and respect from the most corrupted heart without any violence. But what worship is she rendered in practice? What effects do such beautiful ideas produce in the moral order?[44]

Human pride should shrink before this dilemma. While human sciences were impressive, they could not resolve man's situation in its deepest sense:

[They are] a praiseworthy endeavor and worthy of eternal recognition as long as their advances remain within the narrow limits of human reason, as long as they do not hope to probe with their weak light the deepest depths of divinity, and as long as they know their own incapacity and their nothingness in starting to decipher the adorable secrets of grace.[45]

There still were efforts to reconcile the Enlightenment legacy with new directions. This last sermon, the funeral oration following the death of Bishop Cabañas, pronounced six months later on May 20, 1825, was an indication of the new feeling of the Church on this point. In this case reconciliation, insofar as it was possible, was to be found in the terms chosen to exalt the life and works of the late priest. Of course, he had headed up the Church during its difficult discovery of the social questions which weakened its loyalty to reformism. Cabañas, according to the sermon, was "a man decorated with both an ancient and new virtue, who has been able to join the politics of our days to the good faith of our fathers." He had happened to live in an era in which some reduced virtue "to their pleasure" and others ignored "every obligation that did not come from utility or delight." Facing such a situation, he had not only freed himself from such "foolishness," but also managed to cultivate a "true virtue … without fanaticism or impiety." He "foresaw the fatal pitfalls of … audacious and malicious criticism on religious matters … which begins by censuring acts of piety, advances to reform discipline, and ends up attacking doctrine." Dedicated to the useful and the solid, he devoted himself to "serious studies."[46]

Before becoming bishop of Guadalajara, Cabañas had already demonstrated a felicitous ability to "skillfully join the sciences of time and eternity." Since being promoted to the rank of bishop in Spain, he had been obliged to struggle against the forces of the French Revolution, "in which the shadowy spirit of discord easily confused rights with passions, duties with interests, good causes with bad." Yet the moral strength of the Bishop did not embitter or distance him from society, because "benign, gracious, generous," he lived "apart from society without scorning it." He had the vision to support moral and intellectual reform of the Church, letting himself be guided by "the ideas and good taste of the age we live in."[47]

But not everything was resolved by counterposing and balancing the heavenly and the worldly. If the Bishop had turned out to be, in the preacher's words, the personification of generosity in giving all his wealth to the church and the poor, not all of society acted according to such praiseworthy principles. The priest lashed out at the rich in words recalling others spoken by the late Bishop in 1810:

> You, who are overwhelmed by the pleasures of this world, gather up treasures and cares with each step so that riches rule you and fill you with bitterness, you who voluntarily let your disgraceful heart be imprisoned by the formidable chains of infamous avarice....[48]

The rich should follow the prelate's example to uproot unemployment, help the sick, and promote education and the economy.[49]

However, this call for altruistic motives in social action should not be taken as symptomatic of an excessive rigidity in the thinking of this cleric. He was immediately able to stress that, despite criticism against him, Cabañas had only vacillated about Independence while he convinced himself of "the general vote of the nation." As soon as he had grasped "the general will," he came over to the side of Independence. The preacher went on to state that the late Bishop, "always submissive and obedient of the laws, and *enclosed in the sphere of his pastoral ministry*, never wished to mix himself in political events, but always correctly obeyed constituted authorities." However incongruous this may have sounded, as well as elusive in terms of political actions, it allowed the speaker to suggest that the good Bishop had "been able to act with prudence and singular judgment in our political transitions." This would be an even more valuable skill now that the Empire of Iturbide had given way to the first Mexican federation.[50]

With this sermon, the high clergy of Guadalajara closed one cycle, and opened another. The ups and downs of the time had not eliminated its desire to reconcile the old and the new, and to be a participant and a guide in the new order. The double process of closing and opening cycles took place with symbolic justice at the death of the bishop who had lived through the deepest crisis of ideological reformulation at a regional level. From an allegiance to modernization at first sketched out in confident and simple brushstrokes, the passage of time had demanded an ideological discourse of finer strokes, uncertain and tentative. After 1810, the vacillations, growing internal complexity, and partial spread to lower-ranking individuals of clerical discourse showed how the high clergy were drawing closer to new social conditions. Their thoughts reflected both the internal course of modernization and a more conscious understanding of their place within a reordered society. Little could be assumed in this new setting, and down the road everything tended to become subject to arrogant questioning based on logic as audacious as the emerging groups themselves. Driven by self-interest, these groups wanted to make that interest the political basis of the new order.

Without the leadership of a bishop between 1825 and 1831, the Church would pass through an extremely agitated period. The Church in these years was marked by its self-defense and its debates with the forces that wished to confine it to a limited role in the social and political life of the country; the acceptance of popular sovereignty and greater freedom of the press were the greatest pitfalls. For several years, this new discursive cycle brought to the fore pamphlets rather different from the sermons. In the next three chapters, we will examine the even more difficult times this orientation meant for the Church. Yet as far as sermons go, new examples of clerical discourse are found only after 1829; by that point, the upper ranks of the Church were well on their way to recovery, joining their acceptance of the republic and popular sovereignty to an active defense of their own interests and vision.[51] In that year, there were opportunities to speak against the "intoxication of pride" and to recall "that the essence of kingship does not consist of commanding men, but of obeying God."[52] There were clarifications that the Christian God is a "King who is judge and arbiter of Kings."[53] The outlook was sad because man found himself in

a world where all flesh has corrupted its path, where there are very few who do not bear the mark of crime on their brow, where the praise of pleasure rings out, where candor is seen as stupidity, truth as imprudence, piety as superstition, and where there is hardly a single just man who sees the world as if he did not live in it.[54]

The 1820s came to a close not only with the fall of the government of Vicente Guerrero, but also with a reappearance of clerical pessimism about the human condition.[55] During the 1830s, the weariness of the high clergy with Mexican public life undoubtedly deepened. Sermons took on a melodramatic tone. Faced with a situation of open setbacks for the Church, more than one cleric would come down from the abstract heights to set out clearly the specifics of public life.

The celebrations of the appointment of a new bishop for Guadalajara in 1831 were an occasion to rejoice in the salvation of the Church of Jalisco from "the infernal wolves who wished to devour her."[56] There was continual fear of "the explosion of a bomb being prepared against the Altar."

> Frightening shadows that hide the infamous projects of the patricidal [Masonic] lodges! Reveal unto us, yes, tell us what things are being considered against holy rents, against religious establishments, against worship, in a word, against the Church of Jesus Christ![57]

The situation was already quite serious, and difficult to explain. The unity between Church and nation, between religion and the state, was endangered. Perhaps

> Our Lord wishes to test our patience, to humble us, and to purify us through tribulations in order to console us later, and make us understand that we have a bishop, not by men, nor by human means, but by means of his beloved majesty.[58]

In 1833, the death of the recently appointed Bishop Gordoa offered the opportunity for a more measured – but no less forceful – affirmation of the viable relation between religion and society:

> I know well that patriotic love is a virtue we are all obliged to cultivate; I know that obligation comes from the very nature of things, that natural law does not contradict religion, and that our Divine Savior did not come to destroy the social virtues, but to perfect them.[59]

Yet religion should rule over things of this world. Only it was stable and lasting, as well as absolutely transcendent of human life. "Columns crumble, triumphal arches fall down, laurels come undone, and medals wear away," and therefore "only virtue has the power to glorify the dead."[60]

The union between the Church and state remained shaky. Another clerical speaker proclaimed in 1834, after the fall of the liberal government of Valentín Gómez Farías:

> O nineteenth century! How I would like to banish from my memory your terribly baneful sorrows! America, gentlemen, America was resentful, and rightly so, of the usurpation of her rights, rights given her by nature and left intact by Holy Religion, and also convinced that nature itself now makes her able to govern herself, that the elements nature's beneficial hand provides grant her the first place among cultured nations, and that those very elements promise her an easy and certain success in her endeavor. [Thus] she gave in to the vehemence of her patriotic love, planned to break the ties that bound her to Spain, gave a strong shove to break in a single blow the reinforced base of the chain which linked these two hemispheres, resolved at last to be free, and on the memorable day of the sixteenth of September of one thousand eight hundred and ten gave the glorious cry of independence whose echo rang from pole to pole.

Who could have conceived that liberty, the heavenly gift with which the Divine Maker ennobles man, and which religion itself protects, would serve as a pretext for destroying it?[61]

He could only conclude that in Mexico, an "impious and oppressive government lacking feelings of humanity" had fallen, whose greatest sin was a "crime against divine majesty."[62]

If there was still anyone who did not wish to heed the Church, that was not because they had any doubts about its position. The voice of another cleric cried out in 1836:

> Unfortunately, there exists among us an insolent and extremely perverse sect which has constantly declared war on the honor, fortune, rest and tranquility of citizens, on the peace and unity of families, on the success and greatness of the fatherland, on the freedoms and rights of the Church ... a sect which has professed every religious, political and moral error and ... would even dare to climb to the august throne of God on High ... you understand, gentlemen, that I speak of the sect gathered under the banner of York, the fruitful origin of all the disgrace and calamity suffered by the fatherland.[63]

This sect had dug a grave to bury the magnificent unity of the independent nation first founded by Iturbide. "Can the patriot observe the miserable state of the republic without horror?" Agitation and anxiety had culminated in "the final effort of the demagogues," only held back because (right) "opinion always triumphs and moral force is irresistible." But even this salvation was not enough to eliminate the sense of a world "always inconstant, always false and deceptive in its hopes, always in continuous agitation."[64] The true problem was clarified the next year, however, when a cleric pointed to "so many faithless and cowardly souls, who by seeking not God, but themselves" had become "hardened spirits" insensitive to the Church's guidance on Earthly life.[65]

During the 1830s, clerical discourse had passed into a new phase. The meta-historical, Providence-centered, and very general vision of the Independence years had given way to a difficult new period of adjustment to the implications of popular sovereignty. Now, in the midst of growing worry about the effective advance of the positions of its opponents, the Church produced a new and more specific reading from within Mexican historical life. The political arrangement chosen for the exercise of popular sovereignty should allow the practical application of the high virtues the providential interpretation had proposed for the nation. Since they had not been complied with, and had even been openly attacked in order to propose other ideals for building the nation, the Church had to discursively counterattack in order to firm up the efforts of the fatherland and set its own precise outline. Popular sovereignty should not allow a radicalized minority to set the destiny of Mexico. Facing such a clique, the Church felt itself to be a better interpreter and reflection of Mexican popular opinion. It would invoke its constitutional freedom to defend its interests, and also to make use of its voice as authentic guide of the free and sovereign Mexican people.[66]

This new phase would not change greatly during the period ending in 1853/1854 with the return and then the fall of General Santa Anna. Its characteristic features became still clearer. The Church confirmed and deepened its struggle against passion and violence, its search for peace, tranquility and social harmony by means of pious values. In the aftermath of the war with the United States, the Church would reaffirm the role of the priesthood in the social life of the nation, and fight desperately for the abandonment of utopian ideals which assumed that social man was sufficient unto himself without recourse to religion. The ills the nation was lamenting, its defeat and humiliation, were due to its straying from the path of the Virgin of Guadalupe set out since Independence. If this path did promise Mexico a role as the New Israel, it also demanded – under pain of chastisement – that Mexico fully comply with this divine covenant.[67]

When all seemed lost, when the errors of this age ruled over the government and the highest levels of society, when the United States had wrested from Mexico more than half of the national territory, when all pride and all hope were shattered, only then would providence deign to give Mexico a new opportunity, one which demanded that the nation return to the proper path. Every social force – even the most traditional – should assume its responsibility, rectify its errors and "wanderings" with dignity, and serve the fatherland with unselfishness and loyalty. The 1850s had arrived and Mexico would have to be reformed along an authentically Catholic path, recalling its lofty mission as a chosen people. One document from 1850 denounced the "impetuous overflow of corruption and impiety which rots modern societies." It called on "the banner raised by Catholicism" and declared that "Guadalajara justly demands the glory of being at the vanguard of this truly renewing movement, in which the lovers of order and the happiness of the fatherland have placed their hopes."[68] On the death of Bishop Aranda in 1853, another speaker would expound:

> O, if we could only erase from the pages of our history the disgraceful events of 1847, as shameful for the republic as they were disastrous for the Mexican Church, when the temples of other dioceses were robbed of their most precious jewels, the goods of convents and monasteries were taken away, part of Church lands were auctioned off to infamous usurers, to end it all with the sale of more than half of the republic! My God![69]

The problem demanded a solution. Perhaps we should mention that the man the Church supported to politically define and carry out this mission, the man allegedly chosen by the same destiny which guided human affairs, was none other than Antonio López de Santa Anna. This would be the caudillo's last government before the liberal insurgency defeated him with the Plan de Ayutla.

An 1853 sermon celebrating the new presidency of the Mexican general spelled out a feeling then dominant throughout the Church in Guadalajara, and perhaps across the entire country:

> I will speak first as a Mexican, then as a Catholic. As a Mexican I will say that the nation in its deep unease instinctively sought someone to lend a hand to raise it from its baneful collapse. And what did the nation ask for, what did it need? Three things, gentlemen, and nothing more: three things. First: someone to assure its nationality. Second: someone to preserve its worship and religion. Third: someone to organize it internally as a great and strong power. And are not all these pressing and just requirements satisfied with the wise choice the majority of the country has just made?[70]

When the preacher spoke as a Catholic, he said simply that

> God made this change ... but he has placed on us the same conditions as on the children of Israel. If we observe the holy law of God, if we walk with the Lord in spirit and in truth, if we are faithful to his testament, we will reach the happiness born of the harmony and agreement of the magistrate with God, of the people with the law, and of the law with principles of eternal justice."[71]

For this a profound reform in customs and public morality was required. The Guadalajara clergy did not dodge this commitment:

> And since we should all contribute to the good of the nation, with our own oblation, we priests will begin the work, building up the people, weeping for their miseries and our own failures, between the vestibule and the altar, and showing the world with our own testimony and conduct, that we are angels of consolation, angels of peace. And in turn, the judges: administer justice rightly, without forgetting what the apostle has said – you were not given the sword in vain. And the soldier: abuse no one with your power, defame no one, live as the holy Baptist wishes and counsels, "happy with his wages and pay." And all the other classes of society: live honestly and in perfect obedience to God, because he is God, and to Caesar, because God commands it. This conduct is so Christian and so highly worthy, that we will be rewarded with eternal happiness. Amen.[72]

5

A Fundamental Shift

Independence, Popular Sovereignty and Freedom of the Press

Political Geometry

This chapter and the ones that follow address the ways in which liberal spokesmen's overall perspectives on change were intertwined with those of the dominant Church groups. Even though liberalism and clerical ideology were clearly opposed on important issues, they also had significant agreements on social questions. Their forms of addressing those questions, however, differed. While liberals – especially after 1824 – saw all around them a widespread and deep-rooted social rot, with little sign of renewal, clerical observers saw things with a distinct twist. That is, they agreed there was an objective need for change and renewal, and that society's imperfections should be addressed, but they held that the transformation required could be carried out without any drastic change in the social order. From the clerical point of view, popular representation was perfectly compatible with social order and discipline and, therefore, with popular sovereignty exercised primarily by the state. Gradualism and constitutionalism were their banners. Laws had to be observed and time had to pass for things to improve. Wanting to build the perfect world in a single step was an illusion which only proved the ignorance or naïveté of whoever proposed it.

In Guadalajara, it was Francisco Severo Maldonado who best addressed the dilemma these ideological positions created, in the *Nuevo pacto social* he wrote for the 1822/1823 Cortes in Cádiz. National independence surprised him before he could finish the work. In reality, this did not greatly bother the unstoppable cleric; he quickly made the necessary changes so that his project for reforming the Spanish nation would be equally, or even more, applicable to the Mexican nation. Maldonado began with the same premise he had established in his newspaper *El Telégrafo de Guadalajara*: the best reform assumes and requires social peace. Going deeper in his new writings, he quoted Descartes: "Il n'ést past plus aise à un de se défaire de sus préjugés, que de brûler sa maison." He immediately moved on to Rousseau: "Voulez vous regner sur les préjugés? Commencez a regner par eux."[1] Translating these principles into concrete terms, he added later on that "alone among all the nations of Europe," the Spanish monarchy

> like nature reproducing herself from her ruins, had discovered in the very vices, errors and disorders of her previous misgovernment the most effective and sure means of achieving swift and complete restoration.[2]

This was not simply a matter of finding the instruments of renewal among the debris of the past. Citing Jean-Baptiste Say, Maldonado established that "instability produces such dreadful effects that one cannot even pass from a bad system to a good system without suffering serious troubles."[3] He specified that

> ... a good constitution should be like the sun, which by the wisdom and goodness of the Supreme Being rises every day and lights and heats the good and the bad equally. There is no one who does not share, or might not share, in her healthy influences.[4]

Every interest present in corrupted society had the right to be represented in the new, renewed society of the future. In fact, a secure future could only be built on such plurality and care for the past – and the avoidance of "the sophistries of a false and dangerous liberalism." The task to be accomplished was the overall coordination of "state interest with individual interest, a sacred and eternal principle." Here, "there is no room for abstract general wills, but for pragmatic agreements for renewal between the different sectors of society."[5] The preacher wrote:

> O fathers of the fatherland! Do not rush the advance along your majestic course, or try to speed through many centuries in little time. Do not rush to knock down the Gothic edifice of our aged

former government, without first examining all the parts of its ancient construction. Among them you will find many excellent materials to employ, if you only retouch them lightly and clean them of the unfortunate and Baroque forms the ignorance of past centuries disfigured them with. Thus you will build a new edifice incomparably more solid than those palaces of false façades and utterly squalid interior structure which political architects have raised up among the other nations of Europe in recent years.[6]

Thus Maldonado placed himself on the razor's edge. He invoked his fellow clergy's profound traditionalism, on the one hand, and their awareness of the need for change, on the other. He trusted, as he often stated, that his reform project would be a project with truly general support, overcoming the dispute already launched between the "servile" and the liberals.[7]

By contrast, openly liberal pamphlets were radical and decisive, far from the intellectual and social juggling of Maldonado. Their authors chose to protect their radicalism by writing anonymously, keeping themselves safe from any possible personal counterattack. This also allowed them to blend in with the everyday crowd of people in social life, even if this approach implied a certain hypocrisy.[8]

What held social discourse together was the judgment that the colonial order had been seriously deficient and that present conditions offered good opportunities and broad possibilities for improving matters. Independence consolidated this common discursive base. But the anonymity of liberal pamphlets allowed for various analyses, diagnoses and solutions to be tossed out into the public forum without anyone being tied to them directly. Thus liberal pamphlets became the measure of theoretically possible change. The pamphlets proposed transformation according to principles society had not yet accepted in practice. They were a challenge to the status quo, to conformism, and to the lack of imagination. They were the affirmation of a free and sovereign reason, even if reality was stacked against them and difficult to manage. They were also the means of expression of the independent pride of youth with its own power to reason, understand and finally propose and decide. They allowed sovereign thinkers to let their imaginations and pens run wild without the danger of ad hominem attacks, and without any risk for their own private or public lives outside the forum of unrestricted reason. They were also a reflection of youthful admiration for the achievements of

Europe and the United States, and disappointment with Spanish heritage and ecclesiastical thought.

Maldonado, for all his nit-picking positions towards the past and future, captured the peculiarities of this movement.

> Politics is a science as unvarying in its principles as geometry. And just as it would be absurd to say that each people should have their own geometry, so it is absurd to say that each should have their own politics or their peculiar constitution. All these statements prove the general ignorance we are suffering from in the basic and clear principles of the science of association, and how close even the lettered are to doctrines that open the doors to arbitrariness and therefore to tyranny.[9]

In fact, the political geometry being introduced into Mexico originated mostly in literature from north of the Pyrenees, as indicated by the ideas and quotes of Maldonado and the openly declared liberals. It spearheaded critical political debate in Mexico after Independence. Its principles were clearly and constantly felt; one anonymous author proclaimed, in 1823:

> The best government is that under whose influence nations grow and prosper, men enjoy the greatest civil liberty, equality is protected, property is defended, and all the rights of the citizen are assured to the greatest degree.[10]

Pledges "on matters of government," he continued, "are conditional," and they are conditioned precisely by "national confidence." Sovereignty corresponds directly to the nation, which can change governments whenever it pleases, in keeping with "happiness, the only end of every human society."[11]

Thus, the 1820s became an impassioned period when some promoted the idea of a dramatic and definitive change in Mexican life. The declaration of popular sovereignty – moderated at first by the establishment of the Empire, but expanded shortly afterwards with the proclamation of the Federal Republic in 1824 – at once reflected and advanced a new relationship between society and "public affairs." Prisciliano Sánchez said:

> From century to century, there appears for the consolation of humanity a happy moment which passes quickly and never again returns. How unlucky the peoples who uselessly let it escape! Such

is the moment that on the present occasion the heavens in their mercy have offered the nation of Anáhuac [Mexico].

Fellow citizens, ours is a singular epoch: we fortunately find ourselves on the best occasion for happiness if we rightly constitute ourselves in a way dignified and fitting the ideas of the century we are living in.[12]

This vision of things opened and broadened political debate to include social organization, the definition of nationality, the challenges to be faced and the goals to accomplish. The country's problems were blamed on the government's previous lack of representativeness. Now that limitless possibilities opened up before a representative and effective government, many expressed the opinion that no reasonable achievement should be beyond the nation's reach. There were no insurmountable barriers to the progressive development of the nation, only technical difficulties in finding the right mechanism to bring it about, as well as, of course, larger problems in precisely defining desired objectives. Even though such problems might have seemed passing matters, more formalities than realities, in fact the fierce polemics of the 1820s would yield uncertain and worrisome results. This was an impasse, pushing resolution into a more or less distant future. Good faith, optimistic confidence, and the sense of a predictable present and future would have to be severely changed to speed up this process.

The constitutive nature of the 1820s in Mexican life is clear in pamphlets. Leaving aside for the moment pamphlets expressly dedicated to religious matters, the remainder were eloquent testimony to the issues arousing interest and winning the attention of thinkers and legislators. There were treatises on political association, projects and rulings on the financial structure of state and nation, positions on the organization of industry and commerce, many analytical and rhetorical writings about the political transition underway, and finally an assortment of publications about other questions of state organization. To judge by the major thrust of propagandists, public administration drew attention and mobilized political loyalties the most. The press reflected a Guadalajara immersed in the task of defining its personality and public existence in terms of the state and its ideological basis. The structure of society was to be redefined, starting with the state, producing a future unlike the past. Rather than reflecting present-day society, seen as weak and insufficient, the state would bring to life the

elements of transformation and development present within it.[13]
The state was born as a state for the people, but not by the people,
or at the very least not by "the people" according to the strict
definitions of the time, who were not seen as sound and self-sufficient. "Three centuries of tyranny" were why the people were
not able to act for themselves. Now, whatever was not useful had
to be dismantled, in order to reassemble society along appropriate
guidelines set from the heights of the state.

Tradition was no longer seen as a reservoir of wealth, but as a
barrier to making rational and optimal use of all the human and
material resources of society. In between the spontaneous repeti-
tion of the past and the widely recognized need to overcome it, the
state found its place. Just as the transformation of the late medieval
state had made the monarchy base itself on the emerging corps of
"lettered" advisors, so the national state would now depend on a
relatively small number of reformers. These, in turn, would always
aim to place themselves close to a state which historically represented the connection point between the various sectors, layers
and corporations of highly heterogeneous Hispanic society.

It is worth returning to what José María Luis Mora said in
the 1830s:

> If Independence had taken place forty years ago, a man born or
> settled in the territory would not have cared at all for the title of
> *Mexican*, and would have considered himself alone and isolated in
> the world, without any other title. For such a man, the title of high
> court judge [*oidor*], of canon, and even of guild-brother [*cofrade*]
> would have been more worthwhile and we have to agree that he
> would have been right, since it meant something positive: to debate
> *national interests* with him would have been like speaking to him in
> Hebrew; he neither knew nor could he know any other interests
> but those of the *body* or *bodies* he belonged to and he would have
> sacrificed the interests of the rest of society for them, even if they
> were more numerous and important.... Bodies exercise a kind of
> tyranny over the thinking and action of their members, and they
> have quite clear tendencies to monopolize influence and opinion by
> means of the symbol of the doctrine they profess, the commitments
> they demand, and the obligations they impose.[14]

The national state was called to change this situation, replacing
it with a different dynamic based on new principles opposed
to past tradition. Like the axis of a wheel, the state was what

communicated each spoke (corporate body or social layer) with the others in the meantime, while the reforms designed to pull that structure apart were being carried out. That is why the state represented the promise of transformation and became the center of social concerns and debates.

The key role of the state in setting societal goals in the Hispanic world cannot be minimized. The Bourbons assigned the state a central position in the transformation of Spain and its Empire. The liberals only partially deviated from this; they considered the reshaping of the state, its laws and its ethics, to be fundamental for any change in society. But they tried to orient the state's activity towards removing corporate privilege, heavy fiscal burdens, bureaucratic clumsiness and exclusivity – religious or otherwise – in public opinion. Curiously enough, the state should ensure that society avoided falling into past patterns, the ones which – from the liberal point of view – had so terribly narrowed the horizons of previous generations. The task of the new, liberal state was to destroy the outmoded patterns and to establish and oversee the liberating new arrangements promising progress.[15]

Up until then, Mexican life had been connected on every level with the Catholic Church, and so it was only natural that the Church found itself practically at the center of every debate. Politically, how could absolute priority be given to the popular state derived from popular sovereignty without delving into a debate about the Church and its powerful influence over the personal loyalties of many? Socially, how could a reform of society and economy be launched, how could the state be strengthened for the task, without involving the Church and its most concrete manifestations?

The Promise of Independence:
Juggling Nationhood and Freedom

Obviously enough, as already seen, the definition of Mexican nationality sparked disputes between pro-clerical and pro-secular thinkers. If nationality was made a value in itself, that brought out the libertarian and Enlightened aspects of a feisty, popular sovereignty. But if, on the other hand, it was tied to a transcendent mission inspired by Christian messianism, then nationality was turned into a vehicle for achieving something greater than itself. In that case, it would take on a traditional rather than reformist cast coming from sacred respect for the past in which this destiny had been set. Even more importantly, the Church and its authorities, as necessary spokesmen for this transcendent mission, would be positioned as guides of the nation's steps and transformations. In this sense, defining national challenges and goals implied a series of prior assumptions about politics, nationality and social organization. National challenges and goals would be the point where objective reality clashed with the projection of subjective values, a situation which polarized public opinion in Guadalajara, as pamphlets show.

To stress the point, this was the moment for remaking nothing less than the social life of the country. For people of various social outlooks, Independence was a sign that the status quo was no longer adequate. The possibilities emerging with independence brought forth a truly enviable optimism and conceptual clarity, but who had the right to set Mexican destiny? Who represented popular feeling – or the "general will" of the people – and how? Was the people's agreement on matters of custom, belief and conviction a vote of confidence? Or was it a sign of the overwhelming ignorance perpetuated by those who should have represented and overseen the people in days gone by, but who had misruled and defrauded them instead? If that were the case, how could the state promote the liberty and progress of a people who did not fully desire either?

Trying to address these problems amidst mounting disgust with the reign of Agustín de Iturbide, one author called for the consolidation of an authentic public opinion through freedom of the press and enlightenment of the people. His perspective was based on obviously liberal principles which turned every man into a sovereign who had to struggle for his own happiness:

> Without enlightenment, there is no liberty, and so long as men do not know their rights, they will not know how to defend themselves. We must enlighten ourselves, because as long as ignorance is sheltered in our hearts, the rule of despotism will not cease. This monster must be defeated for our happiness, because otherwise, the arbitrariness and injustice of despots will disturb our tranquility at every moment. Our properties will not be secure, our existence will be uncertain, and our lives will only be preserved in exchange for lamentable work in the tyrant's service. In short, so long as the people are ignorant, so long as they do not know their own dignity, and finally so long as they do not know that all power is theirs, that sovereignty dwells in them and that they alone are the legitimate sovereign, everything will

be injustice, everything despotism, everything arbitrariness. Ministers will abuse their power, government will be in disarray, intrigue will do its part, espionage will redouble its watch, bootlickers will increase their perfidy, and in sum: the servile will work with untiring zeal to hold back the enlightenment of the people.[16]

If Independence represented a prolonged crisis of the premises which had guided the social life of man, the 1820s can be seen as a period of deep reflection, ambition, and notable audacity. They held out the hope of a time for Mexico. The moment was right to forge the nation. Years of political apprenticeship and then of political insubordination informed the polemics of those times. Yet for liberals, this was a time that had lasted too long, when they lamented the monotony of a routine that refused to pass away. They rejoiced, nonetheless, at the unsuspected power of the people as it made itself evident. By contrast, the traditionalists demanded a slowdown, because they claimed that a country whose construction was just beginning required understanding and patience to keep the work from spoiling. Two opposing times and their complexities always threatened to smother the object of so many efforts. This was undeniably a very human time, confronting men with a challenging reality that demanded transformation.

For people of liberal leanings, independent Mexico was facing the danger – among others – that civil structures would once again be taken for granted, as worthy in themselves of social loyalties, in keeping with a conservative interpretation of the ancient Christian slogan of "render unto Caesar the things of Caesar, and unto God the things of God." From this standpoint, the state might once again be seen as the sole bearer of sovereignty, a sovereignty understood as not constantly exercised by the people, since at most they would merely monitor the proper behavior of the rulers. The relationship between the civic order and the divine order appeared to be a possibly deadly trap for the republican civic behavior of the young nation. It seemed to free the individual from any lasting and deep commitment to the social order, since that order would be overcome and abandoned as the citizen achieved his goals in another more spiritual and heavenly dimension. Such an orientation threatened to force the social order into virtually replicating civil society exactly as it was constituted at that moment. This would offer the possibility of limiting certain "abuses" by putting pressure on institutions and their representatives, but it provided no real chance to completely renew those institutions through the participation of civil man, eager to achieve self-development and self-fulfillment through worldly institutions.

So long as religious transcendence continued to be presented in terms which relegated civil society to secondary status, it did not seem necessary to take it to heart. From this perspective, William Blake could rightly ask in England a few years earlier: "Are not religion and politics the same thing?"[17] As Groethuysen put it, "a vision of the world is … a creation of the world, a modeling of the world."[18] The relationship between the divine and the worldly set the terms for action in politics. The matter undoubtedly went deep. For some, the deeds which enhanced civil and political society should be judged in light of an essentially theological vision of man and his Earthly surroundings. Society was a means, but not an end in itself. For others, society was hardly a mere stage, but rather the place for achieving human ideals, and the field of battle on which human institutions would increasingly draw closer to their maximum possibilities. For some this was a matter of human transcendence within a given setting, hierarchically subject to God, from whom all Earthly sovereignty came. For others, this was a matter of man's transcendence as a Mexican, in very concrete terms, whose sovereignty came from himself and whose future possibilities depended on his own capacity to develop them intelligently, to transform his reality, and to make clear the way towards a complete improvement of man by man.

It was precisely on the question of the exercise of sovereignty that the rejection of the government of Iturbide in 1823 was based. This struggle would be the forerunner to the emergence of the fight between liberalism and clerical ideology. Iturbide, it was said, had begun with a representative monarchy, but with the passing of time he had merged his state power with his own whims, and not with the free and full interests of his fellow citizens. One author who signed himself "J.J.C." stated

> … that the political existence of Mister Iturbide is incompatible with our happiness, because he has never respected the inviolate rights of man, he has not kept the constitution that was temporarily adopted by the state, he has disdained popular sovereignty, recognizing no law other than his own whims and interest; he has violated the sacred pacts on which public security rests, and he has always perjured, and never kept, what he offered to the nation.[19]

Iturbide had failed precisely in not taking the nation to the higher of the "two steps" necessary to make Independence real: "the first, to be independent of the Spanish government, and the second, to shake off domestic tyranny which should follow it."[20] A pamphlet signed by El Cuerpo de Liberales (The Body of Liberals) insisted that

> [w]e are told that we are now free, and we do not yet enjoy even the freedom to think; we are blessed with electing the government, and we are prohibited from examining it; we are promised a constitution, and our representatives are crushed; enormous contributions are demanded of us, and we are told they are not enough....Against order-givers and tyrants, the healthy portion of Guadalajara ... wants to take active part in public operations ... wants to make effective that wondrous sovereignty spoken of.[21]

The problem was great, they admitted, because such an exercise of sovereignty would confront citizens "with the crowd educated in the tenth century, and with another large segment who live off disorder." But "since when do changes not have their difficulties?" And "should we live badly, because we do not work to live well?"[22]

That same year, José Joaquín Fernández de Lizardi also entered the fray in Guadalajara, by means of the reprinting of an incisive pamphlet. Lizardi set out his argument by sarcasm: "I think that Americans (at least those in Mexico) understand liberty to be nothing more than independence from Spain; the rest they put up with patiently." He claimed that "we were born beneath the sign of the sheep [*sic*], and we accept everything with patience and the love of God, because we are followers and because we are blessed." Only freedom of the press could change things; otherwise, "give me fools, and I will give you slaves."[23]

It was exactly along these lines, placing emphasis on the difficult but necessary participation of citizens in the handling of public affairs, that the governor of Jalisco, Luis Quintanar, argued for the necessarily federal nature of the republic that would succeed Iturbide's imperial regime. In fact, he argued that the social pact had been broken by the insurrection of its signatories – the states – following the general will of those they represented:

> With the power of the congressmen annulled by the general will, their representativeness in the Mexican assembly is truly ephemeral

and worthless, and they should only be considered an isolated and lonely group, without any relationship to the people. If the people played a role in electing congressmen, they did not sign a binding contract to keep them in office, since it should be understood that the people gave their government a provisional form that was tolerated until the people wished to rearrange it.

With the existence of a central government in Mexico thus adulterated, it is necessary as a consequence that the nation is now in its natural state to provide for itself, and in this case the respective provincial governments, elected by the populace, are fully authorized by the people to set the route to be followed.[24]

The governor concluded his statement with the affirmation that "in republics, everyone is born a magistrate."[25] Another author, who signed his name "R.P.," stated that:

> The duties that man has towards society are a product of his convenience and well-being, and each one of them is directly related to the utility it provides for whoever carries it out; therefore egoism in this sense is the best philanthropy, the best and healthiest patriotism; let the individual rightly love the human race above all, but when he assures other citizens of the same rights which he demands from them, then this nation will be the most virtuous and orderly.[26]

Once more he reached federalist conclusions. The "unbearable and baseless primogeniture of Mexico City" – forever "striving to call itself the metropolis" – could be tolerated no longer. All that was left to Guadalajara was to proclaim, as it already had, that "I am equal to the rest of the provinces; all of them together have no rights over me."[27]

The concept of limited state power was stressed by Prisciliano Sánchez, a convinced federalist and shortly afterwards the first governor of the federated state of Jalisco:

> Nothing is more contrary to the dignity and preference of man, to his general vote and to the survival of the social pact, than demanding of him a greater portion of liberty than what is necessary to assure the other portion which is left to him. A well-constituted state should not give its rulers more authority over its subjects than is necessary to maintain social order. Everything beyond those limits is abuse, tyranny, usurpation, because man never gives up freely more than what is strictly necessary to gain a greater good. Therefore the desire to give up [power] should never be assumed.[28]

It was exactly on this point that liberal pamphlets called into question the traditional role of the Church and its upper ranks in the political life and thought of society. Since 1822, Lizardi had entered debates in Guadalajara by means of a reprinting. He proclaimed then "that men have learned that nations are not the patrimony of kings or priests."[29] He insisted on the sovereignty question:

> Yes, sir, pride made kings despots, and ambition made priests fanatics and tyrants.... *Not all* of them, but certainly *many* of them. Monarchs came to need ecclesiastical authority to sanction and sustain them on the throne, and pontiffs so dominated kings that they removed and installed them according to their wishes, relaxing the oath of loyalty of king's vassals as they saw fit, so that any Pope could then say of the kings of Christendom: *per me reges regnant.*
>
> Since royal authority depended on the Church, we can understand that the latter did with royalty as it pleased. From this came the privileges, judicial rights, immunities, and prerogatives which were well-deserved because of the dignity of their ministry, but which were abused to the scandal and harm of the people.
>
> By contrast, the ecclesiastical state, taking advantage of popular ignorance and fanaticism, proclaimed the authority of kings above all others, *after its own*, teaching the people that kings came directly from God, that sovereignty resided in them, and that it was a heresy to think that nations were sovereign or could be free, since kings were absolute lords and masters of the lives and properties of men, who were only their vassals or slaves, born to obey and suffer, even if the king was a tyrant, since doing otherwise would mean resisting the divine order.
>
> These and similar supremely servile maxims, contrary to natural law and the dignity of man, were printed in books, preached from pulpits, and encouraged in confessionals, and with this holy diligence the despotism of kings was promoted with impunity.[30]

In Lizardi's view, the Inquisition had been the faithful instrument of the despotism born of the union of Church and state. Facing such a union of throne and altar, to the detriment of the robust exercise of sovereignty by the people, Lizardi tore sovereignty in civic practice away from its heavenly ties. He chastised Iturbide:

> It is true that kings reign thanks to God, just as everything is done because He allows it and participates as first cause, *omnia per ipsum facta sunt.* That is why Your Majesty is emperor by divine Providence, but according to the natural order, Your Majesty is emperor because

your nation proclaimed you thus, and its legitimate representatives confirmed its sovereign will.[31]

In this context, Lizardi advised the emperor that he "act as a constitutional president- emperor."[32] Shortly afterwards, in response to the crisis sparked by the fall of Iturbide, an author who signed himself "A.R.F." would state:

> In God's name, let us leave behind our foolish worries, and realize that it harms our Holy Religion in nothing if we constitute ourselves under the system of a Republic. This government only looks to establish some laws fitting our customs and situation, and has nothing to do with ecclesiastical doctrine and discipline. Colombia is a republic, and it is Catholic. England is a monarchy, and it is Protestant.[33]

Liberals were worried about the religious concerns of the people, which predisposed them towards traditionalism in political matters and social practices, as is evident in pamphlets within Guadalajara and elsewhere.[34]

It was the elaboration of a Jalisco Constitution in 1824 that launched the richest and most challenging debate about the ties between the Church and public affairs. The debate reached greater intensity because it included the question of not only the free exercise of sovereignty, but also of the financial well-being of the new free and federated state, the development of its economy and its right to international recognition. One pamphlet asserted:

> The priests of every nation and every century have always and forever wished to assume a different status within states and to be governed by rules very different from those governing the mass of the people. They have always wished to dominate all temporal authorities, because by making their authority descend from the heavens, they have tried to place it above all others. The ignorance of the people at first allowed the clergy to abuse its spiritual attributes, dominating them astutely with other faculties which, being temporal in nature, belong to the people themselves. Everything was spiritualized by necessity in order to place even the most precious and sacred rights of nations under the ecclesiastical rod.
>
> The clergy based their enormous power on two great columns which in all times they have tried to make untouchable, *rents and judicial rights*. This is what is frightening about the clergy, and what goes against the grain of the republican equality which the

federation of United Mexican States so prides itself on. If the supreme authorities of the states do not have sufficient [authority] over all the state's inhabitants, of whatever class, status or condition they may be, then it is impossible to keep the people in peace and quiet, because if there are individuals who except themselves from submission to the supreme chief, then that will be enough to agitate and make insolent the rest with impunity.[35]

The administration of justice had to be equitable for all if there was a real desire for concord between ecclesiastical and civil authorities.[36] In addition, the independent wealth of the clergy had to be done away with in order to assure economic development and obedience to the state:

Ecclesiastical rents: that robust and prideful giant which in order to feed its insatiable belly sucks the nurturing juice out of agriculture and leaves the miserable peoples drained, that formidable arm which skillfully moved by the high clergy overcomes the law itself and triumphs over the wisest institutions, that strong shield the authority of sovereigns has always run up against, and that dominating post from whose heights the ecclesiastics have subjected to their influence every branch of public administration. Ecclesiastical rents: I say they cannot remain standing as they are without causing the ruin of the nation. Even clearer: the prosperity of the Mexican nation and its true liberty cannot be realized if the existing system of ecclesiastical rents is not changed.[37]

The author recommended immediate use of state patronage to straighten out the situation, stating that this patronage was "inborn, inherent, and inseparable from the sovereignty of the Mexican nation."[38]

Attacking the clergy effectively, with any chance of weakening its power in society, required undermining the overall prestige it still enjoyed. It required breaking the priesthood's commonly appreciated tie to divinity, and placing members of the priesthood on a level with the other individuals in society, susceptible like them to vices and group interests which went against the general interest. The author known as El Polar proclaimed with severity:

The clergy has tried to place itself outside the circle of society. But they are men like us, they enjoy like us the advantages of society, they live with us and owe their existence to our labors; those of us who break the earth with our arms feed them, those of us who harden our hands in shops clothe them. Is it just that, with such a great debt, with such close ties, they wish to govern themselves without us? There is no reason for doubt: they form part of society, they are members of society and should be entirely subject to the authority of the government just like the rest of us.[39]

Here, as in other liberal authors of the time, an important change takes place. The problem was not religion or the Church as a whole, but the priesthood, and that group should not aspire to more than parity with the other members of society. Society worked and did its duty; when the clergy did the same, it had the right to the corresponding recognition, yet it should not be forgotten that they lived off the efforts of the rest. If the clergy were found to be doing well, that was cause for suggesting their laziness, on the one hand, and the fatigue of lay society, on the other. The canons of the Guadalajara Cathedral were the largest target, here, although any hypothetically abusive and self-interested priest could serve to make the contrast. And the canons in fact embodied a great part of the religious problem under scrutiny. They were the men whose erudition and pens had been at the service of the interests of the Church. They had not lived from the healing of souls at the parish level – a necessary office – but from tithing, which detoured funds from economic development and the state coffers. From this, they enjoyed such economic independence that they could free themselves even of the authority of the state.[40]

The Promise of Independence:
Church Accountability and a Free People

The Political Constitution of Jalisco was where this debate crystallized. Very specific principles and interests were in dispute. This constitution presented the first frontal attack on the internal autonomy of the Church and its union on equal terms with the state. In Article 7, it subjected ecclesiastical financing to state control, which placed all the ministers of the Church under the economic and implicitly moral authority of the government. The article in question read:

> The state Religion is the Apostolic Roman Catholic without tolerance of any other. The state will set and pay all the expenses necessary to promote worship.[41]

The defense of the republican and federal Constitution was easily combined with an attack on the hierarchical character of religious practice. The established interests of the clergy, it was claimed, were alien to true religion and had distorted it. Thus the effort of the "sovereign people," as pointed to in Article 7 of the Constitution, was required to make religion once more "pure, clean, and beautiful, without stains to make her ugly or wrinkles to make her pitiable."[42] The pristine purity of things was to be reestablished. The people

> wanted and want to have ministers who serve them spiritually and whom they maintain bodily. But the people do not want to be hungry for the bread of heaven despite keeping lords to serve, who cannot be spoken to except by written petition, whom the people fear and must fear because they have become potentates with the riches they have acquired through exactions from the poor. In sum, the people wanted and want justice, religion in all its purity, the uprooting of abuses, abundance, prosperity and decorum in all things.[43]

If there were those who did not want to hear such truths, this polemicist, signing his name as the Unbiased Ecclesiastic, challenged them not only to declare him a heretic, but along with him to declare Saint Benedict a heretic as well, since he had spoken even more harshly of the same problem in his time. A careful citation of the saint's words was offered as solid proof.[44]

The demand for a morally unstained clergy was compatible with its subordination to a state emerging from popular sovereignty. The argument appealed to the idea of a Church made up of more than the clergy, consisting of the whole of the faithful. The authentic state, like the ancient Church, was of the people and watched over them. An anonymous defense of Article 7 set out the following "principles of ecclesiastical legislation":

> First: the Church that Jesus Christ founded is a society, whose goal is to obtain eternal happiness for each of its individual members, using the means established by Jesus Christ himself to achieve it. Second: like every society it has a constitution, which is the Gospel; in it are set out the rights and duties of the members, the form of government of that society, and the character, faculties and rights of its governors. Third: in view of the fact that the Church is a society formed by the will of her members since no one can be forced to join her, has an unchangeable constitution because of its divine

origin, its members can use their right to name her rulers (who are the bishops and priests), and these rulers cannot infringe the constitution, we can infer that her government is popular and representative. Fourth: the duties of the members are to believe in the mysteries God has revealed, to worship that same God, according to the rules of worship he himself has established in the Gospel, and to follow the moral precepts he has pointed out; their rights are to name those who should be authorities, to protest and correct religious abuses, to participate in the holy sacraments established by Jesus Christ himself and in the spiritual fruits of common prayer. Fifth: the obligations of the rulers are these: to teach the dogma, morality and doctrine of Jesus Christ; to exclusively administer certain sacraments, and to preside over the faithful when they come together to render God acts of adoration. They are not judges to mete out corporal punishment on the violators of the law of Jesus Christ, since the punishments he himself established are only spiritual. They have the right to be respected by the remainder of the faithful, and to be maintained at their expense.

Priests, therefore, are not the Church, they are only her ministers.[45]

The same document clarified, by means of a denunciation of the clergy who resisted accepting Article 7 of the Constitution, that for practical purposes the people and the government of Jalisco were one and the same thing, precisely because of the latter's new popular representativeness. By contrast, legitimacy was denied to the canons of the Guadalajara cathedral precisely because their authority did *not* come from the people, but wanted to impose itself on them. The secular authorities elected by the people, that is, by the whole of the faithful, had written Article 7, so the clerical authorities could not oppose popular will so expressed without opposing the very principle of representative government. From this standpoint, "the people by means of their legislators" had the right to correct religious abuses. "Abuses are not part of religion; they are acts of corruption that the people are not obligated to follow...." For example, financing the clergy by means of tithing was a corruption of the pristine custom of "voluntary donations and offerings by the faithful in the primitive Church."[46]

Obviously, principles like this pointed to a fundamental shift in the balance of power between the Church and state. If the Church was not responsible to the people, but the state was strengthened by being responsible to and representative of the people, if the representatives of the former were just men like any others, as carnal and as prone to evil as anyone, but state representatives were clear spokesmen for an eminently egalitarian people, then there was no other solution than to ignore the clergy and its statements. Until the Church reformed itself according to the principles of representative government, along the lines of the primitive evangelical Church the liberals conceived of, then it was not worthy of the recognition of free men. Once it had been reformed along those lines, then there would be no doubt of a new union between it and the popular state. Until then, however, the clergy was a caste, a privileged group in a world of collapsing privileges. Its illegitimate character was constantly pointed out, and it was accused of trying to gain a fraudulent power before God and man.[47]

Beyond the fall of the Empire, the writing of the 1824 Constitution and Article 7, three further events sparked controversy midway through the 1820s: the Papal Bull by Leo XII rejecting American independence, the excommunication of the journalist called El Polar, and the conspiracy of Father Arenas. In liberal pamphlets, each in turn served to assert the thinking of previous years and explore its implications.

The state of Mexico gave a firm and swift response to the Bull of Leo XII in the form of a long and learned publication. A contest had been carried out, with a prize given to the author who best wrote on the question: "Within what limits should Papal authority be contained in matters of spiritual power, since such power exercised fully does not damage in any way the sovereignty or independence of nations?"[48] The winning piece was published in Guadalajara. Author Norberto Pérez Cuyado was careful but forceful in his reasoning. He followed the course of Spanish royalist thinking in its struggles to assert its temporal power over the Church. He began from a historical scheme in which problems between Church and state dated back to the time of Constantine, who had wished to protect the Church from persecution. But his praiseworthy goal had led to a less enviable situation. "Every right was disturbed, as Emperors made themselves into judges and teachers of religion and made the ministers of the temple into arbiters and regulators of imperial politics." This process deteriorated further as a result of barbarian invasions and the decay of the Roman Empire. "The mixture and confusion of spiritual and temporal matters was the poisoned root that gave humanity such bitter fruits." From Pérez Cuyado's standpoint, there was only one solution to the resulting problems:

The cure for so many wrongs is breaking up this monstrous and anti-Christian union, and placing each power in its natural place, raising up a wall of bronze at the points where there respective faculties begin and end. That is what experience confirms, and that is what both reason and the Gospel persuade us.[49]

Pérez Cuyado held that the laws, whose making was a task of the government, had the obligation of governing political and civil life. "Political life" referred to the international sphere of the state, in his definition, and "civil life" referred to the internal sphere of the state, having to do with the relationships between members of the society. The laws of the state necessarily had to follow natural and Christian law. Yet while "the propagation and preaching of the general principles of morality, insofar as it orders men's relationships with each other on Earth, is a duty of the priesthood, the application of morality to specific cases has nothing to do with the priesthood, and is even opposed to the nature and goals of that institution." It was beyond any doubt, according to the author, that "the care of secular things, that is, the knowledge and direction of the businesses which occupy men while they live on Earth, did not concern the priesthood."[50]

Such good principles referring to the "distinction and independence between both powers" were observed by "a few wise men" even in the time of the barbarians, with Saint Bernard particularly standing out. Even so, it was "since the renaissance of letters" that these principles had spread and rulers had begun to act in accordance with them. "Such have been the thoughts and actions for the last three centuries in Spain, the country most submissive to the Roman Pontiff in all of Europe. How much more liberty was always exercised by Germany, Venice, Portugal, Naples, and above all, France?" Pérez Cuyado stressed the work of Bishop Bossuet in France in supporting this renewed separation of temporal and ecclesiastical powers. He also insisted that all of this was in keeping with the true spirit of Christianity.[51]

This argument led him to direct an attack on the unrestricted power of the Pope within the Church, because "it should be noted that the Pontiff himself is subject, like the remainder of the faithful, to the entire body of the Church, as declared in sections four and five of the Church Council of Constance."[52] In any case, he continued, the exercise of Papal authority in relations with civil governments is circumscribed by the limits marking the authority of the Church. What is not licit for the Church is not licit for the Pontiff, and since it is beyond any doubt that Jesus Christ did not grant the Church any power over the civil and political affairs of nations, it is equally unmistakable that the Pope does not have the authority to take part in those affairs.[53]

The specific rights accumulated historically by one power relative to the other were another matter, and the author referred this to the diplomacy of concordats between respectively sovereign powers. As Pérez Cuyado stated at the end of his work, he found the Bull of Leo XII simply inappropriate because neither the Church nor its Pontiff had the right to any judgment concerning temporal authority.[54]

Another document attacked the Bull of Leo XII, declaring it "scandalous, null and void." More polemical than learned, this article was clearly liberal rather than statist, and went so far as to affirm that if Leo XII really was the author of the Bull he had committed the sin of "blasphemy, stating that God's cause was that of the princes."[55] The problem was that he

… blended the most perfect sovereignty of God with that of the despotic princes who usurped the sovereignty of the people....The cause and interest of the princes is the brutal ignorance of the people, and could this be God's cause? On the contrary, I affirm that *the devil's cause is one with that of the princes.*

The priests say: if the people are enlightened, everything is lost; and the author of the Ruins writes: if the people are enlightened, everything is won.

What will become of the Pope and other princes enthroned or to be enthroned, if the people become civilized, open their eyes, see the light, learn the sacred rights of God, of the people, and of man? Which are? Give to God what is God's, to the people what is the people's, and to man what is man's.[56]

Writing against a "pamphlet which insults God, men, and the Mexican republic," the author recommended "our separation from the communion of a Pope who is the first to introduce poisonous nourishment into the heritage of the Lord, until the matter is satisfactorily cleared up diplomatically."[57]

The next cause of controversy, the excommunication of El Polar, can only be understood within the course this journalist had followed over the previous years, which had brought it about, as the ruling of the Board of Ecclesiastical Censure stated, that

> from the greatest to the least of the Catholic people, all are scandalized, all are protesting, and all zealously desire that he be subjected to the fitting punishment he has made himself worthy of, and like a rotted member of the mystical body of the Church, he be separated, declared, and reputed to be most lowly, and infamous, so that none be polluted by the noxious fumes his corruption gives off.[58]

The political career of El Polar, profoundly rooted in federalism, culminated in 1825 and 1826 with two pamphlets virulently attacking the cathedral chapters in particular and clerical influence over society in general. Both pamphlets, with some variation, explicitly demanded an important number of changes in the relationships between state, Church and society.

The most illustrative passage of the first of these pamphlets, *Conjuración del polar contra los abusos del clero* (The Polar's Conjuring Against the Church's Abuses), is the following:

> Some time ago, I worked on a general plan for reforms in the ecclesiastical system, and among various things I proposed: the destruction of Cathedral Chapters, the extinction of monasteries and convents, the imposition of certain barriers to stop bishops from banning the reading of books and to keep them from being able to excommunicate or ordain any citizen without government permission. I said that before preaching sermons it was appropriate for them to be reviewed and approved by the government, I designated the number of ecclesiastics to serve in the state of Jalisco, I denied them their privileged judicial status and vested the right of patronage in the supreme government of the state. I also proposed a reform in marriage ceremonies, excluded ecclesiastics from all civil and military employment, removed from them all influence over the education of the young, asked for the confiscation of all the real estate of the religious communities with the prohibition of ever being able to acquire property again under any circumstance, established certain restrictions on the public exercise of the faith such as reducing the excessive number of feast days, processions, private religious obligations [*mandas*] and other superfluous things, arranged a way of administering the viaticum to the ailing. In sum,

I said many other things … but after having seriously thought over this enormous work, I understood that I was publishing reforms in vain if I left standing the origin of the Church's abuses.

I always despair at seeing articles only referring to religion mixed in with our constitutional laws, because as long as our legislators do not give up on this routine, our social order will never advance, and writers will work in vain announcing the best of reforms. These reforms will always be insufficient as long as governments meddle in religious matters, because the people do not have to be told about this; they are free to choose the faith that suits them best, just as they are to choose good or evil. And if the being that created us gave us that freedom, why do we want to enslave all to a single and perpetual faith? These arguments have convinced me that only with universal tolerance, absolute freedom of the press, and the exclusion of every dominant religion, can we decree at once the happiness of the people and forever assure their independence and liberty.[59]

The second of the pamphlets – *Concordatos del Polar con el Estado de Jalisco* (The Polar's Concordats with the state of Jalisco) – basically followed the first, but also included a fierce harangue against clerical celibacy, attacked the capital of chaplaincies – which he considered wasteful – and demanded that the "masses and all the prayers of the Church" be given in Spanish. Seen as a whole, these two pamphlets took the controversy to the highest level, and the Church's rejection could not have been any more absolute, leading to his excommunication.[60]

El Polar himself and another writer calling himself El Otro Polar (the Other Polar) alternated in his defense. They rejected the various considerations made by the ecclesiastical authorities since 1825. In no way did they disguise their total repudiation of ecclesiastical censure and the ways of action of the clerical hierarchy. They deliberately drove open the breach separating their liberal position from clerical thinking. In a pamphlet entitled *El Polar convertido* (The Polar Converted), he accused the canons of moral "bankruptcy" and affirmed they were carrying out a "war against the state." He specifically and systematically accused them of exceeding their authority in trying to censor his pamphlet *Conjuración* because there were legally established procedures which relieved the ecclesiastical authorities of intervening in such matters. Accusing the canons of being a "poor, ignorant council," he drove the point home by arguing that the measures against him only spread his ideas and shamed the council.[61]

By going further in explaining and defending the propositions made in *Conjuración*, the author made the situation worse by using insulting and defiant language, in addition to refusing to retreat on anything essential. Later on, to close with a flourish, he demanded in his new pamphlet that the Popes be popularly elected, just as in the first days of the Church, and in fulfillment of a right inherent to the people. But since the Popes had not been elected in this way, he saw "certain Popes as tyrants ... who thought the people incapable of correct decisions and government."[62] Having landed this blow against the head of the Church, he proceeded to attack the infallibility of General Church Councils (assemblies of bishops) based on the argument that they had never included or represented the congregation of the faithful. And he closed his pamphlet with this withering conclusion:

> In the congregation of all the faithful essentially resides the sovereignty of the Church, therefore nothing done without the vote of those very faithful can be legitimate, since the Church and the General Church Councils must follow the same principles as the Nation and the Congress, and everything that strays from these standards cannot help but bear within it an arbitrary and unjust character. Canons: see what your imprudence has led to, go forward with your whim of offending El Polar, and you will hear far worse things.[63]

El Otro Polar did not hold back in El Polar's defense.[64] He claimed that "tithing, celibacy and impious tolerance are not part of religion," since they are "amendations that you [theologians] have made to the Gospel written by the Apostles who understood better than you the doctrines of our teacher Jesus." His appeal was to reason, above any other authority.[65] Just like El Polar, he ended his article with an exhortation:

> Citizens, do not let yourself be fooled by appearances. These men with crowns and tonsures are men just like you, and just as subject as any to intrigue, error and perversity. And when they rule on a matter they are so involved in, they are more likely than anyone to act with partiality and bad faith. Every matter under debate is as much within the reach of your insight as it is subject to the view of a great and observant talent. So start debating yourselves, and never believe except that which reason tells you is true.[66]

The conclusion of a pamphlet referring to the conspiracy by Father Arenas makes a fitting end for this chapter, since it sums up the core of the debate the liberals kept up all through the 1820s.[67] Written as a dialogue between a traditionalist woman and her liberal son, the pamphlet included the following ironic passage as the final words of the son:

> But do you not understand that there is a vast distance between Church discipline and doctrine, just as between good and bad ministers? What is impious about punishing the horrible crimes of treason, when the public verdict demands it as an overall lesson, even if the delinquents are friars, clerics, bishops, or of higher rank? Then let one of them come along with a portrait of Ferdinand VII, and place it in the plaza, and swear loyalty to it as absolute king and bring down the eagles of the republic, taking away constitutional liberties, and although he commit in his imprudence thousands of idiocies and cause incalculable damage, let nothing be done to him, for he is a minister of God on High.[68]

6

Hegemony Renewed

The Beginnings of a Clerical Counterdiscourse

The Reconstitution of Clerical Discourse
in the Decade after Independence

The Guadajalara Church lost the initiative in social discourse in the 1820s, despite its impressive production of sermons about Independence under Iturbide. It found itself constantly obliged to respond defensively. How could it remain identified with the cause of Independence, popular sovereignty and national progress without accepting a situation that lowered it from its earlier position as the equal of the state?[1] How could it prove itself loyal to popular government and popular sovereignty while at the same time refuse to adhere to a new social order on religious matters?[2] Not only the motto of "throne and altar" was placed in doubt, but also that of "religion and fatherland." The Church had to defend itself through redefinition. Responding to this challenge, the Church made itself present in crucial ways, tenaciously remaking its social discourse and creating new bases of support for its role in society.

The 1824 Political Constitution of the state of Jalisco had presented the first legislative attack under the new federal republic on the Church's internal autonomy and union on equal terms with the state. Article 7 of the Constitution had given the state control of ecclesiastical finances.[3] This set off a battle in the press. By swearing loyalty to the Constitution, the Church would have lost authority, even moral authority, because it became a dependent branch of the state itself. While it is true that the president of the republic offered an opportune political resolution of this dilemma, by means of a decree which allowed citizens to take an oath of loyalty to the Constitution while deferring the question of Article 7, the underlying struggle for ideological hegemony could not be resolved so easily in the future.[4] The freedom which prevailed in the new republic, and the work in course on a constitutional framework, made absolutely necessary an open political debate to win the support of public opinion either for or against Article 7, with all it implied.[5]

What is most notable about the resulting debate is how it confirmed the formation of two alternative and decidedly opposed intellectual groups in the state of Jalisco. Liberal and secularizing intellectuals, heirs to the fiery liberalism of the Cortes of Cádiz, had claimed a space in Jalisco. In its origins, this liberalism was an unexpected byproduct of the climate of change of the Bourbon Reforms, reinforced by the vacuum of legitimate power produced by the Napoleonic invasion. In contrast, there were also republican intellectuals who were more fond of the reformist tradition, more inclined towards individual liberties than towards liberalism as a system, and more desirous of combining authority with the new means of government. Liberalism in Jalisco took shape from the debate between the two.[6]

Curiously enough, while liberalism only explicitly took note of the existence of opposition to its program as an obstacle to be overcome, the Church's defensive ideology presented liberalism as not only a suspicious radicalism but also a source of social renewal whose contributions and understandings could not simply be brushed aside. This was the most problematic aspect of the clearly eclectic direction of this discourse, evident in 1821 and 1822 sermons. In this complex dynamic, the Church lost the initiative in social discourse, but at the same time social practice would prove that liberalism could not do without its opponent, lest it threaten with dissolution the society it wished to liberate.[7]

José María Luis Mora had sensed a key element of this entire process. His approach underscores what was established in Chapter Five:

> The clergy is a corporation dating back to the founding of the colony and deeply rooted in it. Every branch of public administration and the civil acts of life have been and still are more or less subject to its influence. It dictated part of the Laws of the Indies and

has had jurisdiction over the government of Indians and castas who were its faithful servants until Independence, despite the civil government's efforts to emancipate them. Spaniards and their descendants have not escaped it either, falling into the nets it laid in education and the rule of conscience. Everything known in Mexico was taught by the clergy's ministry or subject to its censure. The Inquisition, the bishops and the priests exercised the most absolute dominance over the press, reading, and teaching. The rule of conscience has not been limited to religious duties, but has extended its reach to social, conjugal and domestic duties, to dress and public diversions. Viceroys, magistrates, judges, public administrators, in sum all men of government, have for many years subjected the exercise of public functions to the dictates of a confessor, who even today makes himself heard and effectively influences acts of sovereignty, directing the people who exercise them under his tutelage, acts which ecclesiastics aim to restrict in the final analysis to a matter of mere religious duty.[8]

From this standpoint, not only were the clergy deeply entrenched in society and the state itself, but they ideologically conditioned the power of the state, making it subject to ends unrelated to its Earthly mission.

Paradoxically, Doctor Mora's thinking suggested that the struggle to establish liberalism would simultaneously be a struggle to strengthen the state. Statism and republicanism would blur into one, because without a strong liberal state, society would continue along the same course as always. Mora asked incisively:

In fact, what power can the republic [that is, the republican state] have against a body which has been in the country much longer, directed by bishops, its perpetual and irresponsible [i.e., not responsible to an electorate] heads, whose annual income is at least fifteen and at most one hundred and twenty thousand pesos, and who have at their disposal eighty million pesos of investments whose productive portion yields seven and a half million [pesos per year]? A republic born yesterday, where every branch of public administration is in disarray and the habit of following orders is entirely lost; a republic whose public income barely doubles that of the clergy, and does not remotely suffice to meet its budget; a republic in sum where all is decrepitude, disorder and confusion: can such a republic sustain itself against a body which has the will and the power to destroy its constitution, cripple its laws, and raise up the masses against it?[9]

Above all, the national state had to fortify itself to take up the role of transformer of society.

Considering this, we should assess the Church's efforts to keep from losing its cultural hegemony over society. It is not enough to see the problem from the perspective of liberalism, as in the previous chapter. It would be an error to ignore or downplay the formidable efforts made by the ecclesiastical hierarchy to reshape clerical discourse in a way more in keeping with the times and with the long-term corporatist and ideological interests of the Church.

Evidently, liberal ideology and clerical preference contrasted with one another on key issues. The latter tended to support values promoting work directed to other-worldly ends, obedience, and loyalty to constituted authorities. The former underscored its aspirations of full national transformation with rebellious values and an insistence on individual rights, with the emphasis placed on the shortcomings of civil society and the need to swiftly eliminate them, and with the emergence of a new, imposing and self-reliant voice in every public debate.

The calls for hewing to tradition were countered by irate cries which presented a future based on the denunciation of the past – and its spokesmen. A "progressive" vision of Mexico was forged on the basis of insistent critiques of the inconsistencies, failures and flaws in the practice of Catholic doctrine and in ecclesiastical behavior. As Dale Baum has stressed, liberalism had a negative drive in practice, always opposing some aspect of the established order without offering clear alternatives. Since it set its sights on a libertarian dream of the future, liberalism disdained established values which threatened to endure. The present was seen as composed of an endless series of obstacles to overcome, but since liberalism's conquest of this future was far from complete, it found itself obliged to share the present with the spokesmen for an undying past.[10]

In the 1820s, incipient liberalism demonstrated its capacity for subverting existing ideological loyalties. For a time, it placed the Mexican citizen at the center of a sovereign reflection about the transformation of a shared material and civil existence. But it is essential to point out that in Mexico, one unexpected aspect of this transformation was that practically all of society's thinkers and leaders were agreed on the need for renewal to overcome national weakness.[11] Thus renovation became more complicated. The ideologues of the past could not be so easily discarded, since they, too, had climbed onto the train of progress, were aware of past problems and open to negotiated change, and in short, were at least partly willing to undertake transformation.[12]

This was a transformation which implied the ongoing presence of these ideologues of the past in the new society being forged. How could liberals do away with a long-standing social force which had managed to agree to denounce the past, while remaining present and active in the new social arrangements? There is no worse enemy, one might think, than one who refuses the label. This threatened to take a strong and sustained wind out of the sails of Mexican liberalism.

From one perspective, what we are saying is not entirely new. Jesús Reyes Heroles dedicates the second volume of his magisterial treatment of Mexican liberalism to specifying the nature of what he calls "fluctuating society." But while Reyes Heroles is predisposed to criticize indecisive thinkers with liberal leanings, he overlooks the equivocating nature of the ideologues of the past.[13] Alamán is often believed to have been an exceptional conservative. No doubt he was an extraordinary man, but it is likely that he was closer to the core of Mexican conservatism than is usually suspected. From our standpoint, it is not at all anomalous that a man so "progressive" in many aspects should have finally become the recognized leader of the conservatives, the very man who formed a ministry of development in the last Santa Anna government in 1853. The hatred Alamán provoked among liberals certainly was spurred by his progressive attitudes as much as by his traditionalism, since such attitudes were exactly what frustrated the ideological radicalization and acceleration of social transformation liberal spokesmen were calling for.[14]

The beginnings of this conservative attitude dated back to Bourbon governments. Although conservatives rejected the Bourbon label by the 1820s, this was because the label represented an attempt to portray them as supporters of bringing an heir to the Bourbon dynasty to rule in Mexico – rather than settling on Iturbide or a republican government. This accusation overlooked the real stance that Mexican conservatives developed with considerable coherence: the country had to be changed and developed, but without falling into the ideological commitments and clumsiness of dogmatic liberalism. Instead, the elements promoting change had to be isolated and imposed in such a way that society was perfected without risk of disintegrating or being torn apart. Changes were possible means for overcoming society's contemporary challenges.; they were not a panacea, which only the ignorant expected for humankind. The wisdom of past ages might be incomplete, but its sound judgments never erred. By definition, they were worthy of being incorporated into all present and future arrangements. Why should one assume that only men of the present day were intelligent and knew how to think? Was that not the height of closed-mindedness?[15]

From this perspective, Mexican society was split more clearly over the means and timing of change than over more or less predictable social goals. In general, renewal was accepted as the objective to be achieved. Of course, there was considerable debate about what had to be renewed, and to what extent. But renewal was accepted; the aspiration to perfect man was considered legitimate. The true stumbling block was the principles behind radical change, the arrogance of philosophical reason. If man was held to be self-sufficient, capable of organizing society to fulfill goals he himself set by the lights of his own reason, then obviously this justification was ruled out by conservatives as ridiculous and unacceptable. If, on the contrary, this was a matter of improvement within the limits set by fragile human nature, then it represented a rather notable opportunity. And who was more identified with the progress of civilization than the Catholic Church?[16]

What to renew and how to go about it were moot questions, but not the idea of renewal itself. There was an arguable need to save, to be sure, the sound judgments of the past and the cultural heritage that had made them possible. Such an argument strengthened the idea of Catholic civilization as the greatest of international cultures and a certain and mature bulwark against the errors of reason and the passion of heretics, libertines and adepts of the so-called philosophy of the age. Conservatives did not deny that such errors might produce some positive results. Neither did they deny that the theoretical or practical diatribes launched against the Church had their grain of truth, and at times grew out of the recognition of genuine ills. Such positive insights, however, did not come from the correctness of their premises and procedures, but rather despite their erroneous principles and proceedings.[17]

The evil of humanity, its state of fallen greatness after original sin, produced such seeming contradictions. Man was incapable of advancing along the path of righteousness without stumbling into error and evil, but his stumbling did not indicate that traditional religious beliefs and established society were wrong. They, too, had human failings, but in the case of the Church these could never include dogma, nor the authority, goodness and rightness of traditions properly understood.

Renewal was therefore a matter of containing the scourges of heretics, libertines and "philosophers" so that their better ideas, along with the efforts of people of sounder principles, might serve to improve the established state of things. That is why there was no insistence on flatly rejecting all dissident opinion.[18] Criticisms were annoying and frequently went beyond what was necessary for viable social transformation. They led – in the case of "philosophers" – to fanaticism for change and complete irreverence towards constituted civil and religious authorities. They were a moral and individual matter subject to censure, on the one hand, but they were symptomatic of real flaws needing correction, on the other.[19]

With this attitude, the Church and conservatives yielded the initiative, the radical and brazen initiative, devoid of orthodoxy and respect for what had been achieved, to those dissidents whose power or anonymity allowed them to propose "wayward" alternatives for society. What they could not permit was for those dissidents, with their rudimentary truths, old and new, to establish their ideas in law, in teaching, in religious practice, and in civil and religious custom, without the intervention of the authority, decisive force and moderating reasoning of the Church and the most even-handed and sensible lay leaders. While the Church lost the initiative on the terrain of hypothetically possible changes, it would win it back on the terrain of probable and desired changes. In this view, the praxis of the Church would be strengthened by assuring effective control over societal change.

When the Inquisition existed, the moderating power of the clergy used to keep "errors" from reaching deep into society by blocking them, squeezing out whatever truth they might contain, and making that truth accessible to the flock. Once the Inquisition was abolished, this moderating power was also eliminated. Popular sovereignty and nearly complete freedom of speech and the press had made that impossible, especially within the overall push for social renewal promoted by every government since the Bourbons. Now the fight continued on a new social stage. The desk of the erudite and isolated censor gave way to the defense of "healthy principles" in the public forum of the printed word and on the practical terrain of the civil and religious transformations which would authentically benefit society and represent an improvement. Now the Church would have to struggle to reclaim its role as midwife to social change in Mexico. It could hardly avoid conflict, as a result, with those who wanted to reduce it to the level of a mere body or corporation in political society and themselves assume the role of social pacesetter. In the Church's view, either there would be a properly conceived change, or error would be enshrined as a societal principle. In the first case, the Church would once again occupy the decisive role in society which the Bourbon Reforms had wrested from it. Therefore, it unleashed its greatest efforts to retake the helm of society, demonstrating its gifts for leadership in order to continue as the guide to society's moral existence.[20]

In order to fulfill this role as helmsman in society, the Church needed to recover its own ecclesiastical history and institutional integrity. The critical times of an independent society in transition demanded the presence of a self-critical Church capable of reforming itself and coming to terms with changes. Telling the history of the Church meant establishing the basis of its autonomy from the state and civil society. What role did the Church play in the past? What position did it take towards the state and towards its own weaknesses? What were the prevailing parameters for interaction between the ecclesiastical hierarchy, the priesthood, and the flock – or what should they be? Only a profound self-critique could place the Church on the road to its historical reconstitution, fully up to date with the age and popular aspirations. This was a unique opportunity and a singular challenge. It placed the Church face to face with the history of Councils and Concordats. This self-questioning significantly influenced the basic premises of the Church's polemical pamphlets, and also of its pastoral letters during the period after Independence.[21]

For their part, the liberals, with their tendency to argue from principles and in reference to the United States and Northern Europe, fell easily into a sense of timelessness and placelessness that was dangerous to their cause. Wanting to take things apart, they offered constructive projects which, more often than not, turned out to be impractical and likely to cause society as much trouble as good. In Mexico, unlike other places, liberalism did not harvest the rich set of changes that had already taken place in society. It was a new project, substituting for, rather than fulfilling, older projects. Liberalism could be perceived as quixotic and was in danger of ending up with nothing but pipe dreams without any ties to real society. It partook of the complex character of utopias.[22] If the purest intellectual projects of liberalism turned out to be chimerical, did that not palpably demonstrate the need for moderation and for a respectful adherence to all that was best about the past, whose reliability made it worthy of continuation?[23]

Society matured, adding an element of unfettered reason and defiant rebelliousness against the patterns of the past but making only minor adjustments and emendations in practice. A self-satisfied society gave way to a tense society, prisoner of its own struggle for renewal, but averse to self-destruction. Social reconstitution was thus a more difficult affair than was sometimes thought. It was not simply a matter of adding new values and ideas to society and easily spurring minimal real change. On the contrary, there was a recognized need for fundamental transformations, although their pressing demands had to steer far from a complete liquidation of the past.[24] Mexico was in a quandary.

For the Church, the perfecting of social man was seen to call for deep transformations, but these threatened to lead human subjects astray. When properly understood, the past was a guide for man and an indispensable anchor in storms of rootless reason and passion. Rejecting the past meant negating Catholicism, and therefore the most perfect sources of human civilization and improvement. It meant returning to brutishness and the reign of individual whim. On their way to the final meeting with the Creator, both man and society would have to struggle to achieve and perfect themselves as much as possible. The root problem, original sin, could not be overcome, although the final objective was the restitution of the freedom and ability of primitive man. The history of man was the history of this struggle, continuous and unending in its own right. Only the end of this history, its teleological and theological consummation, could remedy this.[25]

Therefore, the Mexican clergy faced several tasks in their effort to remain present and relevant during the crisis of society in the transition from monarchy to popular sovereignty. The clergy had to forge their own vision of the history of the Church and its relationship with the state and civil society. The clergy had to conceive and put into practice a program to reform the discipline and training of priests. They had to clarify, step by step, their attitude towards the changes proposed by liberal dissidents, promoting or rejecting each in theory and practice. They had to come to terms with the views of Mexican society, in its struggles, triumphs and sacrifices, in order to later offer their own view, thus legitimating major national goals and the transformations directed towards achieving them. They had to maintain and consolidate their multiform presence in political and civil society: to provide guidance on political measures, to participate in elections, to take public posts, to serve in committees formed to study this or that problem, and to make written appeals to the government when political struggle required it.[26] The clergy reprinted treatises about the Church and society, produced or allowed the production of pamphlets defending points judged to be important, accused, applauded, denounced, and, above all, never ceased to stress ecclesiastical autonomy, the Church's sovereign right to reform itself, and its own authority as bellwether and moral guide of political and civil society. The Church asserted itself publicly with great force, to keep from being pushed aside. This aim was incompatible with tolerance for other forms of worship, or acceptance of the image liberals offered of themselves as disinterested philanthropists of society. The goal was the rebirth of a Church of distilled purity and of undisputed hegemony over societal mores. Otherwise, it was sure to be pushed aside, and the dynamic tension between change and continuity, between a past open to criticism and a future best based upon that past, would collapse into chaos, precipitating the ruin of all values and convictions.

The struggle taken up by the Church in Guadalajara may have failed to achieve the drive and success some wished for. Internal dissension among the clergy themselves is still not well understood, but the dynamics of clerical leadership must be considered to be an important element in understanding the real historical development of the country.[27]

From the Praise of Reason and Erudition to Outright Wrangling:
1822–24

Clerical worries about the ideological situation resulting from the principle of popular representation begin to appear in 1822. Once again, the first writings were printed in Mexico City and shipped to Guadalajara. One of these began attacking

> [t]he many talents prostituted to the extreme of endeavoring to confuse liberty with licentiousness, and therefore to persuade [readers] that certain practices of Christian religion which may be in contact with its most respectable dogma are opposed to the healthy principles of liberty today adopted by the people to establish their respective governments.[28]

The problem was more serious still, because those who spread such ideas blended them with fully acceptable ones in such a way as to confuse right thinking "with the indecent errors by which a false zeal has commingled sinful pretense with the precious patrimony of the faithful." Of course, this perfectly fit the pattern of "an age of reason and philosophy in which errors are usually introduced in the shadow of that [Enlightenment]."[29]

The author then dedicated the rest of his publication to reproducing a letter sent to the Spanish newspaper *El Universal* by the auxiliary bishop of Madrid. The tone of argument was not changed by the shift: fulminating against the free and indiscriminate sale of "a multitude of impious books and pamphlets," the bishop called on "whoever wants to keep the faith of their fathers, that is whoever claims to be a constitutionalist."[30] One should avoid reading such publications but for all who succumbed "to the temptation" of reading them, the bishop prayed that they would

[s]uspend judgment and do not give any credit to the events, quotations, and maxims their authors so confidently provide. Instead try to examine them in light of history and reason under the firm knowledge that Christian religion does not flee from the light (as such as these libelously contend), nor does it demand blind and untested obedience, but rather the exact opposite, it asks for rational conviction, the *rationable obsquium* of Saint Paul, since God has deigned, as Saint Jerome says, to subject himself to the examination of reason, rather than to subject the examination of reason to himself.[31]

With the divine foundations of Christian religion proven, reason would have to bend its knee to it, in the tradition of the sages of Christianity.[32]

Another publication, printed in 1823 and reprinted in Guadalajara in 1824, set out to contest Lizardi's defense of Freemasons.[33] The approach did not differ much from what we just analyzed, except that here the rebelliousness of human reason was seen in a more firmly social setting:

Every religion, sect, or community, every spiritual direction which does not recognize the tribunal of the Church (whatever one may think of the tribunal of the Inquisition) as its true legitimate judge, which does not humbly reveal to that tribunal its inner workings, which does not subject itself to that tribunal's direction and correction, is thereby cast out of the heart of the Catholic Church, said Jesus Christ.[34]

As a consequence, and speaking, as the author stated, only to Catholics, leaving aside matters of state and constitution, the pamphlet concluded that "every Catholic ceases to be one in the very act of professing the Masonic sect and swearing his oath to it." Thus not only pagans and self-expressed heretics were outside the framework of the only salvific Church, but also any group that did not explicitly subject itself to the Church. From the standpoint of either the constitutionally Catholic state or simply the true Church, by early 1824 war had been declared on the rebellious reason of individuals and groups in Guadalajara and surrounding areas.[35]

The central theme of clerical thinking would be precisely this stress on clerical authority versus unrestricted reason. This might be seen as the exact counterpoint to the liberal idea that took popular sovereignty to be absolutely free will over matters of both reason and government. Clerical writers were not long in recognizing that the polemics liberals started about various public events – the fall of Iturbide, the establishment of the republic, the elaboration and signing of the state constitution – were products of a broader range of values, attitudes and reasonings which went well beyond the immediate matter under debate. They realized that the true, if not always the most apparent, problem was this new orientation as a whole. It had to be made visible for the Church to criticize it effectively.

When the Guadalajara Church felt strong and secure, its discourse had a notably different tone from the one it would take on in later years. While clearly setting out its viewpoint, clerical discourse was signally even-handed, measured and self-confident. Later on, signs of uncertainty and indignation would become evident, along with a tendency to adopt a more aggressive and cutting discursive style, but there does not seem to be as much change in the content of its statements as in their tone. The clergy's proposals were coherently articulated, with mostly stylistic changes corresponding to shifts in the relative strength of opposing groups. Discursive statements therefore appear as means of struggling for hegemony.

In 1824, the Guadalajara Church clearly set out four themes needing resolution regarding the ties between society and the state, on the one hand, and society and the Church, on the other. Four chapters of Count Muzzarelli's work, *El buen uso de la lógica en materia de religión*, offered a vision which was orthodox, but balanced and open to dialogue, on religious tolerance, the wealth of the clergy, the legal immunity of the clergy, and the intervention of the Church in temporal affairs. Muzzarelli asserted that Catholicism could not be saved if measures were taken which led to turning the secular life of man into an end, not a means. The presence and guidance of the Church in all of social life, including its alliance with the state, were understood to be an integral part of the practice and preservation of the faith, which was the ultimate end of man. In exchange, the Church provided important reinforcement for the secular "city" of mankind and its political government.

In a chapter entitled "Indifference to Religion," Muzzarelli forcefully rejected any religious tolerance towards non-Catholics, identifying it with "scandalous indifference" to questions of faith.[36] The reasons for tolerance did not matter, since it was inappropriate once true religion had been given due weight in the life of man. The Count's text declared:

> If a Catholic Prince or Magistrate cannot block religious freedom without causing a greater harm to the public good, he can tolerate it as a lesser evil in order to avoid a greater evil which would necessarily follow if it were not tolerated. For that reason, in order to avoid greater disorder, in some places public prostitutes are tolerated. Moreover, for the same reason, if in order to end a civil war, which brings great harm to a state and cannot otherwise be concluded, the Prince reaches agreement with heretics to tolerate religious freedom, he should keep his agreement in order to avoid greater public ills and to maintain public confidence. That is what our theologians, along with Saint Thomas and other holy doctors, concede to you. But ... it is contrary to all divine and human laws to introduce into a state dominated by the Catholic religion, without an indispensable need, that religious freedom which tolerates all, which makes all equal without distinction in favor, privilege, employment, and congress, Catholics with Turks and heretics, and which in order to increase the population, make commerce flourish and other similar motives, does not prevent dangers to the faith, nor the scandal and perversion of its own subjects. The Church has always denounced such deplorable charity; reason has always impugned it, and the laws have battled against it countless times.[37]

Muzzarelli's tone was notably more measured when he came to the matter "of the wealth of the clergy."[38] In between the lines, one can sense that the debate among Catholics had already advanced more here than on religious freedom, and tempers flared just as each cited the Scriptures to support a specific position. In fact, disputes about ecclesiastical riches dated back to before the Protestant Reformation and subsequent vitriol. If on matters of tolerance towards Protestants or other religions the argument was ferociously negative, on the question of clerical riches an appreciable space of negotiation opened up. The wealth of the clergy was seen as a divine concession to human weakness, and as a resource potentially useful to the whole of society. Its misuse was a sin, and invited the sacrilegious reprisals that God authorized to purify his Church when it deserved it.

Muzzarelli declared that, once arguments for and against clerical wealth had been "impartially" taken into account, it was clear that divine providence had wisely intervened on the matter:

> [Providence] has seen that not all can follow the counsel of the Gospels in full rigor, and has taken pity on human fragility, permitting a portion of the clergy to possess goods, while providing it at the same time the means to keep from abusing these possessions and to remain useful to others.
>
> [Providence] has seen that a few assisted by divine grace would practice a voluntary and rigorous poverty, and therefore has instituted a few regular orders, separated from the dangers which indigence tends to bring along with it, in which this profession [of poverty] is attended to rigorously. [Providence] has seen that the state of mediocrity was not reducible to a useful and constant practice, and therefore has left each with his own freedom to aid the priest, and to augment his faculties, according to his own prudence, piety and charity. Finally, [providence] has seen that some of His ministers, abusing the riches they were entrusted with, would perhaps reverse divine intentions, and therefore has allowed from time to time that His clergy be dispossessed by violent reprisals, not only of that which was superfluous, but even of that which was necessary. [Providence] permitted the evil of the sin of sacrilegious usurpers of ecclesiastical goods, in order to accomplish a great good by that natural path: in order that His ministers might come to realize they had strayed, and might be alerted to become more faithful in their dispensations from then on.[39]

Muzzarelli based his argument in favor of the personal legal immunity of the clergy on the rights and convenience of the sovereign. One well-formulated question brought both aspects together: "What reason could be given that the officials of the King should be respected by the King himself, receiving abundant reward for their services, yet the Church, spiritual mother of kings, should deserve no affection from those kings for all the ministries it exercises on behalf of their souls?"[40] Insinuating a parallel between service to the King and the transcendental role of the priesthood, Muzzarelli carried his argument so far as to conclude that:

> [w]e find that not only the obligation, but also the interest of princes themselves persuade them to keep ecclesiastics immune from taxes and trials. Suppose that the princes, governing themselves according to the impious maxims of their flatterers, forcefully equaled ecclesiastics with their other subjects. I do not say that in that case the Church should take up arms to defend its rights, but rather I maintain that this would not conform to the spirit and precepts of Jesus Christ. I only entertain the idea that in this case it remove ecclesiastical power from its aid to the temporal power; I do not propose that it drive the people to rebellion, only that it leave them to their own counsel and that, now as lowly as the mass of subjects, it leave the people their common weapons. In my mind, I am saying, I suppose all of this could easily happen, and accepting this fiction, I ask myself: in this case, who would lose more, the clergy losing its privileges, or the prince losing his best defense in the clergy? The clergy in reality would only have to weep over the disdain for its dignity.... But monarchs would suffer because not only would this not enrich them, they would soon find themselves lacking, along with religion, the obedience and fidelity of their remaining vassals.[41]

From this standpoint, it was clear that no sovereignty has such solid foundations so as not to require the aid of Christian doctrine. By means of the priesthood, that doctrine propagated automatic obedience to the legitimate sovereign, without applying too close or prolonged scrutiny dedicated to demanding careful accounts of his lawful bearing and behavior.

The fourth publication by Muzzarelli, nominally concerned with excommunication, became in fact a short treatise on the Church's right and obligation to intervene in certain matters of a temporal nature. First, he justified the prudent, just and exemplary use of the tool of excommunication.[42] Then he went on to affirm:

The mutual commerce between body and soul, the need that each has of the other in our present state, so connects and unites their actions, that thus connected and united they are called the action of man; therefore, if the Church were only to command the spirit its jurisdiction would be invisible, secret, solitary and useless, and no action which is only done through invisible substance can be judged. And if the Prince only commanded over the naked and senseless body, his jurisdiction would be like that the Poets imagined for Orpheus, a jurisdiction over the tops of mountains and the plants of the forest. No, it is not like this: the Church commands men; the Prince commands men. But the Church commands in the spiritual order; the Prince commands in the social order. From this it follows, to return to my proposition, that spiritual actions do not rule out the intervention of the body, nor do temporal ones exclude the intervention of the soul....

There can be no doubt: if ecclesiastical power is restricted to the spirit alone, and temporal power to the body alone, then both become worthless and useless for the ends God created them for.[43]

In opposition to the tendency which would subject the Church to the state, seeing it as an arm of the state, in reality the Church was "prior to the state, in age and dignity." Even more importantly, the Church had primacy in its relative weight in the overall order, because while both Church and state ultimately pursue the same goal, "eternal life," the immediate end of the state was temporal, a "lesser end." Therefore the Church, because of its jurisdiction over the spirit, was authorized "to force the flesh to an honorable and superior end, such as the worship and glory of the Creator." Within this view, excommunication was a powerful instrument of the Church, which perforce had to intervene in temporal, and not only spiritual, life. Despite some lamentable abuses, excommunication should be obeyed as a legitimate power, until errors were corrected in keeping with tradition.[44]

Behind these apparently concrete and specific themes lie great abstract issues about man's life in society. Opposing perceptions produced different categories. The concerns established were different. Since this line of thinking was not properly speculative, but instead practical, directed to defending specific interests of the clergy, the treatment of conflicts was anchored in immediate problems, and therefore partly obscured the underlying theoretical dynamic. But there is no doubt that these writings contained coherent theoretical proposals based on specific ecclesiastical interests. The theme of tolerance, which kept the Catholic clergy in exclusive control of religious matters, was based on a clear hierarchy of social values. Here self-interest, which liberalism saw as a driving motor, had limited room for expression, since the goal of society had to be transcendence, not immanence. The theme of clerical riches allowed the Church to stress the simple truth – a very important point – of the humanity of the clergy and its usefulness to society. Clerical immunity was an issue which allowed stressing the utility of the priesthood and Church not so much to society as a whole, as to the sovereign, that is to say the government, in particular. The Church did not come before the temporal power with empty hands! And finally, the matter of excommunication enabled emphasis once more on the hierarchy of social values, in which the spiritual should order the temporal, and not the other way around.

With the increasing struggle to influence a heterogeneous and partly unwilling public we can better gauge the contentiousness over how social phenomena should be understood. There was a growing need for pamphlets to go beyond their own sociotheoretical system in order to appeal to those influenced by the opposing system. The reach of contrary values had to be thwarted in this way. We have already seen some of this in the sermons and pastoral letters analyzed in the first chapters of this study. In some of these publications, the authors had started from an obviously hegemonic system, in which they could assume the basic agreement of their listeners to a single, shared socio-theoretical scheme. In this context, the voice of the clergy was an authorized voice meriting particular attention. Despite this particularity, before and especially after 1810 a new note emerged, foreshadowing the texture of the polysemic texts after Independence. Worries about how the public perceived reality were already growing, and the clergy did not settle for mere exegesis, moral exhortations, or eloquent restatement of principles considered irrefutable.[45] After 1821, it was no longer a question of teaching an unquestionably loyal public, or of appealing to the goodness and convenience of the King and his counsel of experts. Instead, the Church had to carefully shape how reality itself was understood by a more heterogeneous and less constant public.

For the larger, civil public, the pamphlets created a stage upon which this aspect of the most polemic sermons was even more intensified. Going beyond the framework of exhortation and

implicit threat, or rebuke and instruction, they dedicated themselves to open dispute. They made their point through irony,
frontal and biting attacks, and the clear and detailed exposition of
questions under debate. One reprinting, titled the *Representación
del Arzobispo de Valencia a las Cortes*, is an indication of the discursive transition in pamphlets. In this case, it was a matter of sparring
with the enemy about clerical reforms which, by all indications,
neither the archbishop nor the liberal Cortes were ready to see as
unnecessary or superfluous.[46] How to undertake reforms? What
repercussions would they have for the social order and its very
premises? Was it true that the only way to respond to abuses was
by expunging them with the power of the state, and that such a
state intervention was justified and based on sound precedents?
According to the Archbishop of Valencia, the unmistakable problems did not justify the solution the liberal Cortes wanted. In fact,
he claimed, the two powers had always kept their autonomy on
such matters. He added:

> There were, it is true, in our country, although much less than in
> others, some times of turbulence and misunderstanding between
> the two powers, in which there were attempts like the present one
> to arrange ecclesiastical affairs by civil laws. So it occurred in the
> turbulent years with which the reign of King Philip V began, but
> from that very disorder, order was later even more firmly rees-
> tablished, and so shone truth with greater brightness when that
> religious monarch, rightly informed, … recognized his error, and
> revoked the ill-advised decrees which he had issued contrary to the
> discipline and laws of the Church….
>
>   Therefore it is indisputable that establishing and sanctioning rules
> for its discipline corresponds to the authority of this Church alone;
> that only She can alter already established rules; that only She must
> resolve and decide on ecclesiastical matters and affairs.[47]

The *modus vivendi* the Archbishop of Valencia wished to defend
was legitimated through careful argument that was surely in the
finest tradition of pontifical lawyers. He had to establish through
precedent and logic that there was no reason for "an undue
acquiescence to the Princes of the age." But the Archbishop
characteristically resorted to those he considered true authorities on the matter, that is to say, to the Church Fathers. He
found them "willing to obey [Princes] as their sovereigns in
everything concerning the civil order, but not recognizing them

as more than faithful subjects of the Church, in the order of Religion." How could the bishops of Spain allow the Cortes to treat matters of this nature, when they were only properly treated in an "Ecclesiastical Congress," that is, a Council?[48]

The Archbishop brandished the weapons of the law and the Church's own authorities to make an irrefutable impression. At the time, everything about the life of man in society was controversial. Demands made on the basis of appeals to rights and justice would soon lose their meaning in a world in which different rights, and different justices, were finally emerging from a background of radically opposed visions struggling over the very basis of human life. What influence would this growing breach have over the future course of struggles to win the understanding and allegiance of the people?

Significantly, the task of shaping understandings of reality had to be directed at the lower clergy as well as the lay public. Dennis Ricker states that in the years after Independence, the lower clergy were patriotic "often even to the point of opposing ecclesiastical policies." Yet by the mid-1840s, this had changed. After that point, the lower clergy are seen as more favorable to ecclesiastical policies and ideas than to government preferences. The evolution of clerical discourse and the careful reform of seminaries undoubtedly influenced this change.[49]

In this sense, it is important that the effective tendency of Church discourse was directed towards a broadening of the scope of its general outlook. That is to say, the Church, very much in keeping with tradition, made an effort to keep abreast of the new state of affairs, blending new linguistic terms with its venerable lines of argument. This is not to suggest that the process was uniform or unidirectional. Instead, it took place as a far-sighted and defensive search with deep roots in the Platonic and Scholastic history of the Church which could hardly be fully appreciated from a liberal perspective.[50] Of course, this movement gave ecclesiastical discourse a multiform and shifting character which was especially unsettling for those looking for a completely systematic, internal coherence in thought. This made clerical thinking particularly susceptible to attack as "opportunist." The usual clerical response was, "Opportune, yes; opportunist, never!"

The Archbishop of Valencia, for example, was scandalized that the Cortes wished to do away with monasticism by means of a "mere decree." He recalled the services monks had given to the

Church *and* the state: they were mentors of the state in education and in their vision of social renewal; they also were exemplary not only in holiness but also in the "economic government" of material goods. Their knowledge included necessary and worthwhile Earthly things, not only theology and philosophy, and their lessons contributed to civil, as well as Christian, good conduct. The injustice of the abolition of monasticism, in addition, was shown by the fact that this profession had been "accepted by the Nation so many centuries ago" and that men had entered it "in good faith and by a kind of contract." The expulsion of the Jesuits from Spain was not, as one might think, a precedent justifying the abolition of monasticism; far from the result of free determination, that action had been the product of the "machinations" and "triumphs" of Frederick of Prussia and Voltaire, who had conspired to astutely attack the Church by means of a campaign plotted against the Jesuits. As proof of this, he quoted directly from the correspondence between the two men. In addition, the men of the Jacobin Enlightenment had debased the people rather than enlightening them, making a great mistake.[51]

The text went on to argue that it was unacceptable to put the clergy on state wage, imitating what had been done in France. Bishops, it argued, were not mercenaries: they had works of social charity to perform, and the protection of their dignity was not compatible with their subjection to "lay treasurers, who could retain their salary." The Archbishop resorted to the words of Pius VI in fervently defending the property of the Church, and denying any validity to its alienation on any pretext, or based on any precedent. The legal basis of ecclesiastical power on this matter was once again linked to the Church Councils. In this way, he returned to a more recognizably traditional discourse. But nothing kept him from interweaving one discursive style with another as the argument continued. He could even offer some subtleties, in this regard. Thus he insisted that the Earthly goods of the Church "are like the essence of the Church, maintaining its external worship which are an essential part of it." One could only maintain otherwise, he said, out of ignorance, interest or impiety.[52] But he provided careful historical proof for his argument in French precedents, concluding that:

> we know of the consideration that the clergy of France always received, especially in the age of the greatest lights of that Nation, when the Bossuets, the Fenelons and countless other great men

flourished. Everything we have shown proves sufficiently the inviolable immunity of the goods of the Church.[53]

In opposition to the Enlightenment Voltaire had perverted, another emerged here, no less French and no less worthy of the favorable cultural connotations the name of that nation conjured up. And this Enlightenment was a strictly Catholic phenomenon. There are other fascinating elements to the elaboration of this discourse. Endeavoring to defend the personal immunity of the clergy, the Archbishop of Valencia appealed to special services the clergy and the militia rendered to society. For special services, special privileges were warranted, because "otherwise the good order of society would disappear, and all vocations would be confounded." The fact that there were abuses of personal immunity did not invalidate it; since "ecclesiastics are men ... there must be some criminals among them." What had to be saved at all costs was the bulwark of the priesthood at the heart of society. Punishing criminals should not lead to any scandal, as that would weaken the priesthood's ministry. Doing otherwise threatened to turn that ministry over to "the intrigues of a powerful villain." The Archbishop claimed to have "overwhelming proof of the false testimonies given about priests by those who cannot suffer even their loving rebuke." Thus, the personal immunity of clergy should not be understood as fitting the category of "odious distinctions."[54] Such an error endangered the balance between the two powers, according to the Archbishop, and tore apart the Church's moral leadership of all of society:

> The bishops are tripped up and blocked in their rule by [the usurpation by civil authorities] ... and perhaps ... this ill-disposes the two authorities towards each other while they should be tightly unified for the good of religion and the state. This is the cause of many failings, and of *disdain for the rigor of the Church and mockery of the dignity of the priesthood and the monastic profession.*[55]

The attempt to make priests subject to military service and pay them salaries, thus eliminating tithing, also failed to respect the Church's overall role in society. Once more, the defense of the traditional place of the Church in society was made by appealing to the eighteenth-century Enlightenment. The Archbishop had no problem with citing José Moñino, Count of Floridablanca, in his praise for the charity and public works of the clergy, their activity in the patriotic societies of the reign of Charles III, their generous alms, and their faithfulness and political subordination to the established political regime. If anyone doubted that all this was applicable to independent Jalisco, a note underlined how this last concept specifically applied to the clergy of the state. But the constant appeal to Enlightenment did not indicate a lack of direction in clerical thinking. By making Enlightenment and political reform its own, the clergy reserved the right to rule on their "abuses." In this case, "the abuse of freedom of the press since a few years back" had perverted a principle the Church did not dare attack. The clergy preferred to distinguish between liberty and "licentiousness." The fact that the latter was on the rise made it "indispensable that in the absence of the Inquisition more efficient measures be taken to replace it."[56]

The Archbishop of Valencia was undoubtedly voicing a broader concern that had first appeared in Spain and now in Jalisco, but this thorny matter could easily place the Church in opposition to the state itself, and not only to the most Jacobin factions in civil society. Recognizing that substantial and irreversible changes were taking place in civil life was unavoidable. How could the Church ally itself to the best – or less objectionable – tendencies, and thus forcefully counter the more extreme deviations from the path of Catholicism and the moral leadership of the Church over society? The eloquent Archbishop offered a solution whose achievement would require suspending all innovative laws on the Church–state relationship:

> I already have indicated to the Government the utmost importance or need for the extremely delicate matters of the banning of books and investigations of faith to be always subject in Spain to an authority delegated by both powers which could thus proceed with fitting uniformity, expeditiousness and vigor. At the same time, I have expressed my desires that the Government might arrange this and other matters to the satisfaction of all by reaching an agreement with the common Father of all the faithful, or at least by celebrating the National Church Council already agreed to by the extraordinary Cortes in Cádiz. In this National Church Council, a legitimate authority would at the same time address the purely ecclesiastical matters pointed out at the beginning of this missive and prepare the most effective means for correcting the abuses that may have been introduced in ecclesiastical affairs. Results as healthy for the Church of Spain and its two clergies [secular and regular] as for the state are

to be expected from the resolutions of this Council, once it has been celebrated with due liberty and corresponding legitimacy and solemnity. For that reason I of course ask the Cortes to please quicken the pace in the part corresponding to them, and to facilitate the meeting of the Council. May God see fit to have it meet as soon as possible.[57]

In the writings of both Muzzarelli and the Archbishop of Valencia there was an evident concern with preserving the Church's own sphere of action. This was a practical matter in the now open discussions of clerical reform by the Archbishop, and tolerance, ecclesiastical wealth, clerical immunity and the use of excommunication by Muzzarelli. This was a theoretical matter, as well, both in claiming higher authority for spiritual values and in establishing parallels between state and Church powers. Muzzarelli and the Archbishop recognized the humanity of the clergy, but not the immanent character of its ecclesiastical work. The transcendence of man required that the clergy lead him forward, naturally making use of material goods and the Church's autonomous sphere of authority. Both struggled with the need to make evident that the Church served the interests of the world, and thus its distinctions and privileges were fitting for the exceptional service it gave to society or the state. Both argued from a strong sense of the traditional prerogatives of the Church, and agreed to some extent that adjustments could or should be made, as long as they did not alter the Church's fundamental role in society. The Archbishop, more than the Count, seasoned his discourse with new terminology from the Age of Enlightenment. On this point the archbishop especially, whose discourse followed essentially the same premises as the Count's, was anticipating a new direction for ecclesiastical discourse in Jalisco. In an era of growing pressures from statism and liberalism, the Church had to vary the tone of its discourse to win the loyalty of the people and the government.

Modes of Wrangling:
Indignation

Other 1824 pamphlets pointed out various aspects of public debate and opened a range of options for the dialogue between the Church and the new forces in society. The appearance that year of the new Political Constitution of the state of Jalisco must have made citizens particularly sensitive. Article 7 of the

Constitution would be the specific spark for debate, but what was under debate were the underlying assumptions and fundamental values of society. The tone of these pamphlets is particularly noteworthy, as it reveals the transition to a new social discourse oriented towards a public whose understanding had to be carefully shaped. Indignation was the outstanding tone in one pamphlet. Titled *Pronta y oportuna respuesta al papel titulado "Hereje a la tapatía porque no fía,"* it insisted on the distinction between two powers, one civil and the other ecclesiastical, in the government of society. From this perspective, it was ridiculous to suppose that Congresses function as Church Councils, since the latter were instances of power incomparable to others in their field, despite "the mania for a popular aura ... [which had produced] such an ugly monster." The desire to purify religion was warranted, but first, and above all, religion had to be preserved. Inappropriate readings inspired "impious, irreligious and immoral feelings." The legislator, in particular, drawing on appropriate historical examples, should realize his need to "humble himself before the priest." He had no reason to meddle in ritual or other matters of a religious nature.[58]

Selflessness and Diffident Self-Pity

Another pamphlet about Article 7 of the Jalisco Constitution was no less forceful, and also carried a firm threat of not recognizing the authorities who dared to violate clerical jurisdiction. On ecclesiastical income, it claimed that if the official aim was to take it from the Church, that was wrong, but if there was no intent to change it, then the issue was pointless. The established situation and the rights of the Church had to be respected. The author suggested it was unsuitable for the state to appropriate ecclesiastical income, or to cultivate suspicious interests on the basis of a jumble of ideas derived from dubious books. From the beginning of the pamphlet, the author claimed not to pursue "any pecuniary interest" and argued that the defense the cathedral chapter made of the Church's rights on income matters was not a question of "coffers," but of principles.[59] Moving from a tone of selflessness to diffident self-pity, he argued that if the financial dispute was not resolved in a way acceptable to the Church, that would be enough:

Without waiting to be told, *leave,* I would take up my staff, and whether or not my daughters in confession wept, I would head off looking for some little spot inside or outside the Mexican states where there is more respect for the Holy Apostolic Roman Catholic Church, the fatherland on this Earth which I recognize, venerate and love.[60]

Enlightened Reason and Elitist Restraint

The discourse defending the Church was not limited to indignant and diffident reaction. Fear and suspicion were all too evident in this kind of discourse, along with the sense of rivalry and struggle over society's hierarchy of power and objectives. There was no shortage of other pens proposing a more flexible approach towards contentious issues and their backdrop of general values and attitudes about the structure and direction of society. The Church could skillfully deploy Enlightened reason and elitist restraint in defense of the faith and a moderately representative republic.

One such pamphlet directed at fighting against the editors of *La Fantasma* [*sic*] tried to persuade the public not to follow the errors of the age in their search for enlightenment and change. The Catholic religion did not deny reason and its victories, but neither did it subjugate itself to them. The errors of the editors of *La Fantasma,* the pamphleteer insisted, came from ignorance and lack of knowledge of the "foundations" of religion. The editors wanted to make their reason the measure of all things, leaving behind traditions, the Church Fathers and the Councils. They dared to confuse religion with its vices and moral backsliding. Considering that reason was "so imperfect, weak, and open to error," and therefore should be guided by religion and not try to subdue it, "our religion does not fear the light, nor shrink from the examination of reason, nor demand of us an irrational faith."[61]

The author of this pamphlet reserved the reconciliation of faith and reason to the philosophers and theologians of Christianity, since "it is enough for the common faithful to instruct themselves according to their capacity in religious dogma and morality, to believe both are revealed by God with a sincere, compliant and reverent faith, and to practice both with all the fervor of their spirit and all the strength of their soul."

Thus it was inappropriate to suppose that religious ideas and beliefs were subject to public debate, or that different beliefs could compete among themselves within society. The pamphleteer went into details. He specified that religious tolerance implied the error of believing in salvation through different sects. Religious tolerance was something for atheists and deists and civil tolerance – itself not worthy of condemnation – could only be permitted in certain cases. He conceded that one could speak of a moral or evangelical tolerance, which included "the fraternal charity with which all men should be treated, whatever their nationality or religion," but he maintained that Catholicism had always practiced it.[62]

The author of this *Preservativo contra la irreligión* accused the editors of *La Fantasma* of "artificious bad faith" because they proclaimed themselves Catholics but did not act accordingly. The tolerance they proposed was civil, properly speaking, but had the clear intention of spreading into religious and philosophical tolerance. Catholic Jalisco would be drawn into internal disagreements by the planting of impious, lascivious and sacrilegious ideas "in our cities, in our villages, in our towns, and even in the most hidden ranches in the depths of the forests." That would be the result of denying the Catholic Church its coercive capacity on religious questions, and of ultimately turning education over to men like the anti-clerical Pedro Lissaute.[63]

"Public tranquility" had been based on a united opinion in favor of Independence, after eleven years of "divergences," and such a unity had been prompted by the "schismatic decrees of the Congress of Madrid" of 1820 and everything they augured. Now, countering all that, there emerged the threat of the "fire of a destructive anarchy and most bloody civil wars." And such evil was justified by denouncing the "inhumanity" of Catholics in comparison with the supposed "moderation" of Protestants. The pamphleteer recalled that the Church acted preferentially by "means of persuasion, censure and whatever conciliation is compatible with the truth of dogma." Force was its final resort against "the pride, arrogance, insubordination and whimsy of heretics." Now that the "latter, calling themselves philosophers, follow their own prejudices instead of reason, they must be contained with a healthy barrier," despite "the tastes of the present age." It fell to the Church to apply "spiritual penalties"; it fell to the state to apply the rest.[64]

On this point, he stressed that Catholic religion did not attack reason, since it only aimed to deflate the "bias" of the philosophers, and not their reason, nor did it have anything to do with penalties which were not spiritual. But the state was obliged to defend religion as "the basis of society," since attacks on religion could only be considered "crimes against the nation." "When society has submitted to a religion, giving it the character of social law, as has happened in every Catholic state," then duty and justice demanded that the sovereign repress the impertinent religious dissidents. Following the tradition begun by "the Great Constantine," governments should serve God by combating error. Finally, concluding his pamphlet in a progressively more common, indignant, discursive style, the author of the *Preservativo contra la irreligión* refuted the editors of *La Fantasma* who professed their respect for the opinion of the people on legal matters: "How then could the representatives of the people go against an opinion so widespread across the state?"[65] The people opted for intolerance because the alternative was

> an attack against the most sacred property right. Thus the man who by means of impious writings tries to destroy the true religion of a state is a public bandit, and the one who in conversation tries to uproot religion from the heart of another, is a sacrilegious pickpocket.[66]

Sarcasm and Aggressive Denunciation

A biting, sarcastic tone could be added to the desire to refute new thinkers and force them to listen to the Church. To that end, one pamphleteer wrote *Conversación familiar entre un sacristán y su compadre contra el papel titulado Hereje a la tapatía*. The reader's curiosity was piqued and jarred from the beginning by finding that it was none other than the sexton himself who took the role of *Hereje a la tapatía*, arguing in favor of Article 7.[67] Obviously, the sexton was identified with the Church, because of his office, but he naïvely followed and believed all the arguments of those who would put the Church on the state's payroll. His compadre took pity on him and, understanding his well-intentioned ingenuousness, tried to open his eyes. When offered the argument that now the state was virtually the independent people of Mexico, and that the people had always paid for the Church, the compadre raised a question:

Did I not tell you they would provide common-sense justifications, in order to deceive the ignorant? Tell me: is not the Church of Jalisco composed of the faithful of Jalisco, under the rule of its head? And are not the faithful of Jalisco the ones who have paid the expenses of worship? Therefore, the Church of Jalisco has paid those expenses. Then why don't they write "the Church will pay the expenses for worship?" Moreover, what would you think if they set out a constitutional article like this: The state will pay for and set the domestic expenditures of every family, and due to this, entered into your house to remove, change and set your economic laws?[68]

It was not money that was at stake, but authority and jurisdiction. The congressional deputies might be trying to do the right thing, but there already were many people who had "the same feelings and thoughts" as the Protestants, and might in some future congress turn the best objectives around, "since you can already see that this is done according to the number of votes." Gradually, the sexton saw the light, and in response to the accusation of economic interest on the part of the Church authorities, came to find that the new thinkers must have "some little interest" of their own, and so "the author of that tract was only trying to trick ignorant people like me."[69] Now on the verge of winning the debate, the compadre aggressively changed his tone to denunciation:

Do not let yourself be tricked, compadre, let me tell you. Luther, the implacable enemy of our religion, called its dogmas and principles abuses and prejudices. And you know how he went about things? He extinguished the religious orders, and said he was removing an abuse from religion; he abolished the mass, and said he was removing another abuse from religion; he refused obedience to the Roman Pontiff, and made himself head of the Church, and said he was removing another abuse. In this way, he destroyed the religion of Jesus Christ, saying he was removing abuses. The same path was followed by Voltaire, d'Alembert, Diderot and others who set out to destroy our religion. The words "Enlightenment," "humanity," and "charity" were always on their lips, and they always denounced "superstition," "fanaticism," and "ignorance." And do you know what they understood those words to mean? When they said the first set of words, they meant impiety, licentiousness, and so forth, and when they said the second, religion, its dogma, and its commands.[70]

The author of the pamphlet under attack thought – the compadre claimed – like a Protestant, and went so far as to compare Christianity with other religions. At the same time, he ignored Church authorities. The sexton concluded that "to reach the truth, I should conclude the opposite of everything these tracts say." The compadre closed with this commentary:

> You could do nothing better; that is what I do, and I am not wrong in my calculations: and so when you hear one of these scribblers say that they want religion to be pure, understand that to mean they want it to be a nullity, that is, they want no religion, and you will be right in this before God.[71]

An agreement with the Pope on the matter of patronage was to be expected, and this would allow abuses to be attacked and peace to be kept between the two powers and between citizens.[72]

A Cry of Alarm on Sensitive Matters

One reprint from Puebla underscored the anguish important elements of the clergy must have experienced in trying to come to terms with the unavoidable changes in society without giving up the coherence and dignity of ecclesiastical affairs. The Congress of Veracruz was on its way to modifying the fees associated with the administration of the sacraments and was attacking standard practice in matters of alms and prayers for the dead. It was also attacking abuses in religious matters. The Bishop of Puebla struck a note of alarm on a sensitive issue: he admitted that the civil government had the right to intervene in setting fees, once patronage was agreed to, but he adamantly reserved the rest to ecclesiastical authority.

The Bishop was not worried that new fees be set or that the civil government claimed rights to do so, but that the new fee schedule, lacking clarity and uniformity, would become a motive for debate between priests who administered the sacraments and "the representatives of the people." If a quarrel of this sort was sparked, the priests would seem like mere mercenaries. Everything became thornier still, because the new schedule did not adequately resolve the relationship between custom and formal agreement in established fees, so that conflicting interests could appeal to either local custom or to the overall agreement in defending their positions.[73]

But what we should pay most attention to is that, if parishioners, as they have lost their affection for holy things, have refused to contribute to worship and to the support of their ministers, causing infinite work yet paying little for their services, in keeping with the times in which the current fees were set: what can we expect when they find themselves authorized to enter into contracts and adjustments which, as the law itself states, have been made for their benefit?[74]

In reforming abuses, there was the danger of doing away with good practice as well as bad. But the key to all this was perhaps the "opportunity" of the changes introduced at a moment when all of society was experiencing a major shift:

I am of the opinion that until we have constituted and cemented across the country the federal system we have sworn to uphold, the authorities, and especially the ecclesiastical ones, are too weak – I will painfully say – to make themselves understood and obeyed by the people (pueblos). This is why, even with respect to the clergy immediately subject to me, I am frequently experiencing difficulties and excuses in having my orders followed, even when those orders are not directed in their objective, manner, or circumstances to anything more than common happiness and the assurance that my flock is not lacking for essentials.[75]

Confronted with such a complex and worrisome situation, the Bishop asked for the overturning of the law on fees, committing himself to set a fee schedule to resolve the matter.

Unflinching Impartiality

The new setting of Independent Mexico did indeed worry prominent elements of the clergy, as shown by the pamphlets of another writer attacking Article 7. In one pamphlet, he reminded readers that whoever paid the clergy determined the number of parish priests, for example, and in the final analysis could plunge in and "suppress sermons, the preaching of God's Word, and all the practices and exercises of devotion that the Church admits."[76] The writer insisted on the effects the article would have, not its intentions. In brief, civil power would spread its reach and delve into matters not properly its own. But the pamphleteer avoided addressing more specific issues like tithing and its administration; declaring his desire for an unflinching "impartial examination," he stressed intrinsic concerns rather than formal matters. He was worried about jurisdiction and its consequences, not detailed arrangements. He finished his first pamphlet exhorting readers to "examine words, cut to the core to find if their meaning faithfully corresponds to the objective and ends they state, and to find how far they can extend and reach."[77]

Clarification for the Obstinate

But after seeing his good intentions misunderstood by a "defender of Article 7," this pamphleteer dared to publish a new piece in which he further clarified his position to overcome obstinacy. In this new tone, he emphasized that the discipline of the Church was not subject to the "tribunal of reason," but to "the appropriate ... authority." He went on to say that the important distinction in Article 7 was the difference between "setting" and "paying" the costs of worship. The state, in fact composed of the faithful, had the obligation of paying for the expenses of the Church. That is why part of the question was necessarily complex. But paying did not confer the right to "regulate expenditures," because that invaded ecclesiastical jurisdiction. In the expenses column it made no difference to speak of the state or the faithful, and it was necessary to see that the upkeep of the Church was attended to "in virtue of the obligation all incur by a tacit agreement on entering and remaining in the society of the Church." Just as in "the other political spheres of society," in the Church there was a difference between the representatives and those represented, and the latter had to pay for the former by means of contributions.[78]

> Needless to say, in the first case it is the represented who pay, and also those who set the expenses for their representatives by virtue of contracts stipulated in the Constitution. Beyond the fact that such identification is purely ideal, abstract and metaphysical, while distinctions between certain citizens and others are all too real and effective, causing different attitudes, active in some, passive in others, the same distinction holds in the society of the Church in which the faithful submit and subject themselves to the Church's authority on every point concerning their spiritual government and well-being.[79]

This rash comparison between civil and ecclesiastical affairs insisted on rigorous parallels and avoided assimilating one power to the other at all. To propose otherwise was to flirt with "heterodox propositions."[80]

Annoyance Tempered by Good Faith

Despite what the author of the previous two pamphlets had to say, the exact dividing line between the civil and the religious was not so clear to all. Could one resort to a parallelism between one and the other to support the symmetrical autonomy of both, without changing the content of these related spheres of the social existence of man? The liberal pretense of "democratizing" religious life and subjecting its functioning to the vox populi unsettled more than one clerical spokesman. In one pamphlet, entitled *También los callados suelen hablar*, the author stressed that the new freedom of thought should be restricted to politics, without spilling over into religious questions. It seemed more than evident to him that "the Christian religion is not a system or a problem, and on the contrary, its divinity is sufficiently proven."[81]

This thinker manifested his annoyance at advocacy of any other way of seeing things, which he considered to be "impugning religion at its base." The newspaper *La Estrella Polar*, the spark for his ire, had promised the public exactly "a few rudiments of public law" and "the means for consolidating laws." The newspaper should be dedicated to fulfilling its promise, and to the question of schools. But its authors, feigning an erudition they did not possess, were meddling with religion, causing violent public reactions. This approach meant that the people would not be enlightened but that "over time we would be nothing more than beasts chained to other, larger beasts." In the judgment of the clerical pamphleteer, the imprudent religious toleration upheld by the authors of *La Estrella Polar* promised to bring greater disorder to the nation. In reality, this implied a contest between "the health of the people" and freedom as those journalists understood it. In any case, the laws determined Catholicism to be the religion of state, which should eliminate the arguments of *La Estrella Polar*.

> Without straying from the shining principles of Enlightenment and politics, we know that the People are the legislators, that the laws receive their authority and rigor from them, and ultimately the laws are nothing more than the will and expression of the People themselves. Yet [it is being argued that] the laws cannot determine which should be the religion of state![82]

Apparently, the liberating policies of the Independence period gave the people the right to choose their religion, but not to determine its internal functioning. The author trusted that "a happily faithful people" would freely choose Catholicism as their only religion in such conditions. The author, who confessed he was not "erudite," although he was "a stranger to prejudice," counseled "prudence" and "moderation" on these matters. Sensitive to the pressures exerted by the editors of *La Estrella Polar,* he closed his pamphlet in a tone of good faith:

> I am no more a fanatic than the many who share my ideas, nor am I superstitious, since I am a declared foe of puerile and minimal devotions. I look at religion on the grand scale, convinced that everything directed towards God can be nothing less than sublime. I bring this up because the words "fanatic," "biased," and "superstitious" have become commonplaces.[83]

Self-Defense in the Eyes of the New Republic

Once clerics had realized that the battle of the moment required making popular sovereignty compatible with the Catholic religion, their imaginations could run wild with proposals, since they did not want to fall into openly inflexible, resentful or even reactionary positions. They needed to fight the liberals over the question of popular sovereignty and, by appealing to popular feelings about religion, create a common-sense vision of its reach and limits. At the same time, they had to make the people aware of the real workings of the clergy, so that the people's vision of the Church was not based on what the liberals were saying. But since popular feeling was changing under the new conditions of Independence, they could not carry this out without a certain command of current policies and the principles they were based on.

Another extraordinary example of the Church's discursive efforts to confront contemporary challenges can be seen in the pamphlet titled *La mala fe descubierta y herida con sus propias armas.* After defending the historical rights of the Church concerning the cost of services, the author added in a tone of self-defense:

> The supreme head of the Church, and the remaining pastors, received from Jesus Christ, and not from the people, the power to rule over and govern the society entrusted to them. This is a sovereign legislative power, able to direct and preserve the commonwealth, and in use of that power the Church could and should

designate the means, and set the fees, by which it was supported. It
corresponds to the sovereign legislative power of a society to attempt
by all means to conserve the commonwealth, and one of those indispensable means is the distribution and setting of expenditures. It
corresponds to each member of the commonwealth, as one of his
indispensable obligations, to make the necessary contribution, to free
himself of a portion of his possessions, not according to his own will,
but according to the law established by the sovereign power.[84]

If there were abuses in the distribution of ecclesiastical income,
they should be remedied by Church Councils, and not
Congresses. On this point, the necessary link between the spiritual and the temporal in the real world was clear, but that did
not make it any less evident that the state should pay ecclesiastical expenditures, while the Church should set them. There was
no proper reason to mock the ecclesiastical authorities and show
them disrespect despite their moderation and their status as subjects of the state, in civil affairs, and "ministers of God on High,"
in religious affairs. The canons of the cathedral chapter were
being misunderstood, because they should not be seen as an
aristocracy, but rather as the "senate" of the bishop. They were
not idle, but devoted to worship. There was the same relationship between the canons of the cathedral chapter and the priests
who usually administered the sacraments as between magistrates
(alcaldes) and high-ranking functionaries of the civil government. Each was necessary, in its own right. To highlight the
symmetry of this analysis, the author reminded his readers that
the magnificent palaces in capital cities glorified the sovereignty
of the nation just as the work of the bishop and his cathedral
chapter gave magnificence to worship and divine sovereignty.[85]
The author's tone shifted from self-defense to flattery of the
new republic. Despite the great wealth of America, the canons
received little in income. It was "calumny" to claim otherwise. In
any case, the Church and civil authorities should come together
for any reform the nation wanted. The starting point for this unity
would be the ecclesiastical immunity which was already defended
by the Constitution.[86] Pushing the liberals from the discursive
center of the debate even as he retained their language, the pamphleteer concluded:

> You, Jalisco, who until now were a province of the Viceroyalty of New
> Spain, but now, emancipated like the rest of the nation, find yourself

restored to your pristine state in civil matters and having recovered in
full your civil rights, you are sovereign, free, independent; you must
promote the Earthly well-being of your members: no one, no one
disputes you those rights, no one denies you the attributes of your
civil sovereignty. The bishop, the cathedral chapter, the secular and
regular clergy have subjected themselves to the established system
of government, but keep in mind that you have remained and will
remain Catholic, and so you are now just as you were before in matters of religion; that is to say, you are subject to the Roman Catholic
Apostolic Church; you are bound to recognize her authority, you
must obey her laws, not only out of fear but also out of conscience.[87]

Piety, justice and "true Enlightenment" counseled that a
Concordat be signed within the tradition of shared Church–
state authority over religious matters, so that "with each keeping to the limits of what is just, peace, sweet peace will unite us
with ever-tighter bonds to make us formidable to our enemies,
and strengthen the foundations of our government."[88]

Prudence:
The Appeal to the Harmonious, Social Whole

The author of *Sobre la cuestión del día* went even further in
this debate. He established that the divide was between the
"destructive genius" of societies and the "Americans' efforts in
the difficult task of organizing their social contract." The words
"religious reform" were confusing the issue at hand, and in their
"malice" distorted "the interesting question of appropriate and
necessary reforms" by straying from the established path for such
reforms. Thus Mexico followed the dreadful example of France,
which committed the same error despite being "the most cul-
tured and one of the most humane nations on Earth." The pamphleteer specified the origins of all this confusion: "If liberty,
equality and property are rights seen as sacred, then the inviolability of the conscience of a people is the first of all rights."[89]

The cathedral chapter – so widely criticized by liberals –
oversaw "so many educational, religious, and public charity establishments which owe it their subsistence." Therefore, attacking
the chapter meant going against the interests of the people, and
revealed the ignorance of those who did so: "bold men, presumptuous politicians: you do not know the people you live among,
nor the matters society is truly demanding that you address."

In this, such men were following the bad example given by constitutional Spain, and the result would be upheaval and "the powerful ascendancy of a persecuted Church."[90]

Clerical possessions were the foundation not only of worship, the priesthood and charity, but even the credit of the public treasury. And the association some wished to make between clerical possessions and fanaticism was very suspicious:

> The fear they want to induce, of the influence of fanaticism, is an illusion or a specious pretext; new ideas, and new institutions resist it. If a state wishes to prosper, let it be considerate toward customs, protect letters, cultivate the sciences, and respect religion; thus, we will be philosophers without impiety and pious individuals without fanaticism. Happily, Christianity has never opposed the inalienable rights of human reason; Christianity has civilized the ancient world and the new; Christianity announces that the Earth has been distributed among the sons of man, and leaves the world over to its controversies and nature to its investigations; Christianity gives rules to virtue and places no limits on the human spirit other than its beloved mysteries.[91]

Prudence counseled "a harmonious order," without undue meddling between the Church and the state, "and it does not seem sound that in the name of sovereignty some want to induce them to follow doctrines they themselves resist." The accusation that the cathedral chapter was agitating on behalf of the Bourbons was baseless; the true disturbers of the peace were those who attacked the Church. They resorted to questionable interpretations of the authority of the Holy Fathers and the Councils in their declamations against the clergy, demanding a return to the primitive traditions of the Church. But that was absurd, since the historicity of the clergy was one with the historicity of its people.[92] Thus,

> it is rash and shows a lack of healthy criticism, or sincerity, to want to return the current customs of the ministers of the sanctuary to those of the primitive days of the Church. The passing of time, the prodigious growth of the Church itself, and the successive changes in the customs of nations, have necessarily changed those of ecclesiastics, who have obeyed the influence of the peoples they have lived among, forming with them a single and identical society.[93]

One example of this was the way the Church was governed. From primitive democracy, the Church had taken on "a kind of aristocratic form" to avoid "the confusion produced by the involvement of the multitude of the people in matters of great gravity." In this context, the cathedral chapter dated from the days of the Apostles. This is where the right to tithes came from, even if in the diocese of Guadalajara they were collected "with the greatest leniency and spirit of deference." But it seemed like the historicity of the Church did not imply a new democratization after Mexican Independence. The author of this pamphlet insisted that novelties had to be contained within the political sphere, lest they incur error and agitate consciences by touching the religious. The conclusion was obvious: "let us not break with dangerous experiments that sacred bond which, uniting the Earth to the Heavens, brings us closer in love and in social relations."[94]

Refuting their anticlerical opponents by using their own arguments and symbols, turning them to serve the cause of religion, was not only an ingenious move but a necessary concession to the age and to the men of Mexican Independence. Revealing the breadth and flexible nature of ecclesiastical discourse, this calls into question the vision of a Mexico unavoidably polarized between an obscurantist Church and a popularly supported liberalism. On the other hand, the range of responses by clerical writers to this era is also evident. The variety of opinions and their notable contradictions on certain points are no less interesting than their overall agreement with Count Muzzarelli on the basic points of institutional loyalty. Two more examples of ecclesiastical discourse will point to its ability to question the logic of the spokesmen of liberal reason and even its daring in risking everything by publicly refuting such weighty opposing thinkers as Montesquieu.

Blunt Rebuttal of Wayward Thinkers

The accusations of liberal malice and ignorance were not entirely new, but in *El error despojado de los adornos y aliños de la virtud y presentado bajo su propia forma*, they took on new dimensions. The author began his pamphlet with the statement that some editors were "very poor reasoners" who damaged religion and society, ambushing the people like wolves dressed in sheep's skin. They wanted to do away with the Catholic religion, the only true religion and "the tree of happiness." The blunt rebuttal he offered was succinct and direct: "O philanthropy, much vaunted philanthropy." Reason was subject to disputes, to the most absurd errors and the most monstrous crimes, and demanded the "brightest torch of revelation" to purify it and allow man to find "the true path to happiness." But the writers he was fighting against violated the constitution to attack the intolerance which granted the Catholic religion its proper place in society. By contrast, "what would someone who had written an iota against Independence deserve?" They fallaciously argued that intolerance only held in public, but spoke against it privately.[95] Such inconsistency by wayward thinkers endangered the people's trust in government in this new age:

> Let us be honest, gentlemen editors: all the people have embraced the current system under the firm promise they were given that the Apostolic, Roman, Catholic religion would be kept untouched and without mixture with any sect, and that we would spill our blood in her defense. Under that guarantee, they conferred power upon the deputies, and if we do not honor that promise, the entire world will rightly say we only meant to deceive, and will not give credit to our most solemn vows; from this will be born distrust, insubordination, and frightening division; disorder and endless abominations will prevail.[96]

Intolerance was based on the Gospel, and not on Voltaire, and faith and customs were entrusted to the care of the Church pastors. In the face of this situation, "how is it possible that, when all find protection in the laws, this tender Mother alone [the Church] is persecuted and unprotected?"[97]

Others wanted to "impudently" attack the Church, "flaunting their wisdom" when they spoke without any basis, disregarding the care the civil powers of a Catholic country had to exercise over the faith. They forgot what Saint Thomas had established, that "receiving the faith is voluntary, but retaining it after receiving it, is necessary." Tolerance was to be based on "evangelical charity," and that was the ultimate offense: "Considering you are such excellent logicians, such sublime theologians, such distinguished scribes, and such profound politicians, we wager you do not know: *what is charity?*" God was the first object of charity, and then one's neighbor, but liberals had turned that around. But "why reverse ideas so maliciously, and make humanity the principal or sole object of this virtue and not remember God, or place him last?"[98]

Thus in pursuit of his opponents, peppering his text with expressions like "Excellent logic, gentlemen editors, worthy of the Age of Enlightenment!", the pamphleteer concluded that it was a matter of two opposing cultures: one directed towards God, the other towards man. In this sense, religious tolerance was really "indifference to religious worship."[99] This conclusion was based on the work of famous French thinkers:

> But since you do not read, that is why you do not even know the arguments offered by the most capable opponents of religious intolerance. No wonder our ideas seem abstract and metaphysical to you, because you are like nocturnal birds, who are offended by the light of the sun, and enjoy the shadows of night.[100]

Not content with distorting the Gospels and not knowing the sources of their own thought, wayward writers went so far as to cut short the texts they cited so as to twist their meaning[101]:

> Oh, shame! Oh, the injustice of our Times! Though only a handful of libertines want to introduce sects to decatholicize and demoralize our nation, yet the desires and aims of these immoral and vicious men are listened to and applauded. But those members of an entire nation who only want and seek Earthly and Heavenly happiness are mocked and listened to with distaste.[102]

These "ignorant and prideful scribblers" made fraudulent appeals to the Scriptures in order to mock the public and "a free people who look indignantly on those who protect deception and deceit." Thus the sad conclusion to be drawn was that the pseudo-politicians of the day, "just as they assiduously promise to provide a theory worthy of noble and beautiful beings, ... degrade the dignity of man, to the extent of confusing man at times with beasts, or even with those of lower condition." Or to put it differently: "Truly, between the doctrine of the Holy Fathers and that of our journalists there is the same opposition as between light and darkness, justice and injustice, Christ and Beelzebub!"[103]

Finally, the last publication analyzed in this chapter appeared as a short-lived newspaper, *La Cruz*, of which seven numbers survive. The newspaper dedicated itself to rebutting no less than

Montesquieu himself, based on a close reading of his ideas. First, the author specified that Montesquieu's analysis of religious matters only applied to false religions. After all, "superstitions cannot be universal," and were adapted to local conditions, including the climate, popular feeling, and government type. By contrast, the Catholic religion escaped the fate of superstitions:

> Since the Catholic religion is not created in this way, nor the work of the hands of any man, it happens to be free of all such vices and defects. Since it has come from heaven, there is no country under heaven that can hide from its influence. It perfects all human governments in what they are, according to nature, and it purges all laws of the errors and vices they contract from their authors.... From this, one can see how wrong are those who think it best for only one kind of government, and even more, those who think it prejudicial to all forms of politics.[104]

Directly contradicting Montesquieu in the second number of the paper, the author denied that Catholicism was more appropriate to a monarchy, and Protestantism to a republic. To reinforce his argument, he brought to mind the republics of Catholic Italy. Then he challenged the French author rhetorically: "how will Montesquieu respond to his own principles?" If "virtue is what builds up republics and its absence is what corrupts them, the religion which most truly professes the doctrine and practice of truth will be the best at preserving the vigor of a republic."[105]

Could Montesquieu not know that all of Catholic religion depended on charity? Or that charity is the truest love for the common good, looking beyond one's self, and the ruin of ambition, of avarice, and of all the vices countering perfect love among the citizenry?[106]

Thus, not only did Christianity escape from Montesquieu's decree that all religions were "born and formed in some state," but Catholicism, "without being born in any one state, kept the form of government of each," while Protestantism did the exact opposite. Thus "the Catholic religion is even more effective for aiding good policy, because it does not suffer from any suspicion that it was created by Princes, nor according to their tastes or interests." Catholicism had the good fortune that its "center" was precisely "in an orbit eccentric to the other orbits the world is divided into, each independent of the others, while the Church like the sun is the common center of all."[107]

La Cruz closed its seventh issue with two statements emphasizing how Catholicism had defeated a disoriented Montesquieu
and was useful for all nations and all governments:

> It is quite true that the Catholic religion, which has saved many
> wise and powerful nations, and very strong governments zealous
> of keeping their mutual sovereignty and independence, could not
> place the dignity of the crown on any of these governments, but
> instead was exempt of all and indifferent to all. On this point hangs
> the salvation of many nations and their governments....
>
> Just as by its nature this religion from Heaven is more indepen-
> dent than all Earthly powers, so it is all the more useful to those
> same powers. First, because no man, however wise and astute he
> may be, will find in Her any of the ambitious arts Princes have
> discovered for terrifying and subduing their subjects. What reli-
> gion commands in favor and in honor of the secular powers, has
> not been established or conceived by them....[108]

Conclusion

Behind the growing variety of discursive modes employed by
the Church we can glimpse various perspectives on resolving
pending problems. This variety itself was a response to the need
to shape, for a heterogeneous public, a convincing vision of the
Church's role in society and towards the state. There was clear
agreement on the Church's right to defend itself, but the style and
details of that defense had not yet been set. Since the goal was
not just to establish a coherent ecclesiastical position, but to influence a broad heterogeneous public, this was a sizable challenge.
The declaration of a federal republic based on the principle of
popular sovereignty was a major obstacle for the Church.

The greatest variance among these pamphlets can be stated in
the following way: first, either the republic and the Church would
remain united, in the traditional alliance, or the Church had the
right to resist the state; second, the republic and the Church
are parallel powers, with all comparisons adjusted to the republican style, but their mutual independence assured the divine
sovereignty of the Church; third, if the state did not respect the
Church, the latter could utilize republican principles to bypass the
state to call directly on the people, in the name of the people
and of popular well-being. Beyond this, the points raised by

Count Muzzarelli – on religious intolerance, clerical wealth, personal immunity for the clergy and ecclesiastical jurisdiction – were openly or tacitly held. The Archbishop of Valencia's leaning towards undertaking changes in clerical behavior, but under ecclesiastical jurisdiction, was also generally agreed to. His tendency to employ more up-to-date language was even deepened by other pamphleteers, but we should not assume that different rhetorical positions in the exalted polemics of 1824 were mutually exclusive. In any case, the presence of these differences within clerical discourse suggests a lack of overall cohesion and coordination. Since no officially sanctioned orthodox rhetoric yet existed, there was a range of possibilities, which could be eclectically blended to the taste of individual authors.

7

Verbal Virulence and the Struggle for the State

From Erudition to Biting Invective in Clerical Discourse

In 1824, conservative writings on religious and Church matters had multiplied greatly. These writings were in keeping, as already seen, with the basic premises of the more erudite pamphlets, but such learned publications could not reach a broad and heterogeneous public. Clearly, the pamphlet from the Archbishop of Valencia marked a transition point. Even so, his writing was directed towards the supreme legislative authority in Spain, the Cortes. He did not attempt to address shifting popular attitudes and prejudices, but rather addressed the principles of government understood and employed by men *of* the government. This presupposed a government capacity for making decisions without direct popular involvement.

It was precisely this assumption of the relative autonomy of the government which Mexican Independence placed in crisis. It was now clearly asserted that government should act in accordance with sovereign and popular public opinion. Otherwise, Independence would be for naught, and Mexico might as well return to depending once more on royal sovereignty. In reality, this option was impossible, of course, since even Spain itself was adopting the doctrine of popular sovereignty. Therefore, Mexico could not avoid the issue of self-government without giving up all thought of forming a "people." Either Mexico submitted once more, retreating to form part of the Spanish people, which in any case meant forming part of a self-governing people, or it created its own profile as a people. A return to royal sovereignty in its older sense, now thoroughly anachronistic, was not particularly attractive or likely in either case.[1]

The crisis of principles of government had demanded a different tone in conservative pamphlets. These pamphlets had to multiply feverishly, if they wanted to confront the liberals on every point and plan being presented. At heart, these conservative pamphlets had aimed to combatively occupy the discursive spaces liberal pamphlets wanted to drive them from. They had to set the standards for social meaning and truth in the new, independent society so that this society would choose, by free exercise of its sovereign will, to preserve rather than to transform the Church and religion which were now in question. This was not a superficial change, but a profound one in the nature of power and discourse in Mexico.[2]

This change demanded giving erudition a tone in keeping with the great transition towards popular sovereignty the country was undergoing. Far from being a mere theory, popular sovereignty conditioned even the formulation and expression of ideas in the public sphere. This should not conceal the fact that the degree of academic erudition varied greatly from one pamphlet to the next; but if we review the titles of 1824 pamphlets discussed in the previous chapter, it is clear they have become more polemical than before. The expressive title wording is quite indicative of the pamphlets' discursive stance: *The Silent Also Speak, On the Question of the Day, Bad Faith Uncovered and Wounded by its Own Weapons, Article 7 of the Jalisco Constitution, Another Spanking of the Guadalajaran for Obstinacy and Impiety*.[3] Titles such as these suggest a desire to snatch liberal discursive messages in mid-flight and toss them to the public trimmed and adapted to what was usually called "healthy doctrine." Even the writings which flaunted greater learning showed similar leanings, as can be appreciated once again from their titles: *Error Cleansed of the Adornments and Dressings of Virtue, and Shown As It Is*, and *A Preservative Against Irreligion*.[4]

Two very important trends emerged clearly in these pamphlets. First, they tried to separate ecclesiastical power from any demands for Mexican popular sovereignty, placing it on a higher hierarchical level as an indispensable aid for improving civil life. Second, this implied that Mexicans could only freely exercise their reason and will within a sphere subject to ecclesiastical authority. In this sense, the exact formula for arranging the ties between Church and state was secondary, what was clear was a preference for preserving the ecclesiastical status quo with minimal change, or otherwise for promoting relatively greater clerical autonomy, while clearly recognizing the equality of the two powers. In no case was the state to be excused of its responsibilities towards the Church and the Catholic religion. The partial adoption of a new, republican vocabulary by pamphleteers strengthened the ability of clerical discourse to appeal to the patriotic feelings of Independent Mexico. Anonymity was the perfect resource at a confusing moment, and allowed the pamphleteers to explore various possibilities for adjusting the relationship between Church, state and society, possibilities which differed both in substance and in discursive style.[5]

Even more than the previous year, 1825 would underscore the stylistic shift in Guadalajara clerical pamphlets. From the dignified, circumspect and erudite level of the most carefully pondered pamphlets of 1824, they dropped to another level, more biting and incisive, with a noticeably more popular tone. Liberal attacks and diatribes clearly drove the new style and greater tension evident in clerical discourse; now, the process deepened. In an answer to the liberal pamphlet *El Polar Convertido*, one clerical author responded with almost uncontrollable indignation:

> I agree that men have been capable of abusing the most holy and sacred things and of using religion as a pretext to disturb societies, but is it not an injustice to attribute to religion the disorders it condemns, which indiscrete or wicked men have done under the pretext of propagating or defending religion? If El Polar dared to assert that love for the fatherland, the peoples' wishes for independence and liberty, that the forms of government, the division of powers, the administration of justice, political freedom of the press, the Enlightenment, etcetera, etcetera, had all caused the breakdown of society, everyone would take him for a liar who, without any reasons, causes, or basis, foolishly confused the finest of things with the abuses they are used for.[6]

After refuting various statements by El Polar about religion as the cause of societal disturbances and celibacy as a "cannibalistic establishment," the author moved on to religious tolerance. Following the same vein of argument, he ridiculed El Polar's logic:

God permits the universal tolerance of faiths, therefore they cannot be prohibited. An argument worthy of El Polar! Following these same principles, I'll make these other arguments to you. What God permits cannot be prohibited: God permits all kinds of disorders to happen, therefore these disorders cannot be prohibited. God permits the enemies of the fatherland, permits murders, robberies, and disobedience of the laws, since nothing happens which God does not allow. Therefore, following your same logic, we cannot prohibit murders, robberies, machinations against the fatherland, etc., etc.[7]

In light of Article 171 of the Federal Constitution of the Republic, which made the constitutional articles on Independence and religion unchangeable, the pamphleteer asked why El Polar allowed himself to speak against one, but not the other. After skipping over the matter of tithes – "not because I don't have anything to say, but because I do not want to start with a question that has become so hateful" – he supported ecclesiastical authority on matters of the press, denied that ecclesiastical government was "popular, representative, federal," and insisted on the infallibility of the Church Councils, the legitimacy of Popes not elected by popular vote, and the authority of the Church's pastors over the faithful.

In another pamphlet from that same year, addressed to the publishers of *El Nivel*, the same author returned to the question of tolerance. He reproduced the arguments which emphasized social harmony and the danger of contamination from false doctrines and inappropriate attitudes:

> I have no doubt that the mingling of heretics, deists, and so forth with true Catholics will produce in the latter what communication with idolaters produced in the Hebrews. Ongoing contact, the dissolution of customs which we can unfortunately observe and which in the case of tolerance would not be minor, the inclination towards novelty, the drive to not seem bigoted and to no longer believe such ancient things, the ignorance of the foundations of religion, which is more common than it might seem, and above all our inclination towards evil: what would this produce?[8]

He went on to say that Christian charity at no point authorized tolerance. The idea that Article 171 could ultimately be changed, like any other, was the ultimate affront.

One might hold forth speaking like this to the enemies of our system: Excellent; don't give up hope, enemies of the free press, monarchists, opponents of independence, that every article of the Mexican Constitution can be modified, and so there is no obstacle to changing those articles which bother you. Even though the Mexican people, through its representatives, had wished that the article of independence not be open to change, do not worry: the barrier against change can be removed by the year 1830 and according to what the *nivelistas* are still saying, you can now speak and write against Independence, as long as you do so in theory, without intimidation, and with arguments which will no doubt occur to you....

Attacking Article 171 threatened any hope of stability for the young nation. Jumping from there to attack Independence itself would have been "absurd, impolitic, a crime against the nation." The author closed attacking rebelliousness against the ecclesiastical authorities on matters of faith. If the Church demanded intolerance, that was what had to be done.[9]

In the *Gaceta Diaria de México*, Blanco White wrote that the country should save itself from the religious abuses that had so weakened Spain, and ended up proposing religious tolerance. This was at the heart of the response he drew from a pamphleteer calling himself the True Defender of Our Constitution. "Intolerance is not the source of the ills of Spain," the True Defender argued, "but instead Spain's misfortunes began when she began to cease to be Catholic." Tolerance itself had weakened Spain, through the bad examples and foreign customs which thereby entered the peninsula and reduced it to such a "sad state."[10] He associated unrestricted freedom of thought with "a certain insolence and insubordination in our spirit." It should be understood instead that "it is intolerable impudence for man to dare to defend his rights to freedom if such freedom can even slightly trespass on the rights of God. Let the daring philosopher keep a great distance from denying religion its due, and therefore not fear violating the privileges of his freedom."

From Blanco White's standpoint, full civil liberty could not exclude intellectual liberty. In addition, God himself did not inhibit this, since he allowed all kinds of religions. Considering this argument ridiculous, the conservative pamphleteer did not think that the existence of evil exempted human authorities from "vigilance and zeal" in applying "wise laws and constitutions."

Moreover, "no one should meddle with us, since we are very free to continue with our intolerant system."[11]

For the True Defender, the very publication of Blanco White's writings was an act of audacity. Why should there be recourse to this gentleman, when Guadalajara had "the holiest of writers, the deepest of theologians, and the most excellent polemicists"?

> I'll wager as much as you wish that no one would dare to publish documents against our federation and independence, no matter how important they are, and no matter how wondrous the contents of such documents.
>
> Let whoever would be a man try it, and in Miscalco [at the doors of heaven?] he will see what will happen to him, without any excuses. Since religion is as fundamental a foundation as independence, then why should we keep a respectful and inviolable silence on independence, while we have to allow that the official bulletin itself put forward insulting documents, offensive ideas, and subversive exhortations about our holy religion?[12]

Attempting to change Article 3 of the Constitution meant:[13]

> Offending and insulting to their faces the fathers of the country who unanimously formed our code. Well, are we playing games with government and shifting constitutions like gamblers shift cards? Not only would this scandalize the states of Anáhuac, but every country of the world would rightly conclude that our legislators are weak or indiscreet men.[14]

The author of the pamphlet clearly foresaw the danger of indifference and he closed with a prayer:

> God, by means of your infinite mercy, and by means of that singular love with which you have always watched over the faith of Americans, give strength to the Christian fathers of this land so that they keep our religion pure and intact, as they have sworn to do. Enlighten Withe [sic, for Blanco White] and all who sleep in the darkness and shadows of death. May every nation say with admiration of the states of the federation: blessed the states whose opulence grows together with their faith, and whose happiness is as stable as their religion.[15]

An anonymous pamphlet, without any pseudonym, directed
the editors of *El Nivel* to "rectify their ideas in terms of tolerance" by reading Muzzarelli, *El Error*, and a document sent in by
"The Friend of the Mexican", since – the anonymous pamphlet
claimed – they had not understood anything of those publications, however much they cited them. Later on, the anonymous
author added *La ignorancia descubierta* (Ignorance Uncovered) to
the list of recommended readings. He invoked Saint Augustine
and Saint Leo to justify his defense of intolerance on the part of
civil authority, as well as the prosecution of those who violated
morality or resisted belief. Summarizing the words of Saint Leo,
he recalled that

> real power has been given to you not only for the government of
> the world, but primarily for the protection of the Church.… Once
> princes became Catholic, and incurred the obligation to defend reli-
> gion, they justly punished such crimes with temporal penalties.[16]

If these penalties were cruel and barbarous, that was only a product of the times, and "if there was cruelty it was certainly not
exercised by the Church, but by civil authorities." Civil authority came to reinforce the ecclesiastical authority later expressed
in the Inquisition, although "I am not an apologist for that tribunal, nor do I pretend that it be established among us." The rest
of the pamphlet struck at the editors of *El Nivel*, who in their
ignorance and bad faith wanted to make themselves "mentors of
the religious people of Jalisco" and indicate to ecclesiastics "the
conduct they should follow." Since their errors, like those of all
the impious, were nothing more than "errors a hundred times
refuted," citing appropriate Christian authorities was all that was
required, adds a note at the end of the pamphlet.[17]

Another pamphleteer, who signed himself as "The Invalid,"
entered the fray in Guadalajara by means of a reprint. His point
was to prove that the national sovereignty and dignity of Mexico
required intolerance, which the Constitution also demanded.
Bothered by Lizardi's attacks on the clergy and his support for
tolerance, the pamphleteer opened fire on the positions of the
"Mexican Thinker." By contrast to the infidelity to the young
nation that Lizardi attributed to the clergy, "The Invalid" recalled
that intolerance was an article in the Constitution and, therefore,

Lizardi himself in his writings was in breach of the fundamental law of the nation. Turning the questions Lizardi had directed at the clergy on end, "The Invalid" now asked: "What privileges does the 'Thinker' have to disobey the law publicly and with impunity?"[18]

The author went on to suggest that just as Lizardi had asked for the expulsion of the bishop of Sonora, because he found him opposed to Mexican Independence, so similar proceedings should be essayed for those who attacked "an even more essential article such as the one on religion." Lizardi's opinion that only tolerance was in keeping with freedom of conscience, as an English journalist had declared, awakened absolute repugnance in "The Invalid."

> Are not all peoples free to constitute themselves under the religious form that best suits them? They undoubtedly are: and this is quite in keeping and in accordance with their rights. Then what worry should we have, here, that this foreigner or that does not like our legislation? Do we like it? Then that is more than enough, because everyone should do as he wishes in his own house, without consulting his neighbor's tastes.
>
> It is an undeniable fact that the general will of every state of the federation is to firmly maintain the Catholic religion, excluding any other, just as we have inherited it from our ancestors: [to keep it] to the exclusion of others, as we have done by the grace of God on High, and [to keep it] pure as we have transmitted it to our descendants.[19]

If, despite everything, Lizardi wished to follow foreign opinion on this matter, he ran the risk of falling into "the greatest tyranny and the most cruel despotism on this matter most our own." The English monarch could hardly ask of Mexico what Mexico could not concede, just as Mexico would not ask it of Great Britain, since the form of government, religion and other questions were not subject to any negotiation. Even if England did, the government of Mexico

> should carefully study the matter, as its importance and delicacy demand; should hear the votes of the town councils; should know what is the ruling of the ecclesiastical and secular corporations, since they form the highest echelons of the political hierarchy, and try, finally (if I can explain myself thus) to explore what the states of the federation may say. And if the general will opposes the measure,

then undoubtedly the government, in answering England, should and would oppose it.[20]

Just as Mexico would never give up territory to England to arrange its relationships with that country, it could not and should not budge an inch on religion, "since the purity of our religion merits no less consideration than our territory." By acting with firmness and clarity, Mexico would keep the respect of foreign powers.[21]

Overall, these pamphlets established that the Church's position in Mexico was a patriotic one in the face of mistaken opinions coming in from abroad. The liberal principles some wanted to apply to the Church were thus reoriented to support the self-determination of Mexicans, not only in political matters but also in their right to exercise intolerance towards religious sects competing with Catholicism in national territory. Intolerance was constitutional. Mexico was Catholic by constitution, and therefore had the obligation of watching over the Church and defending it; any position to the contrary was anti-patriotic and anti-constitutional, and threatened the very well-being of the nation. That was the free will of the people.[22]

The new passion and stridency of clerical discourse was evident on another point of public dispute: clerical abuses. This was clear from the refutations made of the writings of a liberal cleric: one pamphleteer responded to him that the key to the question was the "hierarchical order of the Church," the foundation stone on which it was built.[23]

> And if you only pretended to remove from this stone the Earthly crust of luxury, a vice very common in the world today, although not therefore any more excusable in the clergy, then why did you not subtly broach the issue (although you draw attacks) of the ecclesiastical laws on clerical life and honor, and the infractions some commit against these laws?
> … But no, not only do you want a Church without luxury, you also want it to be a ward of others, without rights, without grace, without decorum, without dignity, without possessions – without even those possessions her faithful children have gratefully given and give her of their own volition.[24]

The matter was grave: "although you seem not to want it, you want and want well for the people to call tithe collectors heretics

… and canons … priests … and friars. Enough reticence; is this not how your wishes will be fulfilled?"[25]

The pamphleteer stressed the clergy's works of charity. He pointed out that the mature Church had to take a different form in the contemporary world than the ancient evangelical Church of the first days of Christianity. The pamphleteer went on to attack his opponent personally, insisting that his thinking was worthy of John Wycliff.[26] He made the following comparison:

> The pamphleteer we are combating said that "the minister who does not adjust his life and doctrine to the life and doctrine of the Apostles is not, and cannot call himself, a Minister of the True Church." The Church has condemned the assertion that "if a Bishop or Priest is in mortal sin, he does not ordain, he does not consecrate, he does not administer Sacraments, he does not baptize."[27]

After five copious notes as combative as the text itself, the author concluded in the fifth that

> His inventory of the luxury items of the clergy is so exhaustive that he did not even leave out undergarments; thus, according to Cuña [the liberal cleric], bringing our lives into keeping with those of the Apostles means walking around with our rump uncovered, otherwise we will not be and cannot call ourselves Ministers of the True Church. Assuming this discipline were in force, I would encounter difficulty finding anybody to call to the Orders, except for a few individuals I've seen walking around my neighborhood in the dress they brought out of the belly of their mothers.[28]

The same author produced even more forceful discourse in another pamphlet that same year and on the same theme. This time, he distinguished between two kinds of abuses: those which were committed against canon law and therefore were in opposition to the Church itself, and those "which do not confront the Church proper." Even in the first case, there was much exaggeration, and things were called abuses of luxury which were not. In the end, "who doesn't wear Cordoban shoes, who doesn't use shirts from Britanny, who doesn't have a pair of undergarments of some kind, who doesn't put on a beaver hat or make use of an umbrella to defend himself from the rain?" There was no canon law banning such practices. A more serious offense was mixing up the tithe with this matter of abuses.[29]

Thus you should not compare the Church to a young lady or
a girl (in this case, the same thing) who, having once been beautiful, has been made ugly by smallpox; nor should you say here in
Guadalajara, as I have heard some recounting, what Luther said in
Germany to the world's scandal, that is, that the Church in these
times is as dirty as the diapers of a menstruating woman. The holiness and beauty of the Church can never be changed by the vices
of bad Christians or by the apostasy of the unbelieving.[30]

The so-called abuse of the "sale" of sacraments was another problem.

I certainly do not doubt that there are some, and if you wish
many, for the most part secular clergy, who on the point of contributions, suffrage, and masses behave no differently than if those
sacred objects were merchandise at such-and-such a price. This is
abuse, obviously, and not a light abuse but one very condemned by
extremely severe laws, and terribly anathema to the Church.[31]

But on this point, a just contribution was too often confused
with an abuse. The remainder of the pamphlet was dedicated
to insisting on the parallel the previous pamphlet had set up
between Cuña and Wycliff.[32]
It was difficult for the Church to stick to a single, firm and
convincing course. Accommodating itself to the new situation
of the country without losing its institutional autonomy was a
delicate matter. The gradual tendency was towards deepening
the evident identification of ecclesiastical discourse with rising
Mexican nationalism, while accepting – with many qualifications
– criticism of the clergy. A prominent writer from the period
managed to capture in a few words the new equilibrium the
Church was looking for:

Senseless philosophers, you want a currency, a measure, a language,
and you do not want a religion.
    There are abuses in the Church; it needs reform, we all want it, as
Aquinas and Bonaventure wanted it, but not as Luther wanted it.[33]

But such a balance was difficult to maintain. Discursive spaces
were already being fiercely struggled over, and the authenticity
of the new tone of clerical discourse was impugned. Hesitation
by the conservative pamphleteers would only intensify the dispute. Thus, they had to publicly question the liberals, in their

honesty, depth, and rectitude. Mockery and insinuation could be powerful weapons for this. One pamphlet titled *La Polar embaraz-ada* (The Pregnant Polar) gave a choice example of these discursive tactics. Lady Polar, referred to as an unwed mother, stated:

> You see, I had the good fortune to marry a little polar, which is the same as saying, a little Enlightened philosopher: I have spent eight months in his company, in which I have come to know and admire him for his —I won't say 'well,' but rather abyss of science.[34]

If she had three sons, Lady Polar went on, she would name them in honor of three distinguished Polares (poles). Their father would instruct them:

> To the oldest, that is, the one born first, he will impart an implacable hatred of that thievery they call tithing and a general scorn for all the fanatics of crown and tonsure, and he will teach him to laugh at those Church scaremongers who speak of censure and excommunications. The second ... he will teach how to lie valiantly, to spread foolishness through the press, and to make miserable little arguments that the frailest old lady could demolish, and he will also inculcate in him the worship of all the worst. The third he will command, in imitation of his brothers, trained in Enlightenment, to piously attack all that corruption of paying for masses and prayers, and to confound the false belief that the Pope can concede indulgences, a belief all fanatics live under, when such power is nowhere granted [to the Pope] in all the Gospels. With such doctors, you will quickly see the face of the Earth renewed, and polarism victorious.[35]

And if they were daughters:

> They will be nursed in the coquettishness, the smoothness and the airs that should recommend them to their peers.... [The Little Lady Polars] will dress with the finest taste, that is, with a good part of their legs visible, another with her chest and back uncovered, and always with white shoes, which spark the most comments from the other sex: they will go to Church (which in this Age of Enlightenment is a theater of good opinion), and on entering, they will put all those attending in spiritual commotion; they will snatch up the gazes of all the fanatics.[36]

Any objections to so proceeding were "devilish and hellish sentimentalities," since

> in our system all that is lies, and what we ladies are taught today by the wise young men who surround us is that we should not fear those tales of old ladies and friars, that there is no such prohibition as the Sixth Commandment speaks of, and therefore no reason to resist their entreaties, since everything is natural.[37]

The pamphleteer ended on a note borrowed from Tomás de Iriarte:

> To all and to none
> My warnings apply:
> Whoever feels touched should blame himself,
> And whoever does not, should take heed.[38]

The mocking and provocative tone was evident once more in a pamphlet titled *El Canónigo Bien-pica* [*sic*], *a su Prelado El Polar* (From Canon Strikes-Well to his Prelate, the Polar).[39] In this case, El Polar was under attack for having quoted the Scriptures poorly and having circulated a "pastoral letter" to the people of Jalisco:

> So that Your Lordship sees that I know well how to make applications, and to give writing an obvious, natural and decent meaning (as if I were from *El Nivel*), I'll tell you what happened to me while I was flat on my back after an accident which left me at the edge of the grave. This little story is not very clean, but when so much is tolerated from others, a little bit should be allowed from me. It happened that when the physician came to visit me (I had spent the previous night very badly), and asked me how I felt, I responded, and here you have me stretched out and dried out from evacuations like water (get this), *secus decursus aquarum*, and asking again whether I had grown bitter overnight, I answered him, No, sir, because I have followed the counsel of David: *non accedet ad te malum*, do not grow bitter when you are feeling bad. Here Your Lordship will admire the decency, properness and naturalness with which the texts came to mind, just as today others are often brought to mind − even apparently out of thin air.[40]

Scorn and indignation had now become natural in this dispute for control of the discursive stage. *Un jeringazo al Polar* (A Jolt to El

Polar) adopted both, along with a tone at once plebeian and high-handed. The pamphlet started out with a singular challenge:

> I do not write for the wise, since they surely will not be seduced by the scribblings of sharp schemers; I speak to the average and lesser people, a group full of the gullible, and I use the style they are most used to. I will not follow fashion in what I say, because I am the lord of my own thoughts, and this is not a sermon subject to rules.[41]

The author was repulsed by what El Polar said about religions as the source of the upheavals in society. To El Polar's argument against celibacy – based on the idea that since the clerics had organs, they should use them – the author responded: "as if such a class of organist were so rare among the lay people." He went on:

> But one more thing: I see all the artillery El Polar directs against tithes, canons, baptisms, weddings, funerals and other Church abuses, which he would like to abolish entirely. Let's get to the bottom of this: I also agree with him that there are abuses in the distribution of ecclesiastical income, and other things worthy of great reforms, but who has told this poor man that the canons, priests, friars and other clergy are opposed to reforms? Perhaps they are the most energetic denouncers of such abuses. Remove them, he says, and so it should be, but let it be by the proper means.[42]

The pamphleteer demanded a Concordat with the Pope, so that just as the Church was part of the state, the state would be part of the Church. Once this delicate situation had been attended to in a Concordat, let the reforms go forward. But El Polar was a "little scribbler" with a "certain refined antipathy towards priests." And death – the author asked in passing – how would El Polar face death?

This author – who provocatively signed his pamphlet the "Superstitious and Devoted Fanatic" – was keen to insinuate that he was formally open to dialogue, if there were a basis for it. He conceded that universal tolerance was excellent in itself, in order to compare it to a pair of pants which didn't quite fit Mexico:

> It might be very good for France, England and other countries, where religion is studied by principles, and where a nine year-old boy is a dogmatic theologian. But here, where most only know God is Three-in-One because they heard someone say it, I say that tolerance is not appropriate, and we do not have the legs for this pair of pants.[43]

Still, in 1825, nothing stopped the Church from struggling for discursive space with more calmly aimed attacks and well-rounded arguments. The last pamphlet we will examine from that year set a tone which, while reflecting the growing polemical spirit, stylistically hearkened back to the relatively more reflective and careful tone of 1824. The author defended the Church's right to appeal to citizens' common sense, at the same time bitterly attacking those who claimed to be philosophers but denied the Church any appeal to reason. He worried about the discredit critics had wished to heap on clerics. He rejected the pride and ignorance of certain authors:

> A highly censorious attitude rules over their writings, and they look with scorn upon the authority gathered in all the Bishops of Christendom: they rule on things the Church up to our time has not defined; they deem the highest principles of canon law enshrined in laws everywhere to be prejudicial and vulgar errors; they dictate laws they do not understand, and they want to teach others what they have never learned.[44]

Yet despite everything, and notwithstanding

> the decisive tone with which you dare to pass laws and challenge the universe ... you are nothing but youths puffed up with pride and vain presumption, and you are so backwards in the sciences that you may be among those who have never even greeted them....[45]

But the heart of the matter was the right of the cathedral chapter to defend itself and appeal directly to the people with regard to Article 7 of the Constitution. The Church would do so with an important publication. The way it established this right is very significant.

> When Jalisco declared for the system of a federal republic, there were those who said that this vote was not freely given by the towns, but only by the provincial government [*diputación provincial*]. And what did that government do? It found it necessary, in order to clarify its conduct and vindicate its honor, to print a collection of documents which showed the wishes of the towns regarding the form of government proclaimed, thus clearing the government of the false accusation.
>
> Well, everyone knows the press has spread and continues to spread certain stories which are just as ridiculous as they are insulting to

the cathedral chapter. Then why would it not be proper now for this distinguished corporation to vindicate its honor and maintain its authority by publishing a collection of documents containing the wishes of all the Mexican Church on a matter corresponding to it, which will clear it of all the calumnies and slander that have been cast upon it?[46]

The Church, like even the lowest of the low, could not be denied the right to defend itself. In addition, it was only making objective "good history," and to this "no one can add a thing, except in substance: and what else is this collection we mention, other than the history of a well-known public event?"[47]

If the "scribblers" being attacked were opposed to the publication of the cathedral chapter, they should know they were opposing the Church Councils it was based upon. In addition, the accusation that such a publication constituted an attack against Earthly authorities was false. This was "an atrocious calumny, your favorite weapon, your reason and your entire support" in the task of dividing the two powers and ultimately destroying the ecclesiastical one. "Before and after this event, have ecclesiastical authorities not shown themselves obedient to civil authorities?"[48] If critics intimated anything to the contrary, it was

> because you know you cannot win converts, or destroy the religion of Jesus Christ, which is your whole objective, except by praising the Earthly authorities, fooling the people with false happiness, and exhorting uprisings and rebellion against an authority which you should closely subject yourselves to and obey. Fools deluded by fantastic theories![49]

Since 1824, one could detect that if the Church found itself in danger in its participation in the new national order, it would appeal directly to the people of Jalisco. The change in discursive style, and the adoption of anonymity, already indicated this. The renewal of the clergy's republican vocabulary and the measured acceptance of the need to reform the Church, but from within, advanced this possibility. Finally, the attack on the integrity, intellectual formation, and good will of their opponents made possible a new, more aggressive, discourse on the part of the clergy. In this context, the publication of the cathedral chapter document on correspondence with the state concerning Article 7 of the Jalisco Constitution takes on particular importance.

Discourse and the State:
A Clerical Offensive

In 1826, clerical pamphlets were shot through with indignation. Their sense of urgency and will to resolve the points of contention between the Church and the hard-line liberals would only grow. Ultimately, this was a dispute about the effective control of the state in Jalisco. In its effort to finally discredit the most inflexible liberal thought, the Church focused on the behavior of the new state. The success of clerical thought in appropriating certain outstanding aspects of liberal ideology and in placing anti-clerical discourse in check were the first step towards resolving this matter of state. Instead of pointing towards a new form of constitutional status for the state, this was directed at validating the compromise inherent in the 1824 Constitution between popular sovereignty and ecclesiastical autonomy, except that to make the constitutional compromise stick, the Church had found itself obliged to win over popular allegiance in the public sphere. This was an ironic outcome which could be considered very fitting for the times.

The 1826 pamphlets underscored several key points in what was now a long-standing public debate. They insisted on the hypocrisy of the most hard-line liberals, as well as their anti-constitutional stance and their mockery of the popular will. They stressed the Enlightened and republican character of the clergy and the need to respect the institutional status of the Church. In addition, they demanded that the state respect the terms of the Constitution, and specified the meaning of those terms in such a way that a mature clerical discourse seemed to be gaining effective control over popular interpretations of the Constitution itself.

There was a double irony in this situation. If the Church appealed to the people to place religion beyond the reach of popular sovereignty, the liberals – in name of the people – found themselves tempted to effectively ignore the feelings and wishes of the greater part of the populace of Jalisco. For liberals, the idea of the people was not shaped by a quantitative concept of majority but rather by an ideological sense of what was necessary to speed change up. But since change was neither as absolute nor as wide-spread in practice as it had been in theory, the Church was able to legitimate itself with discourse and behavior in keeping with Independence and the Constitution. Identifying itself with both, as well as with a popular majority ill-disposed towards religious innovations, the Church assured itself of a singular power in the state of Jalisco.[50]

Harmony would have called for general moderation, leading to a sovereignty effectively shared between Church and state. It is true that the Church recognized the sovereignty of the new, popular state, but in such a way that it limited its effective power. Back when the Church and the state were seen as being of divine provenance, the union of throne and altar had fortified the state. Now that only the Church had a divine basis, while sovereignty was based on the people, the Church's disputing control of the people with the state became a rather thorny matter. The state was in danger of ending up much weaker than before, and precisely at the moment when it was expected to be the agent of progress.

Curiously enough, since civil power no longer enjoyed divine support, theocracy threatened to cast a shadow over the secular lives of Mexicans.[51] Only if the Church's protected status within the Constitution were revoked and it was defeated discursively would conditions be ripe for the moral consolidation of the state. In the end, the state had no choice but to remain amorphous and weak, or to follow the ideas of the hard-line liberals down to their final consequences, in order to consolidate itself. Since the new state had to promote collective well-being to legitimate itself as the representative of the people, sooner or later its desire for authority and effectiveness would push it into conflict.

It was the Church's success in adjusting itself to the 1824 Constitution and the new liberal discourse, and not the Church's obscurantism, which would spark the greatest future conflicts. Its adjustments to the terms and tone of the Constitution, along with the preservation of clerical jurisdictional and legal privileges, left the Church with a privileged control over the future goals of man in society. In the scheme of the time, the justification for the liberal state had to be precisely its unique and indisputable capacity for understanding and responding to the demands of the "people."[52]

According to this logic, since the goals of the liberal state were intrinsically bound to the progress of the people, the state could not afford to share its crucial role as interpreter of the wishes and needs of the people with any other institution, lest it be rendered powerless. Nor could it objectively assume a preexisting set of ultimate goals of man. Such goals, if they existed, could not be the objective of the Earthly state, which was nourished by popular sovereignty and by the goals that were theoretically achievable within the parameters of an Earthly national society. Clearly, the goals of the secular state were not based on the idea of an already constituted humanity directed towards pre-set goals. Instead, those goals were still to be defined, as a product of the development or progress of humanity, by means of man's bold seizure of control over his own future. Yet Mexican liberals were unable to remedy the still-flawed communication between those represented and their representatives.

Discourse and activity concerning the state were closely intertwined in 1826. Abstract discourse and learned reflection were starting to wear thin; the moment of truth had arrived. Discourse, never blind to practical considerations, had run its course; now it was the time to definitively unite will and resolution. Fortified by the eloquence accumulated over three years, the opposing discursive forces gave no signs of yielding. Calls to force were the likely outcome. But in 1826 liberals held state power, and the very discourse of the Church still obliged it to observe the Constitution.

Traditionalists therefore set out to win over the popular will. What the Church had launched as a counter-attack turned into an offensive. Two 1826 pamphlets again went after El Polar. One of them accused him of being, like Luther, an ignorant reformer of the Church. By behaving this way, he proved himself to be a dissembler who ultimately scorned the authority of the people, who were Catholic. He was a "wolf cub" who hypocritically appealed to Father Ripalda in attacking tithes but, inconsistently, did not follow the famous Catholic catechist on any other matter.[53] The other pamphlet mocked El Polar as quixotic and ignorant while deeming him a confused and imitative thinker, only convincing to "country bumpkins."[54]

Two other pamphlets defended the mounted escort traditionally offered the Eucharist when it was taken out for public processions. One pamphlet limited itself to denouncing those who attacked the escort as "factious libertines" who should leave if they did not like the current situation under a constitutional government.[55] From the author's standpoint, no position was above the law, and the law authorized Catholic practices. On the same theme, another author detected "an insufferable stink and prestilence."[56] Number 29 of the official government *Gaceta* had published an "accursed communique protecting El Polar." Those who did not agree with Catholic practices should leave; perhaps they would be enlightened by their departure. "Let El Polar go to the United States, and there break the laws of the country, and we will see if he has a very happy trip; and let him not reply that adoring Jesus Christ is not the law, because he will be disappointed." The ongoing attack on public Catholic ritual had to be resisted. "How good it was, just as he called us 'factious and religious,' to return the favor with the epithet of a 'factious libertine,' which will not perish with the victory he longs for!" But in any case all of this was ridiculous.[57] Under the guise of simply reporting a conversation, the author closed with a sharp attack:

> I started to laugh deeply at both the heated dedication with which one speaker defended Catholic worship and your foolish project as you brandish your sword against an entire people firmly attached to their ancient belief and willing to give a thousand lives in its defense.[58]

He asked the publisher of the *Gaceta* to not publish "such insolent nonsense" again.

Several pamphlets attempted to thwart liberal diatribes against the clergy, portrayed as tyrannical, oppressive and ignorant. One insisted that the people were not so ignorant as to require "philosophers." Inspired, undoubtedly, by Cicero, he claimed there was nothing so absurd that a philosopher had not said it. Conceding that there were abuses in the Church, he insisted that the way to uproot them was by returning to the Church's true principles, not by abandoning them. Against the "scribblers who were abortive offspring of the Church" he asserted that the clergy was not an agitator, but simply enjoyed the support of the "people," and this allowed him to suggest that on these grounds the Church would defend itself.[59]

Another pamphleteer asserted that the "levelers" at *El Nivel* could not even "argue properly" and were "very far from being able to call themselves mentors of the American people." They quoted the Holy Scriptures without even understanding them. With no logic, they misunderstood what they were told, and "held forth without any rule other than their own whim, or any guide other than their passions." Understanding the Scriptures demanded the same kind of knowledge as the natural sciences or even "cruder arts." Like Luther, the *El Nivel* writers introduced a "private spirit" into scriptural interpretation, while the Church since the Council of Trent had reserved for itself the right to set the "meaning and interpretation" of the Scriptures. When people hostile to the doctrines of the Church made such incursions, thus violating the Constitution, they had to be punished in order to protect the Church.[60]

And now that he had entered into matters of Church and Constitution, the author claimed:

> It is false, it is slanderous to say that ecclesiastics have not adapted to the present system; they have respected and obeyed its laws as they pertain to them, and have not opposed them. What hurts them is that this very same system and its beneficial laws should be used to oppress, assault, and if possible, even destroy religion. What hurts them is that under the pretext of liberty, new criteria are invented every day for discrediting the Church, its laws, its customs, and its standards, and making them hateful. What hurts them is that no occasion or means is lost to insult, slur and calumniate the Church's ministers, to knock them down and treat them not as ministers of the true faith, or even as mere citizens, but to make them live – in the country where they were born and among those who are their brothers by nature and faith – a life more tragic than even foreigners have to suffer. All this hurts us, and although we can overlook what is merely aimed at our persons, we cannot do the same for things aimed at the faith, and at the rights of the Church, because they are so sacred and inviolable that they demand to be defended even at the cost of our lives.[61]

The author recalled that penalties applied in defense of the Church had to be material as well as spiritual, just like the nature of man, but this would never grant the secular power dominance over the church.

In this same vein, attacking liberals and defending the priesthood as the people's guide, another pamphleteer denounced the "calumny" against the clergy. In defending the property of the Church, he invoked the "contract" between the two powers on the matter, and the authority of Samuel Pufendorf on the power of the Church.[62] He told *El Nivel*: "If you could read, you would speak more carefully." But in the end, little more could be expected from these "modern-day savants." The wealth of the Church was in the service of the "public welfare," and it was protected by canon and civil laws which reserved the Church's rights as property owner. If, despite all this, liberals went against the Church, then it would be a case of "not accepting it [expropriation] in order not to be traitors to God." Faithless attacks should not be published anymore, since they were "viewed very poorly by the faithful."[63]

The pamphleteer called for the state to join the assault on liberal zealots in order to keep their audacious proposals from gaining ground among the "common people." El Polar was an "indecent pygmy," but since he expressed himself freely and there was no one to oppose him in such vulgar language, there was the risk he would win support. With his "most crude language and phrases," a ponderous style full of "nasty terms … directed at ministers of God on High," he freely held forth against clerical abuses, tithes, and canons. "With what authority did he vilify gentlemen who, even leaving aside their elevated and venerable state, are honorable citizens?" With or without tithes, it was unjust to cover such men with epithets. Thus,

> it is to be expected that the government, knowing of such undue personal slander, should punish them according to the law, and repress the audaciousness of these writers, especially when they speak of a body worthy of dignity beyond any dispute, since it is a venerable institution.[64]

The writer asserted that the "puerile and superficial" discourse of El Polar was now reaching deep into many states. Like "mad animals," the persons who professed such ideas trod upon the "most sacred things." The result, incidentally, was that El Polar had become "a servant of others."[65] Monarchists rejoiced in the way El Polar identified independence with irreligion. The state should silence him, and make each federal state see

> that the problem is not to be found – nor could it be – in our current system, but in the swarm of *nivelistas*, *polaristas* and worse creatures such as deists, materialists, atheists, the indifferent [agnostics?], etcetera, which in all governments are like the moths that eat away at all governments, at every class of garment in the world, without concern for its nobility and cost or for the dignity and circumstances of the dreams [it represents].[66]

Whoever chose to step outside the Constitution and the wishes of the people placed himself outside of the law. There was no reason to tolerate such men. Then why did the government not act in keeping with the people's wishes and the Constitution? In 1824, the state government had overstepped the bounds of the federal Constitution by appropriating for itself financial control over the clergy. The clergy of Jalisco had appealed to the federal government, and won the dispute; in 1825, the Church had published the correspondence on the matter.[67] During the same year, they published correspondence relating to conflict and subsequent agreement over direct contributions (income taxes).[68] In 1826, the Church still faced several options: it could appeal once more to federal authorities, or it could openly and directly call into question the actions and judgment of the government of Jalisco. It stood on the right of self-defense guaranteed to Mexican citizens. Having firmly established the republican character of the clergy and cast doubt upon the hard-line liberals, the Church might now even deepen its activities.

A citizen named Francisco Semería brought two years of frictions with the Jalisco government to a head with the publication of a pamphlet suggesting that neither liberal editors nor the government were following liberal republicanism. According to Semería, the law compelled him to swear an oath to the Jalisco Constitution before the cathedral chapter, since he was employed by the latter. The government and the liberal publication *La Palanca* called on him to take his oath in the presence of government authorities. Semería challenged the editors of *La Palanca* to confirm that the law demanded he do so. "In the face of the sublimity of the law, all else is subordinate; that is, governors, presidents, and in sum all men are under the law...." He added, "the law commanded me to swear the oath before the cathedral chapter; that is why I did not do so before the government" and "prove to me that the governor of this state is above the law, and then you can tell me fully that I do not understand what baseness is."[69]

Semería insisted that "in my opinion, liberalism is irreproachable." He challenged the editors of *La Palanca*: "If you attack reason with mockery and liberalism with satire, do not doubt that we will tell you the fruits of this are servility and ignorance ... and someday you will lift up the thrones of despotism and ignorance." Semería's message appeared to be clear: "Do not be so zealous in honoring the government as to wish to canonize even its aberrations." The executive power should ensure that laws were obeyed: "This power must not be allowed to diverge one iota from the legal path."

The municipal council of Guadalajara also entered the struggle. In open support of the Church, it asked the Jalisco government to enforce the restrictions on freedom of the press for "impious pamphlets." Unsatisfied with the governor's responses, it directed itself to the president of the Republic. The municipal council quoted the heretical assertions made by *El Polar* and the newspaper *El Nivel*.[70]

The president of the municipal council declared to the head of the nation that "a general law has been violated, harming things vital to Mexicans: and if Your Excellence deigns to declare so, this corporation asks that from now on this law be enforced." The municipal council recommended the renewal of editorial juries, aiming for "them to be of general trustworthiness," but then it immediately devoted three pages of the document to declaring to the president that its attempt to effect such a renewal had faced irregularities in procedures for voting and the frank opposition of the Vice Governor of Jalisco.[71]

Clerical discourse had wide-ranging aims, and there can be no doubt that its effectiveness worried the government. The final pamphlet from 1826 we will cite is proof of this. Printed in the shop of the liberal Urbano Sanromán, it contained two documents referring to the intervention of the civil government in ecclesiastical appointments. The first document was a statement by José Miguel Gordoa, just named Governor of the Mitre, the highest-ranking official in the Jalisco Church after the death of Bishop Cabañas in late 1824. The second was the letter which Prisciliano Sánchez, governor of Jalisco, wrote to preface Gordoa's document when he forwarded it to the Jalisco Congress. Within a single pamphlet, public opinion once again had the opportunity to assess two confronting discourses, two viewpoints about Church–state relations and the new modus operandi of the republican government.[72]

Gordoa set out a basic principle of the relationship between the two powers:

> Not even the princes reserved for themselves more power of intervention than that which was necessary to impede disorder; nor did they go any further except when the Church asked them to, admonishing them that peace and good harmony between both authorities consists only in mutual aid and respect, and not in attempts by one to rule over the other, impeding in some way the full and free exercise of its authority.[73]

What was appropriate in ecclesiastical appointments was for the corresponding clerical authorities to name individuals deemed competent and suitable for each post. If the state had any reason to suspect that the cleric graced with a position had "attacked or disturbed public order," a case should be made against him with "positive facts." Proceeding by any other means would be arbitrary and would tend to cause ill will within the ecclesiastical body. Dealing a hard blow to the government's position, Gordoa stated that

> In the just and liberal system governing us, no one can be harmed by suspicion – not even murderers themselves can have their rights as citizens removed – until they are proven to have committed the crime they are accused of; thus until then, the accused are just as suitable for any post in their career as the most honorable man.[74]

Fully aware of the force of his words, and making use of his own distinguished political career, Gordoa added, "I use this language, Your Excellency, with the certainty and satisfaction that it has always been my language since the fatherland saw fit to employ me in public positions."

The Governor of the Mitre demanded that the same conditions be applied to candidates for ecclesiastical posts as were applied to candidates for civil posts. Thus, he posed the rhetorical question: "Can it be that the eternal principles of universal and unchanging justice which favor lay people in achieving their rights and destinies do not favor ecclesiastics in achieving theirs?"[75] The government was within its rights to want to exclude delinquents from ecclesiastical posts, but the right to exclude candidatures that it was claiming meant

> an undefined extension [of prerogatives] which gives the civil government a scope not even held by those who exercised privileged patronage rights accorded by the Apostolic See, and implies a shameful rejection that would undoubtedly defame anyone excluded, crippling him for life from obtaining benefits and therefore impeding any Bishop from proposing him again.[76]

With the "rights of man as well known and respected as they are today," the government's aim was still more aberrant. In addition, the Jalisco and Federal Constitutions recognized Catholicism, which brought "governors and governed" together beneath "the same rules in ecclesiastical matters, which can be no other than canon law."[77]

Gordoa was determined to win this battle based on liberal principles. He immediately charged that Article 3 of the decree on Church appointments "seems to induce the suspicion that neither the ecclesiastical prelate nor his subjects fulfill their sacred duties." But "I protest that I have no reservations about the entire public being judge of my private conduct." He referred to a letter from the government itself recognizing that he worthily fulfilled the duties of his position.[78]

> Even less could the suspicion the decree insinuates diminish the respectable state of the clergy, whose efforts to comply with the charge of their ministry amidst the current lack of ecclesiastics are so well known, whose sincere adherence to the system of government in which we have constituted ourselves is beyond any doubt, whose circumspection and prudence in each disagreement that has occurred is worthy of the greatest praise and, in sum, whose moderate and ecclesiastical conduct provides no basis for such slanderous suspicions.[79]

Appealing in passing to the authority of Jacques Bénigne Bossuet, Gordoa brought up the clergy's legal privileges on this matter. Insisting that authorities and clerics complied with and would comply with their ecclesiastical and civic duties, he nonetheless demanded to know "what penal laws are indicated in the article referred to." The Governor of the Mitre professed due respect to civil authorities, but he demanded that because of his investiture and according to the laws, he had the authority to defend "the rights and prerogatives the Church has [traditionally] possessed, which have been left in force and effect by our general Constitution and sovereign rulings." Gordoa closed his document with the request that the Governor revoke the decree in exchange for his personal commitment to dedicate himself to "avoiding the ills which may have worsened at the moment it was published."[80]

Prisciliano Sánchez' response is extremely interesting. He conceded that Gordoa had cooperated with the government, and that "both clergies" (that is, the diocesan clergy and the regular orders) had shown "good behavior." While satisfied with the situation, Sánchez nonetheless drew a different conclusion from it: "Therefore, if such favorable circumstances were to persist forever, we could be sure that the precaution of this right to exclude candidates would be unnecessary, since there would never be occasion to apply it."[81]

But this was not certain; therefore, for the good of the people the government had the duty of foreseeing and prudently forestalling unfortunate situations by means of the law.

Sánchez set out his own views from the standpoint of civil power and the new impulses of secular Mexican society:

This right is the incontestable ability the sovereign Earthly power should have to prevent and block any damages even remotely threatening its people, coming under whatever pretext and from wherever they may come. Just as a physical individual has a natural right to survival and well-being which no power on Earth is able to hamper without resorting to tyranny, so a moral individual, such as society, has its natural right to survival and proper order which cannot be taken away by any authority under even the most sacred pretext.[82]

By absorbing civil society into the state, Sánchez skirted the "odiousness" of the theme under discussion, and rushed to recognize other merits in Gordoa's argument. Both powers were effectively "independent ... [and] equally sovereign." The ecclesiastical power had full authority in defending its jurisdiction, but this did not block the civil power from resisting an ecclesiastical appointment "as long as they had solid reasons to fear that such a person, abusing his authority, would compromise public tranquility." This was a matter of the survival of the secular power of the state.[83] This was self-defense and not intrusion, he suggested:

The history of all nations and all times does not leave any room for doubt on this point, offering to our eyes a thousand scandalous attacks which horrify our imagination. The events of our revolution are not far off, when the confessionals and pulpits were often the fulcrum on which the levers of power of our oppressors stood. The consoling voice of the pastor became the cries of the lion, and the healthy waters of penitence came to be poisoned in such a way that from there spread the deadly venom which blighted our poor patriots.[84]

The dangers of ecclesiastical abuses were not hypothetical, but corroborated by past history. The resulting "damage to states and their governments" was dealt with "with impunity from the advantageous posts they [the priests] hold when they cause the damage, and there was great difficulty in judicially convicting them of deeds which, however scandalous, they know how to astutely cover with the cloak of religion."[85]

The Governor of Jalisco wanted to win over the Congress by establishing himself as the defender of the new popular government:

Otherwise who can calculate, much less compensate for, the sum of evils that one parish priest opposed to the system of government can foolishly cause from his confessional? What measure could erase the prestige occasioned among the simple folk by an indiscreet preacher who launches from the pulpit the most indecorous and denigrating expressions against the constituted authorities and their actions?[86]

The laws which aimed to save society were striving for "the health of the fatherland which is the supreme law." They did not meddle in matters of instituting ecclesiastical authorities, responsibilities of the Church which only patronage could change, but attempted only to "resist the placement of those ecclesiastics who could be prejudicial [to the government]." Just as it was not acceptable for Mexico to allow the Pope to name bishops who professed loyalty to Ferdinand VII, so the state of Jalisco could not be a "mindless spectator to the evils which could threaten the people by standing by as perhaps its greatest enemies were placed in the most dangerous positions."[87]

Sánchez had no difficulties in recognizing the weakness of the new, popular state in comparison with a Church whose deep-rootedness gave it singular popular support.

It would be a very unequal struggle, if one were joined between the governor of a state and an ecclesiastic who set out to oppose the system of government, or the most vital aspects of the urgent reform of many abuses, and if the prelate could without any coercion place his supporters in the most valuable positions as he saw fit, and the civil authority could not prevent this in any way.[88]

In addition, the government's decreed right to unilaterally reject a candidate was convenient because it avoided the problem of a trial. After all, there would be no chance of an impartial trial, since the Church as well as the state – both responsible for the only available courts – would be directly involved in the case.[89]

This last argument seemed to place the role of the courts in a liberal government in check overall. Yet the most effective part of Gordoa's argument still had not received a response from Sánchez: the rights of man under a liberal government should not be violated on mere suspicion, and a career employment was the right of every citizen, and, in this case, of clerics. Sánchez went on to clarify the point, and then counterattack:

This reasoning is brilliant when considered superficially. Denying an individual the rights he has to pursue the possibilities his career offers him on the basis of mere conjectures is an entirely different thing from resisting his placement in a given post, on the basis of well-founded suspicions, while leaving him able to occupy another post where those suspicions do not apply.[90]

The Governor granted the cleric's right in principle, but extended the state's shadow in this particular case. This argument might not be convincing on its own, so Sánchez shifted to the defensive:

> If the government or the people participated in the election of their pastors, as they did in the primitive Church and continued to do for several centuries, then we can see there would be no need to recur to the nominal exclusion the political authority definitely exercises as a right, since the election of one [candidate] tacitly excludes the others. This muddle of difficulties, present since the people were denied involvement in elections, undoubtedly was what prompted the invention of the Concordats and Royal Patronage. These were not conferred on the princes so much out of grace and favor, as through a transaction which was beneficial to the ecclesiastical power because in its absence the ecclesiastical power would have had to give way to the just demands of the civil power.[91]

Sánchez now seemed to be unwittingly confusing popular government with government at all, a confusion which underscores how this dilemma defined the Mexican state. Just beginning its existence, the state was weak; from its weakness, it forged a powerful and oft-repeated argument which gave it strength. As the representative of the people, the state had discretional rights over the liberalism that inspired it. Ultimately, the people could be conceived of as the common folk, and those who managed to exercise power over it, independent of the state, could be seen as a threat to the state and to its representation of the people. Curiously enough, there was no reflection here at all about the separation of powers within the government. The seed of a statism even more powerful than Bourbon absolutism was being sown, here. In the new liberal model of the Mexican state being implemented in Jalisco, the state not only watched over the people; through the unique representation it was granted, the state *was* the people. Only a Church which opened up its appointments to popular means of election could hope to come abreast of this virtual monolith: the government viewed as the will of a united people. In the meantime, the state called for the right to expunge clerical abuses.

Sánchez offered the argument that the ecclesiastics who were eliminated from consideration for a given post due to suspicion might ask to be appointed to another. Considering that what they were suspected of was disloyalty to the political system, suspicion would surely last as long as the hint of disloyalty did. Traditionally, the royal government had exercised patronage by choosing from *ternas* (lists of three candidates) which the clergy proposed, but this was not a useful point of reference now. The exclusion of a cleric from a post in those cases could be due to an indefinite range of reasons, and did not defame anyone. An exclusive right to deny appointments on suspicions of political disloyalty was an entirely different business. Sánchez was, in effect, giving the state supreme discretionary power without the traditional mechanisms of patronage. Considering that neither the state nor the Church were particularly inclined to mutual trust, Sánchez insisted on the rights of the former: "The health and tranquility of the people are too precious to be abandoned to the embrace of blind trust. States are not worrying over trifles when they take precautions on behalf of their sacred rights."[92]

The governor placed the two possibilities in the balance: that of a potential injustice done to a cleric, and that of commotion among the people. Deciding that the second was more weighty, he ruled that the state could not tolerate the risk. He argued that, in comparison, the civil government was less prone to abusing its power in this sense. The governor was responsible to the people, he had a non-renewable term of four years, and he was subject to criticism by the press and the citizenry. These restrictions which bore down upon the power of the Jalisco governor did not, he said, burden the ecclesiastical authorities. The Governor insisted on the "inborn ability of each society to look to its preservation and prevent its ruin." He expressed amazement that, "defending the inalienable rights of the people and avoiding damage required the blessing of Rome." This time, the civil government triumphed: the Legislature voted to maintain the government's authority to exclude candidates from Church appointments.[93]

Beyond this immediate result, however, the long-range consequences of the Church–state debate that raged through 1825 and 1826 were far from clear. Proceeding frequently with salty derision and jocularity, Church spokesmen had made many popular appeals, showing at the same time a spirit of moderation and reform-mindedness. Yet while the Church battled for its institutional rights and autonomy in relation to the state, it decidedly resisted opening the Church to the overhaul accepted for temporal politics. By seeking the high ground of supporting the independence as a sacred pact in which the defense of religion was the surest guarantee of liberty, it ultimately questioned the identification of both its adversaries and the state over their claims to represent popular sovereignty and the liberal rule of law. Whither this would lead was still to be decided.

8

The Great
Unresolved Issues

The Patronage and Tithes during the
Constitutional Regime, 1827–33

Plumbing the Depths
Sparring between the Temporal and Ecclesiastical Powers

In 1827, the problem of tithes came to the fore once again, in the midst of the economic and fiscal crisis brought on by the War for Independence and deepened under the Empire and the Early Republic.[1] Events took an ironic course. Up to that point, the local clergy had blocked fiery Jalisco liberalism by appealing to the federal government. National authorities had intervened in local events to insist that modifications of Church affairs in Jalisco would have to await the national solution of the patronage issue. From 1825 on, the Jalisco government demanded that the Church pay property taxes on its wealth – which demand the Church disputed by once more appealing to federal authorities.[2] But the National Congress had given the states the power to tax in 1824.[3] In 1827, various states fought the Church for effective control of tithes, and a new restlessness was unleashed in Jalisco. In the midst of a long-standing fiscal crisis, the states were attempting to collect tithes through the local civil administration.[4] A decision of the National Congress had enabled the state to confront the Church on a local level.

At this moment, opposition between civil authorities and the clergy grew more intense. Once again, immediate material concerns were interwoven with abstract concepts and arguments struggling for discursive hegemony. To be sure, the economic question had already emerged in 1824, but Article 7 of the 1824

Jalisco Constitution, an article never enacted, had threatened ecclesiastical jurisdiction by asserting the state's economic power over the Church. The clergy had maneuvered to demonstrate that it was inappropriate for the state to determine expenses for worship. This was not its place; it indeed had the obligation – if not always the ability – to cover those expenses. Proposing anything else meant violating the Church's jurisdiction.

After the state lost this conflict, there began several years of intense public debate to clarify the role of the Church in light of national independence and in relation to the new state based on popular sovereignty. Paying taxes on the wealth of the Church now sparked debate, but this was far from putting the clergy on the payroll and at the disposition of the state. The interests of the state and the Church could be sensed behind the struggles over principles in pamphlets and newspapers, but neither had been blocked, yet. In 1826, and despite a brilliant discursive campaign by the clergy, Governor Sánchez had been able to assert the rights of the government in clerical appointments, with the approval of his Legislature. In the clash between the government and the clergy, both sides had continued to struggle to win popular adherence. The executive power had made relentless advances in 1826. In 1827, it now returned to economic matters with an initiative that was extremely threatening to the clergy, since the state proposed to collect tithes based on federal legislation, without technically affecting either ecclesiastical jurisdiction or the portion of the tithes it was due to receive.[5]

We should remember that all across the nation, resolving the matter of the patronage was becoming increasingly more urgent. The various aspects of the religious question were growing more and more unsettling.

The full reach of government authority was unclear; in Jalisco, this was precisely the problem. The religious and ethical bases of the young state had not been defined before the people, a situation which conflicted with the effective exercise of sovereignty, and especially of "popular sovereignty."[6]

Pedro Lissaute clearly signaled this dilemma in a statement made in Jalisco in 1830. He presented the crisis of the young state and the reemergence of Church–state conflict in a context that was not solely ideological and constitutional. In light of state power and the goals of civil society, he pointed out the inability of the new state to fulfill its most elementary duties. The tax problems demonstrated how right he was. Lissaute viewed the problem of Church wealth and influence within not only the national, but also the international, context of a transformation in the relationship between popular enlightenment and politics. He held that international trends Mexico clearly was a part of were showing how useful knowledge could be placed at the service of the people, allowing democracy to be truly realized for the first time. His was a decidedly liberal perspective.[7]

Lissaute's analysis saw the government, the state, at the head of this great task. It had to carry out a revolution in popular education. Such a revolution would end up producing what was earlier thought impossible – and this is worth repeating – a democratic and free society. Through the development of science and technology, a "certain level of correspondence" would be achieved "between our moral faculties and our physical strength." Lissaute suggested that "with some help from the public administration, the Institute [of Sciences in Jalisco] could be the most powerful agent to improve this state of affairs." If no such transformation was undertaken, "would those whose only place [in society] is to humbly lend their muscle power to others be able to reason?" But the government had no funds to meet this need. Thus those who represented the injustices and mistaken cultural orientations of the past continued to enjoy power and riches of dubious provenance. They maintained a monopoly over culture which was hardly appropriate to modern times, blocking the "great social revolution."[8]

Lissaute assigned the state a central role in creating the new social and political order. That is why the question of loyalty to the new government, its constitution, and its laws, became particularly sensitive. Obedience to the government should not be in conflict with freedom of conscience, he judged, because the new government stood for a free system. In this context, he praised the

> condemnation the philosophy of this age levels at everything that does not tend to inculcate love for work, for principles of order, *for obedience to the law, and for independence from the will of any particular individual no matter how respectable.*[9]

Obedience to the government was the guarantee of freedom of conscience against the unjust defenders of outdated orthodoxies. Lissaute imagined Mexico might be "a country in which each individual participates in sovereignty, and therefore is destined to directly influence the resolution of all questions touching public administration."[10]

Nonetheless, this process was far from taking place in practice, as he himself noted, and this weakened the effective foundation of the liberal state.[11]

Within the framework marked out by Lissaute, the people exercised their liberty and supported the government naturally, and simultaneously. If such were not the case, they could be accused of behaving like the mob, or of advancing the interests of antisocial groups. Such groups placed their narrow interests above those of an entire free society. Both haste to strengthen the state and disgust towards the opposition are evident in Lissaute's perspective. The transition from Absolutist reformism to reformism based on the doctrine of popular sovereignty was going through a difficult moment.[12]

The Governor had already mentioned the economic crisis and fiscal problems of Jalisco in his 1826 *Memoria* (Report). The economic crisis had emerged as a result of the minimal growth of new economic activities together with the decline of traditional businesses. Commerce in Jalisco had taken on a "passive" character, "because it exports very few articles to other states, while consuming infinite products introduced here, whether from various points in the [Mexican] Federation or from overseas." The minting of money had diminished substantially and Jalisco suffered from a "shortage of coin."[13] In another section of his *Memoria*, the Governor remarked that

> the government has faced unspeakable work in every one of the measures taken in the different branches of public administration, because all of them have been neglected, experiencing more than ever the dreadful effects of oppression, the worst of which is the lack of resources with which to promote the most interesting establishments.

Yet the new government hoped to awaken and guide public opinion in a liberal direction.[14] But government's authority to do so was still weak, in the face of deep-rooted, popular support for the Church.[15] Sánchez asserted that

> Of the many ills the Spanish government left us as our patrimony, placing the interests of the clergy in opposition to the interests of the people was certainly not the least. Thus, the latter could not be promoted without the former being demoted, and if one still wishes them to continue as they are, one must give up all hope of making any improvement or progress for the public cause.[16]

Overwhelmed by "exhausting tasks," the government suffered insolvency in the midst of

> the novelty of the system, the blameless ignorance of the multitude and other difficulties which necessarily must be felt in leading a people still bowed down by the heavy chains they bore for three hundred years.[17]

By the time Vice Governor Juan Nepomuceno Cumplido offered his *Memoria*, 1 February 1827, the coffers of the state of Jalisco were in a "distressing situation," the educational work of the Institute of Sciences was making slow progress because of economic obstacles, and there was a serious problem of "murders and robberies" in Guadalajara and its surroundings.[18] In 1828, the same Vice Governor reported the existence of many "vagabonds" and beggars.[19] The government was trying to organize a civic militia and attend to matters of "public health and comfort," although it confessed to a "lack of funds" for the latter. The Vice Governor announced advances in introducing the Lancaster Method of primary instruction in the state, but it is unclear whether the information provided demonstrates a truly first-class effort on this point.[20]

By 1831, the situation did not seem to have significantly improved. In his report for that year, Governor José Ignacio Herrera bitterly reminded all that

> a new people, and therefore a miserable one, only in its infancy in industry, science and commerce, which sees half of what it earns from such hard work wrested from it, will only progress slowly, and for a long time will barely be able to purchase future comforts.[21]

He asserted that the state was free of political disturbances, but banditry was still on the rise. "For the first time," he went on to say, "an economic year is beginning without predictions of bankruptcy." While there was a serious lack of coinage, the new civil administration of tithes was resolving the problems of the public coffers. The governor reported problems with the officials of the civic militia and a lack of advances in primary education, but also material improvements in the San Miguel hospital.[22]

The Church, in turn, found itself without a leader and clear coherence in its public thinking, battling – however astutely – against an ideological and institutional siege. The absence of a clear direction and the decline in the number of priests made the Church progressively more vulnerable to the demands of both the Catholic faithful and the state, which was constitutionally obligated to watch over it.[23] While it is true that clerical discourse was forceful and vigorous in 1825 and 1826 even without a bishop, the advances of the Jalisco government on tax matters and its achievement of discretionary power over ecclesiastical appointments by legislative vote indicated the need for a change. The Church was not unnerved, and its discourse showed a willingness to make use of new elements to firmly assert its positions, but now it needed to take the ideological dispute one step further, clearly establishing official guidelines for thought. Facing the new assault by the government on the matter of tithes, it had to take an unmistakably clear stance. Looking beyond this particular matter, the Church once again had to resort to the national political level, and call for a Concordat specifying the terms of its relationship with the state – along the way easing the appointment of a new bishop to reaffirm the ecclesiastical hierarchy and ordain priests for parochial work.

In fact, ecclesiastical anxiety over the patronage had been evident in Guadalajara since 1826. A pamphlet had then been reprinted in the city attacking the premises underlying the instructions the federal government intended to give its emissary to Rome.[24] The pamphlet argued that

> even in the days of the absolutist kings, when sovereigns were said to be lords of all lives, honors, and possessions, they were never believed to be the true owners of the lands and goods existing within a nation, nor were they granted any rights other than high or eminent ones, which are very different from what is properly called property....
>
> Since it is thus evident that the nation, in the name of sovereignty, has only high or eminent domain over the land and goods existing within the republic, and not property rights truly and properly understood, then how could it have the right of patronage, which canon law grants only to whoever ceded his property, and thereby established or endowed these or other temples? This right of lay persons to name people for ecclesiastical posts is in reality a burden on the Church; it is a weight, a servitude, and that is why canon law [only] concedes it as a recompense for the favor done to the Church in granting it a property.[25]

Further on, the pamphlet spelled out the implications of its statements for Church–state relations:

> The state gives protection to the Church, that is true. But for this favor, the Church gratefully offers a tribute to civil authorities of all the honor, distinction, prerogatives and considerations a benefactor is due. Additionally, this is a very powerful argument for granting it [the state] the right of patronage, yet this will always be a favor, a grace, a privilege, because such protection is not a voluntary act that can be rightly omitted, but an obligation and a responsibility that the secular Catholic power has before God and Man to defend and protect the Church, independent of the patronage over presentation [of candidates for posts].[26]

The launching of the newspaper *El Defensor de la Religión* – planned since 1826 and finally published in 1827 – was symptomatic of the high clergy's growing sense of the need to clarify both the terms of debate and the institutional position of the Church relative to the state and to society.[27] Orthodox opinions were offered carefully and with weighty arguments, frequently in response to heterodox proposals. What they were saying was not so different from previous years. Instead, just as the government's struggle for discretionary power over ecclesiastical appointments and later for control of tithes constituted an entire phase of state formation, so the ideas expressed in *El Defensor* played the same role in reconstituting ecclesiastical discursive forces. With the publication of *El Defensor*, clerical pamphlets themselves were transformed, turned into even more open weapons of the high clergy in its struggle to keep abreast of the young republic. But it is important to point out that while the forum for pro-state ideas became constrained to the legislative chambers and the votes of legislators, the language of the Church was no less clearly directed to setting standards for members of the ecclesiastical corporation and the faithful among the legislators.[28]

El Defensor employed various tactics worthy of note. One could be considered a spectacle of horrors, a parade of the wayward ideas of the great minds of European thought: from John Calvin (1509–1564) and Philipp Melanchthon (1497–1560) to Hugo Grotius (1583–1645), Thomas Hobbes (1588–1679), Pasquier Quesnel (1634–1719), John Toland (1670–1772), Denis Diderot (1713–1784), Guillaume Thomas François Raynal (1713–1796),

Honoré GabrielVictor Riqueti, Comte de Mirabeau (1749–1791), and Louis Marie Prudhomme (1752–1830). After a condensed biography which recognized some personal merit, each distinguished figure of European thought was measured up against the plumb-line of Catholic orthodoxy. In general, their theoretical divergences were associated directly with defects in character.[29]

Another line of articles returned to central questions of Catholic orthodoxy. This originally began in response to 1827 challenges regarding the patronage, which led it to refute the attacks of Church opponents.[30] Before the year ended, *El Defensor* was discussing the legislative authority of the Church and the existence of God.[31] In 1828, the paper dwelled at length, in an article extending over several issues, on the immortality of the soul and revelation.[32] But perhaps what stood out most was the paper's constant recourse to themes that not only enhanced orthodoxy and the continuing relevance of religion and the faith, but also underscored the Church's role as the sacramental and legitimate institution of Catholic religiosity.

In 1828, the newspaper went further with this approach. Spread across the pages of *El Defensor* were such concerns as the legislative power of the Church and the history of Councils, oral confession, impediments to marriage, book banning, patronage once more, and the French precedents for rearranging Church–state relations.[33] There was even occasion for discussing certain papal scandals and offering guidance on how to handle such embarrassing events. *El Defensor* not only indicated orthodox opinion in theory, themes and authors, but it also provided the basis for an elemental historical perspective – not new, by the way – through which Mexican Catholics could contemplate the errors made by ancient Catholics without feeling themselves forcefully bound to them. The times and the weakness of man might explain some pitfalls, but the Church as an institution could never be contemplated within such pedestrian and temporal frameworks. Thus, the Church was removed from the critical gaze that it so enthusiastically turned towards contrary thinkers of the present and the past.[34]

In this way, clerical discourse after 1827 lost in apparent spontaneity and plebeian style what it gained in coherence and thoughtfulness. Its triumph in terms of clear and orthodox thinking – even though oriented towards reconciliation with the First Republic – had the defect of turning significantly away from language accessible to a wide range of the populace. The difficulties of this moment would seem to indicate not so much the exclusive defects or closed character of ecclesiastical discourse as the effective limits of the new discourse emerging with popular sovereignty. It was easier to debate popular sovereignty than to make the exercise of sovereignty effectively popular! In practice, the legislature and the cathedral chapter could handle national affairs without having constant recourse to the opinions and leanings of the majority. The legislature captured the sovereign power of civil society no less than the cathedral chapter did so for the body faithful. In both cases, the "people" and the flock were notable for their absence, however much they were invoked discursively. The representation of popular interests was "virtual" – that is, carried out with an eye towards the well-being of the people – but it was not direct representation, nor was it effectively carried out by the people.[35]

Between Constitutionalism and the Exercise of Full Ecclesiastical Sovereignty

José Miguel Gordoa, who in 1831 would come to be the first bishop of Jalisco appointed during the Republic, had already expressed in 1827 the Church's dilemma in facing the state. Called to pass judgment on the establishment of a diocese in Zacatecas, his home state, Gordoa carefully weighed the implications any decision of his would have.[36] If he approved of the creation of a new diocese, this would ipso facto provide support for those who wanted to make this action a power of the state. Yet if he rejected the new diocese, he would appear to be someone lacking patriotism, even for his native state. He declared of the proposed bishopric: "I promoted it in Spain, and I have longed for it in the intimacy of my heart." Underscoring his point, he added: "I yield to no one in my love for my dearest homeland, and for everything that favors its true good and exaltation." But he demanded that Zacatecas avoid the "confusion of powers." To establish a diocese required, he asserted, agreement between both powers – civil and religious. In this case, the appropriate religious power could only be the Papacy. Gordoa found himself obliged to specify that popular sovereignty ruled over civil affairs, but not over religious ones:[37]

> Thus, let the worthy representatives of this state make the arrangements, let them forcefully uphold the rights of those they represent in civil matters, carrying them to the highest point of human

happiness. But we must not forget that the rights of man as citizen are one thing, and the duties of the same man as a child of the Church are another.[38]

Gordoa rejected the general "spirit of innovation" on this point, obviously fearing its "capriciousness" and "arbitrariness." He let himself be guided by sources denouncing the "irreligion" promoted by "the false politicians and adulators of secular powers." On the one hand, he denounced the desire to impose the authority of the new popular state on the Church. On the other, he insisted that "our lack of communication with the Apostolic See is not so absolute, since we are seeing, and quite frequently, papal directives to Mexican members of religious orders authorizing their secularization."[39]

On the matter of income, Gordoa saw the same embroilment. He lamented that "if ecclesiastics speak, of course they are thought to do so out of interest, and if they remain quiet, they are said to have no support for their argument." The solution here was no different than in the establishment of a Zacatecas diocese: Gordoa proposed to join the wills of both powers by means of a Concordat. He expressed his dissatisfaction in stating that "as for me, I frankly protest that the day on which I retire to eat the bread my parents obtained with the sweat of their brows will be the happiest of my life."[40]

As a priest, Gordoa was indignant because others spoke as if the Mexican nation and Catholicism were two things that were independent of each other. In fact, on the religious issue, the nation was now definitively committed.[41] Referring to the congressman whose speech had motivated the request by the Zacatecas Congress, Gordoa proclaimed:

> Let us elevate together, Representative Gómez Huerta and the signer of this reverent exposition, let us elevate to the sovereign general Congress our ardent wishes and humble supplications that by accelerating their work they give the fatherland the day so longed for on which relations will be established with the Holy See. This is how the congressman will respond to public expectations. In this way, he will fulfill that intimate and precious confidence that the district of the village of Tlaltenango placed in his activity and zeal, and I will also have the glory and the sweet satisfaction of cooperating in his designs.[42]

Within this polemical setting, which threatened to broaden disputes between Church and state and to lead towards a confrontation over principles or the Concordat issue, the thorniest problem that emerged in these years was the extinction of the Church's tithe offices. They were how the cathedral chapter had administered everything related to tithes, and their suppression by civil authorities threatened the jurisdiction and economic solvency of the high clergy. This led to a concrete discussion of the matter of parochial fees. The money that reformists wanted to use to replace those fees would come from the tithes now collected by the state.[43]

The set of interconnected themes discussed once the polemic over tithes and fees began showed that the aggressive overall approaches – still present from earlier years – were more than just the context for specific disputes. Alongside the careful and detailed debate about ecclesiastical monies, it became clearer and clearer that more general debates had to descend from abstraction and become more concrete. The way of doing this was by taking up the patronage issue once more. This virtual protectorate that the state exercised over the Church hinted at a solution for all the pending theoretical questions about Church, state and society. From 1827 to 1831, tithes were the main testing point for these debates, as a sequel to the mooted Article 7 of the 1824 Constitution and to the 1825–26 disputes about Church income and ecclesiastical appointments. The agitated ideological stage, the fiscal crisis of the state, the crisis of the ecclesiastical hierarchy as the ranks of bishops dwindled one by one, and the crisis of the democratic program of the new government after 1827: all pushed the matter of tithes towards a more general, supposedly final, solution of the patronage question. After being a matter of state on a national level since 1824, patronage now clearly descended to the level of popular sovereignty, but the handling of that sovereignty in the federal states allowed the full blast of liberal polemics to finally enter the patronage debate. After being a matter of state, patronage clearly became captive to ideological polemics.

By means of Decree 77, on 16 February 1827, Jalisco had suppressed the Church's tithe offices. The same decree, composed during a secret session, replaced them with a Board of Tithes.[44] In the debate this change provoked, one publication counterbalanced a statement of opposition by the cathedral chapter of Guadalajara with the special ruling produced by a legislative committee.[45] While the Cabildo's statement insisted that the shift required an agreement between ecclesiastical and civil authorities and should await the decision of the National Congress on patronage, the ruling was based on radically opposed theoretical assumptions. The committee clearly affirmed that tithes had their origin in royal authority, which was secular, and not in ecclesiastical authority. Appealing to Papal Bulls and similar arguments, it added, "does this not deserve to be classified as seditious?" "Who does not see in this statement the subversion of all the social achievements of Mexicans?" According to the ruling, it was clear that because of historical continuity, the sovereignty of Mexicans was absolute on this matter. The National Congress, the committee insisted, had declared tithes to be profane income. As a consequence, either tithes would be administered by the state, or this income would have no meaning whatsoever. The abolition of the Church's tithe offices in Jalisco was in keeping with what had been decided in the National Congress. There had been no alteration in payments and no different application of tithes, only change on an administrative level. However, the committee recommended that the Congress form a special commission, and the cathedral chapter form another, in order to address the abolition of certain parochial rights and payments. It ordered that the "testimony of this file" be sent to the National Congress.[46]

The Church in Jalisco was ready to complain once more, and to defend itself with the weapons at hand, on 2 March 1827. Feeling strapped by temporal imperatives, the cathedral chapter began by expressing its astonishment and surprise. The chapter insisted that "it was unable on principle to agree to the establishment of the Board, the naming of the only ecclesiastical individual it was authorized to choose, and the concession of a place for the office of the Board." At the same time, the chapter protested to the governor with "full sincerity, the respect and submission due to the supreme powers of the state." But this was a difficult balance to maintain, since this formal act of submission was accompanied by such harsh criticism and rejection of the government decree. For the chapter, the proposed make-up of the new Board and the distribution of votes among its members was a scandal, because "far from granting the Church's intervention in the administration of its income, instead this seems testimony" to the government's "dishonorable and offensive disdain of episcopal dignity and of the venerable chapter in which its jurisdiction is deposited."[47]

In the eyes of the chapter, the result was a plundering of the Church. Recalling a similar attempt at change at the end of the eighteenth century, the chapter allowed itself a reflection on state politics:

> And if the Spanish government, with even less basis, and even under the aegis of the patronage, absolute authority and ministerial abuse which we have often bitterly wept over, saw fit to admit the written complaints of all the Churches of America, then what should this Chapter not expect from a frankly liberal republican government, whose foremost characteristic, as a political body, should be the respect of property that all its constitutions guarantee, and as an Apostolic Roman Catholic body, the fulfillment and protection of ecclesiastical laws and Concordats? That is what this Chapter should expect, just as the supreme powers of the state have solemnly protested.[48]

However, the chapter did not seem to want a confrontation with the state in Jalisco. It declared that it found itself facing the dilemma of either "abandoning its duties" towards the Church or displeasing the government, but wished to do neither. That is why the chapter "has no other option than appealing to the judgment and discretion of Your Excellency himself [the governor] and the Honorable Congress, so that you might be convinced and persuaded that, very far from opposing [the decree] out of willful obstinacy, the chapter finds itself in a bitter and painful conflict it cannot obviate." In order to do so, the chapter accepted that the Church's tithe offices cease operating "on contentious and judicial" matters not only in Jalisco, but also in the other states of the diocese. However, the chapter did not freely accept conceding facilities for the new Board of Tithes, as the government had demanded. They dryly remarked to the governor that "Your Excellency may act as you deem fit, as you have already done in installing the Board and taking over the archives."[49]

The chapter offered to give up its portion of the decimal tithe – pointing out that "by the same measure, our obligations and rights will also cease" – in order to prove "that our resistance does not come from a miserable clinging to the interests in dispute." It insisted that it was "ready for any reform carried out according to canon law" in search of a "rational compromise." For that reason, the chapter said, they had asked several times to

enter into "conference with civil authorities" in keeping with
the 18 December 1824 decree which had pegged the resolution
of ecclesiastical income matters to the national settlement of the
patronage issue, allowing for interim changes only where the
clergy and the state governments were entirely aligned. Therefore,
the chapter's statement continued to insist that there should be no
changes until the matter of a Concordat at a national level had
been resolved. Accepting the forceful acts of the state government
so as not to be proven to desire subversion, the chapter nonetheless salvaged the principle of ecclesiastical rights. Following this
line of thinking, one could hardly fail to reach the conclusion that
the state of Jalisco was transgressing against not only the rights
of the Church but also the decisions of the National Congress.
Similarly, the chapter's decision to give up the tithes was a dou-
ble-edged weapon. If the state government accepted the offer,
Jalisco was left without religious leadership, since the "obligations and rights" of the cathedral chapter members were to cease
along with the tithe. While ecclesiastical diplomacy was formally
submissive to the state government, the challenge implied in its
response placed the state before a difficult dilemma in which its
authority and effective power were once again put to the test.

Another pamphlet, titled *Defensa del Venerable Cabildo Eclesiástico
de Guadalajara*, included the 5 July 1827 report by the Board of
Tithes. In the report, the Board contrasted "the humble, submissive
and plaintive language of the cathedral chapter" with its "system
of opposition and resistance, uninterrupted until now." The Board
sustained the fine it had in fact imposed on the chapter because
of the ecclesiastical statement issued on 2 March. On the basis of
the debate about one of the terms employed in that document,
the Board was able to brand the members of the cathedral chapter
as among those who, in their dealings with the Board, "were dis-
respectful and disobedient and did not comply with orders."[50]

The report argued categorically that the Board was planning
to give the members of the chapter their share of the tithes collected in full and on time. Contradicting opposing suggestions,
the Board placed all the blame on this point on the chapter, all of
whose members – save one – refused to collect their tithe allot-
ment because of their vehement resistance to the change.

But the Church would not give up so easily. Armed with the
concepts developed over the previous years, it once more tried
to turn the government's liberalism against it. The same pamphlet
which included the report contained the "Última representación

del apoderado del cabildo eclesiástico" of 15 September 1827.[51] The starting point for this statement was the sharp denunciation that, since 1824, the Jalisco government had tried to achieve the "debasement and humiliation" of the cathedral chapter. This time, the statement was made directly to President Guadalupe Victoria, following the same tactic of appealing to the federal government used in opposing Article 7 of the 1824 Jalisco Constitution and in the disputes of 1825–26. In fact, the spokesman for the chapter declared that this had already been tried, fruitlessly, and his statement took on a despondent tone which seemed to underscore the point.[52] The statement argued that it seemed

> that no other recourse was left to the chapter but the Heavens, and that on Earth, when respectable individuals remain firm in their principles, they have no other hope or path, except that of pain and torment, until they come to see the extermination of their Church, their authority, and their persons if they do not rush to abandon their posts.[53]

Nevertheless, such a negative outlook for the Church would not make it give up. The spokesman defiantly insisted that "the Venerable Cathedral Chapter will follow ... the path it has chosen until it reaches the will of the True God who sustains it."[54]

The spokesman continued his statement, guided by this same spirit of the chapter. He denounced the fact that in the National Congress, the president of the ecclesiastical commission was the congressman from Jalisco, José de Jesús Huerta. Although the spokesman did not mention it, Huerta was a priest. But the spokesman clearly pointed out his trajectory as liberal thinker and suggested that he was conspiring with the Jalisco authorities on this matter.[55] The action taken by the Jalisco government was contrary to the mandate of the National Congress, he declared. For him, it made no sense and was legally inappropriate to separate the "authority, administration, and distribution of tithes" from the very question of Church income whose resolution depended on the National Congress. He objected that a greater portion of tithes was being assigned to the states than had previously been granted to the King of Spain, and that the government of Jalisco was assuming this power over the Church without legal or constitutional precedents.[56]

The spokesman for the cathedral chapter underscored his assertions by stating that

I would also like you to tell me if it is in keeping with the Constitution, and our liberal system, to debate in secret sessions about the extinction of said tribunal and to put the law into effect the same day without publishing it, without allowing any excuses or delays from the Venerable Cathedral Chapter.[57]

Defending the right of the cathedral chapter to assert and present its rights, he also condemned in passing the fine that had been imposed on it: "representing one's own rights, writing formal complaints to superiors, and maintaining one's own authority could never be judged disrespectfulness and disobedience."[58]

The accusation the spokesman was making depended on his capacity to reconcile the legal order with the ecclesiastical position. Thus the Church's submission to the Constitution and popular sovereignty would be compatible with its strong defense of its own interests. "For the Holy Church to recognize and yield before the sovereignty of the people is very just, and order requires it," he conceded, but he demanded an "attention and attentiveness" for the Church that was no less than what was given to individuals. In this context, the spokesman expressed deep indignation in the matter of the fine placed on the chapter. Considering the context of misunderstandings between governors and governed, "no such equal case could be cited, *even from the times of despotism and arbitrariness*."[59] The spokesman went on to insist that the point under debate was the right of citizens to defend themselves against arbitrary acts by the government:

Even if ancient laws, the practice and customs of many years, the Constitution, which reserved these matters for the National Congress, and the Congress itself, which required the agreement of the Churches for each innovation, did not speak in favor of that very respectable body [the cathedral chapter], the most general rules with which we have tried to uproot from among us despotism and that absolute domination over the properties and rights *of [corporate] bodies and particular individuals* would be enough for the Board to have found itself embarrassed to explain freely and confidently what it wishes to show in its apology, or defense, which it voluntarily made. Because if a new system in the handling, distribution and collection of this branch of the administration were to be created, the representative voices of the Church should be heard, as sharers of the tithes, and therefore interested parties in the collection, administration, and distribution.[60]

Convenience, and not only adherence to the "liberal, just, and equal" Constitution, should have inclined the government towards consulting the Church on this matter. The Church's knowledge of the matter, gained over time, was useful. Instead, the state had acted in secrecy and reduced the ecclesiastical presence on the new Board of Tithes to only one of four total votes. The new rules made it virtually impossible for an ecclesiastic to preside over the Board or have the deciding vote. The sites occupied without permission by the new Board of Tithes had served various functions and housed a variety of materials which the Church could only with great difficult accommodate elsewhere.[61]

> Where are the rules governing us today? Is this how we are assured of possessing our goods, our properties, our rights? This is certainly the most damaging example that could be given, for the government to act in such a way against constitutional laws which so flatter and exalt the people.[62]

The spokesman also accused the Board of including deception in its report. The Board had accused the members of the cathedral chapter of not collecting their portion of the tithes by their own decision. On the one hand, this avoided the underlying problem. On the other:

> The regulation which determined the distribution that should be made of the decimal tithe, and the aid that should be provided to the members of this Venerable Cathedral Chapter, was published on 9 May, four days after my statement was presented to the supreme government. And could it be carried out before it was published?[63]

What is more, the published regulation was not directly communicated to the chapter. In denouncing the rebelliousness of the chapter, the Board was being insolent and overreaching its authority. The Board was also revealing a "narrow-minded understanding" of the matter. The chapter justified its actions in civil terms on the basis of the National Constitution, the 18 December 1824 decree and the laws in effect. In ecclesiastical terms, the chapter clung to "the dispositions of canon law" and "the current discipline of the Church": "A religious, honorable, and praiseworthy course of action, worthy of your veneration!"[64]

The spokesman also denounced variations in the distribution of tithes, and justified a dignified and honorable resistance on the part of the chapter until its "pending appeals to the sovereign General Congress" were resolved. Attacking the Board's reasoning as insincere, he underscored "the artfulness, cunning and injustice of that report." After various additional notes designed to further fortify his argument, he praised Article 3 of the National Constitution on the question of the inalienably Catholic character of the Mexican nation, adding: "and without the Church, without a Holy Pontiff, without ministers, without canon law, the Councils, the rules, and the current discipline, the Apostolic Roman Catholic religion is a chimera, an insignificant trifle, a mockery."[65]

This seemed to be the culmination of this declaration, with the Church upholding popular sovereignty as much as strict adherence to its religious duties. But it was not. Instead, the spokesman went further, in a direction full of ambiguities. He had defended the chapter by appealing to liberal ideas of citizen's rights and the right to defend one's own property and principles, but now he asserted a more traditional idea, quite rash in the context of the time:

> The Church has its sovereignty, its power, its jurisdiction, its laws, its discipline, its own weapons and its ministers – in principle the highest and most sublime. The nation which confesses, constitutes and swears to the religion of Jesus Christ must from that very moment recognize, respect, maintain and protect the sovereignty, power, jurisdiction, laws, discipline, weapons and ministers of that Church. The Church is not an individual, a citizen, who lives only under the protection and power of the civil government, but a sovereign who obtains and must exercise, in the midst of civil society, its power, its jurisdiction, its laws, its discipline and weapons, must name and maintain its ministers, working on some points in complete freedom, and on others in accordance with civil sovereignty.[66]

Giving priority to another range of considerations weakened the recourse to constitutional freedoms. The chapter did not respond on a single plane, but kept shifting belligerently from one to the other.[67] Was the Church justified in demanding the rights of an individual and later demanding to be treated as sovereign? How could these two lines of thinking be reconciled? How could the Church take the position of a subject, turned citizen, on the one hand, and of a parallel power, on the other? This might be traditional, but at this moment of crisis, the internal coherence of clerical discourse was sharply weakened. This could only limit the effectiveness of this discourse and, later on, push the Church towards a position as an embittered detractor of the triumphant liberal state. For now, its concrete message was only the requirement that "ecclesiastical discipline" be maintained "without alterations until the exercise of patronage was settled."[68]

Another 1827 pamphlet was dedicated precisely to laying the foundations, from a different perspective, for this same idea of freezing change until a Concordat governing the patronage had been reached. Arroyo, the author, summarized a historical and gradualist vision of human events. Society and its standards were fragile and uncertain; society needed to be careful that – whatever happened – changes took place in an orderly fashion and with "exact calculations." "One need not try hard to ruin things: it is done with a stroke of the pen. But raising up and fortifying afterwards what was so swiftly and imprudently ruined does not tend to be so easy." This was true of tithes and of the future of parish fees, as it was more generally true of the state's attempt to invade the Church's legitimate sphere of action. Question by question, "each one of enormous dimensions, this was invariably a matter of affairs which deserved careful study and appropriate decisions." However, instead of this, a "mass of enormous and vast ideas" were presented without "precise, determined, specific, exact goals, which could be called initiatives, bills or decrees, and subjected to a vote." The pamphlet intended to forestall the threat that liberal ideology, in full expansion, would dominate the legislature and drive the future course of events. The immediate spur for the pamphlet was a wide-ranging speech about clerical questions presented by Congressman Gómez Huerta in the neighboring legislature of Zacatecas. The response was originally presented to the Congress of Nuevo León, but it was later printed in Guadalajara.[69]

The unmitigated liberal approach of Gómez Huerta, the pamphlet argued, could not be the way to proceed. It was inappropriate to lump everything together. Historically, many governments had later retreated from such rash steps, and "I cannot persuade myself that all of this is as simple and straightforward as representative Gómez Huerta believes." This congressman, the pamphleteer stated, simply repeated the ideas of the Mexican Thinker, whose ideas came from liberal Spaniards established in London. Behind them were the ideas of very debatable authors: "only this is surprising."[70]

"To form a proper judgment," one had to read the other side, the rebuttal of these ideas. For example, it happened that the Church was criticized for a supposed medley of impediments to marriage, but critics exaggerated their number and did not take into account the means for overcoming them. "The exaggeration is, one can see, so far-fetched that it would barely be forgiven coming from an Andalusian." There was no reason for "such bitter and resentful complaints."[71]

According to this pamphlet, it could not be more evident that only men of true learning could resolve these matters, but provincial legislatures were not apt places to find such men or to carry out the decisive deliberations on these issues: "up in the Federal Congress there are wise men who understand all these points more than representative Gómez Huerta and more than all of us." The Federal Congress was very aware of the pros and contras of all these questions, and there was no need to bother its members in an attempt to illuminate them. From all of this, the author concluded simply that "no ill comes from remaining silent, but some may indeed come from speaking out."[72]

It is symptomatic and significant that *El Defensor* picked up on Arroyo's ideas in its articles.[73] His approach was consistent with the vision clearly forged by the cathedral chapter of Guadalajara: the sovereign right to express opinions and formulate judgments was legitimate. But on ecclesiastical matters, the decisions derived from Mexican sovereignty should be taken at a national level, in the lofty chambers of the National Congress. Just as the cathedral chapter had been referring its conflicts with the state government of Jalisco to the national presidency, so the Concordat itself would finally have to pass through the National Congress. The imperative push was invariably for this to take place at the national level. Once more, the Church revealed that it was only partially committed to popular sovereignty. The Church accepted that state legislatures had the rights popular sovereignty granted, but it thought they should delay their exercise of those rights not only on behalf of a national solution, but also in deference to the supreme wisdom of the national legislature and of the national executive in Mexico City.

A Delicate Balance:
A Free Church in a Free Nation

But if the Church of Jalisco slipped a little in adjusting itself to the implications of its theoretically and officially patriotic adherence to national sovereignty and the 1824 Constitution, it was not about to suffer criticism or reproach. When José de Jesús Huerta accused the Church of being ultramontane, he sparked the publication of a harsh response, another 1827 pamphlet, apparently from the pen of José Ramírez.[74]

Ramírez spoke for more than the Jalisco Church in his insistence that no exercise of patronage was licit until a Concordat had been signed with the Papacy. But he could hardly contain his indignation at being accused of being ultramontane. The good of the fatherland, he suggested, required a careful detachment on matters of Church–state relations. Despite this, he alleged, Huerta proceeded to attack, implicating all by accusing them indiscriminately of surrender to the Roman Curia. Using phrases like "a foreign power" to refer to the Papacy was incendiary and irresponsible, yet they were employed by "our politicians, some of them with a quite unforgivable lack of reflection."[75]

Ramírez denounced Huerta for speaking of an ecclesiastical aristocracy, when he himself called the majority of the citizens "the people" only if they supported "the Enlightened portion of the Republic." If they did otherwise, he wrote them off as "the rabble" – "an ominous specter." He also asserted that Huerta had quite inexact knowledge of the authors on whom he based his arguments. *El Defensor* was a more trustworthy source, Ramírez suggested, "so that the use of [ecclesiastical] authorities not become a weapon that turns against whoever fires it." Ramírez showed his impatience before what he clearly saw as the obstinacy of Huerta, as well as his poor handling and "muddling" of sources. Huerta, he suggested, had surrendered to "reasons of state" and was mistaken. And, as this whole business bordered on mutual accusations, Ramírez felt free to denounce Huerta as a Yorkino and Freemason. If one had to choose between being Yorkino and ultramontane, Ramírez added, he would find himself obliged to choose the latter. But he added that at this level (which he obviously found to be vulgar and unrefined), he would certainly find himself in the company of Miguel Ramos Arizpe, Francisco Pablo Vázquez and José Miguel Guridi y Alcocer.[76]

No longer wishing to descend to Huerta's level, Ramírez turned with arrogance and exasperation to boast of his own knowledge on the patronage question, to denounce Huerta's position as puerile, and to appeal to "public judgment" as his final resort. Undoubtedly enraged, this member of the Guadalajara cathedral chapter was not only defending his erudition, but also – and with singular determination – his patriotism, his commitment to republican ideas, and his confidence in the people. Up to what point? It was unclear, but the intentions behind his pamphlet, and its likely political effects, were more obvious.[77]

Ramírez' peculiar conception of the 1824 Constitution and the role of Mexican popular sovereignty can be seen in another pamphlet he published in 1827. This was his report on the patronage, originally written as a substantiated "vote" for the National Congress in 1824. Its publication in Jalisco in 1827 was undoubtedly significant, coming at a moment when the question of patronage came up locally once more and was under consideration by the committee Huerta presided over in the Federal Congress. Ramírez' openly patriotic and optimistic language in this document resembled the welcome given to national Independence in many sermons during 1821 and 1822. Ramírez saw the 1824 Constitution as the Church's solution against unbridled liberalism, and celebrated Catholicism's elevation to the status of national religion. He said the Constitution was an

> immortal act for that article [Article 3] alone which, expressing the most legitimate and true general will, sanctioned and made as eternal as anything human can be, its sovereignty, independence and liberty, and gave full reign to the best hopes and greatest confidence deposited in their representatives by eminently Roman Catholic peoples.[78]

Evidently, for Ramírez the union of religion with independence expressed "the national will, in what is most recommendable and precious about it, which is its faith, its hierarchical order, its essential discipline, and the sole true religion it professes" against indifference and opposing dogmas.[79]

In 1824, Ramírez had called for restraint in avoiding the sudden changes which he thought damaged society:

> When we have passed from a despotic and arbitrary government to a liberal and lawful one, we see that liberty, rights, and citizenship are proclaimed and sustained all over in every aspect and in every

possible way, by the means and to the degree we all know. But we also observe, as shown by a multitude of very evident events, that this enthusiasm for the system nears true fanaticism, and on the sole basis of repeating that word and applying it exclusively to the clergy, we see the very advantages of the system denied in practice, and without any further grounds, the clergy are presented as a class of enemies of society deserving oppression and the despotic exercise of civil authority.[80]

Ramírez demanded a well-developed Concordat between the national state and the Papacy, so that patronage might be exercised. He insisted on a "middle way" between the "ultrareligious" and "political fanatics." He appealed to the moderation of Bentham, "who I will never tire of citing." And he goaded Mexican patriotism by emphatically declaring that, in religious matters, "I would not wish us to be such servile imitators of the Spaniards any longer." In both temporal and religious spheres, then, Mexico had to set out its own honorable and sovereign course. In the "political infancy" of Mexico, adherence to Catholic religion would be an irreplaceable foundation of reason and stability. A Concordat was thus the matter of the hour.[81] The consecration of political life in the First Mexican Republic was the ideal means for countering the force of Jacobin liberalism. The union of fatherland and religion by means of the constitutive act of the nation was the most secure barrier against the arbitrariness of kings and assemblies. Royal arbitrariness came more out of weakness than conviction; that of assemblies responded to Jacobin pressures. The middle way was a representative republic, preferably with emphasis on the National Constitution and the Federal Congress.[82]

If this Mexican constitutional solution was clearly laid out in Ramírez' writings, *El Defensor* did not miss the opportunity to reinforce this idea in 1828–29 with a long article about the French Revolution and the civil constitution revolutionaries had wished to impose on the French clergy.[83] It is worth stressing that the article on the French clergy and civil constitution removed the last bit of innocence from the Church–state conflict in Jalisco. Centered on the confiscatory measures taken against the property of the French clergy, the article declared that those measures had tried to destroy the Church. In addition, the article argued that in this way the French government had taken over "considerable coffers with which to foment rebellion more and more, in sum, to pay the costs of revolution with the loot from the altar, the priest-hood, and the suffering members of Jesus Christ." This exposed the clergy to becoming

> the toy of the people, subject to the whims of the multitude and so-called legislators, irreconcilable enemies of Catholicism, and to make use of the expression of the [French] Assembly itself, a troop of wage workers and mercenaries, who could hope for nothing more from a corrupt nation than swift collapse into the greatest indigence and misery.[84]

The civil constitution to be imposed on the French clergy had been the careful product of an alliance between *Encylopédie* atheists, Protestants, and Jansenists. The article claimed that

> a plan existed, and was to be carried out in due time. The idea was to make many innovations, to alter and even destroy ancient institutions, but at the same time they [such individuals] wanted to pretend these mutations were true to the rules of the Church, so the destruction were seen as a means of perfection in the eyes of the ignorant, who everywhere are the majority, and finally [the idea was] to be schismatic, heretical and impious, although appearing Catholic for some time.[85]

The article said the solution to the abuses of the French clergy was a call for a national Church Council. This would have allowed abuses to be attacked, while protecting ecclesiastical jurisdiction and the institutions of canon law. Neither denying the existence of abuses nor trying to correct them by inappropriate methods was suitable, the author argued. The French civil constitution's attack on ecclesiastical authority and the clerical hierarchy, the "slow death" assigned to cathedral chapters, the assault on cloistered life, and the insistence on civic oaths: all these faced the dignified rejection of the greater part of the French clergy. Threatened by the "patriotic fanaticism" of the rabble, the clergy of France resisted, vicars and the simple priests of rural areas as well. Bishops responded similarly. The clergy placed its principles above its ambitions and abandoned the short-term pursuit of public recognition and promotions.[86]

The supplement to issue 105 of *El Defensor*, on 16 January 1829, was dedicated to contrasting the economic and numerical weakness of the Mexican clergy with its importance for the state and excellent morale and patriotism. There were foreign countries which pursued "the clumsy objective of corrupting the Americas, of demoralizing them, of weakening their forces with vice and disorder, and of thus achieving a victory otherwise impossible."[87] Towards this end,

> they have tried to break the sacred bonds joining the interests of Church and state, to spark the most stubborn war between priesthood and empire, in short, to renew the bloody scenes played out in France in the last days of the past century in order to destroy us and tear us apart so that, oppressed by the most cruel desperation, we might offer our innocent hands to the most shameful chains and bend our necks to once again bear a yoke far more ignominious than the one we finally managed, at the cost of uncounted sacrifices, to shake off gloriously.... Woe unto us if we second their liberty-killing plans; misery unto us if we let ourselves be seduced![88]

The author clearly asserted that the Church could coexist perfectly well with the Mexican federal republic.

The author of the supplement insisted that the Church found itself weakened. In fact, "the appearance of the Mexican Church was pitiful." The lack of communications with the Papacy, the advance of anti-clerical thinking, and the stalling on the matter of the patronage due to a lack of instructions from the federal government all left the Church without a clear direction and with a significant shortage of priests. There was only a single bishop left in the Republic, the cathedral chapters were emptying out, the parishes were in the hands of interim priests and with an insufficient number of ministers. If the federal government did not act because of a lack of funds, it could count on a donation on the part of the clergy and well-disposed individuals. It was not advisable for the cathedral chapters to fade away, "those august senates where the pastoral rod rests in the absence of the bishop, sole depositaries [under such circumstances] of episcopal power." The problem with priests was also grave:

> Ah, three thousand, six hundred, and seventy-nine ecclesiastics: will they be enough to attend to eight million faithful scattered across great distances? Well, that is the number of priests there are in the republic, without excepting the sick and injured....[89]

An air of desperation and weariness invaded clerical discourse due to the unresolved religious situation of the republic, and therefore the unresolved role of the clergy itself in national life. The clergy were as worried about growing weakness as about uncertainty and attacks:

> In fact, the clergy have completely fulfilled the obligations the fatherland imposes on its individual members, have effectively and powerfully cooperated in Independence and in the establishment of the current form of government. And what rewards have they received? Have their cries been heard? Have their fortunes improved? Ah! Today it is the same as it was in 1821, and so it will be as long as we have no communication with the Apostolic See.[90]

Thus the decade closed in a way not so different from 1821–22. On both occasions, clerical discourse resorted to consecrating the bonds between Church and state amidst political crisis in Mexico. On the first occasion, this solution was achieved despite the transition from the Iturbide regime to republican politics. On the second, clerical discourse was simply trying to get the republican solution to fulfill its promise to the Church, but the pressures to exclude the Church from the republican pact were very strong, by this point. The lack of resolution on the patronage matter between 1824 and 1826 had allowed this topic to become more popular in state legislatures, as in Jalisco, becoming mixed up with questions such as tithing, the borders of dioceses and states, and so forth. The issue of patronage in the hands of local legislatures promised to push Church–state relations to the breaking point. While clerical discourse showed the same theocratic tendencies at the end of the 1820s as it had at the beginning, the tone of clerical discourse was now far less optimistic.

The Golden Rule:
Constitution, Patronage and Mutual Cooperation

From 1829 to 1833 this new tone spread through debate on the Church–state question. In 1831 and 1832, several documents were produced in this vein. Examining them will allow us to bring this chapter to a close, and to set the stage for the major changes associated with the years 1833 and 1834 and their immediate consequences in the conservative and moderate governments in power until 1853.

The liberal point of view, quite solidified by 1831, could be seen in pamphlets like one entitled *Observaciones sobre la Bula de su Santidad el Señor Gregorio XVI* (Observations on the Bull of His Holiness Gregory XVI), published in Mexico City. The pamphleteer signed his name "A Secular Priest" and managed to provide a new liberal synthesis by rejecting a Papal Bull in reference to the reform of religious orders in Mexico. Concerned over the sovereignty of "Mexican borders," the author lamented that a Bull which nowhere recognized the Mexican government should have been allowed into the country. This allowed the Pope easier direct handling of ecclesiastical questions in Mexico without recognizing the country's political regime. The danger of such actions was that the clergy would consolidate their dominion over the people and economy of the country independently of the government and, in fact, with effective power over the unenlightened citizenry.[91] The supremacy that Mexican historian Reyes Heroles saw as indispensable for the new liberal state had only been a chimera.[92]

In opposition to this position, which did not add much to what Lissaute had set out in 1830, there emerged new versions of an equally consolidated clerical stance. These included two pamphlets by Pedro Espinosa, a prominent member of the cathedral chapter, and later the bishop of Guadalajara, and several more folksy writings recalling the old days of 1824–26 when the Church was still struggling to give coherence and formality to its position in the face of a growing liberal threat and the aftermath of the death of Bishop Cabañas. In his writings, Pedro Espinosa addressed the issues of tithes and fees. On the first issue, he returned to the recurrent position that the liberal government was pushing for more power than an absolutist king, and that republican liberty therefore benefited everyone but the Church.[93] Espinosa accepted that the state should reassume civil legal jurisdiction over tithing, but not that it should directly administer it. Thus, coercion in tithing fell to the state. Espinosa claimed that administration of tithes by the Church was more efficient and productive; any other procedure would be marred by un-republican arbitrariness and excess. The author insinuated that liberal self-interest also favored direct Church administration of tithes, since it would yield better results than administration by bureaucrats on state salaries. Espinosa insisted on the existence of two sovereignties – temporal and spiritual – in Catholic society like in any other. From this standpoint, tithes were clearly argued to be ecclesiastical income, due to their origin, their purpose, and the intent of contributors, whatever the specific arrangements between Church and state might be. That was why contributors responded so positively.[94]

The King of Spain himself had asked the Church to control tithing, which underscored this line of argument. The Church's support of the independent Mexican government led it to acquiesce to de facto state control over tithes, since "the Church never looks upon the well-being of peoples with indifference." Later changes had not fundamentally altered that situation. For Espinosa, the legal reference point for the new republic was the 1824 Constitution and the Federal Congress, but he did not fail to point out, in keeping with more recent clerical feeling, that "I am not unaware that the sovereign Federal Congress might one day err, since it does not have the gift of infallibility."[95]

Stressing that the Church was a legitimate property owner, he argued that in the new legal order the state was no longer lord of "lives and possessions." The anti-statism of Espinosa became evident in his attack on the contradictions of a liberal state that was stronger than the former absolutist state so loathed at the time.[96]

In a way, Espinosa's other pamphlet on parochial fees was an extension of the previous one. Basically, he argued that even all tithes combined were not enough to meet the needs of the parishes, and therefore fees were indispensable in sustaining the ecclesiastical work of the parishes. In addition, to remove fees only to later restore them out of necessity would only stir up the matter unnecessarily, while diminishing the force of custom. Espinosa called for fees to be revised within an atmosphere of cooperation between Church and state. But his clear intention was to show that, far from having an excess of money at their disposal, parish priests and their churches were in a situation of "penury." There was "a great scarcity of ecclesiastics," and priests found themselves obliged to work in non-ecclesiastical activities because of the lack of adequate income. In any case, "a just and rational reform does not only consist of taking away what is abundant, but also of providing what is lacking."[97]

Although Espinosa still believed that the woes of the clergy were occurring in "the land of riches," he did not fail to mention that the state of Jalisco did not even have enough money to make its contribution to the federation, and therefore could not be expected to aid the Church at this difficult moment. He recalled that certain expropriations of Church possessions by the government before 1810 had already reduced the once-flourishing resources of the clergy. Again, Espinosa did not offer a new approach, but he did restate matters in a succinct, persuasive, and graphic way.[98]

The remaining pamphlets also addressed tithes and patronage. One called for the disappearance of the Board of Tithes the state had established in Jalisco. Justice, the rights of the Church, and general utility demanded this step be taken. Administration of tithes by the cathedral chapter meant that those most interested in receiving tithes would be directly involved in collecting them; the pamphlet suggested this was a good idea. Current denunciations of avarice, on the one hand, and negligence, on the other, were contradictory and anything but impartial, the pamphlet emphasized. Real problems with the tithe were minor and could be addressed within the prior system of Church administration.[99]

Another pamphlet went to the heart of the matter – in republican and legal terms – by inquiring whether the law protecting the new Board was truly a law,

> because to be the law, a law must be just, as a man must be free and a circle must be round. An unjust law is the same as a circle that is not round, a man who is not free. But, let us say the law is not unjust: does that mean it is immutable? Such a quality is not possessed by any law other than natural law.[100]

In addition, the drop in tithe collections after the Board's creation was due to its lack of public esteem, the pamphlet argued, and if the prior situation was not restored, tithes would end up disappearing entirely. The argument closed with a set of calculations showing that the tithe did not meet the ecclesiastical needs that had inspired its creation.[101]

A third pamphlet also justified Church administration of tithes, but it did so within a many-sided argument: the priesthood was seen as a divine creation, not a creation of society; the Council of Trent was presented as the basis for this doctrine; divine rights were stated to be equivalent not to "virtue" but to "what has been immediately established by God." Therefore, the Scriptures, tradition and the Church Councils were the pillars of the dogma and principles of the Catholic Church. Priests were thus the interpreters entrusted with the sacramental and doctrinal life this established.[102]

> The priesthood does not directly serve the national body ... it serves divine worship, and for this there are priests in the Catholic

Church entrusted with the instruction and sanctification of man. Their functions, directed immediately at the spirit, have nothing to do with society, whose object is temporal matters. The Church is a society independent of civil society; combated by civil society, it endures. The first statement is a truth of faith, while the second is proven by history.[103]

Tithes were seen as the income proper to this independent society. Coming from the people, this income – once given – duly belonged to the Church. Ecclesiastics were not "employees of the nation," and Church dogma and discipline – that is, the temporal organization of the Church, and even its possessions – were inextricably bound together. To reinforce his statements, the author of this pamphlet cited Article 3 and Article 50, Faculty XII, of the 1824 Constitution, which established the Catholic Church and pointed the way towards a Concordat for the exercise of patronage. Similarly, he cited the General Decree of 18 December 1824, which stated that there would be no variation on matters of ecclesiastical income unless mutually agreed to by Church and state until the exercise of patronage had been arranged.[104]

The last pamphlet from 1831 demanded that patronage be resolved in order to achieve the necessary balance between the temporal and spiritual aspects of "man." Recognition of Mexican Independence and patronage by the Pope was already under way, so there would be no problem in that respect. On the other hand, the bishops had sworn an oath to uphold the 1824 Constitution, without being obliged to do so by any Article of that Constitution. The real problem was not between Church and state, the author asserted, but between the Church and a handful of agitators who were trying to do damage to "a nation still in swaddling clothes, because of the egoism of certain public writers." Those writers did not respect the Constitutional Articles which joined Church and state in preserving and protecting worship. The pamphlet's author appealed to the now-familiar name of the "Enlightened Bossuet" to mark the exact divide: orthodoxy in the faith should go along with due respect for the civil sovereignty of the state. He seemed to suggest that the fortitude of an independent Mexico would come from proper cooperation between both powers, thus resolving conflicts.[105]

In concluding, it might be said that the late 1820s and early 1830s had witnessed the rapid application of abstract principles guiding the relations between Church and state in the new republic to the key outstanding economic questions faced by any Catholic state. In this process, the political and diplomatic questions of patronage and Concordat worked their way to the fore. While Church voices continued to battle in favor of a recognition of separate spheres of action for the Church and the government within a Catholic state, and availed themselves of liberal principles in their arguments, the times were quite definitely those of conflict, confrontation and even acrimony. There was intense debate over the interpretation of the 1824 Constitution, orthodoxy in the Catholic faith, and equity under the law. The Church did, however, successfully assert the golden rule which the clergy hoped would solve the problem: patronage and mutual cooperation under the Constitution of 1824.

9

Clerical Discourse Claims for Itself

The Representation of the National Will, 1833–53

The Church on Trial

Better days seemed to await the Church in Guadalajara when, in 1831, it received the first bishop appointed since Independence. The federal government and the Papacy had accommodated themselves to a Catholic country's need for prelates for its Church. Although the future of patronage – and therefore Church–state relations – remained unresolved, a significant step had been taken towards a de facto agreement.[1] On 17 June 1831, the official *Gaceta* expressed its optimism:

> Cheerful and happy the holy Church of the federation, since it has succeeded in having Peter's successor grant it a prelate of holy piety and virtue. His Enlightenment, his ardent patriotism, his halo of peace will be a comfort to the Mexican flock, which asks the heavens for the fervent bond of union.[2]

Bishop José Miguel Gordoa himself sensed that, in fact, the situation was more delicate. Gordoa confessed that he had doubts about accepting "a mitre ringed by sharp and penetrating thorns." He stated that he accepted out of a sense of obligation, well aware that "we are taking on a burden whose enormous weight strains even the most robust men." Gordoa was sensitive to the advance in Jalisco of doctrines and attitudes opposed to the Church. He warned the faithful against the "ruinous systems of Lutherans, Calvinists and Jansenists." He demanded respect for the authority of the Church, and especially of the Pope.[3] Yet despite the problems, he declared that

> in the midst of so many errors that have spread across our beloved fatherland, and at the mercy of the books that incredulity and heresy have unleashed like a devastating torrent, we have the greatest pleasure, and we give the most humble thanks to the father of mercies, that the greater part of those who make up our beloved flock have not bent their knees to Baal, but have remained firm in their faith.[4]

Gordoa was not completely consoled by the faithfulness to the Church of most Jaliscans. He counseled against the reading of books "of perverse doctrines" and demanded that Catholics be fully obedient in "these times of tribulation." He attacked the spread of atheism, the rejection of worship and the Holy Scriptures, and mockery of the faith. No less dangerous was the nominal Catholicism practiced by some which "denied the rights of the Church, fought against its prerogatives, impugned its discipline, and by confusing ideas of spiritual and temporal power, made the latter grow on the ruins of the former."[5]

Addressing himself to priests, the new bishop continued to counsel against "novelties" and "error." He insisted on preaching "the word of God with full strength and valor," without impatience, "because we live in times when men do not suffer truth … but they find themselves animated by a burning desire to hear doctrines which succor their intemperate passions, and they anxiously think up and search out maxims satisfying their disorderly appetites." The Bishop called priests to irreproachable and spiritual conduct, in light of existing enemies ready to exploit any deviation:

> O venerable priests, our sins, our scandals excite the fury of the Heavens, and we are responsible before the Almighty God for our errors and all our public calamities. By contrast, our virtues disarm the arm of vengeance, and draw to the Earth the forgiveness of our most merciful God.[6]

The strained tone evident throughout the new Bishop's pastoral letter grew even sharper in the final pages. Addressing the members of the government, Gordoa asserted

Fulfilling one of our principal obligations, and justly persuaded of the religiousness of those who serve in the major posts of the states which our Diocese embraces, who therefore should always strive for the true happiness of their fellows and rule over the people with fairness and justice, we frankly exhort you from the depths of our soul to unity and the fulfillment of your duties as Catholics with the greatest exactness, so that joining your care and vigilance to that of the Pastor, we might preserve and sustain public morality, so important for the good of society, and for that very reason *you must uphold the purity of customs and due respect for Religion with your utmost consideration. Oh, you who are placed at the head of government! Render your homage to the Catholic Church, act according to the dictates of a righteous and delicate conscience,* and give your assistance when the spiritual power implores you. Just as the Princes of the Church pay you the honor due to the high post you occupy, so give them what they deserve due to their august character and sublime dignity. Let the greatest harmony reign between both powers; let the limits God has placed on both be respected; let us all work for the undisturbed happiness of the people.[7]

Evidently, the controversies of previous years were not lost on the new Bishop, nor did he try to hypocritically pretend they were. With apparent good faith, he addressed the problem energetically, insisting on "the balance, so necessary and just," between Church and state:

How happy we will be, and how blessed, if the rebukes and disputes customary between both authorities do not appear, and if, *with both mutually respecting each other,* unity and true harmony prevail. Would that our Merciful God, in the time his beloved Providence keeps us at the head of his flock, never let peace be disturbed, or order altered! Those are our desires, and the object of our most ardent prayers.[8]

Finally, he called the faithful to respect "constituted authorities," to follow good Christian conduct, and to properly educate their children. But he did not fail to chide those who were attacking Catholicism and the authority of the Church. He now made no allusions to problems with statism or state incursions into Church rights. He simply spoke of the loss of faith:

To you who have abandoned the faith, and live subject to the tyrannical domination of your passions, to you, ungrateful children of the most loving Mother, we finally direct our words with tears in our eyes and our heart overwhelmed by your sad fate in an immense sea of suffering. Hear the voice of your Pastor, wayward sheep, or better stated, hear the voice of your most loving God who invites you with his grace. Ah, passion obscured your understanding, pride carried you to the extreme of denying the mysteries of our belief, your lips have blasphemed against the Holy and terrible Name of God. You wanted to fathom Divinity, and you have been oppressed by the immense weight of his glory. Where is the sweetness you enjoyed in the bosom of the Church in your first years of candor and innocence?[9]

An equilibrium between the two powers was a remote possibility at best, and the reconciliation Gordoa called for, with each respective jurisdiction carefully acknowledged, would not be achieved at that time. The danger he sensed of a growing lack of respect for the Church would grow deeper, but the Bishop – who died on 12 June 1832 – would not live to see the greatest confrontation yet between Church and state. Jalisco would face 1833 once again without a bishop.[10]

The funeral oration for the Bishop clearly marked out the problems to come. Pedro Barajas, the preacher, spoke of the balance between the spiritual and the temporal, noticeably disdaining the latter while primarily turning towards the former. He would not allow Earthly happiness and glory to be the measure of the late Gordoa:

Inspired by eternal truth, can I occupy myself in offering a panegyric to Earthly happiness without betraying my ministry and profaning the authority of the Gospels? Would I employ my time rightly in exalting the passing glories of the age? Let us leave behind this habit of celebrating oneself, let us leave to vanity the art of praising vanity, let us leave behind the carnal and vulgar man who on his own authority raises altars to those who do not even deserve tombs, who crowns injustice, and who bows to burn incense to vice. Before this God who is not pleased by the praise of sinners, I cannot pay tribute to sin, because it would be a kind of sacrilege to mix the smoke rising from a profane fire with the incense of religion. I will speak of a man, yes, but his positive virtues will give me my subject, without any need to resort to human greatness to praise him.[11]

Further on, the speaker stressed that "the remains of human greatness are an unhappy crown for the dead, nothing more than some dried flowers drained of their fragrance and beauty, destined only to thicken the soil covering cadavers." The glory of Gordoa was better found in virtue and wisdom. He could not overlook the "civic glories" of Gordoa, with regard to his participation in the Cortes in Cádiz and his role there in keeping with "Mexican honor."[12] For a brief moment, it seemed as though he was going to shore up the ancient balance between the spiritual and the temporal, but he did not allow that to happen:

> I know very well that love of the fatherland is a virtue we are obliged to cultivate; I know that this obligation comes from the very nature of things, that natural law is not contradicted by religion, and that our Divine Savior did not come to destroy social virtues, but to perfect them. *Yet they would be nothing if religion and morality had a secondary place in the life of Gordoa....*[13]

The faith of Gordoa was invulnerable to "the philosophes, that infamous plague," and "if his liberal ideas did not give ground to a Villanueva, in religiosity he was a [La] Rochefoucaul[d]."[14]

> Such is the conduct of a disciple of the Gospels: knowing how to reconcile fidelity due to God with obedience to Caesar, and to intertwine one's duties so that fulfilling one does not mean failing the others. That is how to respect the rights of the prince with no detriment to those of the Creator, and to strive for the well-being of society without denying the Sovereign who is society's author.[15]

The preacher was calling for a virtue that was much more than civic. He preached selflessness along clearly Christian and otherworldly lines. He underscored the late Bishop's lack of personal ambition, and his acceptance of the life divine providence had assigned him, even when this meant a separation from power and greatness. "Ambition," the speaker insisted, is "one of the hardest servitudes:"[16]

> Our most illustrious prelate was deeply convinced of this truth, and due to that, he never wished to take advantage of revolutions. He ardently desired the liberty and happiness of his fatherland, and when this great event was verified, he rejoiced in happiness like every good Mexican. But since his wishes were directed towards the

public good, and not his own, he never tried to take a place on the political stage.[17]

The ecclesiastical speaker saw Gordoa afflicted by the "ravages of the philosophes." While always inclined towards clemency, the Bishop had nonetheless been zealous in the "conservation of religion and sacred discipline." Subjected to attacks and denunciations when he arrived in Guadalajara for what would be his short (eleven-month) episcopal tenure, he ignored them. Struck down by a deadly disease when he made a pastoral visit to his diocese, he took comfort in religious piety and the Virgin of Zapopan. So he died as he had lived, the speaker indicated, while the "incredulous who hold disdain for the faith to be strength of spirit" are often seen making an "odd shift" at the last minute, "in order to die as believers."[18]

> And you, foolish age, tell me: which of your glories reaches beyond the fleeting days of this present life? What monuments capable of enduring forever will you establish? The columns of victory collapse, the triumphal arch comes undone, the laurels shed their leaves, and the medals wear away. Can the splendor of human greatness become even a weak dawn light reflecting beyond the dark shadows of the tomb? Will the trumpets of fame interrupt for one second the silence of those perpetually dormant walls? No, everything perishes with this present life: and how can such glories seduce mortals, entertain them, occupy them in playing with the interests of eternity? Deplorable blindness! Let us open our eyes, gentlemen: only virtue has the power to glorify the dead.[19]

It is true that Gordoa's demise shortly after being consecrated bishop of Guadalajara was a chance event, but his reservations about accepting the post and the sharp contrasts drawn in his funeral oration were symptomatic of the deep disgust the Guadalajara Church felt after years of friction with the civil authorities and anti-clerical pamphleteers. The Church still aspired to restoring the ancient Church–state balance formally preserved in Articles 3 and 171 of the 1824 Constitution. Yet there was no longer any certainty on the part of the clergy. Both Gordoa and Barajas recognized in their own ways that this was a deep problem related to social attitudes of the citizenry, and not merely to the government's overstepping its authority.

They do not seem to have gauged each individual factor or fully measured their interaction, but even so, the opinions of Gordoa and Barajas serve very well as an introduction to the dynamics of the following years.

Many 1833 pamphlets were directed at refuting opinions expressed in current newspapers due to the political rise of forces contrary to the Church in Jalisco and the nation. The new liberal vice-president, Valentín Gómez Farías, had taken over the executive on 1 April, as the elected president, Antonio López de Santa Anna, preferred to request a leave of absence. On 15 April, there appeared a pamphlet aiming to counter the viewpoint of the liberal newspaper *El Fénix.* The pamphleteer lamented that "our reformers" want to appropriate the goods of the Church for themselves, and suppress its income. The project was not new, he argued, as could be seen in publications from earlier years. The destruction of the clergy would lead, he stated, to that of religion itself. The "perverse gaze" of those who attacked what they disparagingly called "the clerical race" had to be unveiled. The reformers were not to be believed in their supposed intentions of purifying religion, aiding the needy, protecting agricultural producers, and solving national "urgencies."[20]

If they truly wanted this, they would undoubtedly propose to reduce the bureaucratic posts that have scandalously multiplied doing very serious damage to the treasury without benefiting anyone other than those who secure them; they would not promote discord and the internal divisions for which the blood of unfortunate thousands has been spilled and the money missing from the treasury has been wasted, when it should have been invested towards the utility of the nation; they would have proposed effective measures so that, once authority had taken them, foreign commerce were not to the detriment of our artisans and merchants, nearly all of whom find themselves almost ruined and many of whom find themselves reduced to the sad need to beg or rob so as not to die of hunger. That is what they would do if their patriotism were true. If they so desired us to return to apostolic times, they already would have sold their goods and placed their earnings at the feet of the bishops, like the faithful did in the primitive age [of the Church]."[21]

On the contrary, they wanted the money of the Church for themselves:

> The zeal of our [reformers] is none other [than greed] … and I say the same of their love for the fatherland. No one is unaware of what fatherland means to them. They have believed that with Independence they earned the right for the nation to maintain them, in exchange for political harangues, as a writing published in recent days rightly said. Since the treasury cannot support so many expenses, they want ecclesiastical wealth to pass into it.[22]

In this, they were following the precedent of certain European countries of the previous century which had similar aims and a similar philosophical inspiration rooted in the thinking of Voltaire, but however much money there was, it would run out before long, just as had happened in England centuries before.[23]

The author of the pamphlet demanded his freedom as a Mexican to denounce what the reformers wanted to do to the Church with the support of "a multitude of low and truly servile adulators who are as common here as under the kings of Spain, France and elsewhere."

> We must understand that civil authority, however supreme, has certain limits it may not go beyond. *Not only Popes and Kings have had their adulators, Congresses have them as well*, and we need not see something as just and fair simply because a Congress does it. They are not infallible, they are not impeccable, and just as absolutist kings have sometimes allowed others to tell them the truth, why should liberal congresses be offended to hear it?[24]

This writer defended the Church's rights over its property, its influence over temporal affairs, and its faculty for establishing its own fundamental laws.[25] He added that this applied to the relation between Church property and national finances:

> Of course I agree that there is nothing useful which is not just.… Not public credit, not the immense guarantee it would offer to the nation's creditors, not the confidence it would awaken at a moment when our hopes seem to slip away every day: none of these are a sufficient motive for sanctioning a usurpation.[26]

On the other hand, and countering the preferences of Congress, he denied that private testaments could be broken on the pretext of the ignorance of their authors. Regarding the origins of property, he argued that "even before all civil law, even before all public will, property already existed." Setting any other tenets for testaments and property was unacceptable: "there were no such principles even in the days of absolutist kings who claimed to be lords of houses and possessions."[27]

Finally he stressed the rights of the clergy by appealing to another kind of argument already seen in this study. Utility and republican rights were not the only discursive resources available for defending the Church.

> It is also necessary to understand that the clergy is not a political body whose existence is due to civil laws. It has higher origins: Jesus Christ himself established it, and it cannot help but be present wherever the Catholic religion is professed. Professing this divine religion is an unavoidable obligation born from a principle of divine truth. That is, men are obligated to worship God, and we must give him the tribute his Majesty commands. We are not free to profess the religion that suits us, but solely, exactly and unavoidably the religion which is true. This is the principle we must start from in order to determine whether or not the clergy is necessary: and who can doubt that it is any less necessary in the religious order than governors are in the civil order?[28]

Once again, clerical polemics thus laid out an appeal to a different order of things in which the Church and its goals were evidently higher and more stable in the life of man than whatever governments and their human objectives might be.

Another newspaper that sparked great controversy that year was *El Siglo XIX*, which had attacked the clergy stating that there was no need for the Pope to fill the vacant ecclesiastical benefices and questioning a series of practices of worship. The paper's outlook was not especially new, but the advance of such opinions and new government measures against the Church drew a stern response. One author declared:

> You yourselves confess that without the [clergy] there is no religion, without religion there is no morality, and without morality there is no society: therefore, by destroying the clergy you destroy society. Does committing such an attack not horrify you? You should tremble, yes, tremble at the certainty that in the ruin of the nation you will be the first victims immolated by the disorder you have promoted. Put down the little hardback books containing antisocial errors, read the history of the ages, even if it's only bound in

parchment and scrolls, and it will teach you beyond any doubt that the end of those who perturb society has always been disastrous. Slander the clergy, make the people hateful, and on the day of the upheaval, the philosophers will be missing the refuge they would have found with the ecclesiastics. Who but a man blinded by anti-religious fervor would deny the services the clergy have rendered, I won't even say all over the Republic, but in this very city in different eras?... How many times – I know too well, I have gathered information scrupulously, and I have evidence I could present to the public – how many times have ecclesiastics pulled back the knife aimed infallibly at the heart of these philosophers the people abhor for their shameless evil and blasphemies against religion? And these are the ecclesiastic enemies of the people, the rabid canons, those with whom there can be no security? Ungrateful editors of *Siglo XIX*! Is this the clergy you want to annihilate?[29]

This pamphleteer went on to deny that the clergy was rich. To the contrary, he argued, it suffered from widespread poverty, including the bishop, canons and parish priests. "I do not know where those 'immense riches' of the clergy are, and where that lavish luxury could be found, except in your imagination." In any case, it was better for the clergy to have money, because it spent that money on works, and thus "sooner or later it ended up falling into the hands of the poor." In comparison, those who proclaimed their love of liberty, humanity, and the fatherland could not show anything similar. "I have heard it said that love is works, not good intentions, and for that very reason I do not want to believe in your tales." Since the wealth of the clergy was insufficient, and yet it supported works of great social importance, the only explanation for anti-clerical discourse was that its spreaders were coming to "loot." The author closed his article asking: "Pastors of the Church, when will you break your silence, and tell the faithful who are the wolves tearing apart the flock of Jesus Christ?" He called for resistance by all the clergy, like that the French clergy had given (apparently referring to the French Revolution), and without any internal divisions under any pretext. "It is time for us to learn who is of God, and who is of the Devil."[30]

Before and after this particular polemic, *El Siglo XIX* was also the object of other responses opposing its positions on Church matters. One pamphlet sardonically referred to its editors as the "Solomons of the nineteenth century." Fighting against the appropriation of Church income some now encouraged, this pamphlet tried to make the public see this appropriation as theft.[31] Considering how the editors of *El Siglo XIX* mocked theological knowledge, this pamphleteer made use of popular wisdom:

> At least recall a saying very common among old women: "he who holds the leg sins as much as he who kills the cow." According to this, the state sins no less by watching and consenting than the Church does by committing, according to you, theft in collecting tithes. The state also takes a very large part of the spoils, while forcing poor laborers to pay up by means of the Board of Tithes. Then let the state pay its share, and the Church will immediately pay its share. And how happy the state must be with you, dear editors, for the "honor" you do it by supposing that the income of which the state itself collects and takes a great part is robbery! This will not be the only restitution the state is obliged to make. Another would be for the *alcabala*, since the merchant's calculations are the same as those of the laborer.[32]

The pamphleteer questioned the estimates by the editors of *El Siglo XIX* of the amount of tithes, and wondered whether the term "robbery" should be applied to a payment the faithful made out of piety. He also pointed out that the state still collected part of the tithes for very dubious purposes, such as royal debts from before Independence, savings for Spanish soldiers' widows, and the distinguished Caroline order "established against the so-called insurgents which it is shameful to continue to collect after Independence." What was the justification for this? Perhaps these contradictions were due to something else. "Could it be that with Independence, everyone won their liberty except for the Church, which [reformers] are trying to weaken, even by means of the signs and countersigns given to night patrols in this city, such as "idle canons," "priestly pride," "mysterious masses," and so on and so forth?"[33]

He argued that the language used to refer to the clergy was contradictory. On the one hand, clerics were portrayed as "servants of the people" who therefore had to earn their wages; on the other hand, clerics were referred to as "beggars." He claimed they could not be both at the same time. In so far as the clergy gave the ecclesiastical services the people paid for, there should be no complaints. Finally, the pamphleteer could not understand certain discriminatory taxes reformers wanted to impose on several kinds of popular worship and ecclesiastical wills. He said:

Why should the wills of ecclesiastics be taxed fifteen percent, when those of lay people are only taxed five percent? It occurs to me that this must be in order to establish "equality" between the clergy and lay people and the author of the project must understand "five to be equal to fifteen," however much "those who burn their eyelashes reading folio books covered in parchment and written in Latin" try to prove the contrary. Dear Gentlemen Editors, please enlighten me, spread your beneficial light, so that the shadows might fade away from this poor fanatic....[34]

The editors of *El Siglo XIX* continued to draw attention. One pamphlet, dated 22 May 1833, ended its first paragraph like this: "Oh, sublime genius, deepest talent! Eternal praise to the state of Jalisco, which has the glory of counting such wise men among its sons!" Undoubtedly going too far, the pamphleteer added that "due to your prowess, Gentlemen, you certainly deserve to be deputies in the Honorable Congress of the state." Continuing in this confrontational language, the author dared to state that "Solomon was a dolt in comparison with these wise men." Later, he added a series of comments on the ideas expressed by the newspaper editors. The first comments were oriented towards proving the ignorance of the editors and the triviality of their arguments about the Church. Immediately afterwards, the pamphleteer shifted to another line of attack, demanding irrefutable proof from the editors on matters such as the election of bishops they advocated and the exercise of patronage rights by civil authority they proposed. The author questioned how much obedience of Catholic pastors by their flock the editors were willing to accept, and he asked them to clarify how it was permissible for civil authority to constantly meddle in Church matters if there was no parallel Church meddling in civil matters.[35]

And finally. Demonstrate that the Church of God is not a truly sovereign and independent society in its sphere, but a mere subordinate brotherhood or confraternity of prayerful devotion entirely subject to the inspection and laws of the political governments across whose territory it has spread. And with this you gentlemen will have demonstrated that "the existence of" this corporation or union of organized men, with its particular make up, absolutely depends on the consent of the sovereign.[36]

The author closed in the same provocative tone running throughout his pamphlet: "Gentlemen Editors, for your own credit and that of the party you belong to, you must respond: it is unbearable to be so provoked by a fanatic and to have to keep your silence."[37]

A further two pamphlets would be directed against *El Siglo XIX*. *Dogma and Discipline* clarified the errors the newspaper had committed in its reading of the Bible, and defended public prayer, kneeling, and the use of religious images in worship. It closed suggesting that some of the editors of *El Siglo XIX* were in the courts or legislature of Jalisco.[38] *The Day of Bitter Disappointments, Or the Triumph of Our Religion* carried on the battle in another pamphlet dated 7 June 1833.[39] In general, it was directed against "the mad efforts those fools have made to decatholicize a people standing firm on the sacrosanct commands of Jesus Christ" by means of "poisoned papers." But it only specifically mentioned *El Siglo XIX*. Even though the Church had resisted attacking liberals, they had "soiled so many sheets of paper" that they had generated "a wave of indignation against the enemies of the Church which almost reaches madness." Despite this, the Church had insisted that the personal safety of liberals should be respected. Only the Church had been able to hold back the people from resorting to violence against their detractors, and for that, the Church should be thanked, or at least left in peace. This last pamphlet pointed out:

It is said that you still have some hope that the first Magistrate of the Republic will sign the preposterous patronage law, but since this is not credible because of his religiosity and thoughtfulness, once more you will be defrauded by your mad hopes, and our triumph will be majestic. Let us suppose, however, that by one of those incomprehensible designs of Providence, the law passes, and the Most Excellent President ignores the endless counsel given to him on this point; in that case, our clergy, following what it has already expressed, would offer opposition with positive acts, would subject itself to suffering the sorrows of exile and whatever was to come, and even if the Churches were closed and profaned, God ... would not lack for altars and temples. And on the contrary, he would have many more, and more dignified ones.

The Mexican Church places its best hopes in the Great Love of our adorable Religion and the protection of her august Mother who saw fit to visit this happy soil to save us from all errors and divisions.[40]

It was one thing to have to deal with liberal newspapers, however, and quite another to discover their editors represented in the highest spheres of government. Even worse was discovering that the official *Gaceta* dared to print the same kind of opinions clerical spokesmen were refuting in private newspapers. One pamphleteer said:

> I am not surprised by … what has come out of such pens; but I do find striking a communique I saw in the *Gaceta* of the state government which atrociously slandered ecclesiastical authority, combated preachers, and set forth doctrines opposed to Catholic dogma.[41]

The clergy was "a respectable corporation" that accepted government authority and watched over social peace. Attacking its members in the official bulletin, and without any proper basis, was inappropriate, because "ecclesiastics do not have fewer rights than other citizens because they belong to the clergy." A citizen had the right to expect any accusation to follow due legal process, lest that accusation slip into calumny and arbitrariness. Those who attacked the Church did so out of bad faith or hatred for preachers. They felt condemned by sermons attacking impiety, immorality and vice because they "always see themselves portrayed" there. If a preacher spoke of virtue, they were ashamed because they did not practice it. Unbelievers and libertines would always be offended, but religious men would always feel themselves instructed and edified. Therefore, the government should not be offended by the teachings of the clergy.

> This is not sedition, but rather the most appropriate means to establish the peace that restless and turbulent spirits wish to destroy, to assure obedience to the authorities, and to conserve the well-being of a state which can only be happy under the beneficial shadow of the only true religion existing on the face of the Earth.[42]

Another pamphlet attacked the same article as this last one, together with another article the *Gaceta* published on 2 April. How could writers like Voltaire and Rousseau and "other writers of that stripe" be the basis for matters of religion? The pamphlet affirmed "the dogma of the supremacy and independence of both powers" and its "sacred and indisputable" character for Catholics. The two powers were no less supreme and independent under a Catholic government than under a pagan one. The pamphleteer went on to say that he did not consider the authors of the controversial articles to be heretics, because their ignorance excused them of any such accusation.[43] He asked, in relation to certain Biblical allusions:

> And if tomorrow a usurper should take over the government, ejecting the legitimate holder of office, if another comes with a formidable army to lay siege to this city, if another comes to subjugate us and take away our independence and liberty, would it not be licit for any Mexican to remove and, if necessary, kill them?[44]

This author rejected the attacks on "abuses and cruelties sometimes committed in the name of religion" which failed to recall that "philosophical fanaticism is stronger than false religious zeal." He defended the attacks on impiety and the defense of Article 3 of the Constitution in sermons. The clergy were within their rights and within constitutional standards:

> I say and will repeat a thousand times: the clergy are not the enemy of you gentlemen, much less of the nation; the clergy recognize and fully respect the civil authorities; if the clergy feel harmed in their interests or honor, they will suffer and keep silent a thousand times, or else speak with all possible moderation; but they never are seditious nor do they disturb the peace, and if some [members of the clergy] in this state have been accused by their enemies, of whom there is no shortage, nothing has been proven. Their suffering has been taken to the limit; they are insulted in public papers which distort events; no other class of citizens has felt such an attempt to weaken it, and it seems that for some [reformers], it now is a crime just to be an ecclesiastic.[45]

The author closed underscoring the religiosity and patriotism of the Jalisco clergy.[46]

When the Law Fails
The Right to Strike Back

This discursive assertiveness adopted towards both the authors of private newspapers and the official *Gaceta* leaves no doubt that the Church was no longer going to yield in defending what it considered its rights. The Church still expended efforts to defend its image and intentions, as well as to discredit its opponents inside the government and out. But this served its purpose of setting the limits of what its conduct could be if it faced a new confrontation with anti-clerical forces. This was not an empty exercise, nor words in vain: clerical discourse clearly announced the path being laid out, and at what point the Church would consider itself attacked by people who did not even respect the Constitution or know the meaning of authentically disinterested patriotism.

It is not surprising, in this context, that several publications that year clearly represented the views of the ecclesiastical hierarchy. Two key pamphlets about the patronage appeared; they used undoubtedly strong language. The first pamphlet began like this:

> When religion finds itself embattled, everyone who claims to be Catholic should come to its defense. Respect for constituted authorities does not compel us to remain silent in this case. The fear of punishment, whatever it may be, should not hold us back in any way. Insults, disdain, expulsion itself and even death cannot save us from speaking with the clarity the apostles had, speaking to those who forced silence upon them. *These are the circumstances every Mexican worthy of the name finds himself in today.*[47]

The author made it clear that opposition to the government on this matter was not only right, but fully patriotic and constitutional.

> What public papers are announcing, what can be heard in conversations, what we ourselves see: everything reveals the existence of a party trying to decatholicize the Mexican nation, to secularize the Church and leave us like France with a shadow of religion. It fully wishes for Article 3 to be erased from the Federal Constitution, and if it does not dare propose this, that is because it fears the people. Yes, this is the only reason, not the respect due to the widespread general will of the entire nation, expressed in a clear and firm way since the moment of our happy emancipation, and later repeated on different occasions.[48]

The "Protestant's apprentices" were pushing a "wicked project."
While their activities aimed to damage the Catholic religion, the
defense of religion – promised by the 1824 Constitution – was
nowhere evident. A "cold indifference" prevailed. Everywhere,
the Church and its dogmas were attacked. "Tolerating such circumstances is a crime."[49] The pamphleteer denounced French-
style "philosophy" and the work of the "great lodge" [of
Freemasons]. What was coming next was a civil constitution for
the clergy. Just like in France, an attempt was now being made
to split the clergy, but the clergy should not allow it: "Shame on
those who let themselves be seduced! Today they fire on canons,
tomorrow beneficed priests will be next; they will try to make the
rest of the clergy rise up against them, then it will be the remaining clergy, and the people will be left without priests at all."[50]

The writer considered that the government had not only the
right, but also the obligation, to protect the Church – but it did
not have the right to govern it. He insisted that there were two
powers, and that their mutual support was convenient for the
good of society, whether the government was Catholic or not.
He rejected the worship of secular power and the idea that the
people had the right to elect their ecclesiastical pastors. "As if
our congresses and governments had more than civil powers!
As if they had the powers the Christian people might have –
although if they did, it would not be as a nation, but as part of
the Catholic Church!" He forcefully underscored the difference
between the government's eminent domain over ecclesiastical
wealth, and ownership in a narrower sense. The author seemed to
greatly limit the possibility that the Mexican government might
obtain effective exercise of patronage by arguing that since the
Council of Trent, "there has been and can be no other way of
acquiring it other than subvention" [of the Church]. Since the
Mexican treasury had not occupied itself in building or repairing
temples since Independence, the government really had nothing
to argue in terms of patronage.[51]

Speaking "with the freedom proper to a Mexican and a
Catholic," in his second publication on patronage the pamphleteer challenged the Federal Congress to clearly demonstrate its
rights over patronage. Denouncing the "infamous reformers,"
he demanded that Mexicans follow a line like the "enlightened
French clergy" which, without ever becoming ultramontane,
recognized the just rights of the Papacy. He accused the government of tyranny and absolutism in imposing an exercise of

patronage it did not deserve. With his arguments, he laid waste the idea that patronage was inherent to the nation and that it was not the Church's place to modify its own internal rules. He concluded with a quotation from Bossuet about the rights of the pope, and a separate note denying the constitutionality of patronage and stating "to speak correctly it is not enough to be a senator or congressman; something more is needed." Clearly, he was rising up against the authority of the members of congress, appealing to the reason and information at the disposition of simple citizens.[52]

More formal rejections by the Church were not lacking. On 14 May 1833, the cathedral chapter of the Archdiocese of Mexico blamed the national changes in religious matters for the epidemic that had entered national territory: "Yes, sin is the source of every calamity plaguing the Earth: vices ... dissolution ... licentiousness ... impiety ... cannot help but enflame His [God's] rage.... Mexico, in other times Catholic and religious, Mexico, privileged vine of the Lord, how have you become the vine of another, strange and odious to your God?"[53]

A minority of Mexicans were to blame.[54] They dazzled the people with unfounded ideas:

> Let our supposed philosophers cease to brag of being the deposi-
> taries of literature; there are no connections between science and
> impiety; there are no affinities between Enlightenment and irreli-
> gion; but there are, yes, and very tight ones, between disbelief and
> corruption of customs.[55]

Mexicans should reject all impiety without fear of distancing themselves from advances in knowledge of all kinds:

> This longing for amassing knowledge, this striving to record even
> the most hidden objects, this entirely philosophical freedom to
> speak freely of all the beings of nature, is not opposed, to say the
> least, is friendly to just submission, to the healthy servanthood due
> unto revelation.[56]

On 30 May 1833, two long letters to President Santa Anna would be signed by the cathedral chapter and general clergy of the Guadalajara Diocese. Both rejected the new law declaring patronage inherent to the nation. They declared the willingness of all signers to lose everything before yielding on this point. The first indicated the impossibility of supporting what amounted to a virtual schism. To avoid criticism, the cathedral chapter promised to instruct the people in obedience to authorities in all which "does not oppose the rights of God." It insisted on keeping "the greatest jewel we have received from our parents, which is the Apostolic Roman Catholic religion." Besides using nearly identical language, the second letter warned against the attempt to "destroy the majestic edifice of the Catholic Church and to convert it into a merely human society." The statement assured readers that no more than two or three percent of the Guadalajara clergy thought differently.[57]

On 19 December 1833, Diego Aranda, the governor of the mitre of the Guadalajara Church, found himself obliged to resist still another encroachment of the government on ecclesiastical rights: this was the law concerning Church property in mortmain.[58] Aranda demanded the repeal of a law which he saw as violating the constitutional statutes and convictions of the Mexican people, as well as attacking the Church. He immediately appealed to the constitutions of the state of Jalisco and the nation on the matter of ecclesiastical property and jurisdiction. Aranda recalled the sad history of the loans the Church had contributed to the state in the past, and insisted that a Catholic people could not make their political system independent of their religious beliefs. He did not believe the terms of the law forcing the Church to sell its properties could be met. Even if several obstacles were overcome and

> even if those presently vested with authority went beyond themselves in religiously fulfilling their commitments, as should be expected, who could promise the same in the circumstantial vicissitudes during which the individuals in whom supreme powers are vested necessarily change?[59]

In closing, Aranda called for harmony between the powers and referred to the authority of the Council of Trent. However, if the state did not yield, and even though he proclaimed himself "a subject" in civil terms, he threatened "terrible censure" on religious grounds.[60]

The convergence of radical liberal thinking and government action, both in Jalisco and the nation, had finally taken place in 1833. In this context, the appeal to state and national constitutions sounded hollow. Discrediting and threatening opponents seemed more in keeping with the moment, but did not resolve the ecclesiastical dilemma. The Church was waiting for and depending on events outside its sphere of control. One measure of this situation can be captured in a brief pamphlet from the middle of the year, when Pedro Tamés assumed the governorship of Jalisco. The document began with this – freely translated – verse:

> Without much fantasy
> Even the roughest reader
> Will see a certain analogy
> Between a good governor,
> And an ornamental comb.[61]

The document astutely suggested that new governor would find himself the subject of a struggle to determine his political direction. And it added:

> Poor young man, placed in the drag of human vicissitudes! It will not be easy for him to finish his term without feeling wounded by the insults of sanguinary pens. Such insults are very much in fashion.

This dilemma allowed the writer to "elaborate on the elegant comb" and his analogy with the course of the new governor:

> Because of its elevation, an ornamental comb is in the view of even the most indifferent observers, and subject to their examination. Such are the good and bad actions of a governor, which due to his high office cannot be hidden from the curious eyes of the people observing him. A comb is composed of a few teeth which hold back the hair and sometimes irritate the scalp. The government also has thorns which constantly prick whoever is holding its difficult reins. A well-placed comb is impervious to winds, which cannot move it out of place. That is how the governor should stand firm against the winds of adulation or mordacity, letting them all blow through freely. In sum, the more lovely the comb, the more delicate and breakable it is, a turn of the head can throw it to the ground, and shatter it into a thousand pieces.[62]

However, even though the fate of the Church depended on the weighty decisions the governor would take, pamphlets did not leave any room to doubt that what one called "the Polaresque race" was behind every measure contrary to the Church.[63] And the governor's situation could not be separated from the question at hand. Another pamphlet began with a different –also freely translated– verse:

Even if the Governor is not Polar
Taking what isn't yours is theft.
And if the owner is a Church or college
Beyond stealing, it's a sacrilege.
Saying this snatch is not impious
Is theft, is sacrilege, is heresy.[64]

This pamphlet alleged that the "reprehensible depredation" of the Church was continuing, despite the arrival of the new governor, as well as the attacks on the cathedral chapter, Guadalajara clergy, and the Church in general. Most of the pamphlet was dedicated to supporting the opening verse, condemning not only the sale of ecclesiastical property, but also its purchase, made on the pretext that the purchaser was not directly involved in obtaining it from the Church. Later on, the pamphlet explained and justified why the Governor was still allowed to take communion in the Church, despite everything that had been said, referring the matter to the consciences of the Governor, his confessor, the priest officiating the mass, and in the final analysis, to the ecclesiastical authorities.

A second pamphlet by the same author referred to "Polaresque sordidness" and the "leprousy of Polarism."[65] The pamphleteer refused to excuse the Governor, unless he distanced himself from both; he set out to detail once more the ideas of the previous pamphlet. He defended the clergy's property rights on the basis of ecclesiastical and civil arguments.

In a well-regulated republic, no one is denied this right, unless he has incurred the penalty of confiscation, or unless he is ruled incapable of governing himself wisely due to some vice of age, illness, foolishness, or madness. Supposing this, taking the wealth of the Church means stealing it, and denying the Church the right to administer what it is left, adds insult to injury. Such is the situation of the poor Church of Jalisco.[66]

Although Pedro Tamés had assumed the governorship on 1 March 1833, the situation was getting so difficult that he was not expected to last. The liberal legislation of the state of Jalisco pushed ahead, in April restricting the rights of Spaniards to own

and administer property, and by the end of the year passing the
law mandating sale of Church lands. Finally, on 13 June 1834, the
Governor belatedly began proceedings to derogate Decree 525,
on the sale of Church lands, but his initiative was blocked by the
Legislature. Faced with this dilemma, Tamés chose to resign.[67]

On 12 August 1834, as the direct result of the ouster of Vice-
President Valentín Gómez Farías, consummated by mid-June, José
Antonio Romero took office as the provisional governor of Jalisco;
on 29 November, he was legally elected governor. Immediately
after entering office, Romero launched anti-liberal policies, overturning the law on sale of Church lands, suppressing the civic militia
that sustained federalism, and closing the Institute of Sciences to
reopen instead the University and the College of San Juan.[68]

Constructing a New Legitimacy

In this new setting, the Guadalajara Church evidently moved
with singular gusto and resolution, looking to strike a suitable
political alliance. The words of disgust with liberal power in
1833 became, after 1834, solidarity with its overthrow and with
the establishment of a government that would restore the most
important parts of the previous balance of power. The attempt
to reconcile Church and state can be seen in one pamphlet from
this period. The pamphlet attacked the "brazenness of the riff-
raff" in trying to pass off as a product of the people something
which came solely from *Yorkinismo* (York Rite Masonry). Such
liberal pamphlets hardly reflected, the author claimed, even one
tenth as much popular support as the Cuernavaca Plan had
received in Guadalajara: "but now you see: the sanscullottes
figure that they alone make up the sovereign people...."[69] The
pamphleteer denounced the abuses of the former liberal government of Jalisco towards the press and the clergy, and in public
borrowing. "It was rightly said" of the fallen government "that
it could give the tyrants of Constantinople lessons in despotism."
The sale of Church lands, the abuse of government jobs, and the
manipulation of elections by a "government of demagogy" had
meant that the only ones lamenting the overthrow were members of "that loathsome and justly detested party [the York Rite
Masons], while the rest enjoy the liberty they had lost ... [and
which] they had anxiously longed for."

The legitimacy of the new government was not initially electoral, but the pamphleteer assured readers that it was authentic:

The claims to legitimacy of the government that fell were: intrigue, bribes to control elections, jobs to those who helped them, in a word, the votes of the [Masonic] lodges. With the people tired of suffering, the Central Army entered the capital, and immediately issued a pronouncement and named a junta of honorable subjects, lovers of the public good, to elect a new governor, district head, [and] municipal council – all made up of select men (who find themselves driven by the most lively wishes for the good of the community, and in order to achieve it, have set out to persecute the Masonic lodges, which is why they do not let anyone walk the streets without reason outside the normal hours, why they have banned fireworks, and why they have taken other measures the Freemasons complain of).[70]

The state of Jalisco supported the new government and exercised its popular will directly, without recourse to elections:

The pronouncement of the capital was seconded by the remaining towns in the state; and here is manifest the will of a free and sovereign people, which can forego whenever it wishes the rituals and formulas foreseen in the Constitution, since it has seen the fundamental pacts to which it owed its political existence shattered in a thousand ways, and finally when a sad and constant experience has taught it that those rituals and formulas have only served the triumph of bold sanscullottism.[71]

The new government immediately abused the power of decree as much as the previous government had: the legislation from 1833 was overturned. Juntas in each neighborhood chose the magistrates instead of the Masonic lodges the pamphlet claimed had formerly done so.

The author of this pamphlet defended the return of the Church's property and rights and also "that it might inherit just like even coachmen and prostitutes do." He demanded that Spaniards be returned their rights to property, condemned the right to inheritance granted to illegitimate children, and attacked the secret juntas and the Institute of Sciences "whose science is entirely coded in imposture." He denounced the fact that the public treasury was in complete disarray despite the appropriation of tithes and the floating of "enormous loans." He judged the past administration of justice to be anti-clerical and past promotion of education to be anti-religious. Decrying "that espionage in which the last government indisputably exceeded the despotic Spanish" regime, he praised "true liberty, which we will never confuse with its abuse, which demagogy so tenderly longs for." Against the "factious" who "wanted to call themselves the people of Guadalajara," a "virtuous army, honor and glory of Mexicans" had acted, "shattering with a single blow the ominous chains shackling the people and as a result giving them the precious gift of the sweet justice and moderated freedom which they now enjoy."[72]

The Church hastened to give its official approval to the new government. On 20 August 1834 it issued an edict; this expressly stated:

> The Lord took mercy on the latest of our ills, stretched out his merciful hand to dry our tears, and from one moment to the next allowed us to see in the capital of the Republic, sent by God, the Most Excellent Gentleman Antonio López de Santa Anna....[73]

The cathedral chapter saw Santa Anna as providentially inspired by the best sentiments of piety and religion, and thus,

> persuaded of the opinion of the Mexican people, he sliced with his invincible sword through the bonds which trapped the Church, restored Her peace, took Her under his protection, and with his energetic measures has since filled the flock of the pastor of our souls with joy.[74]

From "oppression," the Church had returned to "freedom," protected by "fundamental laws." Jalisco had been in the vanguard of "error" towards the Church, now, God had sent "the consolation we yearned for with such powerful longing: a government established by the votes of people, a government friendly to the dearest interests of its subjects, a government fully aware of the ills this Church has suffered." The chapter called for unity, peace and respect for the state and Church in their respective matters. They accepted that, even with the new government, there would not be civil enforcement of the payment of tithes or the fulfillment of religious vows which had been derogated the previous year. But they placed all the moral force of the Church behind the faithful's full compliance with both. Finally, the chapter invited all to a solemn religious ceremony in the cathedral on 28 August, where the "most divine Sacrament of our Lord" [the Eucharist] would be displayed all day. Similar ceremonies should be promoted across the diocese, the chapter suggested, and plenary indulgence was promised to anyone who confessed and took communion on these occasions.

Taking this further, the Guadalajara Church ended the year by printing a sermon preached on 12 December in honor of the Virgin of Guadalupe. This sermon demanded a ban on exporting metal coins from the country, an end to speculative loans, and, in dealing with foreigners, "avoiding direct contact, the origin of the most disastrous effects."[75] In addition to telling the history of the Virgin of Guadalupe's appearance in Mexico and recalling her meaning for Mexicans before and after independence, the preacher tied her to the unfortunate luck of the recently fallen "tyrannical government."[76] He asserted that

> Mary, under the name of Guadalupe, has become the special mother of Mexicans, and has taken us under her protection to cover us with gifts. Mary of Guadalupe has taken charge in America of the cultivation of the Religion of her beloved son, establishing it in a firm, certain, and constant way, defending it in all times against the blows of its enemies. But if Anáhuac, in general, has been at all times the object of the motherly tenderness of Mary, Jalisco, a noble and integral part of this illustrious Nation, has this time seen the proof of her decisive protection. When Guadalajara was waiting to see its streets bathed in blood, entering the buildings and covering the floors, it saw this theater of disasters transformed by the intercession of Mary of Guadalupe into the greatest of pleasures. Yes, Jaliscans, by the intercession of Mary your troubles have ceased.[77]

The reorganization of the foundations of politics in Jalisco and the federal government began in parallel with the Church's consecration of the overthrow of the 1833–34 liberal government. The new governor of the state insisted on the need for this change in his report at the beginning of 1835. He admitted the lack of solid advances for the moment "because of the countless ills brought to this soil by the barbarous and opprobrious domination of a disorganized, immoral, and impious faction, whose disastrous and malign influence had spread all across the republic." Yet order and public tranquility, the basis of all future progress, had been restored thanks to the "revolution" carried out based on the "saving plan of Cuernavaca." According to the Governor, this revolution had been "the most general, the most interesting, the most free and simultaneous one confirmed on our soil since that of independence." Its great promise for the future of the administration and the economy was because "everything had come from the people, and they never err in their true interests." From "oppression and tyranny," Jalisco had passed over to the "gentle yoke of justice and law." The state took its distance from "political fanaticism" and the "dazzling and cunning theories" which offered no firm foundation for the destiny of man.[78]

Romero claimed he had had to face a series of written complaints by the defeated faction, all vitiated in his view by the political record of their authors and by "the notorious slander they were riddled with, as well as the use of forged signatures" and like abuses, which constituted fraud. Yet the government had ultimately freed all those tried for this wrongdoing, at their own request. The success the government had achieved in this regard had not fully extended to the gangs "infesting the roads due to the general misery." Romero recognized that even if the law on persecution and conviction of delinquents was passed – as he was requesting – the greater need was for creating "means of subsistence and teaching proper morals."[79]

The "almost complete replacement ... of mayors and other functionaries" of Jalisco towns had already taken place, but the administration of justice by courts and the deteriorated prison system still caused the Governor worries. The prisons were far from readying criminals for a useful life, he insisted, and they also generated expenses for the public treasury. The disarray of public finance was credited to the dishonesty of the previous administration, to the high number of government employees, and to "excessive smuggling." The floating of a governmental loan was being arranged, and this would seek to "redeem ... all those individuals who, during the past administration, were attacked and extorted of substantial sums demanded by force." Recognizing that the public treasury "demanded a new organization or a significant reform," he also admitted he had not yet been able to achieve it. The Governor went over the need for a more functional reorganization of the tobacco monopoly, mentioned in passing the everyday work of the mint, and emphasized the support given to education along more traditional lines. He lamented that "the greater part of the towns in the state still" lacked "the first rudiments of public education." Pointing out that the government was struggling with a difficult situation in terms of hospitals, he allowed himself to "gleefully" note that the civic militia no longer existed.[80]

Concentrating on the question of government, Romero announced with evident joy that "the greatest intelligence and harmony reigns between this and the other authorities of the state, civil as well as military and ecclesiastical." A "council of government made up of individuals selected for their virtues and education" and a "reformed cabinet" were in charge of directing state affairs in Jalisco. He found it notable, especially in terms of the cabinet, that now "one no longer notes, as in the previous administration, odious rivalries, heated religious-political questions, and small-scale favoritism." Bureaucratic issues were no longer blurred into political ones. The politician admitted that agriculture was offering no appreciable signs of growth, and even if commerce was being promisingly reestablished after the return of peace, industry in particular was lagging behind; it had been negatively affected by previous recruitment for the civic militia and by the "excessive and shocking introduction of countless foreign goods." Once more, as he had done in his previous year's report, he demanded that the National Development Bank (Banco de Avío, created in 1830) be set straight to improve this situation. Mexico should not continue to be a volatile and scarcely profitable economy dominated by the mining industry, which produced wealth only for foreigners. Finally, he estimated that the growth of the population was nil, due to the effects of the cholera epidemic Guadalajara had just suffered. He closed with these ponderous words:

> I have told you with sincerity what is the current state of public administration in Jalisco. Here you have seen whether the state has improved or worsened during the period of my government, as well as the grave problems that are still present and weigh us down. With this knowledge, and since the people have declared that the time of reforms has arrived, there is nothing for you to do but apply opportune remedies.[81]

On 23 June of that year, the Jalisco Congress did in fact propose some remedies. The Congress' proposal began with a peculiar declaration of the rights of man:

> It is undeniable that, when for a long time a people have been unable, under the institutions that govern them, to achieve the joys

of free men and to find themselves protected, secure, prosperous, and happy, but instead have found themselves persecuted, attacked, miserable and unfortunate, then they are in need of unavoidably changing their form of government....[82]

In accord with the "general will, which is what forms true opinion and what gives life to governments and consolidates them," adhering to many written statements received from all parts of Jalisco, and at the initiative of the federal government, the Congress reached the well-founded conclusion that the establishment of a central government was necessary. The Congress noted the great differences between Jaliscans in property, talent, virtue, and religion, all of which promoted discord among the citizenry. The 1824 Constitution had not managed to resolve this situation,

and having as its basis the ominous equality it wanted to establish at any cost over all the classes in Jalisco, which Providence had separated to construct the harmony of society, republicanism formed a set of deceptive illusions so that a gang of ambitious and delusionary men might dominate the nation by decatholicizing it first.[83]

In practice, the republican system set up in 1824 had turned out to be "essentially anarchic, designed for intrigue, seduction, ambition, evil and disorder." The nation found itself stirred up by "the hurricane of armchair theories agitated by the most indecent and anti-social passions."[84]

Religion, property, liberty, safety, Church, order, decency: everything was attacked, profaned, and almost destroyed by the force of that rabble of anarchists who pompously called themselves federalists, constitutionalists, free thinkers, liberals, and so forth, invoking for their protection the 1824 Constitution with all its evils, which people of their ilk had broken and torn apart since 1828, which was always rendered null as soon as some partisan activity demanded its complete or partial overturning. Thus, since its existence was a sham, the entire nation found itself turned into a windmill exposed to the gales of the most reckless anarchism, from whose gusts we would have perished if the Heavens had not granted us such visible protection making ... appear that genius who today governs the destiny of the fatherland and who, with a strong hand, will stop, defeat, and destroy the monster of anarchy, giving a most decisive blow to sansculotism, tearing from the faces of false patriots the masks that concealed them, and removing from all [such] aspirants even the most remote hopes of ever again figuring on the public stage and prospering at the expenses of the people so vilely sacrificed until now.[85]

The Congress of Jalisco specifically requested a "central popular representative" government policy. It upheld religious intolerance along with independence, territorial integrity, the division of powers, and freedom of the press. It demanded the convocation of a constitutional congress, with the current members of the Federal Congress not excluded from candidacy. The standards for constitutional delegates should be set, they insisted, in such a way as to include

the three classes of the military, the clergy, and the property owners, with the last understood to include not only those with territorial property but also those who have an income, industry or profession which provides them with enough to live honestly, with no one who is not included in these classes being allowed to enter the constitutional congress.[86]

This Congress should be made up of a limited number of delegates, who would meet in a single chamber. The new national constitution should be written in a six-month period. It should allow for a presidency with a term of ten or more years, subject to reelection, and the first president – the Jalisco Congress proposed – should be Antonio López de Santa Anna himself. The proposed Federal Congress would be made up of two chambers, with representatives elected for four-year terms, but eligible for reelection without restrictions. Governors and political heads of states should have appropriately long terms – which were not specified – and superior magistrates should hold office perpetually. Instead of state congresses, there would be provincial councils (*diputaciones provinciales*) just like there had been at Independence.

In this way, political arrangements were meant to eliminate the possibility of new liberal agitation threatening the rights of the Church, property owners or the army.[87] The highest ranks of the Church were duly pleased. One 1836 sermon reinforced the support already given; the speaker, Francisco Espinosa, suggested that Mexico was on the verge of returning to the happy unity and harmony of 1821:

Oh, those happy days in which all Mexicans only longed for the freedom and greatness of their homeland! What unity in the Army! What fraternity among the citizenry! All were moved by the same spirit, all were led by the same interests. Days of peace and serenity! Days of glory and fortune! You passed by, like the lightning which shows the walker in a dense wood the way forward, then disappears, leaving him in the depths of a stormy night. What malign genius has destroyed our unity? Who has turned those who were friends into enemies? Detestable ambition, blind avarice, reckless impiety![88]

Everything had been destroyed by party spirit and tyrannical actions, above all in 1833–34. According to Espinosa, in the case of Jalisco it was the deceased General Miguel Barragán himself – now being honored – who had brought the Cuernavaca Plan to the state and made the righteous change without failing to be "patient and moderate with the factious, [and] contrary to persecution." In the eyes of Espinosa, this was what had earned Barragán the recognition of the people and the Church in the hour of his death.[89]

A Troubled Victory

Nevertheless, there are reasons to believe the high clergy of Guadalajara was exaggerating the restoration that had taken place, and underestimating the gradual shift that public opinion was undergoing. A change of government could not hold back this subtle transformation. In the following years, ecclesiastical discourse seemed to realize this. In 1837 and 1838 the Church published sermons with singularly other-worldly leanings, apparently signaling its growing anxiety.[90] In 1838, it published a long document which sought to refute opposition to Papal jurisdiction, the ecclesiastical hierarchy, and the sovereignty of the Church.[91] Similarly, the recently appointed new bishop, Diego Aranda, expressed mixed feelings in his first pastoral letter in 1837:

> What a sweet pleasure fills our spirit when we see all of you in the bosom of the Catholic Church, imbued with the Holy precepts of our Religion, animated by its spirit, nursed by its breasts and its doctrine, and far from the principles of impiety and licentiousness which have ruined so many, taking away their security and disturbing the peace and calm of their hearts! What unspeakable

satisfaction we experience in directing our words to a truly Catholic people, to so many wise and virtuous priests hard at work in the vineyards of the Lord, to so many faithful who have freed themselves from temptation and resisted the attempts to draw them away from the faith, and also to those *whose lips may blaspheme the holy and terrible name of the Lord but whose hearts are not ruled by impiety!*[92]

But he later became more cautious in his choice of words:

Circumstances are in fact very difficult, since we have to fight: against the devastating torrent of perverse books that has spread across our diocese, sweeping away with its poisoned waters many who have let themselves be seduced, more by adopting licentiousness in their customs than by adopting the maxims of impiety; against the corruption of customs which, in more than a few, has produced a neglect of the eternal precepts of the Gospels, which has separated them from their duties, and which has made them contradict in their actions the holy obligations they were joined to by Baptism; against the declared enemies of the Church who lose no opportunity to fight its respectable laws and its holy discipline; against … but *alas, we are not capable of enumerating all the obstacles and difficulties appearing everywhere we have a pastoral duty*, and we must render accounts of the sheep entrusted to our care at the severe tribunal of the Supreme Judge.[93]

Faced with such dilemmas, Aranda reminded priests that "we are the light of the world and we must shine like burning lamps in the temple of the Lord, dissipating the shadows of error and enlightening the people with truth…."[94]

At the beginning of 1840, Bishop Aranda once again expressed himself in terms which indicated that indeed, all was not well in Jalisco. He said his "heart was deeply afflicted at seeing the damage the errors of recent times – condemned by faith, reason, and good sense – have done to the heritage of Jesus Christ, and very especially to our beloved flock."[95] Later on, the Bishop commented with dismay that people preferred to celebrate civic heroes instead of those of the Church:

Ah, yes, let us celebrate enthusiastically the memorable events of the fatherland…. But shall we not celebrate those of our holy religion?… Let us remember with pleasure the days in which our liberty was proclaimed…. But shall we not remember those days in which the ominous chains of our servitude to the devil fell apart, in which the liberty of the children of God was declared? ... Let us bring to memory the heroes of the republic.... But shall we forget those the Church venerates, whose actions are more illustrious, more glorious?[96]

The Bishop lamented the lack of observance of religious holidays by the faithful. He was also scandalized by their use of free time during those holidays to devote themselves "to criminal laziness, to forbidden games, to profane entertainment, to indecent pleasures, to the excesses of gluttony ... and to all those disorders we see with bitter feeling to be the occupation of a considerable part of the people." The Bishop called Mexicans to remember the days in which religion and the Mexican people had been inseparable. He asked them to return to penitence and Communion at Easter, while he noted that not even on that occasion did "the greater part of the faithful in our diocese" confess, due to a lack of faith, misconduct, or mere laziness. On the other hand, he found cause for worry in the "unworthy communion" of people who could be considered "scandalous sinners."[97]

And do we lament [under such circumstances] that our misfortunes are multiplying, that peace has left us, that divisions torment us, that impiety and disbelief constantly threaten us, that wars tear us apart, that poverty is spreading, and that we are stricken by evils and misery?[98]

Aranda was aghast that many did not pay even a portion of the tithes they owed the Church. And he pointed to "wealthy landowners" in particular, who were supposedly the political allies of the Church since 1834, since "the poor ... generally make an effort to pay the tithe."[99]

Clearly, Bishop Aranda was witnessing a significant change in the social values of his diocese. But this was not happening only on a religious plane. Just as the political arrangement of 1834–35 had not managed to resolve all the differences between Church and society, or between Church and state, neither had it been able to shore up, as Governor Romero had promised, the economic and social well-being of Jalisco. The signs of discontent or sheer lack of interest in the new political situation began to be evident.[100] In parallel to Bishop Aranda's misgivings, a political movement emerged, marked by the revolt of Mariano Paredes y Arrillaga on 8 August 1841. Paredes, the military commander of the Jalisco garrison, painted an economic and social scene no less depressing than politically disconcerting. His vision was the perfect counterpoint to Bishop Aranda's views on religion. He foresaw foreign interventions and the dismemberment of the country. In matters of national defense, he considered things to be in utter disarray. The treasury overwhelmed the people, harming commerce, industry and territorial property. Copper coins were a cause of popular frustration, without any response from the government. Public credit was worth less "than that of the poorest citizen."[101] Paredes held that

> the new Constitution [of 1836] did not satisfy any of the hopes it had fed for the future of the fatherland; other hopes are conceived, desires are thrust forward, and there is not enough energy to suffocate excesses or enough dignity to listen to complaints.[102]

In Paredes' words, "the certain ruin of the fatherland" was on the verge of being consummated, and this went beyond any party allegiances.[103]

As a product of this movement in Jalisco and similar ones in other parts of the republic, the "Bases of Tacubaya" were produced on 28 September 1841. This political plan called for a national congress with the power to reform the Constitution of the Seven Laws. The year ended with Antonio López de Santa Anna installed in the presidency of the republic, and with Mariano Paredes serving as governor of Jalisco. When the elections for this congress were held in May 1842, the liberals won in Jalisco, and managed to control the Federal Congress. Mariano Otero became a congressman for Jalisco. He had already taken the opportunity to clearly show the strong idealism still held by certain liberal sectors. In a public speech in Guadalajara in late 1841, he emphasized the idea of an unavoidable, but orderly, march towards perfectibility. Remarking on the colonial era, for example, he noted that "once a man has thought, whatever the object of his meditations, he will learn to doubt, and to discern what is true from what is false. Then no tyranny, no power could introduce itself inside his head to scream at him in the impenetrable mystery of thought: DO NOT EXAMINE THIS!" The high ranks of bureaucracy, the army, the high clergy and the merchants had opposed independence, an action that was symptomatic because "this miserable fraction … lived off tyranny and abuses." But the change took place, gathering force despite the failure of its first sponsors, and the attempts to detain change by establishing a Mexican monarchy did not prosper.[104]

Otero went on to offer a vision of the unstoppable change Mexico had experienced since then. He firmly stated that "the republic is a fait accompli, against which the absolute power of one man will not prevail, whatever the title by which he calls his despotism...." Despite the constant struggle of factions and the maladies of the country, "social elements have improved greatly in this prolonged and painful drama, slowly changing the face of society."[105] No longer could parties captivate Mexicans with ancient "prestige":

> The time of words has passed, that of deeds is coming soon and – whatever the current complications of interests – Liberty, daughter of justice and preserver of order, and Equality, the most precious and fruitful of human rights, will be solidly established, aided by Christianity, whose spirit is eminently liberal and democratic. Such is the march followed today by free and civilized peoples, who have achieved the rule of liberty without terror or anarchy, and the influence of the Catholic religion without fanaticism or barbarism.[106]

Otero declared that "though we do not know the means for obtaining these results, we should doubt our own lights, and not those of God."[107]

But liberal ideals still had to contend with the anguish they provoked in the Church itself. The project for reforms presented to the Congress in 1842 caused deep unease among the high clergy of Jalisco. Perhaps the canons were behind a pamphlet questioning the foundation of this project. This pamphlet expressed fear that "anarchy" would be unleashed, which was exactly what a constitution should "prevent." The pamphlet's author, Juan Rodríguez de San Miguel, objected to the civil liberty decreed by the project, its implications for religion, and finally the regulating authority it proposed. Rodríguez rejected unlimited civil liberty, since this allowed attacks on the very constitutional statutes which were being established and, in his view, went beyond what France had allowed, not only in the 1830 Constitution but even in the Declaration of the Rights of Man in 1791.[108]

If the seeds of "sedition" and "anarchy" were being planted in the civil sphere, according to Rodríguez, then the same was being done in the religious sphere. The proposal sought to make only "direct" attacks on religion and morality illicit, and prohibited only the "public" exercise of another religious belief. The Catholicity of the Mexican nation was mentioned in Paragraph V and not in Paragraph I where, in Rodríguez' opinion, it should be, "as soon as it [the Constitution] speaks of the political being of the free and independent nation." Mexico owed "its civilization, its being, its institutions ... and its customs" to Catholicism. This was the "singular glory" of the Republic, and now reformers sought to spread "the seed of eternal disunity among future generations."[109]

A clear break between the temporal and the spiritual was not acceptable to Rodríguez, and he demanded that "the interests of religion and those of the state" be seen "as one and the same." Making an analogy to the Jewish people of the Old Testament, Rodríguez asked: "a people favored by the light of the Gospel, are they not a chosen and privileged people whose obligations are greater in proportion to the inestimable favor they have been given?"[110]

He immediately denounced the project's lack of limitations on freedom of the press and the fact that it left private education in complete freedom to choose an orientation, so long as it did not attack morality. He closed with the criticism that the regulatory power which blocked the excesses of the executive, judicial, and legislative powers was ruined by being set up in "an irregular and incomplete manner." The danger of abuses was still too strong.[111]

Shortly after Rodríguez' pamphlet was published, the Guadalajara Church published its own comment on this constitutional project, explicitly praising what Rodríguez had said. Dated 6 December 1842, this document sought to reconcile the patriotism of the cathedral chapter and its support for "the utmost prosperity, power and grandeur for the country" with its rejection of certain articles of the project. Significantly, in light of changing national opinions, the chapter declared that its statement would ignore political concerns, "concentrating on strictly religious ones." Then it went on to recapitulate, with a few modifications, what Rodríguez had written. One thing that had struck the chapter about the project was that, by establishing a single jury to address freedom of expression, it removed from the clergy the ability to classify abuses in religious matters. The chapter put its finger on this problem more clearly than Rodríguez: "From this it follows that a meeting of frequently illiterate lay people will decide what is contrary to dogma, therefore ruling on dogma like a judge."[112]

This was intolerable: "Who, no matter how much he wor-shipped civil authority, would dare to defend it?"[113]

The chapter also demanded greater protection of the property of corporations. Although the project guaranteed such property, it did so in language that lacked the clarity time had proven to be necessary to counter changing public opinions. The language in the Article about the exercise of patronage also caused the chapter worries; the chapter asked that it be modified. While its language might once have seemed innocent, "today we cannot let it pass, when later events [after the 1824 Constitution] have caused so much and such tremendous disillusion." The chapter wanted it to be perfectly clear that patronage was not inherent to national sovereignty. In addition, it insisted on questioning the govern-ment's right to permit or to block Papal communications with the Mexican flock.[114] The canons asked:

> In this age when so many generous efforts to spread enlightenment are made, and when anyone who impedes the spread of light among the people is seen as an enemy of society, in this very age, will keep-ing knowledge of the truths of the faith from men be considered a just, legitimate and rational right?[115]

Finally, the chapter objected to the extension of power granted to the Congress to oversee ecclesiastical affairs, drew attention to the dangers of a schism like that of England in the sixteenth cen-tury, and closed with a long quotation from the document by the Archbishop of Valencia already analyzed in Chapter Six above.[116]

The chapter's sensitivity to the need to adapt its defense of the rights of the Church to the ever more pronounced statist and liberalizing convictions of Mexican society should not be underestimated. This kind of tension has been evident throughout this study, and endured to the end of the period examined here. Before the end of 1842, a well-known Jalisco cleric made one more effort in this direction. He exclaimed:

> The Catholic religion! The nineteenth century! What a necessary connection! What a brilliant bond! What an important union for the human race! Who could detain, gentlemen, the race of time, to prove it to you with all simplicity, but with such truth as to neces-sarily win over every understanding capable of grasping it. I would invoke the century we live in; I would make it come to this very Temple; and before anything else, we would see it worship the cross

above our altar, and that action should be enough for all, a demon-
stration. What does this nineteenth century want? Does it love the
sciences? Geniuses admire Christianity, the sciences see it as their
benefactor, they follow it like a guide that does not let them stray....
Does the nineteenth century love liberty? With a cross in its hand,
religion congregates Jew and Gentiles, Greek and Barbarian, slave
and free: it tells all they are the same in Jesus Christ ...

What! Does the nineteenth century love glory? Christianity has
glory, that of the arts, that of literature, that of the sciences. If
our century is proud of its advances, let it see where the inspiration came from.[117]
And so the preacher went on for several pages more. It is worth
noting, and underscoring, that the moment the Church was celebrating with the resonant words of this friar was the dissolving, on
19 December 1842, of the Constitutional Congress the Church
had so objected to.[118]
Considering what we have just seen, it is surprising that on 1
May 1843, barely a month and a few days before the publication
of the Constitution of the Bases Orgánicas, product of the new
political situation, the Guadalajara Church should once again raise
its voice against this latest project. Even in political circumstances
now ill-disposed towards liberalism, the Church still found articles
it feared would be "pernicious." Freedom of expression and the
press was too broad and unrestricted for the Church, opening
the nation to suffering both in temporal and spiritual affairs. The
country was exposed to being divided on crucial matters, and in
consequence, to being immediately stirred up "by the action of
sectarians and the reaction of the faithful." The implications of
this complete freedom of expression, the Church suggested, was
government indifference towards "anti-social and disastrous atheism," while sectarians would begin to secretly "decatholicize" the
nation under the aegis of virtually official protection. This despite
the fact that the new constitutional project provided for the censorship of writings directly addressing dogma. "Catholic doctrine
is not fought only by attacking dogma, but also by attacking discipline and morality." The high clergy of Guadalajara insisted that
the circulation of banned books and irreligious imprints was not
fully eliminated, as it should be, in the new project. Even the
project the Church had opposed the year before had been more
explicit in blocking abuses of freedom of the press against dogma
and morality.[119]

Once again, the Church was excluded from deciding on what did – or did not – violate the law in religious terms. This time judges and not juries would rule on hypothetical infractions, but the result was essentially the same, with the corresponding ecclesiastical authorities excluded from the process. Putting the best face on the situation, the Church stated this must be a matter of a flawed phrasing of the article in question. It is likely, however, that that was not the case. On the following point, related to patronage, the Church found the new project slipping into the very same problems as the previous one. Once again, the high clergy spelled it out: the nation could not exercise patronage as an inherent sovereign right. The ideas of the "innovators" on this had already been sufficiently refuted, and the unified opinion of the bishops of Mexico had been shown to oppose such proposals in 1834. The document repeated the same objections as the previous year.[120]

It was strange to find such continuity between the two impugned projects, even at a moment of a political reaction against the authors of the first, but matters grew worse for the Church, since in the opinion of the high clergy of Guadalajara the new project even took away its special tax exemptions. Denying that the clergy was acting out of "personal views" and stating that they had suffered similar attacks in the past, which had not ceased, the clergy nonetheless rejected the opinion that they had the authority to accept this new legislation. The high clergy stated: "as for taxes, we have always been the first to pay them, even though the Mexican clergy has always been most taxed during all public emergencies, suffering special and strong levies above and beyond what the common citizenry have paid."[121]

In the face of the new tax policy, they hinted at passive resistance; they would not recognize its lawfulness, but they would not incite to violence. Any change of this nature had to be arranged directly with the Pope.[122]

This document also objected to the phrasing of the article granting discretionary power over Church appointments to the state and specifying governmental protection for Catholicism in Mexico, suggesting that the wording opened the door to religious tolerance, especially considering that another Article allowed foreigners to acquire real estate and become naturalized without any further requirement beyond requesting it.[123] The high clergy decreed:

> When dictating fundamental laws assuring the happiness of the Republic, it is unavoidably necessary to foresee all the evils which

could befall *the innocent Mexican people* in the future, it is necessary
to keep them from the scandal they would suffer with the establishment of sects, it is necessary to free them from the insolence
and daring of sectarians, and it is finally necessary to keep intact
the guarantee of Religion that was offered to them from the act
of independence, *along with their independence and liberty*. Everything
opposed to this, everything which opens the door to innovations
on religious matters, everything which attacks the rights of the
Church, everything that does not conform to the holy laws that
have directed the people until now, *is against the will of an immense
majority of the nation, which must always be respected.*[124]

The Bases Orgánicas of the Mexican Republic were passed on
12 June 1843. On 31 August, a decree made a government
license necessary for the sale of Church property, capping off
a series of similar measures. Jan Bazant states that the result of
these actions was that the government now controlled the whole
of ecclesiastical wealth, and so the Church could do little more
than await an open or hidden nationalization of its properties.[125]
Once again, the clergy recoiled. The Guadalajara Church was
not the first to dispute this right with the government, but it
closely followed the protest by the Bishop of Michoacán and the
responses of the corresponding government minister. By early
1844, despite the overturning of the decree in dispute, the high
clergy of Guadalajara supported the position of the Michoacán
clergy.[126] But the problem did not end there; 1844 was marked
by a series of deeply resented general tax assessments. If there
was still uncertainty in religious questions, the weight of a bankrupt economy could only worsen political disagreements.[127]

The response was not long in coming. On 26 October 1844,
the Departmental Assembly of Jalisco, with Pedro Barajas – cathedral canon – as its spokesman, demanded the government take
responsibility for the situation of the country and suppress the
extraordinary tax law of August of that year.[128] Another document
from the Assembly on 30 October, with Pedro Barajas again as
spokesman, called the ongoing situation "a dictatorship without
responsibility." If they had known this would be the result of the
1841 rebellion and the Plan of Tacubaya, "the nation would never
have adopted it, because among Mexicans no one who seeks
limitless power and [a political] organization without guarantees
can ever lead – or will ever be allowed to." The document
demanded that the treasury be brought under control, denounced

the actions of speculators, and called for the government to take "effective responsibility." In addition to overturning the tax law, the Assembly asked for the reform of those constitutional articles which were "contrary to the prosperity of the Departments."[129]

The words that Governor Antonio Escobedo added on this matter made it clear that unease was quite widespread in Jalisco.[130] The general commander of the Department of Jalisco, Pánfilo Galindo, seconded the actions of the Assembly, and General Paredes y Arrillaga did the same, by means of a special manifiesto.[131] Paredes proclaimed that

> today, the bankrupt nation resembles a cadaver abandoned to the voracity of the vultures. The treasury of opulent Mexico finds itself surrounded by inexorable creditors, by avid and insatiable speculators, by naked soldiers and hungry employees. What has become of public funds?[132]

The municipal council of Guadalajara, declaring that "the people were not made for the government," also joined the rebellion of Jalisco against the central government of General Antonio López de Santa Anna.[133] In early 1845, the Departmental Assembly demanded that the central government carry out constitutional reforms which would strengthen the fiscal, judicial, and politico-economic power of the departments. Frictions between Jalisco and the central government and instability in the departmental government continued through the rest of the year.[134] Beginning in early 1846, Jalisco found itself involved in a national struggle between monarchists and those who favored a return to the 1824 Constitution, until the latter triumphed in August.[135]

Church, Government, and People:
The Elusive Compromise

Returning to the 1824 federal Constitution on the verge of war with the United States meant that Mexican liberalism and statism, which had never been entirely opposed, would be firmly reunited. Once more, as in 1833–34, they could be allied both in the federal and state government, making it more difficult for the Church to resort to one or another level of government as an arbiter. The liberal statism of 1833–34 had been pushed aside with denunciations of its demagogy and dishonesty, which – opponents said – had allowed a handful of men to assume national sovereignty and grant themselves the spoils and offices of the state. Conservative statism after 1835 never fully came together, and in Jalisco led to the ironic situation of members of the high clergy linking up with federalist-inspired malcontents to attack and weaken the Santa Anna dictatorship, which absorbed money without any apparent limits. When faced with the threat of the United States, there seemed for a brief moment to be a possibility that Jalisco society would unite, the rich and the poor, laity and the clergy, pooling their efforts to meet the challenge of the moment. But the state's temptation to seize ecclesiastical properties was too great. Once more, 1847 marked a great confrontation between the clergy and the reborn liberal state — materially bankrupt and with its sovereignty threatened — and ultimately precipitated debate over the now long-standing issue of national goals. Pamphlets on this point, while not particularly innovative, were very numerous.[136]

It seems pointless to review here the well-known clerical arguments about Church property, but one small pamphlet directed to a large public is particularly interesting. The pamphleteer asked:

> Until when, privileged nation, worthy of being the first of all the nations of the globe, will you be a toy for the whims of one demagogue or tyrant or another? How far have you fallen, once magnanimous people, that you do not see, that you do not sense, they are leading you to the slaughterhouse, like a flock of sheep? Do you not realize that those who today unfortunately rule your destiny are the same ones who in other bitter times made you cry rivers of tears?[137]

The pamphlet accused the liberals of violating the 1824 Constitution in the 1846 legislative elections, but, it added, that was the least of their sins. The larger problem was that the possibility of national union was once again slipping away:

> Unfortunate nation! What genius of the abyss always mocks your most agreeable and solid wishes? When you thought that by reestablishing the 1824 Constitution a new era of fortune and prosperity would open up to you; when you promised yourself that a congress of wise, patriotic and judicious representatives would cure such deep and still-open wounds, would close the doors through which countless evils have been introduced, and would constitute you as a stable nation analogous to your circumstances, you find yourselves with some men affected by revolutionary vertigo and the mortal

contagion of party spirit, who instead of uniting, divide, who instead of building, destroy, who instead of dedicating themselves to fixing various branches of political and civil order, ignore them and overturn everything because they won't lift their thumb from proposals for ecclesiastical reforms which are not their responsibility.[138]

The pamphlet continued to question the legitimacy of the attack on Church wealth, especially the law of 13 January 1848, which made it the guarantee for a loan the federal government would arrange for up to fifteen million pesos. There was the insinuation of fraud in the vote of the National Congress, and the suggestion that the wealth of the Church would be subject to the avarice of speculators because of this "sacrilegious looting." Resorting to the now well-known arguments about the protection the 1824 Constitution promised the Church, the pamphlet asked how the Church would survive without clergy, and how the clergy would survive without wealth to sustain it. It ended by referring to Article 112 of the Constitution itself, which expressly stipulated that "the president cannot occupy the property of any individual owner, or corporation, nor disturb their possession, use or employment of it." In addition, the government was failing in its duty, as announced in Article 101, of ensuring adherence to the Constitution.[139] Therefore,

if the Constitution is not kept by the supreme powers themselves, if they do not measure their actions against it; if we are not to be ruled by wise laws, but by whim; if the rights of citizens are invaded, if there is no public or individual safety; if properties are no longer guaranteed, then social ties have now been broken, citizens' obligations towards society have ended; each of us has the right to arm himself in self-defense; and in this case, the life of a savage offers a thousand times more advantages to hapless man than life in society.[140]

In the opinion of this pamphleteer, Mexican political life was on the verge of dissolution.

If political life was in such dire shape, with such important consequences for Church–state relations, then what was taking place inside the Church and in its bonds with society? Judging by the pastoral letters of Bishop Aranda between the mid-1840s and his death in 1853, one would have to conclude that the religious situation was no less agitated than the political one. In 1845 the Bishop called priests to live exemplary lives and periodically take spiritual retreats. He wanted priests to be "clear mirrors where the beautiful splendor of holy actions are reflected."[141] And this can be properly understood to respond not only to the abuses he recognized had made their way into the priesthood, but also to the slackening of religious practice of the faithful he had denounced in another pastoral letter shortly before.[142]

By 1847, the bishop found himself immersed, like all Mexicans, in the difficult problem of the war with the United States. While willing to cooperate economically and morally in the war effort, he was not willing – as already seen – to entirely sacrifice the Church's property rights over its goods. Aranda interpreted the misfortunes of war and the "threat to our nationality" as products of Mexicans' straying from the Christian path. In his pastoral letter of that year, he asked, "What precept of the holy and immaculate law has not been scandalously broken? What commandment of the Church is not scorned?" The Church was under attack. "Woe unto this sinful nation!"[143]

In 1848, the Bishop denounced the existence of a "spirit of delusion and lies" in the nation. Novel ideas were spreading "imaginary notions of enlightenment" along with "specious notions of happiness," flattering people with "deceptive hopes for wealth and abundance, with false theories, with sublime discourses...." Because of the damage being done to the republic, the bishop allowed himself to speak of a "homicidal sect," opposed to "our religion ... our fatherland ... and our families...." Due to the "gullible leanings of the people towards novelties," these ideas had reached "colossal stature." In the middle of his pastoral letter, the Bishop addressed himself to the president of the republic, speaking out against "tolerance" as he stressed the country's social and constitutional commitments to the Catholic religion.[144]

Rejecting the colonization of the country by non-Catholics under any pretext, the Bishop argued that Catholicism had harmonized the coexistence of different races in Mexico and avoided a caste war. He sternly assured the president that "truth and justice are not what must be reconciled to the times; the times must be reconciled to truth and justice." The separation some wanted to make between individual man and social man was totally specious, he added. All of society should be consecrated to God, not exclusively dedicated to temporal matters, and "society, no less than individuals, should offer adoration to its God."[145] In another pastoral letter from 1848, the Bishop had declared that "the enemies who at one time fled now have prevailed, and in order to punish our presumptuous confidence, God has afflicted a nation once glorious and flourishing with healthy humiliations."[146] At the end of the year, Aranda condemned the fact that

> there reigns everywhere, and *in every class*, a certain spirit of tolerance and indifference which endures everything and tolerates anything except the truth which, in the midst of such a striking alteration of ideas and principles, lies beaten down and scorned, even by the very ones who, without having joined under the banners of error and impiety, follow in full, or pretend to follow a middle road between religion and the age....[147]

Surprisingly, the Bishop did not only attack the reading of openly heretical or impious books; the prelate was looking further still:

> The present century has inherited more than it might at first seem of the vices which afflicted the last century: atheism in principles and sensualism, or better stated, materialism in customs. On the last point, one could even say that the current century goes further in perversity than its father. Impious and irreligious as the last century was, it did however have a greater abundance of noble, moral and decent ideas, and literature had not been corrupted to the degree we see today.
>
> Since a few years back, literature under the name of "romanticism" has not only strayed from the path, not only forgotten decency in all its details or aspects, but also has openly and shamelessly proclaimed and enshrined the most scandalous and impious cynicism, striving to establish, so to speak, another morality in opposition to that of the Ten Commandments developed and perfected in the Gospel.[148]

But the bishop did not waver from the Church's struggle to reconcile "Enlightenment properly understood" to Catholic beliefs, a struggle underway for a harried half-century. He quoted Saint Jerome to support his opinion on the matter:

> No one takes his daughters to a bordello so they might learn to detest prostitution there; no one entrusts his son to a band of thieves so they might teach him to be valiant and bold; no one knowingly raises the sail on a broken ship to teach themselves how to escape a shipwreck, and you: you propose to read impious and

heretical books, at no risk to your souls, in order to study the truth in them?[149]

As late as 1852, in his last pastoral letter, Bishop Aranda continued to be almost obsessed by these same religious problems. Once more he reminded his flock:

Luxury, which we did not know, and which is already starting to make its fatal effects felt, which augments as public misery grows; the multitude of houses of iniquity, where the poor and the neediest are sacrificed by means of fraud and usury, which is condemned by every law: do these not clearly manifest the degree of moral degeneration we have reached? Sordid interest, whimsy and individual opinion, regulators of the limits of the just and unjust; the general lack of restraint of this century which rushes on, without finding any dam to hold it back; the mad presumption of thinking ourselves better than our parents, more enlightened than all the centuries which have come before us; our tenacious obstinacy in rejecting at once the lessons of experience and the warnings of misfortune. These are the excesses which have risen up to the throne of the living God.[150]

But the Bishop immediately went on to offer, by means of a new encyclical from Pope Pius IX, whose own rule was so difficult, means for the flock of Guadalajara to obtain plenary indulgence for their sins.[151] For Aranda, impelled by his office, never lost hope of making his flock respond to the "honor and religion which the Mexican nation boasts of in all the world."[152] This is the underlying message of the strong theocratic accent assumed by the sermons of the Guadalajara Church, as noted in Chapter Four. This is also the reason why one of those sermons, on 12 December at the commemoration of the appearance of the Virgin of Guadalupe, could assure listeners – perhaps with a certain excess of optimism – that "Mexicans have passed through furious storms, and their beliefs have emerged pure and unmixed with any others. Everything has changed ... [but] in this country God is not invoked with the lips and denied with the heart." In the Virgin of Guadalupe, incontestably, "in you the bedrock of principle which will save Mexico is being revealed ... and whoever follows her, will rise to the Heavens."[153]

In supporting the return of Antonio López de Santa Anna to the presidency in 1853, the Church of Guadalajara seemed

authentically inspired by hope for the political and social regen-
eration of Mexico, but we must recognize that the background
for this political action was far from calm or reassuring. While
the war with the United States seemed to have brought about a
political turning point in which Mexican conservatism could try
to provide a definitive solution to the prolonged national crisis,
the inability of traditionalism to adapt to changes in the years
after 1835 and to other shifts, not only liberal and statist ones, but
also the less noisy appearance of a new social morality in Mexico,
seemed to augur poorly both for clerical conservatives and innovators in 1853. Everything indicates that the victory of the Plan of
Ayutla took place within a much more complicated social setting than its authors could have foreseen. Even those supporting
the Santa Anna government in order to bring precipitous change
to a halt had themselves been caught up in the complex process
of cultural renovation and nation-building that so characterized
the nineteenth century. Different and antagonistic tendencies had
rocked the Santa Anna government from the start. Its demise, in
the midst of the triumph of its most dictatorial tendencies, not
only defrauded outright conservatives, but left moderate liberals
and progressive conservatives equally adrift.[154]

Previously, in 1833, the Guadalajara Church had located its
problems in Mexico in the abuses of a government all too ready
to exceed its popular mandate in questions of religion. When
the constitutional pact of 1824 had worn thin, Churchmen had
appealed both to the higher purpose of religion and to its stabiliz-
ing effect on human society to guarantee its privileged position in
Mexican society. But the conservative government which followed
had been unable to stem economic crisis and resorted to increasing fiscal pressure on the Church. Thereafter, the Constitution
of 1843 and the return to the Constitution of 1824 in 1846
failed to right the balance in Church–state affairs. As the pastoral
letters of Bishop Diego Aranda so graphically show, increasingly
the Church realized that the problem was not simply in government. The people of Mexico were showing signs of new values
which were either indifferent or hostile to the Church. Aranda
suspected that European trends against the Church were making
themselves felt in Mexico. He died in the midst of a crisis, holding
fast to his belief in the deep Catholic faith of the Mexican people
but fearing the devil had been unleashed in his beloved nation.

The initially limited political goals of the revolution of Ayutla would quickly be surpassed in questions regarding the Church. To explain this, it may be necessary to grant that Bishop Aranda was right in seeing not only legislative excess but also new popular values as twin sources of a tidal change in the Mexican socio-political arrangement. Yet he desperately held to the long-standing belief in a providential role for the Mexican people in history, and he chose to trust in their defense of the nation's Catholic faith.

Conclusion

D uring half a century of Bourbon Reforms, independence struggles, and nation-building, the Guadalajara Church had sought to find a way to positively and creatively address the modernization of Mexico. As new social goals and values came to the fore, creeping secularization threatened to dislodge the Church from its privileged role in Mexican society and to diminish its status relative to the state. The Guadalajara Church responded energetically and enthusiastically to the demand for regional economic development and accountable governance and sensitively to the cry for renewal in intellectual life and education. Yet the clergy were hampered in their adjustments once the independence struggle made clear that the changes might mark a potentially absolute dividing line between the past and the present.

Once the clergy had reconciled with Independence, after 1821, the major stumbling block was persistent and growing anti-clericalism under the federal republic, between 1824 and 1834. While fighting to maintain a constitutionalist and progressive stance during those years, clerics evinced a growing sense of defensiveness and even embitterment. As they became convinced that Jacobin politicians would not listen to their arguments, they increasingly resorted to the Mexican public at large as the audience for their ideas and the aim of their political actions. In so doing, they elaborated the idea of a Mexican nation with a divine calling.

Still espousing the need for economic development and responsible government, the clergy appealed to a holistic concept of the nation which might counter a narrowed notion of "the people" manipulated by Jacobin political actors. This propelled the clergy toward the ideological justification of the ouster of Vice-president Valentín Gómez Farías in 1834, and a deep commitment to the governments which followed. Significantly, this political mobilization did not resolve pending issues between the Church and the state in Mexico, nor did it eliminate those movements in Mexican society and values which were pushing toward secularization. Churchmen were forced to defend the traditional links between the Church and the state, and between the Church and the Mexican people.

Not surprisingly, the Church was prepared for the challenge. Already during the independence struggles, and especially in the discourse welcoming the achievement of Independence in 1821, the clergy had worked out key aspects of a vision of the Mexican people with a providential destiny. This discourse would consolidate in the 1830s, as the Church witnessed the liberal program of 1833–34 and the unstoppable secularizing drift of society and the state thereafter. In fact, this holistic idea was the basis for clerical traditionalism, which was broad enough to accommodate a wide spectrum of political ideas and modernizing notions.

During the first ten years after independence, Church thinkers increasingly pointed to the need to resolve the patronage issue in order to settle outstanding problems between Church and state. In 1833, these traditionalists shifted from the multi-faceted theme of patronage to a single, key concept: now they spoke of "religiosity." The idea of "religiosity" was the clerical response to patronage claimed by the state on the basis of popular sovereignty. If the state could subsume the will of the people by way of popular sovereignty, then the Church could absorb the people into the "religious" people, the faithful people. There are clear parallels between sermons from 1821–23 consecrating Independence before the rise of the republic and those made after the Gómez Farías-Mora government, when clerical orators once again raised up the Mexican people as standard-bearers of a divine mission.[1]

Between 1824 and 1826, in keeping with the agitated first phase of the republic, anonymous clerical spokesmen had disputed radical liberals' supposed representation of the people. Yet even while trying to check the liberal advance and its ascendance over the state, the Church also insinuated its willingness to confirm a state power of such dubious popular lineage. The believing people, the numerical majority of the people, clerical spokesmen suggested, had no quarrel with the Church or Catholicism, so long as changes made to the state respected this, no problems were foreseen. In this sense, while clerical spokesmen may have underestimated the extent of the real change in the sovereignty exercised by the state, they can hardly be thought to have been fundamentally wrong. They can be called skeptics about this Mexican political transition, but one must admit they were also realists.[2]

The reorganization of the Mexican state was successful within very limited parameters. Its true reach remained to be defined, but it definitely did not extend so far as liberals came to assert. Out of realism and skepticism, the Church supported the new transition. The new citizenry with a voice, a category which did not clearly include all Mexicans, should include the Church itself. If the extension of civil rights encompassed the Church, then just like other beneficiaries, the Church could defend itself against potentially arbitrary power exercised by the state. In general, clerical spokesmen saw an unassailable and popular – although hardly universal – benefit in this change. What they feared was that liberals would appeal to the "people," arbitrarily and demagogically, to seize control of the state.

Thus was born the specter of a new statism even more absolutist and more threatening than the one that was dying. This process had to be stopped, and the changes orchestrated by the state had to be limited, by questioning what the popular will truly was. The Church basically applied this astute judgment to matters affecting Catholicism and the Church. In so doing, it defended its interests in the way preached by the liberalism then in vogue. Only with great difficulty could the Church reach agreement with other privileged groups in society since, given the grave economic and social crisis of the nation, no individual group wished to bear the cost of healing national ills. The Church claimed that its interests coincided with the interests and convictions of the majority who were opposed to a strong, arbitrary and fiscally taxing state and to any change in the official national religion, but other groups would have to defend their own special interests and bring them into line with the rest of the nation.

Between 1833 and 1834, all the questions related to patronage came to a head, thanks to the actions of a state determined to assert its ideological and political hegemony and resolve its fiscal crisis. By contrast, between 1835 and 1846 a new state with limited representation took power. Access to political office was first limited by income and literacy requirements. Later on, in 1846 –

perhaps too late to matter – a proportional formula was used to allocate political representation among various groups, according to their perceived political and social weight: property-owners, merchants, miners, industrialists, magistrates, administrators, clergy and military officers. Voting was indirect and restricted, and official posts were not effectively open to any Mexican.

The Church struggled to regain control of the spiritual destiny of society by means of sermons and pastoral letters, while the previous, agitated period continued to have a lasting impact. The language of religious nationalism grew more intense. Attempts at reform followed, even of ecclesiastical education, but contradictions were prevalent. The state that emerged from the Constitution of the Seven Laws (1836) did not support Church efforts to continue collecting tithes, even if overall ecclesiastical administration of tithes was restored. Other notable internal divisions delayed and complicated the unification of traditionalist forces. There were differences of opinion about the constitution of a supreme conservative power, a certain lingering political deference towards the liberal or statist tradition, and, to be sure, the still-evident influence of liberal forces themselves, on behalf of individual rather than corporate representation. In the end, traditionalists became vulnerable to the reemergence of the Mexican liberalism whose radical expression they had fought against.[3]

The 1830s clearly show the danger of using liberal movements as period markers and defining all other political activities on their basis. This approach fixes on making exalted liberalism the paragon of political virtue in Mexico; it threatens to divert a scholar from truly examining the forces in opposition and analyzing the social structure on its own merits. Such an approach predisposes the historian toward a self-fulfilling vision of doom. It is eminently teleological and therefore anything but truly historical: reducing the possibilities of analysis, instead of opening them up, it overemphasizes a single type of confrontational documentation. Rather than sparking questions, this approach turns the history of Mexico over to the complacency of established knowledge, judging the whole of its historical movements from a position of interpretative intransigence.

The rising liberal movement appears to have split after 1827, a year which had seemed to promise a splendid future by marking the eclipse of the more conservative Scottish Rite Freemasons. Liberal fortunes peaked and declined due to liberalism's own internal divisions. The government of Vicente Guerrero did not enjoy the support of all liberals. When it was overthrown, the former vice-president, Anastasio Bustamante, could take the presidency with quite widespread support. Yet the turn taken by the new government, leading it further and further away from liberalism, did not spark a swift and coordinated response.[4] Instead, there was a panorama of confusion and opposing opinions. The new liberal government of 1833–34 did not fundamentally alter this situation; what the government did was attempt to shore up the dwindling strength of the national state. Lacking a solid fiscal base and overshadowed by the authority and omnipresence of the ecclesiastical bureaucracy, the state would be strengthened by appropriating part of the Church's wealth and by restricting the Church's multiple roles in civil society. The forced sale of clerical property would generate taxes for the government. Once ecclesiastical property and lands were in the hands of private owners, they would be subject to direct taxation by the state, without any debate about legal principles. Thus the liberal program of 1833–34, which included a cultural component in plans for revamping education, promised to grant the national state a power it had never known.[5] The state was on its way to becoming the great articulator of national life. It would have a power that neither the passive Hapsburg nor even the newly active Bourbon state had known. Thus came the paradox of a national state that became strong and interventionist in the name of liberalism.

The inherent problem with this process was that it assumed strong popular support for the state and discounted the clerical capacity for response. The program had the gift of simplicity in its outline and clarity in its goals, but it was not politically viable, because even though the state opted for the path of confrontation, it lacked the support necessary to win. Instead of serving to close up differences between liberals, already evident for some time, this unraveled them further. Since the program did not enjoy solid support even among its likely adherents, its proponents were open to accusations of factionalism and "tyranny" which were not long in coming. The clergy could seek alliance with all those forces who, adhering to the republican tradition so carefully cultivated by clerical pamphlets since the 1820s, might reconcile themselves to the Church as an active institution with a voice in the new society.[6]

The Church was definitely opposed to an overly strong state – the Bourbon version of absolutism had done it serious harm – and it did not turn towards anti-republican state formulas at this time. The Bourbons had first used the Church and then denied it a portion of its power, only to immediately prove incapable of leading civil society, which slipped out of its control after the Napoleonic invasion and the Cortes in Cádiz. After the failure of a Mexican monarchy under Agustín de Iturbide, a republic in Mexico, by contrast, promised that the state would never again lose its bond with the people. The Mexican people were the best guarantee that this form of government would protect the Church. The question then became one of eliminating the possibility that "factious" politicians might control the republic.

This ecclesiastical discourse appeared during the mid-1820s and became deeply entrenched after 1833. As a result of this, what the Church ultimately proposed was a republic under the tutelage of the national government. This tutelage had already been tested in the 1820s, with the constant recourse to federal power in Church–state conflicts, in Jalisco. Once the Church had found Mexican liberalism wanting, it pushed for a centralized republic which might ensure the "truly representative" character of the government. Mechanisms for judging and overseeing government acts had to be created, since the federal government of the first republic had ultimately failed to effectively do so. After the presidency of Guadalupe Victoria (1824–28), the clergy held, the rise of the most hard-line liberals had subordinated the government to them.

There were no effective intermediaries between the people and the government, so once control of the government was lost, there were no guarantees. The existence of such mediating spaces between the people and the government had to be ensured, so that no government could ignore them. One of those spaces would naturally be the Church, but the Church did not think of assuming for itself all popular representation; it joined other social sectors at this socio-political conjuncture. In addition, the structure of government should include mechanisms for "slow" representation and others for "swift" representation – that is to say, representation should be divided into short- and long-term aspects. In this way, no sudden and surprising movement could use the government to carry out arbitrary acts, since long-term representatives would block it. If short-term movements advanced projects that took root, there was the hypothetical possibility that they could be implemented directly or with the slow transformation of the long-term watchdog representation. The formula of basically bifurcated representation, which ended up being repeated on different levels, allowed an appropriate and necessary – according to its proponents

– path to be opened between the clergy's now long-standing adherence to republicanism and their growing anger and indignation at attempts to marginalize and discredit them. The Mexican Church had not yet been so discredited among the people as to be easily eliminated from the political arena.[7]

Only a revival of intermediary bodies and a surgical intervention on the model of political representation could make the Mexican Church and state compatible once again. By carrying out this transition, however, the Church found itself in a position of openly returning to the Hapsburg model of the state as an arbiter which drew strength from its mediation between rivals within civil society. The Bourbon state had made a partial transition towards a clearly hierarchical state, following the French model; liberalism in the 1820s and 1830s threatened to consummate this process by making everyone equal to the common people and establishing the state as their transparent representative.[8] The problem was that once the corporate bodies had disappeared, who were the people? If civil society was not strong and dense enough to imprint its hegemonic seal on the government, then anyone who momentarily occupied the government could effectively declare himself the spokesman of the people. That is to say, from this perspective the liberal state postulating itself as emerging from popular sovereignty could turn out to be an arbitrary government momentarily in charge of the state due to the need for administrative renewal set by electoral law. Liberal demagogy could take over, altering the natural course of events.

By the mid-1830s, clerical republicanism became an attempt to rebuild the old basis of Mexican civil society. The republic of the Seven Laws was a corporatist republic on Hapsburg lines guided by the clergy. It was not openly aristocratic, since there was no tradition and no foundation for aristocracy, as Otero and De la Rosa had rightly argued.[9] It was an attempt to bind the leading lights of civil society to the pattern of republican government, and to block the mandate of latter-day savants and whimsical men of letters. Mexico in the 1820s had been the country of reason finally set free, the country of untrammeled debates where ideas flowed swiftly clothed in satire, irony, and biting wit. In the late 1830s, Mexico was not oriented toward reason as a liberating force in itself, but ordered around the nature of popular sovereignty and truth. Reason and rationality were capable of error; the people, guided by demagogues, was also prone to err. Only when guided by providence would reason and the people be oriented

towards truth and appropriate representation. Thus the Mexican
people – as a whole – once more had to be elevated to the level
of the new Israel that had been glimpsed in the early baptism
of Independence by the Church. However, the Church did not
wish to struggle with the state for temporal power in too direct
or constant a fashion.

The appeal to Providence as the guide for Mexicans and the
accompanying self-criticism of the Church as a human institution
were fully compatible, however curious this may seem at first.[10]
Paradoxically, this logic allowed the Church to endorse earlier calls
for improving itself at the same moment when it effectively gave
signs of directing civil society. At this moment of apparent satisfaction, the Church's moderation and ongoing efforts to respond to
critics are evident. Once more this revealed that the Church recognized the need to respond to the political and moral demands
of society. More effective internal cohesion required this; the
Church's social prestige and search for social hegemony made it
indispensable.[11] What this demanded was maintaining a constant
presence in the political shifts of the new nation. The immediate
outcome of political events forced the Church to take on a more
active role than previously in discourse about political power. It
now went from being the conscience of Mexican politics to being
its *eminence grise*, but this very step would weaken the Church in
the long run, by burdening it with the responsibility for political
actions that it could have otherwise avoided.

A more lasting contribution would be elevating the Mexican
people to a new level in political discourse. The clerical critique
of the representative character of the state would collapse along
with the Mexican state and army under the weight of their failure
to stop the U. S. invasion in 1847. After that date, the imperative
need for a strong state was unavoidable. The two sturdiest bodies
of society, the one almost civil (the Church) and the other a more
direct part of the government apparatus (the army), had proved
worthless in the face of external threat. Now, the representativeness of government – relative to civil society – took a back seat
to the need to defend the integrity of the Mexican nation, and
it was precisely the Church which, with its discourse from the
mid-1830s forward, had given real and independent life to the
concept of the "Mexican nation." By seeking protection in the
heart of the people, the Church resorted to the idea of a chosen
and privileged nation which did not depend on itself, but on
divine providence.

From the 1850s forward, liberal governments would have to reconcile their growing strength with the idea of defending the divine mission and transcendence of the Mexican nation against outside threats of extinction. The violent and aggressive foreign presence on the Mexican stage would end up weakening the Church as a political force, but not before elevating its nationalist message to new heights. The opposing Mexican positions of universalist liberalism and religious nationalism would start off down a long path of conflicting interactions.

It is true that the Mexican Church had important influence over civil society, which it tried to mobilize as it had instinctively done in the 1830s, but it is strangely appropriate that its deepest ideological impact was on how Mexicans viewed their destiny as a nation. The Church created for Mexico a line of continuity from an ethnic indigenous past, passing through providential Hispanic Christianization, down to the independence and republicanism of a people who had hypothetically reached adulthood.[12] The government of Mexico had gone from imperfectly reflecting the opinions of the corporate bodies and other component groups of society to tentatively representing the "people," but since there was no quick solution to the ancient problem of who the Mexican people were, only the idea of a providentially chosen nation could resolve this dilemma and enable the option for the whole to overcome the problem of the parts. The concept of nation provided the mold for containing the still-smoking and shifting lava of the heterogeneous elements of Mexico. While the Mexican bourgeoisie turned to governing with the help of foreign capital in the last quarter of the nineteenth century, the sense of a "nation" with a destiny could effectively hold back any assault on the state as such. The government in power could be seen as in the service of national destiny.

In many ways, the government continued to be the bureaucratic shell inherited from the Bourbons, lacking effective popular sovereignty to guide it, since it hardly mattered that sovereignty was popular if there was no effective definition of who the people were who should orient it. The great contribution of the Mexican Church was to provide the missing link that finally substituted for Spanish royal sovereignty: the providential nation. This created a bridge between a people who apparently could not be reduced to a common denominator and a government which was not politically accountable because of the fragmentation of civil society. In the providential vision, the "Mexican nation" both already existed and was being remade. It was a reality and a project for the future. From this point forward, no government could, in principle, be irresponsible, given this paragon of legitimacy; every government would have to legitimate itself in the eyes of the nation in the making. No portion of the people was paramount over the great, providential nation. The government would not be responsible to any one group in particular, and thus would enjoy some of the well-known leeway of the old Spanish regime, but it would no longer be accountable to no one: it now had to justify its actions before all sectors by appealing to the course and project of the nation. In this discourse, the modern popular Mexican state was born.

Notes*

Notes to Introduction

1. See Lesley B. Simpson, "Mexico's Forgotten Century," *Pacific Historical Review* 19 (1953): 113–21; Andrés Lira and Luis Muro, "El siglo de la integración," and Enrique Florescano and Isabel Gil Sánchez, "La época de las reformas borbónicas y el crecimiento económico, 1750–1808," in *Historia General de México* (Mexico: El Colegio de México, 1976), vol. 2., 83–181, 183–301. It is true that historical studies on the nineteenth century are making significant advances, as can be seen in Leslie Bethell (ed.), *The Cambridge History of Latin America, Volume III: From Independence to c. 1870* (Cambridge: Cambridge University Press, 1985), 841–913; Stephen R. Niblo and Laurens B. Perry, "Recent Additions to Nineteenth-Century Mexican Historiography," *Latin American Research Review* 12 (1978): 3–45; and Robert Potash, "Historiography of Mexico since 1821," *Hispanic American Historical Review* 40 (1960), 383–424. Even so, for the Mexican case there is still nothing which covers the first half of the century as well as Daniel Cosio Villegas (ed.), *Historia moderna de México* (Mexico: Hermes, 1955) covers the period from 1867 to 1910.

2. For the seventeenth century, for example, I am thinking of works like those of Peter Bakewell, *Silver Mining and Society in Colonial Mexico: Zacatecas, 1546–1700* (New York: Cambridge University Press, 1971) and Jonathan Israel, *Race, Class, and Politics in Colonial Mexico, 1610–1670* (New York: Oxford University Press, 1975). For the nineteenth century, I am thinking of Fernando Díaz y Díaz, *Caudillos y Caciques: AntonioLópez de Santa Anna y Juan Alvarez* (Mexico City: 1972) and Andrés Lira González, *Comunidades indígenas frente a la Ciudad de México, Tenochtitlan y Tlatelolco, sus pueblos y barrios, 1812–1919* (Mexico City: El Colegio de Michoacán/Conacyt, 1983), as well as other works cited over the course of this study.

---

* Reprinting was an intense business in nineteenth-century Mexico. Wherever possible, I have attempted to include reference to the first printing. However, when the origin of printed material is not specified in the original, the term "reprint" is simply placed at the end of each entry.

3. William B. Taylor, *Magistrates of the Sacred. Priests and Parishioners in Eighteenth-Century Mexico* (Palo Alto: Stanford University Press, 1996).
4. William B. Taylor, *Entre el proceso global y el conocimiento local: ensayos sobre el estado, la sociedad y la cultura en el México del siglo XVIII* (Mexico City: UAM-Iztapalapa and Miguel Ángel Porrúa, forthcoming).
5. Virginia Guedea, *En busca de un gobierno alterno: los guadalupes de México* Mexico City: UNAM, 1992; Manuel Chust, *La cuestión nacional americana en las Cortes de Cádiz* (Valencia: Fundación Instituto Historia Social and IIH/Universidad Nacional Autónoma de México, 1999); Jaime E. Rodríguez O., *The Independence of Spanish America* (Cambridge, Cambridge University Press, 1998); Josefina Zoraida Vázquez (ed.), *Interpretaciones del siglo XVIII mexicano. El impacto de las reformas borbónicas* (Mexico City: Nueva Imagen, 1992); Josefina Zoraida Vázquez (ed.), *Interpretaciones de la Historia de México. La fundación del Estado mexicano, 1821–1855* (Mexico City: Nueva Imagen, 1994); Josefina Zoraida Vázquez (ed.), *Interpretaciones sobre la Independencia de México* (Mexico City: Nueva Imagen, 1997).
6. François-Xavier Guerra, *Modernidad e independencias. Ensayos sobre las revoluciones hispánicas* (Mexico City: Fondo de Cultura Económica, 1993); François-Xavier Guerra, "La independencia de México y las revoluciones hispánicas," in Antonio Annino and Raymond Buve (ed.), *El liberalismo en México, Cuadernos de Historia Latinoamericana* (Münster: Lit) 1 (1993): 15–48; Annick Lempérière, "Nación moderna o república barroca?" in François-Xavier Guerra and Mónica Quijada (ed.), *Imaginar la Nación, Cuadernos de Historia Latinoamericana* (Münster: Lit) 2 (1994): 135–77; Brian F. Connaughton, "Ágape en disputa: fiesta cívica, cultura política regional y la frágil urdimbre nacional antes del Plan de Ayutla," *Historia Mexicana* 65, no. 2 (Oct.–Dec. 1995): 281–316; Verónica Zárate Toscano, "Tradición y modernidad: la Orden Imperial de Guadalupe. Su organización y sus rituales", *Historia Mexicana* 65, no. 2 (Oct.–Dec. 1995): 191–220; Mariano E. Torres Bautista, "De la fiesta monárquica a la fiesta cívica: el tránsito del poder en Puebla, 1821–1822," *Historia Mexicana* 65, no. 2 (Oct.–Dec. 1995): 221–39; François-Xavier Guerra and Annick Lempérière (ed.), *Los espacios públicos en Iberoamérica. Ambigüedades y problemas. Siglos XVIII y XIX* (Mexico City: Centro Francés de Estudios Mexicanos y Centroamericanos and Fondo de Cultura Económica, 1998); Humberto Morales and William Fowler (ed.), *El conservadurismo mexicano en el siglo XIX (1810–1910)* (Puebla: Benemérita Universidad Autónoma de Puebla/Saint Andrews University/Secretaría de Cultura del Gobierno del Estado de Puebla, 1999).
7. Peter F. Guardino, *Peasants, Politics and the Formation of Mexico's National State: Guerrero, 1800–1857* (Palo Alto: Stanford University Press, 1996); Florencia E. Mallon, *Peasant and Nation. The Making of Postcolonial Mexico and Peru* (Berkeley and Los Angeles: University of California Press, 1995); Guy P. C. Thomson, "Los indios y el servicio militar en el México decimonónico. ¿Leva o ciudadanía?" in Antonio Escobar (ed.), *Indio, Nación y Comunidad en el México del Siglo XIX* (Mexico City: CEMCA/CIESAS, 1993), 207–51; Guy P. C. Thomson with David G. Lafrance, *Patriotism, Politics and Popular Liberalism in Nineteenth-Century Mexico, Juan Francisco Lucas and the Puebla Sierra* (Wilmington, Delaware: Scholarly Resources, 1999); Dorothy Tanck de Estrada, *Pueblos de indios y educación en el México colonial, 1750–1821* (Mexico City: El Colegio de México, 1999).
8. Christon I. Archer, "Politicization of the Army of New Spain during the War of Independence, 1810–1821" in Jaime E. Rodríguez O. (ed.), *The Origins of Mexican National Politics, 1808–1847* (Wilmington, Delaware: Scholarly

Resources, 1997); José Antonio Serrano Ortega, "Liberalismo gaditano y milicias cívicas en Guanajuato, 1820–1836", in Brian Connaughton, Carlos Illades and Sonia Pérez Toledo (ed.), *Construcción de la legitimidad política en México en el siglo XIX* (Mexico City: El Colegio de Michoacán/Universidad Autónoma Metropolitana/Universidad Nacional Autónoma de México/El Colegio de México, 1999), 169–92; Juan Ortiz Escamilla, *Guerra y Gobierno. Los pueblos y la independencia de México,* (Seville, Spain: Universidad Internacional de Andalucía/ Universidad de Sevilla/Colegio de México/Instituto Mora, 1997).

9. Donald Fithian Stevens, *Origins of Instability in Early Republican Mexico* (Durham: Duke University Press, 1991); Michael Costeloe, *The Central Republic in Mexico, 1835–1846* (Cambridge: Cambridge University Press, 1993); Richard Warren, "Elections and Popular Political Participation in Mexico, 1808–1836" in Vincent Peloso and Barbara A. Tenenbaum, *Liberals, Politics, and Power. State Formation in Nineteenth-Century Latin America* (Athens: University of Georgia Press, 1996), 30–57; Eric Van Young, *The Other Rebellion: Popular Violence, Ideology, and the Mexican Struggle for Independence, 1810–1821* (Palo Alto: Stanford University Press, 2001); Antonio Annino, "Soberanías en lucha," in Antonio Annino, L. Castro Leiva, and François-Xavier Guerra (ed.), *De los imperios a las naciones: Iberoamérica* (Zaragoza: iberCaja, 1994), 229–53; Antonio Annino, "Cádiz y la revolución territorial de los pueblos mexicanos 1812–1821," in Antonio Annino (ed.), *Historia de las elecciones en Iberoamérica, siglo XIX, De la formación del espacio político nacional* (Buenos Aires, Fondo de Cultura Económica, 1995), 177–226; Antonio Annino, "Otras naciones: sincretismo político en el México decimonónico," in *Imaginar la Nación, Cuadernos de Historia Latinoamericana 1* (1994), 216–55; Antonio Annino, "Ciudadanía 'versus' gobernabilidad republicana en México. Los orígenes de un dilema," in Hilda Sábato (ed.), *Ciudadanía política y formación de las naciones. Perspectivas históricas de América Latina* (Mexico City: El Colegio de México, Fideicomiso Historia de las Américas, and Fondo de Cultura Económica, 1999), 62–93; Marcello Carmagnani, "Finanzas y Estado en México, 1820–1880," in Enrique Montalvo Ortega (ed.), *El águila bifronte. Poder y liberalismo en México* (Mexico City: INAH, 1995), 121–76; Marcello Carmagnani, "Del territorio a la región. Líneas de un proceso en la primera mitad del siglo XIX," in Alicia Hernández Chávez and Manuel Miño Grijalva (ed.), *Cincuenta Años de Historia de México,* vol. 2 (Mexico: El Colegio de México, 1991): 221–41; Pedro Pérez Herrero, "'Crecimiento' colonial vs. 'crisis' nacional en México, 1765–1854. Notas a un modelo económico explicativo," in Virginia Guedea and Jaime E. Rodríguez O. (ed.), *Cinco Siglos de Historia de México,* vol. 2, (Mexico City: Instituto de Investigaciones Dr. José María Luis Mora and University of California, Irvine, 1992), 81–105; Reynaldo Sordo Cedeño, *El Congreso en la primera república centralista* (Mexico City: El Colegio de México e Instituto Tecnológico Autónomo de México, 1993).

10. David A. Brading, *Una Iglesia Asediada: el obispado de Michoacán, 1749–1810* (Mexico City: Fondo de Cultura Económica, 1994); Luisa Zahino Peñafort, *Iglesia y sociedad en México, 1755–1800. Tradición, reforma y reacciones* (Mexico City: UNAM, 1996); Juvenal Jaramillo Magaña, *Hacia una Iglesia beligerante. La gestión episcopal de Fray Antonio de San Miguel en Michoacán, (1784–1804). Los proyectos ilustrados y las defensas canónicas* (Mexico City: El Colegio de Michoacán, 1996); Cristina Gómez Álvarez, *El alto clero poblano y la revolución de Independencia, 1808–1821* (Mexico City: Facultad de Filosofía y Letras, UNAM and Benemérita Universidad Autónoma de Puebla, 1997); Ana Carolina Ibarra,

El Cabildo Catedral de Antequera, Oaxaca y el movimiento insurgente (Mexico City: El Colegio de Michoacán, 2000). An excellent earlier work that I discovered after writing this study in Spanish is Oscar Mazín Gómez, *Entre dos majestades: El obispo y la iglesia del Gran Michoacán ante las reformas borbónicas, 1758–1772* (Zamora, Michoacán, El Colegio de Michoacán, 1987).

11. Eric Van Young, "Recent Anglophone Scholarship on Mexico and Central America in the Age of Revolution (1750–1850)," *Hispanic American Historical Review* 45, no. 4 (1985): 725–43; Woodrow Borah, "Discontinuity and Continuity in Mexican History," *Pacific Historical Review* 38, no. 1 (1979): 1–25; Donald F. Stevens, "Economic Fluctuations and Political Instability in Early Republican Mexico," *Journal of Interdisciplinary History* 16, no. 4 (1986): 645–65.

12. Charles Hale, "The Reconstruction of Nineteenth-Century Politics in Spanish America: A Case for the History of Ideas," *Latin American Research Review* 8, no. 2 (1973): 53–73, particularly 59.

13. Ibid., 59–61.

14. Ibid., 60–61.

15. Ibid., 61–63.

16. Quoted in Richard V. Burks, "A Conception of Ideology for Historians," *Journal of the History of Ideas* 10, no. 2 (1949): 197.

17. Ibid., 183–98.

18. Georges Duby, "Ideologies in Social History," in Jacques Le Goff and Pierre Nora (ed.), *Constructing the Past: Essays in Historical Methodology* (Cambridge: Cambridge University Press, 1985), 154.

19. Ibid., 154–55.

20. Ibid., 155.

21. Ibid., 164.

22. Fernando García de Cortázar, "La Nueva Historia de la Iglesia Contemporánea en España" in Manuel Tuñón de Lara (ed.), *Historiografía española contemporánea* (Madrid: Siglo XXI, 1980), 207.

23. Ibid., 212–14, 216.

24. Ibid., 225.

25. For the Spanish case, an important overall study of the adaptations – and lack thereof – by the Church in the face of liberal–conservative polarization is José Manuel Cuenca Toribio, *Estudios sobre la iglesia española del XIX* (Madrid: Ediciones Rialp, 1973).

26. Gérard Mairet, "Pueblo y Nación," in François Châtelet (ed.), *Historia de las Ideologías*, vol. 3 (Mexico City: Premia Editora, 1981), 43.

27. Ibid., 56.

28. Gérard Mairet, "El liberalismo: Presupuestos y Significaciones," in Châtelet, *Historia de las Ideologías*, 116–39.

29. Margaret E. Crahan, "Spanish and American Counterpoint: Problems and Possibilities in Spanish Colonial Administrative History," in Richard Graham and Peter Smith (ed.), *New Approaches to Latin American History* (Austin: University of Texas Press, 1974), 36–70.

30. Mairet, "El liberalismo," 123.

31. Ivan Vallier, *Catholicism, Social Control and Modernization in Latin America* (Englewood Cliffs, NJ: Prentice Hall, 1970), 7.

32. Ibid., 7–9, 17.

33. Frederick Pike, "Spanish Origins of the Social-Political Ideology of the Catholic Church in Nineteenth-Century Spanish America," *The Americas* 29, no. 1 (1972): 1–16.

34. E. Bradford Burns, *The Poverty of Progress, Latin America in the Nineteenth Century* (Berkeley: The University of California Press, 1980).

35. Pike, "Spanish Origins," 2.

36. Howard J. Wiarda, "Corporatist Theory and Ideology: A Latin American Development Paradigm," *Journal of Church and State* 20, no. 1 (1978): 47.

37. Hugh Hamill, "The Rector to the Rescue: Royalist Pamphleteers in the Defense of Mexico, 1808–1821," in Roderic A. Camp, Charles A. Hale and Josefina Zoraida Vázquez (ed.), *Los intelectuales y el poder en México/Intellectuals and Power in Mexico* (Mexico: El Colegio de México and UCLA Latin American Center Publications, 1991), 49–61, particularly 49.

38. Hamill, 60. On the role of Benito Jerónimo Feijóo in innovative Spanish thinking, see chapter 1.

39. Hamill, "The Rector," 60–61.

40. Quoted in Arno J. Mayer, *Dynamics of Counterrevolution in Europe, 1870–1956, An Analytical Framework* (New York: Harper Torchbooks, 1971), 54.

41. Mayer, *Dynamics*, 55.

42. Ibid., 35, 86, 84.

43. Gastón García Cantú, *El pensamiento de la reacción mexicana, Historia documental 1810–1962* (Mexico City: Empresas Editoriales, 1965).

44. Carlos Pereyra, *Configuraciones: Teoría e historia* (Mexico City: Edicol, 1979), 59. Pereyra, *El sujeto de la historia* (Madrid: Alianza Editorial, 1984).

45. For example, Wilfrid Hardy Calcott, *Church and State in Mexico, 1822–1857* (New York: Octagon Books, 1971 [1926]) is a book which, in my opinion, follows too closely liberal preconceptions about the role of the Church in Mexican life.

46. Juan Carlos Portantiero, *Los usos de Gramsci* (Mexico City: Folios Ediciones, 1981), 151. See also Hughes Portelli, *Gramsci y el bloque histórico* (Mexico City: Siglo XIX, 1973).

47. See Carlos Sempat Assadourian, et al., *Modos de producción en América Latina* (Mexico City: Cuadernos de Pasado y Presente #40, 1973).

48. Karl Mannheim, *Ideology and Utopia: An Introduction to the Sociology of Knowledge* (London & Henley: Routledge & Kegan Paul, 1979 [1936]), 75, 83.

49. D. A. Brading, *The First America, The Spanish Monarchy, Creole Patriots, and the Liberal State, 1492–1867* (Cambridge: Cambridge University Press, 1993), 343–61 and passim.

50. Ibid., 571.

51. Brian F. Connaughton, *Dimensiones de la identidad patriótica, Religión, política y regiones en México. Siglo XIX*, Mexico, UAM-I/Miguel Ángel Porrúa, 2001, 146–54.

52. Ibid., 73–98.

53. Ibid., 123–65.

54. Benedict Anderson, *Imagined Communities. Reflections on the Origin and Spread of Nationalism* (New York, Verso, 1991/2000).

55. Ibid., 24–36, but also 67–82, 163–206. Anderson borrows time-related concepts from Walter Benjamin, *Illuminations* (London, Fontana, 1973).

56. Ibid., 113–14.

57. Ibid., 109–10.

58. Claudio Lomnitz, in his *Deep Mexico, Silent Mexico: An Anthropology of Nationalism*, (Minneapolis, MN, University of Minnesota Press, 2001), 3–34, discusses the religious content of Spanish national identity within the context of Mexican history. I discuss the Mexican development upon this theme in my article "Conjuring the Body Politic from the 'Corpus Mysticum': The Post-independent Pursuit of Public Opinion in Mexico, 1821–1854," in *The Americas*, 55: 3 (1998), 459–79.

59. *El Despertador Americano*, Reprinted in Mexico City, INAH, 1964, p. 5, No. 1, Dec. 20, 1810.
60. Ibid., p. 17, No. 2 Dec. 27, 1810.
61. Ibid., p. 29, No. 4, Jan. 3, 1811.
62. Lucas Alamán, *Historia de Méjico* (Mexico; Editorial Jus, 1942), 5 vols. Published originally between 1849 and 1852, this work deals extensively with the turmoils of the time. See especially volumes 2 and 5. In this last volume, for example on p. 787, Alamán speaks of the peril of caste war. A recent work emphasizing the violent nature of the independence war is Eric Van Young's *The Other Rebellion*.
63. William Taylor, "The Virgin of Guadalupe in New Spain: An Inquiry into the Social History of Marian Devotion," *American Ethnologist* 14, no. 1 (1987): 9–33.
64. Juan Marichal, *El secreto de España. Ensayos de historia intelectual y política*, Madrid: Santillana, S. A. Taurus, 1995, pp. 13–28 and passim; Andrés Barcala Muñoz, *Censuras Inquisitoriales a las obras de P. Tamburini y al Sínodo de Pistoya*, Madrid: Centro de Estudios Históricos, 1985.
65. Certainly Abad y Queipo and Servando Teresa de Mier were part of this story. As Vergés and Díaz-Thomé have shown, in 1820 Mier would openly defend the Council of Pistoia and the closely related Civil Constitution of the French clergy of 1791. See Brading, *The First America*, 572, 585–90; David A. Brading, "El jansenismo español y la caída de la monarquía católica en México, in Josefina Zoraida Vázquez (ed.), *Interpretaciones del siglo XVIII mexicano. El impacto de las reformas borbónicas*, México: Nueva Imagen, 1992, 187–215; J. M. Miquel I. Vergés and Hugo Díaz-Thomé, *Escritos inéditos de Fray Servando Teresa de Mier*, Mexico: El Colegio de México, 1994, 31, 91–92.
66. Lomnitz, *Deep Mexico*, 3.
67. Adrian Hastings, *The Construction of Nationhood. Ethnicity, Religion and Nationalism*, (Cambridge: Cambridge University Press, 1997), 2.
68. Ibid., 3.
69. Ibid., 4, 18.
70. Ibid., 25.
71. Ibid., 185.
72. Taylor, *Magistrates*.
73. B. F. Connaughton, "A Most Delicate Balance: Representative Government, Public Opinion and Priests in Mexico, 1821–1834," *Mexican Studies/Estudios Mexicanos*, 17, no. (2001), 41–69.
74. Hastings, *The Construction*, 196.
75. Ibid., 198.
76. J. M. Gutiérrez de Estada, *Méjico en 1840 y en 1847 por Don…*, Paris: Imprenta de Lacrampe Hijo Y [sic], Calle Damiette, No. 2, 1848.
77. Erika Pani, *Para mexicanizar el Segundo Imperio. El imaginario político de los imperialistas*, Mexico: El Colegio de México e Instituto Mora, 2001.
78. Charles Hale, *The Transformation of Liberalism in Late Nineteenth-Century Mexico*, Princeton: Princeton University Press, 1989.
79. Laurens Ballard Perry, *Juárez and Díaz: Machine Politics in Mexico*, DeKalb: Northern Illinois University Press, 1978.
80. William Beezley, Cheryl English Martin, and William French (ed.), *Rituals of Rule, Rituals of Resistance: Public Celebrations and Popular Culture in Mexico*, Wilmington, Del.: SR Books, 1994.
81. Lomnitz, *Deep Mexico*, 156, summing up his interpretation of Mary Kay Vaughn, "The Construction of the Patriotic Festival in Tecamachalco: Puebla, 1900–1946", in ibid., 213–45.

Notes to Chapter 1

1. These themes have been studied for the European case, across a long historical period, by Antonio Gramsci. In *Gramsci y la cuestión religiosa: una sociología marxista de la religión* (Barcelona: Laia, 1977), Hughes Portelli has summarized Gramsci's thoughts on this, drawing mainly on *The Prison Notebooks*.

2. Besides the mutual support Church and state offered each other, the former typically took care of social services – education, hospitals, and charity – while individual clerics occasionally held political office. Yet beyond this, the interrelations between Church and state permeated the entire socio-political, economic and cultural structure of power. Effective summaries are offered in Charles Haring, *The Spanish Empire in America* (New York: Harbinger Books, 1963), 166–93; Charles Gibson, *Spain in America* (New York: Harper Torchbooks, 1967); and Mario Góngora, *Studies in the Colonial History of Latin America* (London: Cambridge University Press, 1975), 33–126. Some aspects of these relations in urban and social settings are treated in Paul Ganster, "Churchmen," in Louisa Schell Hoberman and Susan Migden Socolow, (ed.), *Cities and Society in Colonial Latin America* (Albuquerque: University of New Mexico Press, 1986), 137–63, and Rosa Camelo, "El cura y el alcalde mayor," in Woodrow Borah (ed.), *El gobierno provincial en la Nueva España 1570–1787* (Mexico City:UNAM, 1985), 149–65. An overall economic history is offered in Arnold J. Bauer(ed.), *La Iglesia en la economía de América Latina* (Mexico City: INAH, 1986).

3. To follow this process, see John H. Elliot, *Imperial Spain, 1469–1716* (Harmondsworth: Pelican Books, 1970); Stanley and Barbara Stein, *The Colonial Heritage of Latin America* (New York: Oxford University Press, 1970); Richard Herr, *The Eighteenth Century Revolution in Spain* (Princeton: Princeton University Press, 1969); and Jean Sarrailh, *La España ilustrada de la segunda mitad del siglo XVIII* (Madrid: Fondo de Cultura Económica, 1974).

4. See Chapter Five below.

5. The new daring of lay opinion is given great importance in the ideological formation of the French bourgeoisie by Bernhard Groethuysen, *La formación de la conciencia burguesa en Francia durante el siglo XVIII* (México: Fondo de Cultura Económica, 1981).

6. Aubrey F.G. Bell, *El Renacimiento español* (Zaragoza: Ebro, 1944); José Miranda, *Las ideas y las instituciones políticas mexicanas* (Mexico City: UNAM, 1978).

7. Some idea of the breadth and sincerity of Spanish reformist ideas can be gained by looking at Benito Jerónimo Feijóo, *Teatro crítico universal*, 3 vols. (Madrid: Espasa-Calpe, 1975). Marcelo Bitar Letayf, in *Los economistas españoles del siglo XVIII y sus ideas sobre el comercio con las Indias* (Mexico City: IMCE, 1975), concentrates on changes in economic ideas through a comparative critique of Spanish economic practices with those of some foreign countries.

8. Arthur Young, "An Enquiry into the State of the Public Mind among the Lower Classes (1798)" in Christopher Hill, *Reformation to Industrial Revolution* (Harmondsworth: Pelican Books, 1969), 275.

9. This theme is treated for an earlier period in Brian Connaughton, *España y Nueva España ante la crisis de la modernidad* (Mexico City: SEP/FCE, 1983).

10. Both Herr and Margarita Urías emphasize that this change was directed from above, and that the productive bourgeoisie had little direct participation in elaborating government policy. See Herr, *Eighteenth Century Revolution*, and

Margarita Urías, et al., *Formación y desarrollo de la burguesía en México, Siglo XIX* (Mexico City: Siglo XXI, 1978).

11. For Charles Hale, the dynamic we are describing could be summarized as follows: "Mexican political liberalism, both in its constitutionalist and in its anti-corporate phases, contained a set of basic assumptions about society. These assumptions were derived from utilitarianism, essentially a theory of morals and human nature, which permeated the philosophy of the Enlightenment in Europe, and which became systematically developed as a doctrine by Jeremy Bentham between 1780 and 1815." He adds: "In broadest terms, utilitarianism was based on a secular view of human nature in which the individual forms his ideas from experience and, if left free, will act rationally in his own interest and in the interests of others." But Hale underscores that the state, based on an efficient central administration, would attend to the greater good of society. See Charles A. Hale, *Mexican Liberalism in the Age of Mora, 1821–1853* (New Haven: Yale University Press, 1968), 148–59.

12. Pablo González Casanova, *El misoneísmo y la modernidad cristiana en el siglo XVIII* (Mexico City: Colegio de México, 1948), studied the adaptations Mexican Catholic thought made towards new ideas before Independence, but assumed that these adaptations ceased afterwards. Jesús Reyes Heroles admitted that the privileged classes in Mexico, even the high clergy, "possessed neither the ideas nor the bulwark of coordinated and interlocked interests" to hold back the advance of liberal ideas. But he held that they tried to mount closed resistance anyway. See Reyes Heroles, *El liberalismo mexicano* (Mexico City: FCE, 1974), 1: 113. Francisco Morales, however, suggestively extended the reach of his study, taking in the Bourbon period and the first Mexican republic. Extending our conceptual and temporal categories seems to offer the best possibilities for analysis. Francisco Morales, *Clero y política en México (1767–1834) Algunas ideas sobre la autoridad, la independencia y la reforma eclesiástica* (Mexico City: SEP, 1975).

13. Ample evidence of the struggle between traditional and innovative orientations will be given throughout this work.

14. On commerce and industry in Guadalajara and its region during this period, see José Ramírez Flores, "El Real Consulado de Guadalajara, notas históricas" in R. Smith (ed.), *Los consulados de comerciantes en Nueva España* (Mexico City: IMCE, 1976), 65–171; Rubén Villaseñor Bordes, *El mercantil consulado de Guadalajara* (Guadalajara, 1970); José Fernando Abascal y Sousa "Provincia de Guadalajara, Estado que demuestra los frutos y los efectos de agricultura, industria y comercio ... en el año de 1803" in Enrique Florescano and Isabel Gil Sánchez (ed.), *Descripciones económicas regionales de Nueva España: Provincias del Centro, Sureste y Sur, 1766–1827* (Mexico City: INAH, 1976). Additional information on the organization of commerce and guilds in Guadalajara is provided by Brian Hamnett, *Roots of Insurgency: Mexican Regions, 1750–1824* (Cambridge: Cambridge University Press, 1986).

15. Richard Lindley, *Haciendas and Economic Development: Guadalajara, Mexico, at Independence* (Austin: University of Texas Press, 1983). See also M. A. Burkholder and D. S. Chandler, "Creole Appointments and the Sale of Audiencia Positions in the Spanish Empire under the Early Bourbons, 1701–1750," *Journal of Latin American Studies* 4, no. 2 (Nov. 1972): 187–206, and by the same authors, *De la impotencia a la autoridad: La corona española en América 1687–1808* (Mexico City: FCE, 1984). The commercial drive of the Spaniards in the area might have provoked some frictions with affected interests, as Hamnett suggests, but this likely did not alter the nature of the alliance at the top of local society.

16. See Chapter Two and following.
17. See Jean Pierre Berthe, "Introducción a la historia de Guadalajara y su región" in Jean Piel, et al., *Regiones y ciudades en América Latina* (Mexico City: SEP, 1973), 130–47; Hélène Riviére D'Arc, *Guadalajara y su región* (Mexico City: SEP, 1973); Eric Van Young, *Hacienda and Market in Eighteenth-Century Mexico: The Rural Economy of the Guadalajara Region, 1675–1820* (Berkeley: University of California, 1981); Eric Van Young, "Urban Markets," *Hispanic American Historical Review*, 54, no. 4 (Nov. 1979): 593–635; Eric Van Young, "Conflict and Solidarity in Indian Village Life: The Guadalajara Region in the Late Colonial Period," *Hispanic American Historical Review*, 54, no. 1 (1984): 55–79; Ramón María Serrera Contreras, "La región de Guadalajara en el virreinato de la Nueva España (1760–1805): estudio de actividad ganadera" (Ph.D. diss., Universidad de Sevilla, 1975); William Taylor, "Sacarse de pobre, el bandolerismo en Nueva Galicia, 1794–1821," *Revista Jalisco* 2, no. 1–2 (1981), 34–45; and William Taylor, "Indian Pueblos of Central Jalisco on the Eve of Independence," in Richard Garner and William Taylor(ed), *Iberian Colonies, New World Societies: Essays in Memory of Charles Gibson* (1986), 161–63.
18. All these aspects are discussed in the books cited in the last footnote, as well as in Luis Páez Brotchie, *Guadalajara, Jalisco, México, su crecimiento, división y nomenclatura durante la época colonial 1542–1821* (Guadalajara: 1951).
19. On the concept of "prominent clerics," see note 37 below.
20. See Chapter Two.
21. Vicente Rodríguez Casado, "Iglesia y Estado en el reino de Carlos III," *Estudios Americanos* I, no. 1 (Sep. 1948): 5–57; William J. Callahan, *Church, Politics and Society in Spain 1750–1874* (Cambridge: Harvard University Press, 1984), 3; Herr, *Eighteenth Century Revolution*, 13 and 34–35; Góngora, *Studies*, 194–205; Nancy M. Farriss, *Crown and Clergy in Colonial Mexico 1759–1821: the Crisis of Ecclesiastical Privilege* (London: Athlone Press, 1968); Fernando Pérez Memen, *El episcopado y la Independencia de México (1810–1836)* (Mexico City: Editorial Jus, 1977), 15–26; Morales, *Clero y política,* passim.
22. About the French background, see Pérez Memen, "La Revolución francesa," 26–40; Herr, *Eighteenth Century Revolution*, 439–42. Concerning Guadalajara, see Chapter 3 below.
23. See Chapters Four, Six, and Seven of this study in particular.
24. Michael Costeloe, *Church and State in Independent Mexico: A Study of the Patronage Debate, 1821–1857* (London: Royal Historical Society, 1978).
25. See Chapter Nine of this study.
26. Groethuysen, *La formación*, sets out a contrast between detachment and reverence towards the past in the French case. Harold J. Laski maintains the following view of liberalism: "In its essence, it is the outlook of a new class which, given authority, is convinced that it can remould more adequately than in the past the destinies of man." See Laski, *The Rise of European Liberalism, An Essay in Interpretation* (London: George Allen & Unwin Ltd., 1958), 85. José Luis Romero has underscored that in Latin America "conservative political thought was essentially pragmatic," in his prologue to *Pensamiento conservador (1815–1898)* (Caracas: Biblioteca Ayacucho, 1978), xiv; this allowed it to take heterogeneous and ambivalent forms. It was "rooted on a level that was pre-intellectual, imprecise, contradictory, and differed according to the aspects of reality which in each circumstance, time, and country emerged and called for polemics. At base, it was as doctrinaire as was conceivable since, in the final analysis, it appealed to divine order" (ibid., xix). "What was most subtly hidden behind

the preoccupation with order was something that had a singular meaning: the perception that Independence had provoked the formation of a new society, different from the traditional one, of uncertain direction, and – in the eyes of conservatives – pregnant with dangers" (ibid., xxiii–xxiv). Thus, the contradictory course of conservative thought was as inevitable as was the failure of the "principled" ultramontane ideology. "In the world of principles, differences were deep, and sometimes appeared irreconcilable; but in the world of social and economic realities, agreements became evident little by little, and *many principles came to become valid by losing their original labels. In truth, nothing seems more difficult, when one analyzes nineteenth-century Latin American political thought, than distinguishing a liberal conservative from a conservative liberal*" (ibid., xxviii; italics mine).

27. On this process before the eighteenth century, see Connaughton, *España y Nueva España*. On the relationship between liberalism and absolutism in eighteenth-century Spain, and the ties between Spanish and Mexican liberalism, see José Miranda, "El liberalismo español hasta mediados del siglo XIX," *Historia Mexicana* 6, no. 2 (1956): 161–99, and "El liberalismo mexicano y el liberalismo europeo," *Historia Mexicana* 8, no. 4 (1959): 512–23.

28. Many examples of this ecclesiastical position will be provided throughout this book.

29. The radical implications of the doctrine of popular sovereignty in Guadalajara are considered in Chapter Five of this work.

30. Ciro Cardoso (ed.), *México en el siglo XIX (1821–1910), Historia económica y de la estructura social* (Mexico City: Editorial Nueva Imagen, 1980); David Bushnell and Neill Macaulay, *The Emergence of Latin America in the Nineteenth Century* (New York: Oxford University Press, 1988); Torcuato Di Tella, "Las Clases Peligrosas a comienzos del siglo XIX en México," *Desarrollo Económico* 12, no. 48 (1972): 761–91; L. N. McAlister, "Social Structure and Social Change in New Spain," *Hispanic American Historical Review* 43, no. 3 (1963): 349–70; Hale, *Mexican Liberalism*.

31. So argued, convincingly, two important nineteenth-century Mexican authors. See Mariano Otero, *Consideraciones sobre la situación política y social de la República Mexicana en el año 1847* (Mexico City, 1848) and his *Ensayo sobre el verdadero estado de la cuestión social y política que se agita en la República Mexicana* (Mexico City, 1842); and Luis de la Rosa, *La política de los Editores del Tiempo analizada ante la nación* (Guadalajara: J. Manuel Brambila, 1846).

32. Hale, *Mexican Liberalism*, 11–38 and "The War with the United States and the Crisis in Mexican Thought," *The Americas* 14, no. 2 (1957): 153–73.

33. About the rush to make the principle of popular sovereignty effective and extensive, see Chapter Five. Leading liberal José María Luis Mora would come to lament in 1827 that "absolutism has not been able to leave our habits or ideas, much less our government." It also undermined popular elections. "Among us there have been doctrines which it was not licit to touch; this has been said over and over again, and we have even been of the idea that it was a crime to attack what were called the bases of the system, by revealing the true or supposed problems to which they were subject...." See Mora, "Ensayo filosófico sobre nuestra revolución constitucional," in *Obras sueltas de José María Luis Mora, ciudadano mexicano* (Paris: Librería de Rosa, 1837), II: 281–83.

34. See Mora, "Ensayo filosófico," and *Méjico y sus Revoluciones* (Mexico City: EUFESA, 1981 [1836]). Reyes Heroles, *El liberalismo mexicano*, is also worth consulting.

35. Mora wrote in his *Revista Política* in 1837: "The corporate bodies exercise a kind of tyranny of mind and action over their members, and they have quite marked tendencies to monopolize influence and opinion by means of the symbol of doctrine they profess, the commitments they demand, and the obligations they impose." He added that "the corporate bodies exercise over their members a true tyranny which makes illusory the civil liberty and personal independence that corresponds to their members as citizens." Mora, *Obras sueltas*, xcix–c, ci.

36. See Luis González y González, "El optimismo nacionalista como factor de la Independencia de México," *Estudios de la historiografía americana* (Mexico City: El Colegio de México, 1948), 155–215; Hale, "The War with the United States."

37. Oscar Terán analyzes the importance of a new way of seeing historical subjects in social struggles in his prologue to Michel Foucault, *El discurso de poder* (Mexico City: Folios, 1983), 11–50. An understanding of what is meant by *high clergy* or *prominent clerics* is germane to this discussion. On the one hand, Pérez Memen considers "bishops, the cathedral chapter in vacant bishoprics, the Governors of the Mitre and Vicars General in episcopal roles" as members of the high clergy. See Pérez Memen, *El episcopado*. Similarly, Schmitt held that "bishops, members of cathedral chapters, Inquisition officials, and the major officials of the religious orders and institutions made up the high clergy." See Karl Schmitt, "The Clergy and the Independence of New Spain," *Hispanic American Historical Review* 34, no. 3 (1954): 289. But Juan B. Iguíniz offered, perhaps accidentally, the possibility of a more flexible definition of the high clergy in his extensive *Catálogo Biobibliográfico de los Doctores, Licenciados y Maestros de la Antigua Universidad de Guadalajara* (Mexico City: UNAM, 1963). In a detailed work on the educational institutions of Guadalajara and their graduates, Carmen Castañeda García has pointed in a similar direction. See Carmen Castañeda García, "La educación en Guadalajara durante la colonia, 1552–1821" (Ph.D. diss., El Colegio de México, 1974). The educational elite of Guadalajara – and especially at a time when the future direction was by definition unknown – was made up of religious figures to an extent which requires a careful definition of our current notions of "high clergy." I propose that, beyond debating which church posts this notion could be applied to (for example, even curates or chaplains with good placement and income), we should reconstruct an idea of the high clergy as the "clergy with authority," possessed of high educational merits and the right to aspire to – but not always achieve – church posts of the highest rank. In a situation marked by polemics and indecision, authority was won by clarity of expression, arguments based on "sound doctrine," and gifts of persuasion. Ecclesiastical decisions at the level of the bishop or his cathedral chapter were, in this sense, the product of a debate among a lettered minority, which struggled to determine Catholic outlooks and authoritative decisions.

38. See Chapter Five below.

39. See Juan B. Iguíniz, "La imprenta en la Nueva Galicia 1793–1821. Apuntes Bibliográficos," *Anales del Museo Nacional de Arqueología, Historia, y Etnología*, 3, no. 4–5 (1911): 249–336, and "Adiciones" *Boletín de la Biblioteca Nacional de México* 12, no. 8 (octubre 1919–junio 1920): 57–76, for a list of known publications from before 1821.

40. This study will show the breadth and diversity of genres of clerical writings, including first printings and reprints. For a general view of publishing, see Juan B. Iguíniz, *El periodismo en Guadalajara 1809–1915* (Guadalajara: Universidad de Guadalajara, 1955), 2 vols.

41. See Chapters Two and Three.

42. One liberal current would identify popular sovereignty with an authentically representative state, yet this insistence only led to a de facto liberal statism. The less effective popular participation was, the deeper this statism would grow. If the state was not renewed on the basis of liberal principles, the burden of custom would perpetuate state power at the expense of the people in any case. In addition to the works of Mora already cited, see Chapters Five and Eight of this work. The Jalisco Church, as will be seen, made an effort to call for the protection of the new republican regime, but this effort was made in response to strong denunciations of its non-democratic character.

43. Of course, the groundwork was laid. See David A. Brading, *Los orígenes del nacionalismo mexicano*, (Mexico City: Colección SepSetentas, 1973) and Jacques Lafaye, *Quetzalcóatl and Guadalup: The Formation of Mexican National Consciousness 1531–1813* (Chicago: University of Chicago Press, 1976).

44. McAlister, "Social Structure and Social Change."

45. See Magnus Mörner, *Estado, razas y cambio social en la Hispanoamérica Colonial* (Mexico City: Colección SepSetentas, 1974); Israel, *Race, Class, and Politics*.

46. That is why the dilemma of ideological forces from the end of the 1820s was about how to give a clearer form to the regime by reinterpreting or perhaps reforming the constitution. See Michael P. Costeloe, *La primera república federal de México (1824–1835)* (Mexico City: Fondo de Cultura Económica, 1975). From a theoretical perspective, "discourse appears like an item – finite, limited, desireable, useful – which has its rules of appearance, but also its conditions of appropriation and use; an item which sets out, therefore, by its existence (and not simply in its practical applications) a question of power; an item which is, by nature, the object of a struggle, and of a political struggle." Michel Foucault, *La arqueología del saber* (Mexico City: Siglo XXI, 1970), 204.

47. For the United States case, Bernard Bailyn has stressed that "[t]he pamphlet's greatest asset was perhaps its flexibility in size, for while it could contain only a very few pages and hence be used for publishing short squibs and sharp, quick rebuttals, it could also accommodate much longer, more serious and permanent writing as well." In addition, "[t]he best of the writing that appeared in this form ... had a rare combination of spontaneity, of dash and detail, of casualness and care." The Mexican case adds greater force to Bailyn's statement. Bernard Bailyn(ed.), *Pamphlets of the American Revolution 1750–1776* (Cambridge: Harvard University Press, 1965), I: 4–5.

48. On the interrelationship between national and international affairs, see Jan Bazant, *A Concise History of Mexico* (New York: Cambridge University Press, 1977) and Ann Staples, *La iglesia en la primera república federal mexicana(1824–1835)* (Mexico City: Colección SepSetentas, 1976). For the disputes among liberals, see Reyes Heroles, *El liberalismo mexicano*, vol. 2.

49. See also: Feijoó, *Teatro crítico universal*; Morales, *Clero y política*; Góngora, *Studies*; González Casanova, *El misoneísmo*; Germán Cardoso Galué, *Michoacán en el siglo de las luces* (Mexico City: El Colegio de México, 1973). Not even the Inquisition could disconnect itself from its social environment to define what should be understood as orthodox behavior, as shown in Monalisa Lina Pérez-Marchand, *Dos etapas ideológicas del siglo XVIII en México a través de los papeles de la Inquisición* (Mexico City: El Colegio de México, 1945). In his *Obras sueltas*, Mora had no problem with reproducing writings of Bishop-elect Manuel Abad y Queipo of Michoacán.

50. David Brading has analyzed the structural and ideological complexity of pre-Independence Mexico in "El clero mexicano y el movimiento insurgente de 1810," *Relaciones* 2, no. 5 (1981): 5–26 and "Tridentine Catholicism and Enlightened Despotism in Bourbon Mexico," *Journal of Latin American Studies* 15 (1983): 1–22. The complex structure of Mexican conservativism has been studied from a rich legal point of view by Alfonso Noriega, *El pensamiento conservador y el conservadurismo mexicano* (Mexico City: UNAM, 1972), 2 vols.

51. See note 37 above.

Notes to Chapter 2

1. Alejandra Moreno Toscano and Enrique Florescano, *El sector externo y la organización espacial y regional de México (1821–1910)* (Mexico City: UAP, 1977).

2. See John Lynch, *Spanish Colonial Administration 1782–1820* (New York: Greenwood Press, 1969); Herr, *Eighteenth Century Revolution*, 120–53; Stein and Stein, *La herencia colonial*; Marcelo Bitar Letayf, *Los economistas españoles*; Nettie Lee Benson, *La diputación provincial y el federalismo mexicano* (Mexico City: El Colegio de México, 1955); Brian Hamnett, "Obstáculos a la politica agraria del despotismo ilustrado," *Historia Mexicana* 20, no. 2 (1970); Enrique Florescano, "El problema agrario en los últimos años del virreinato, 1820–1821," *Historia Mexicana* 20, no. 4 (1971).

3. See María del Carmen Velázquez, "La comandancia general de las provincias internas," *Historia Mexicana* 27, no. 2 (1977) and "La jurisdicción militar en la Nueva Galicia," *Historia Mexicana* 9, no. 1 (1959); Michael Thurman, "The Founding of the Naval Department of San Blas and its First Fleet: 1767–1770," *Hispanic American Historical Review* 33 (1963) and *The Naval Department of San Blas: New Spain's Bastion for Alta California and Nootka, 1767 to 1798* (Glendale, CA: Arthur H. Clark Co., 1967); José Ramírez Flores, "El Real Consulado"; Rubén Villaseñor Bordes, *El mercantil consulado*; José Fernando Abascal y Souza, "Provincia de Guadalajara."

4. Lynch, *Spanish Colonial Administration*; Velázquez, "La comandancia general"; José María Muriá, *Historia de las divisiones territoriales de Jalisco* (Mexico City: INAH, 1976); Luis Navarro García, *Intendencias en Indias* (Sevilla: Escuela de Estudios Hispanoamericanos, 1959) and *José de Gálvez y la comandancia general de las provincias internas*, prologue by José Antonio Calderón (Sevilla: Escuela de Estudios Hispanoamericanos, 1964); Ricardo Rees Jones, *El despotismo ilustrado y los intendentes de Nueva España* (Mexico City: UNAM, 1979).

5. Muriá, *Historia de las divisiones*; Villaseñor Bordes, *El mercantil consulado*, 66–68; Carmen Castañeda García, "La educación en Guadalajara," 257–433; Edmundo O'Gorman, *Historia de las divisiones territoriales de México* (Mexico City: Porrúa, 1966), 3–25; Van Young, *Hacienda and Market* and "Urban Markets"; José María Muriá (ed.), *Historia de Jalisco* (Guadalajara: Gobierno de Jalisco, 1981), II: 17–323. Key writings for the colonial history of Jalisco are reproduced in Muriá, et al., *Lecturas históricas de Jalisco*.

6. See Serrera Contreras, *La región de Guadalajara*, 14; Muriá, *Historia de las divisiones*, 44–45.

7. Saying this of the high clergy does not imply reducing the importance of the work of Intendants Jacobo Ugarte y Loyola and José Fernando Abascal y Souza. To get an idea of the best inspiration behind these ideas of government reform,

Rees Jones offers the following observation from a minister of the Spanish state: "Since the sole object of this work is limited to treating everything which might lead to give America new possibilities, and to make of men who were barely counted among the rational an industrious nation, dedicated to agriculture and the arts, much of the perfection of all of this lies in how to conduct such a large operation. So as not to err in this, what seems most appropriate is to establish there the same form of government we have in Spain. That is, to place Intendants in those provinces." José del Campillo y Cosío, *Nuevo sistema de gobierno económico para la América: con los males y daños que le causa el que hoy tiene, de los que participa copiosamente España, y remedios universales para que la primera tenga considerables ventajas, y la segunda mayores intereses* (Madrid: Benito Cano, 1789), quoted in Rees Jones, *El despotismo ilustrado*, 77–78. Part of the work of the Intendants is reflected in José Menéndez Valdez, *Descripción y censo general*; Ramón Serrera Contretas, "Estado económico de la intendencia de Guadalajara." *Jahrbüch fur Geschichte von Staat, Wirtschaft und Gesellschaft* 11 (1974): 134–36; and Abascal y Souza, "Provincia de Guadalajara."

8. Gaspar González de Cándamo, *Sermón de honras del rey nuestro señor* (Guadalajara: n.p., n.d.), 6. The titles of all sermons and pamphlets will be given in abbreviated form in the notes; for complete titles, see the Bibliography.
9. Ibid., 17.
10. Ibid., 17–18.
11. Ibid., 18–20. Unless otherwise noted, all italics are mine.
12. Ibid., 21–22.
13. Ibid., 23.
14. Ibid., 23, 25.
15. Ibid., 25.
16. Ibid., 25–30.
17. Ibid., 31.
18. Ibid., 31–32.
19. Ibid., 32–34.
20. Ibid., 34–35.
21. Ibid., 36–42.
22. Ibid., 43.
23. Ibid., 46.
24. The document is reproduced in Villaseñor Bordes, *El mercantil consulado*, 34–36.
25. Ibid., 37.
26. Ibid., 37.
27. Ibid., 37–38.
28. Ibid., 38–40.
29. Ibid., 41–43.
30. Ibid., 45, 54–55.
31. Juan Joseph Moreno, *Sermón predicado el día 10 de noviembre de 1792* (Guadalajara: n.p. n.d.), 21–22. Moreno himself commented on Charles III's approval. For the dates the Bishops of Guadalajara governed the diocese, see Muriá, et al., *Lecturas históricas*, II: 177–78.
32. Moreno, *Sermón predicado el día 10 de noviembre de 1792*, 22.
33. Ibid., 21–23. The Anchorites were a medieval group of religious recluses.
34. Ibid., 21–23, 43. The list of the deceased Bishop's donations appears under the title "Extracto de las donaciones," 34–41. A substantial donation can be seen here to the Royal and Literary University of Guadalajara, which opened its doors the same year in which Alcalde died.

35. Juan Joseph Moreno, *Sermón predicado en la solemne acción de gracias* (Mexico City: Imprenta Nueva Madrileña, 1789), 16.
36. Ibid., 16.
37. Ibid., 24–25, 37, 39, 55.
38. Fernando Cevallos, *Observaciones sobre reforma eclesiástica* (Puebla: Oficina del Gobierno, 1820 [1812]). This work is found in the Jalisco State Public Library in Guadalajara, in the Miscellany Collection.
39. His extensive index contains the words in quotes.
40. Manuel Abad y Queipo, *Representación sobre la inmunidad personal del clero*, reproduced in Mora, *Obras sueltas*. For a profound reflection on the general dynamics of the clergy's response to Bourbon reforms in New Spain, see Farriss, *Crown and Clergy*.
41. Alberto Santoscoy, "Veinte años de beneficiencia y sus efectos durante un siglo," in *Obras Completas* (Guadalajara: Gobierno del Estado, 1983), 1: 171–288. The appendix contains edicts, pastoral letters and other materials by the Bishop, 261–88.
42. Ibid., 263–67.
43. Ibid., 257–70.
44. Ibid., 270–75.
45. Ibid., 278–79.
46. Ibid., 280–81.
47. Ibid., 281–83.
48. Ibid., 281–82.
49. Ibid., 283–88.
50. Agustín Joseph Mariano del Río de Loza, *La más clara idea del más oscuro misterio* (Mexico City: Don Felipe Zúñiga y Ontiveros, 1789).
51. Ibid., iii–iv.
52. Ibid., iv–v.
53. Ibid., vii–viii
54. Ibid., ix.
55. Ibid., x. Literally, "to force them to enter."
56. Ibid., xviii–xix.
57. Ibid., xx–xxi.
58. Ibid., xxii.
59. Agustín Joseph Mariano del Río de Loza, *Continuo espiritual* (Guadalajara: Oficina de don Mariano Valdez Téllez Girón, 1798).
60. Ibid., 14–15, 19.
61. Ibid., 19–20.
62. Ibid., 26.
63. Ibid., 30.
64. Ibid., 35–36.
65. José Ignacio María de Nava, *Sermón de la Purísima* ... (Guadalajara: Oficina de don Mariano Valdez Téllez Girón, 1806); Juan Bautista José Román y Bugarin, *Oración panegírica de Nuestra Señora de Guadalupe* ... *el día 12 de diciembre del año de 1806* (Guadalajara: Tipografía de Rodríguez, 1852); Román y Bugarín, *Oración panegírica de Nuestra Señora del Refugio* ... *en el día cuatro de julio del año de 1807* (Guadalajara: Tipografía de Rodríguez, 1852). On Marian devotion at the end of the colonial period, see Taylor, "The Virgin of Guadalupe", 9–33.
66. Nava, *Sermón de la Purísima*, 35–38.
67. Román y Bugarin, *Nuestra Señora de Guadalupe*, 2, 17.

68. Ibid., 9–10, 15.
69. Ibid., 15, 20–21.
70. Ibid., 27–28.
71. Ibid., 28–30.
72. Román y Bugarin, *Nuestra Señora del Refugio*, 21.
73. Gaspar González de Cándamo, *Sermón de honras,*(Mexico City: n.p., n.d.), xii, xxi, xxiii–xxiv, xxvi–xxvii, xxvii.
74. Ibid., xxxix–xl.
75. Ibid., xl.
76. Ibid., xli.
77. Ibid., xlii.
78. Ibid., xliii–xliv.
79. J. Ignacio Dávila Garibi, *Apuntes para la historia de la iglesia en Guadalajara* (Mexico City: Cultura, 1966), IV: 1. See also Serrera Contreras, *La región de Guadalajara*, 127–30.
80. Dávila Garibi, *Apuntes*, IV:1, 445–82, reproduces some interesting documents.
81. Juan Cruz Ruiz de Cabañas, *Nos el doctor don … a todo el venerable clero secular* (Guadalajara: n.p., 30 April 1810), 13.
82. Ibid., 14–15.
83. Ibid.
84. Ibid., 16, 20, 23.
85. Juan Cruz Ruiz de Cabañas, *Nos el doctor D … en el Nuevo Reino de Galicia* (Guadalajara: n.p., 4 April 1812). Unpaginated.
86. Ibid.
87. Ibid.
88. Luis Pérez Verdia, *Biografías: fray Antonio Alcalde, Prisciliano Sánchez* (Guadalajara: Ediciones ITG, 1952), 46–50.
89. See "Disposiciones que da el obispo de Guadalajara a los señores curas para prevenirse de la peste que asoló en 1813" and "Circular a todos los curas párrocos de las ciudades y villas del obispado de Guadalajara sobre el establecimiento de cementerios fuera de los poblados, año de 1814," in *Misceláneas*, 95–96 and 774–4.
90. Juan Cruz Ruiz de Cabañas, *Nos el doctor D … en el Nuevo Reino de Galicia* (Guadalajara: n.p., 3 September 1815), 2.
91. Ibid., 6–9, 15–16.
92. In P. Eucario López, *Centenario de la arquidiócesis de Guadalajara* (Guadalajara: n.p., 1964), 36.
93. Ibid.
94. Ibid., 28.
95. Ibid., 29–30.
96. Ibid., 30–34.
97. Castañeda García, "La educación en Guadalajara," 136–73.
98. In addition to the sources already mentioned, see the preliminary study by Ramón Serrera Contreras in José Menéndez Valdez, *Descripción y censo general*, 27, and Villaseñor Bordes, *El mercantil consulado*, 14, 107–8.
99. The figures here are based on tables 23 and 24 in Castañeda García, "La educación en Guadalajara."
100. Correspondence between Cabañas and village priests during this period tends to support the portrait offered here. See Archivo Histórico de Jalisco, folders G-4-802, JAL/3163; G-4-808, JAL/3159; and G-4-719, GUA/4.

101. Villaseñor Bordes, *El mercantil consulado*, 24–25.
102. Van Young, *Haciendas and Markets*, 217–74, 318–19.
103. Carmen Castañeda García, "La formación de la burguesía...," in *Primer Encuentro de Investigación Jalisciense, Economía y Sociedad* (Conference Proceedings, 11–14 August 1981), volume entitled Theme V. *La Cultura Regional*, Presiding Chair Manuel Rodríguez Lapuente, 21–32 [each paper paginated independently]; *Reseña de la solemne fiesta*, esp. 7–18. On Maldonado and other prominent clerics in this period, see Chapter Three.
104. John Tutino, "Hacienda Social Relations in Mexico," *Hispanic American Historical Review* 45, no. 3 (1975); T.G. Powell, "Priests and Peasants in Central Mexico," *Hispanic American Historical Review* 47, no. 2 (1977); Van Young, *Haciendas and Markets*, 308–9, 315; Luis Pérez Verdia, *Historia particular del estado de Jalisco* (Guadalajara, 1951), 1: 488.
105. See Villaseñor Bordes, *El mercantil consulado*, 47 and following; Ramírez Flores, "El Real Consulado," 78–80; Lindley, *Haciendas and Economic Development;* Van Young, *Haciendas and Markets*, 232, 254–55, 263. The priest referred to is Francisco Severo Maldonado.
106. See Menéndez Valdez, *Descripción y censo general*, 33–35; Serrera Contreras, *La región de Guadalajara*, 134–36.
107. Urías. et al., *Formación y desarrollo*.

Notes to Chapter 3

1. Morales, *Clero y política*, 11–54.
2. See Chapter One.
3. In addition to what was presented in the previous chapter, the actions of the cathedral chapter and the bishop in supporting the extension of the ecclesiastical jurisdiction of Guadalajara – and reducing the jurisdiction of the bishop of Valladolid, in New Spain – are interesting. See AGN, Ramo de Obispos y Arzobispos, tomos 5 and 17.
4. See Callahan, *Church, Politics and Society in Spain*, 108–85, for an analysis of these dynamics in Spain.
5. Later on in this chapter, this dynamic will be analyzed for the second decade of the nineteenth century.
6. Many sermons bore an explicit authorization on the early pages.
7. On Maldonado, see Alfonso Noriega, *Francisco Severo Maldonado* (Mexico City: UNAM, 1980) and Juan B. Iguíniz, "Apuntes biográficos," *Anales del Museo Nacional de Arqueología, Historia y Etnología* 3, no. 1 (1911).
8. Morales, *Clero y política*, 90.
9. See chapters Six, Seven and Eight.
10. Cabañas, *Nos el doctor don ... a todo el venerable clero secular*. Incidentally, he insisted on giving to Spain in another pastoral letter on 10 September 1810. See Cabañas, *Excitativa*, in Alma Dorantes, et al. (ed.), *Inventario e índice de las Misceláneas de la Biblioteca Pública del Estado de Jalisco* (Guadalajara: INAH-CRO, 1978), 3 vols., III, No. 774-2.
11. Ibid., 15, 10–17.
12. Ibid., 20, 22–23.
13. Cabañas, *Nos el doctor D ... en el Nuevo Reino de Galicia*.
14. Ibid.

15. See Schmitt, "The Clergy and the Independence of New Spain," 299.
16. Cabañas, *Nos el Dr. ..., por la gracia de Dios y de la Santa Sede Apostólica*, 2–3.
17. Ibid., 7–8, 9, 15–16. Italics mine.
18. Morales notes that this is a general characteristic of the higher clergy's stances from the end of the eighteenth century. Morales, *Clero y política*, 31.
19. Cabañas, *Nos el Dr. ..., por la gracia de Dios y de la Santa Sede Apostólica*, 13, 16. Italics mine.
20. Hamnett, *Revolución y contrarrevolución en México y el Perú (Liberalismo, realeza y separatismo 1800–1824)* (Mexico City: Fondo de Cultura Económica, 1978).
21. Tomás Blanco y Navarro, *Canción elegiaca* (Guadalajara: por orden superior sin editora, 1811), 4–5.
22. Ibid., 5, 6, 8–10.
23. José María Hidalgo y Badillo, *Sermón eucarístico* (Guadalajara: Por orden superior sin editora, 1811), 24–25.
24. Ibid., 25, 38–40, 42, 44–46.
25. José María Hidalgo y Badillo, *Sermón panegírico* (Guadalajara: Oficina de José Fructo Romero, 1816), 21–22.
26. Ibid., 6.
27. Ibid., 13–14.
28. *El Telégrafo de Guadalajara*, edited by Francisco Severo Maldonado, appeared from 27 May 1811 until 15 February 1813.
29. *Telégrafo* 1, no. 7 (8 July 1811): 51–53.
30. *Telégrafo* 1, no. 7 (8 July 1811): 53–54; *Telégrafo* 1, no. 12 (12 Aug 1811): 93–94; *Telégrafo* 1, no. 13–23 (19 Aug.–20 Oct. 1811): 97–184; *Telégrafo* 1, no. 15 (11 Nov. 1811): 199; *Telégrafo* 2, no. 46–48 (11–25 Jun. 1812): 361–83.
31. *Telégrafo*, 1, no. 4 (17 Jun. 1811): 25–31. See also facsimile reproduction of *El Despertador Americano*.
32. Ibid., 29.
33. Ibid., 30.
34. *Telégrafo*, 1, no. 5–6 (24 Jun.–1 Jul. 1811): 33–48.
35. *Telégrafo*, 1, no. 7 (8 Jul. 1811): 51–53.
36. *Telégrafo*, 1, no. 7–11 (8 Jul.–5 Aug. 1811): 55–81.
37. *Telégrafo*, 1, no. 12 (12 Aug. 1811): 89.
38. Ibid., 93–94.
39. *Telégrafo*, 1, no. 13–23 (19 Aug.–28 Oct. 1811): 97–184.
40. *Telégrafo*, 1, no. 25 (11 Nov. 1811): 197.
41. *Telégrafo*, 2, no. 46 (11 Jun. 1812): 361–63; *Telégrafo* 2, no. 48 (25 Jun. 1812): 378–83.
42. *Telégrafo*, 2, no. 25 (11 Nov. 1811): 199.
43. *Telégrafo*, 2, no. 47 (18 Jun. 1811): 371.
44. See Noriega, *Francisco Severo Maldonado*; Iguíniz, "Apuntes biográficos" on Maldonado's education and the official support received by *El Telégrafo de Guadalajara*.
45. See Hamnett, *Revolución y contrarrevolución*.
46. Manuel Tiburcio Orosco y Albares [*sic*], *Oración eucarístico moral* (Guadalajara: Oficina de José Fructo Romero, 1817).
47. Ibid., 2, 5, 8, 9.
48. Ibid., 10–11.
49. Ibid., 22. The thinkers being criticized are Denis Diderot (1713–1784), Claude Adrien Helvetius (1715–1771), and Pierre Bayle (1647–1706).
50. Ibid., 23–25.

51. José Simeón de Uría, *Oración fúnebre* (Guadalajara: Imprenta de la Viuda y Herederos de Don José Romero, 1819).
52. Ibid., 1.
53. Ibid., 3.
54. Ibid., 10–13, 15.
55. Ibid., 15, 18–19, 28.
56. José Miguel Ramírez y Torres, *Elogio fúnebre* (Guadalajara: Imprenta de la Viuda y Herederos de Don José Romero, 1820).
57. Ibid., 7, 27.
58. Ibid., 18.
59. Ibid., 21–22.
60. Ibid., 10.
61. Ibid., 28.
62. Ibid., 20–22, 29–30, 40, 45.
63. José Domingo Sánchez Reza, *Elogio fúnebre* (Guadalajara: Imprenta de la Viuda y Herederos de Don José Romero, ca. 1820).
64. Ibid., 4, 8.
65. Ibid., 19. Italics mine.
66. Ibid., 21, 24.
67. Ibid., 24–27.
68. Ibid., 28–29.
69. Ibid., 29–30.
70. Ibid., 34–36.
71. Ibid., 36.
72. Ibid., 37–38.
73. José María Hidalgo y Badillo, *Sermón predicado* (Guadalajara: Oficina de D. Mariano Rodríguez, ca.1820), 5–6.
74. Ibid., 8–10.
75. Ibid., 11–12.
76. Ibid., 4, 12, 19–20, 22, 26.

Notes to Chapter 4

1. In addition to the preceding chapter, see Brading, "El clero mexicano"; Schmitt, "The Clergy and the Independence"; José Bravo Ugarte, "El Clero y la Independencia," *Abside* 15, no. 2 (1951): 199–218; Farriss, *Crown and Clergy*, 201, 249–50.
2. Farriss writes that "the prerogatives demanded in virtue of royal patronage were designed to assure that the Church would function as an auxiliary of the Crown, and to transform the clergy into a branch of the state bureaucracy which could be depended on to faithfully execute royal mandates." Farriss, *Crown and Clergy*, 15. But the legal immunity and internal autonomy of the clergy kept this from effectively being the case. Chapters Two and Three of this work underscore that this situation of the clergy did not necessarily associate it with a generalized reactionary outlook. Farriss demonstrates that the fear of change in the status of the clergy had a powerful influence over the opinions of the high and low clergy and guided its action in the Independence period.
3. In addition to what was quoted in Chapter Two about regional interests, smallpox inoculation and other points of cooperation between Church and state,

see the exchange of letters in 1814 between General De la Cruz and Bishop
Cabañas about public health in the intendancy of Guadalajara in 1813 and 1814.
The letters are reproduced in Francisco Orozco y Jiménez (ed.), *Colección de
documentos históricos inéditos o muy raros referentes al Arzobispado de Guadalajara*, IV,
Núm. 4 (Guadalajara, 1 October 1925).

4.   Farriss, *Crown and Clergy*, 32–38; C. C. Noel, "The Clerical Confrontation with the
Enlightenment in Spain," *European Studies Review* 5, no. 2 (April 1975): 103–22.

5.   William Callahan has portrayed the Spanish Church as having lost its historical
relevance. See Callahan, "The Origins of the Conservative Church in Spain,
1793–1823," *European Studies Review* 1, no. 2 (April 1979): 199–223, and "Two
Spains and Two Churches, 1760–1835," *Historical Reflections* 2, no. 2 (Winter
1976): 158–81. Chapters Two and Five of this study deal with similar problems
in the Mexican Church.

6.   In *Crown and Clergy*, Farriss gives many examples of the impossibility of setting
clear limits. In "El clero mexicano," Brading has suggested that this imprecision
was an increasingly delicate problem during the Bourbon period. This viewpoint
has been more fully developed by William Taylor, in his "Conflict and Balance
in District Politics; Tecali and the Sierra Norte de Puebla in the Eighteenth
Century," in Ronald Spores and Ross Hassig (ed.), *Five Centuries of Law and
Politics in Central Mexico* (Nashville, Tennessee: Publications in Anthropology No.
30, 1984), and in his *Magistrates of the Sacred: Priests and Parishioners in Eighteenth-
Century Mexico* (Palo Alto: Stanford University Press, 1996).

7.   For education in the intendancy of Guadalajara, see Castañeda García, "La
educación" and "La formación de la burguesía"; Juan B. Iguíniz, *La antigua
universidad de Guadalajara* (Mexico City: UNAM, 1959); Muriá (ed.), *Historia de
Jalisco*, II: 215–36. As for vital statistics, it is worth noting that this only changed
with the Reforma. About the role of priests in towns, see Taylor, *Magistrates*,
Thomas Powell, "Priests and Peasants," and *El liberalismo*, 59–65. Powell suggests
that the clergy was in the process of losing its traditional support over the course
of the nineteenth century. Others add force to this contention: Staples, *La iglesia*,
25; Farriss, *Crown and Clergy*. On the Church and the economy, see: Van Young,
Hacienda and Market; Bazant, *Alienation*; Bauer (ed.), *La iglesia en la economía*. On
cemeteries, ideas of modern hygiene or matters of the correct practice of the
faith could intervene in considerations of the matter.

8.   See the studies cited in notes 1, 2, and 5.

9.   In the *Modern Catholic Dictionary* (Garden City, New York: Doubleday, 1980),
John A. Hardon, S. J. offers the following definitions of anathema and excommunion. Anathema is a "[s]olemn condemnation, of biblical origin, used by the
Church to declare that some position or teaching contradicts Catholic faith and
doctrine." Excommunion is an "ecclesiastical censure by which one is more
or less excluded from communion with the faithful. It is also called *anathema*,
especially if it inflicted with formal solemnities on persons notoriously obstinate
to reconciliation. Some excommunicated persons are *vitandi* (to be avoided),
others *tolerati* (tolerated). No one is *vitandus* unless that person has been publicly
excommunicated by name by the Holy See, and it is expressly stated that the
person is "to be avoided." "In order for an excommunion to take effect, the
person must have been *objectively guilty* of the crime charged" (italics mine).
Since in Mexico, and specifically in Guadalajara, the situation the clergy faced
was of formal Catholic orthodoxy, solely modified by a new orientation of
public opinion, these ecclesiastical weapons were difficult to apply effectively.

The context of change in European culture, of Bourbon Reforms and later of a liberalism which was still flexible in the 1812 Cádiz Constitution and the 1824 Mexican Constitution, made recourse to such extraordinary measures difficult. Yet see Chapter Five for specific cases of its use in Guadalajara.

10. The study of the discursive dynamics of the high clergy of Guadalajara could benefit from theoretical works on discourse, action and power. For an overall vision of the complex nature of discourse, see Teun A. Van Dijk, *Estructuras y funciones del discurso* (Mexico City: Siglo XXI, 1980). On discourse and power in a more specific sense, see Foucault, *El discurso del poder*, and Gilberto Giménez, *Poder, estado y discurso, Perspectivas sociológicas y semiológicas del discurso político-jurídico* (Mexico City: UNAM, 1983).

11. In the *Modern Catholic Dictionary*, Hardon defines the homily as a "sermon or informal discourse on some part of the Sacred Scriptures. It aims to explain in an instructive commentary the literal meaning of the *chosen* text or subject and from this develop a *practical application* for the moral or spiritual life." (Italics mine). *The New Catholic Encyclopedia* (New York: McGraw–Hill, 1967) defines the sermon as "any discourse or address given in connection with an ecclesiastical function. Thus, it is taken to include the homily, a commentary on Sacred Scripture; instruction, given from the pulpit, on matters of faith, morals, liturgical practice, etc; the panegyric, a talk generally given on a great feast, on the virtues of a saint; the eulogy, a funeral speech extolling the life and accomplishments of a dead person; the 'occasional' sermon, an address to honor a special event, such as the dedication of a church, or the consecration of a bishop." *The New Catholic Encyclopedia* defines pastoral letters as "[f]ormal letters, doctrinal, devotional, or disciplinary in their purpose, written by a bishop for the faithful of his diocese." It goes on to say that the pastoral letter is a more solemn teaching than the sermon. It adds that "just as encyclicals are today a common expression of the pope's ordinary magisterium, so too pastoral letters are the most common expression of the ordinary magisterium of the bishops throughout the world. Thus, pastorals are similar to encyclicals insofar as they are per se an expression of the Church's ordinary teaching authority." By contrast, *The Catholic Encyclopedia* (New York: Encyclopedia Press, 1913) divides episcopal documents into different types: "pastoral letters, synodal and diocesan statutes, mandates, or ordinances, or decrees." I will prefer the broad definition of pastoral letter in this book.

12. See the works already cited by Morales, *Clero y política*, 90; Pérez Memen, *El episcopado*, 191–209; Farriss, *Crown and Clergy*, 248–53.

13. José de San Martín, *Sermón ...* (Guadalajara: Oficina de Don Mariano Rodríguez, 1821).

14. Ibid., 5–6.

15. Ibid., 6–7.

16. Ibid., 8–9.

17. Ibid., 12. To weigh the influence of a theocratic vision in Independence leaders like Hidalgo and Morelos, see Hugh Hamill, *The Hidalgo Revolt, Prelude to Mexican Independence* (Westport, Connecticut: Greenwood Press Publishers, 1981); Agustín Churruca Peláez, S. J., *El pensamiento insurgente de Morelos*. (Mexico City: Editorial Porrúa, S.A., 1983); Lillian Briseño Senosiain (ed.), *La Independencia de México, Textos de su Historia* (Mexico City: SEP/Instituto de Investigaciones Dr. José María Luis Mora, 1985).

18. Fernando García Diego, *Sermón ....* (Guadalajara: Imprenta de D. Mariano Rodríguez, 1822), 24.

19. Ibid., 29–30. Italics mine.

20. Ibid., 30–32.

21. On Guerrero and Iturbide, see William Spence Robertson, *Rise of the Spanish-American Republics as Told in the Lives of their Liberators* (New York: The Free Press, 1965), 111–40; Jan Bazant, *A Concise History of Mexico* (New York: Cambridge University Press, 1977), 5–29. Briseño Senosiain (ed.), *La Independencia de México*, reproduces some interesting documents on this.

22. See Chapter Two on Marian devotion and the importance of the Virgin of Guadalupe at the beginning of the nineteenth century. Further along in this chapter, as in the rest of this work, many examples of this tendency will be cited. William Taylor has studied the richness of the spread of popular veneration of the Virgin Mary in the late eighteenth and early nineteenth century. See his "The Virgin of Guadalupe in New Spain."

23. José de Jesús Huerta, *Sermón que en la solemne bendición* (Guadalajara: Imprenta de Urbano Sanromán, 1822), 9. Italics mine. This priest was from Santa Ana Acatlán, Jalisco. He had a doctorate in theology from the University of Guadalajara and was a leading figure of the Conciliar Seminary and of the university at the beginning of the nineteenth century. He failed to be named canon at the Guadalajara and Durango cathedrals, and had two parishes of his own before arriving at Atononilco el Alto in 1819, a post he retained until his death in 1859. "During the War of Independence he criticized the movement and favored in various ways the royalist side, but on the verge of emancipation, the tragic death of a brother, apparently for political motives, made him change his mind, passing to the other side and bitterly attacking Spanish domination." Iguíniz, *Catálogo biobibliográfico*, 192–94.

24. Huerta, *Sermón*, 18–19, 20. Italics mine.

25. Nicolás de Santa María, *Sermón que predicaba en la Santa Iglesia Catedral ...* (Guadalajara: Imprenta de D. Urbano Sanromán, 1822), 10–11.

26. Jaime Santiago Mariano Landeríbar, *Sermón patriótico ... julio de 1821*, cited in Morales, *Clero y política*, 91–93.

27. Tomás Blasco y Navarro, *Sermón gratulatorio ...* (Guadalajara: Imprenta de D. Urbano Sanromán, 1821). This is the same Blasco y Navarro quoted in the previous chapter. To the information contained in the title of the sermon, Iguíniz adds that he was of Spanish birth and a participant in the Sociedad Patriótica de Guadalajara in 1821. Iguíniz, *Catálogo biobibliográfico*, 86–87.

28. The later efforts of Lucas Alamán to deny Hidalgo this honor are treated in Hale, "The War with the United States," and Hale, *Mexican Liberalism*, 11–38.

29. The Church showed itself able to take part in the elaboration of Mexican nationalism, a process whose overall outline is traced in Brading, *Los orígenes*. This allowed it to uphold important elements of the defense of Mexican values and rights. Its acceptance first of regionalism and later of independent nationalism implied at the very least a "geographical" or horizontal dimension to the promotion of its self-interest. The Church was able to do this without authorizing the destruction of a theocratic vision of the social life of man and his knowledge.

30. For the European background for this debate, see Groethuysen, *La formación*; Paul Hazard, *The European Mind [1680–1715]* (New York: World, 1963) and *European Thought in the Eighteenth Century* (Cleveland: Meridian Books, 1963); Ernst Cassirer, *La Filosofía de la Ilustración* (Mexico City: Fondo de Cultura Económica, 1972) and Franklin L. Baumer, *El pensamiento europeo moderno,*

Continuidad y Cambio en las Ideas, 1600–1950 (Mexico City: Fondo de Cultura Económica, 1985), 158–77. Related questions are discussed in greater detail in Chapters Three and Five. For now, we should stress that the leaders of Mexican society were much more likely than the leaders of European secular thought to respond eclectically to calls for a new political and cultural ethics. For useful documents on this, see Briseño Senosiain (ed.), *La Independencia de México*, vol 2. Noel has suggested that in Spain, the Enlightenment's practical aspects were more important than its implications of intellectual liberation and toleration. See Noel, "The Clerical Confrontation," 103–6. It was the latter implications which pointed towards complete secularization, turning man himself into the measure and goal of all. The same seems to be true of Mexico. The Cortes of Cádiz and the independence movement in Mexico deepened the tensions inherent to bringing together the Hispano-Mexican world and the legacy of the Enlightenment.

31. About the context of growing political dispute after the mid-1820s, see Costeloe, *La primera república federal*, and Stanley C. Green, *The Mexican Republic: The First Decade 1823–1832* (Pittsburg, Pa.: University of Pittsburgh Press, 1987). Chapters Five, Six, and Seven of this work explore this process with regard to the Church in Guadalajara.

32. Noriega, *El pensamiento conservador*, vol. 1.

33. Hale, *Mexican Liberalism*, 34–35 and 241, debates this connection. On the other hand, widespread evidence of the fury that tolerance produced in Jalisco is offered in Dorantes, et al., *Inventario*.

34. Consider this sample: "in truth, rulings pronounced by the Church are not monuments, always vain, and always fleeting, but sentences which contain the happiness they announce." For loyal clerics: "religion will give true immortality to those priests who, like the heroes of the ancient alliance, died in the faith, confessing that they were pilgrims and guests upon this Earth." José M. Cayetano Orozco, *Sermón de honras* (Mexico City: Imprenta de J.M. Lara, 1849), 7. See also Chapter Five and following in this work. Orozco, from Cocula, Jalisco, was ordained in 1838 and was granted the degree of doctor in theology by the University of Guadalajara in 1839. He had an important career in the Church and in politics in Guadalajara and Mexico City. See Iguíniz, *Catálogo biobibliográfico*, 221–23.

35. See Chapter Five of this work.

36. On the fiscal obligations imposed on the Church, see Carlos Marichal, "La Iglesia y la crisis financiera del virreinato, 1780–1808: Apuntes sobre un tema viejo y nuevo," *Relaciones 10*, no. 40 (1989): 103–29. Regarding disentailment in New Spain, see Brian R. Hamnett, "The Appropriation of Mexican Church Wealth by the Spanish Bourbon Government: The 'Consolidación de Vales Reales,' 1805–1808," *Journal of Latin American Studies* 1, no. 2 (Nov. 1969): 85–113; C. C. Noel, "Opposition to Enlightened Reform in Spain: Campomanes and the Clergy, 1765–1775," *Societas* 3, no. 1 (Winter 1973): 21–43. Noel has suggested that conservatism in the Spanish clergy dated from the 1760s forward. From early on, the clergy would be at the center of a mobilization of the conservative forces of society. The implications of this for the Mexican case are important, and deserve careful study in different sources than the ones used for this study. Noel found opposition in correspondence between the clergy and the Crown, in various attempts to exert pressure, and even in publications supported by opposition clergy, but this author underestimates

certain important questions. His own analysis would seem to permit a different perspective from his. Due to the influence exercised by discontented clergy, the Bourbon government gave in on key points, such as the law of disentailment of ecclesiastical property and on some of the more excessive aspects of royalist advance on clerical privileges. The clerical opposition proved capable of going over the heads of the reformist members of the Bourbon government, and reaching the King. This created a split between the reformist orientation of the government and its specific results at any given moment. Thus, as long as recourse to the King was assured, the possibility of an effective audience with him pointed towards a governing attitude of negotiation. In this sense, the clergy was more deeply indebted to the King, and saw itself even more implicated in the reforms. This did not do away with all dissatisfaction, but it allowed practical cooperation between the Church and the reformist state to go forward. One should not forget that the Crown had control over the appointment and promotion of bishops and canons in the Empire. This panorama must have weakened any alliance of traditional interests against Bourbon Reforms, especially in America, where there were so many Creole and mercantile interests wanting to take advantage of them. The Church's caution and defense of its own territory – ideologicallly and materially – are real factors that should be considered. In addition, its sense of hierarchy and organic unity certainly have a conservative aspect. For that reason, the Church seemed more to follow than to initiate changes taking place at an institutional level. A more systematic and sustained response on the part of the Mexican clergy would await the moment of Independence, in 1810 and even more so in 1824.

37.   Ramírez y Torres, *Elogio fúnebre*, 7 and 22, cited in Chapter Three. This priest was originally from Durango. He graduated with a doctorate in theology from the University of Guadalajara in 1808 and the Audiencia granted him a law degree in 1818. He acted as canon of the Guadalajara cathedral, and his political career included participation in the Spanish Cortes in 1820 and 1821 and in the Constituent Congress of 1823 and 1824. See Iguíniz, *Catálogo biobibliográfico*, 273–74.

38.   Ibid., 10.

39.   Ibid., 28.

40.   Huerta, *Sermón*, 18–19; García Diego, *Sermón*, 29–30.

41.   José María Esparza, *Sermón predicado el día 1 de marzo de 1825* (Guadalajara: Oficina de C. Mariano Rodríguez, 1825), 13.

42.   Ibid.

43.   José Domingo Sánchez Reza, *Elogio fúnebre* (Guadalajara: Imprenta del C. Mariano Rodríguez, 1825), 42. For details about Sánchez Reza himself, see Iguíniz, *Catálogo biobibliográfico*, 284–86. This is the same Sánchez Reza dealt with in Chapter Three. He was from Zacatecas, received a doctorate in canon law from the University of Guadalajara, and a law degree from the Royal Audiencia. He joined the cathedral chapter of Guadalajara in 1815, to later take prominence in Church life. He took active part in politics from his election to the Cortes of 1820–21 for Guadalajara to his position as member of the department government in 1835. Over the course of his political career, Sánchez Reza, like the Church, seems to have gradually become more traditionalist.

44.   Sánchez Reza, *Elogio*, 42.

45.   Ibid., 49–50.

46. Ibid., 40, 42–43, 46, 48–49. See also José Ignacio Dávila Garibi, *Biografía de un gran prelado*, (Guadalajara: Tipografía C. M. Sainz, 1925), 400, regarding the ceremony in which this sermon was preached.

47. Ibid., 57, 58, 66–68.

48. Ibid., 71.

49. Ibid., 70–75

50. Ibid., 76–78. Italics mine.

51. See Chapters Five, Seven and Eight of this study.

52. Juan de Aguirre, *Panegírico* (Guadalajara: Oficina a cargo del C. Dionisio Rodríguez, 1829), 3–4.

53. Ibid., 6.

54. Ibid., 17.

55. The background to this situation is presented in the following chapters. As will be seen, clerical pessimism was also combined with a significant discursive appeal, very capable of reaching out to patriotism or even liberalism itself in its efforts to defend the Church's interests.

56. Francisco Espinosa, *Sermón predicado* (Guadalajara: Imprenta de la Casa de Misericordia, a cargo del C. Jesús Portillo, 1832), unpaginated. Originally from Tepic, Espinosa graduated with a doctorate in theology from the University of Guadalajara in 1834. He would go on to an active ecclesiastical and political career. For more details, see Iguíniz, *Catálogo biobibliográfico*, 142–44, and Chapter Eight of this work.

57. F. Espinosa, *Sermón*.

58. Ibid.

59. Pedro Barajas, *Elogio fúnebre* (Guadalajara: Imprenta de Rodríguez, a cargo de Trinidad Buitrón, 1833), 12. Originally from Lagos, Barajas fought in the royalist ranks at the beginning of the Independence struggle. He consolidated his ecclesiastical and later political career starting in the 1820s, standing out because of his erudition as a clerical thinker. He would graduate with a doctorate from the University of Guadalajara in 1839 and be named the first bishop of San Luis Potosí in 1855. See Iguíniz, *Catálogo biobibliográfico*, 80–84.

60. Ibid., 22–23.

61. José Antonio González Plata, *Sermón predicado* (Guadalajara: Imprenta del Supremo Gobierno a cargo de D. Nicolás España, 1834), 14–15. González Plata was a member of the Royal Military Order of Our Lady of Mercy, in which he seems to have had a modest ecclesiastical career, but not without holding "various posts" in his order. He received the degree of doctor in theology from the University of Guadalajara in 1835. See Iguíniz, *Catálogo biobibliográfico*, 165–66.

62. González Plata, *Sermón*, 19–20.

63. Francisco Espinosa, *Oración* (Guadalajara: Imprenta del Gobierno a cargo de don Nicolás España, 1836), 6–7. Italics mine. The "sect" is the Masons.

64. Ibid., 15, 19–22.

65. Pedro Cobieya, *Oración panegírica* (Guadalajara: Imprenta de M. Brambila, 1837), 21–22. Born in Guadalajara, he was ordained in 1834 and was a distinguished member of the Franciscan Order. In 1849 he received a doctorate in theology from the University of Guadalajara. His ecclesiastical career continued in the cathedral chapter of Guadalajara.

66. See Chapters Seven and Eight to fill out the overview sketched here.

67. See Casiano Espinosa, *Sermón predicado* (Guadalajara: Imprenta de Manuel Brambilia, 1840); Juan Nepomuceno Camacho, *Sermón predicado* (Guadalajara: Oficina de Dionisio Rodríguez, 1841); Pedro Barajas, *Sermón que en la solemne* (Mexico City: Imprenta del Águila, 1841); Manuel de San Juan Crisóstomo, *Sermón* (Guadalajara: Imprenta del Gobierno, 1842); Juan N. Camacho, *Sermón* (Guadalajara: Imprenta de M. Brambila, 1845); Pedro Barajas, *Sermon predicado* (Guadalajara: Imprenta de Dionisio Rodríguez, 1848) and Orozco, *Sermón de honras.*

68. Jesús Ortiz, *Historia, progreso* (Guadalajara: Tipografía de Rodríguez, 1851). See also Orozco, *Sermón que en la solemne festividad de la Concepción de María* (Guadalajara: Tipografía de Rodríguez, 1851). It is also worth pointing out that the sermons dedicated to Our Lady of Refuge and Our Lady of Guadalupe by Román y Bugarín, which were discussed in Chapter Two, were published in 1852.

69. Francisco Espinosa, *Elogio fúnebre* (Guadalajara: Tipografía de Dionisio Rodríguez, 1853), 100.

70. Pablo Antonio del Niño Jesús, *Sermón predicado* (Guadalajara: Tipografía del Gobierno, a cargo de J. Santos Orosco, 1853), 12.

71. Ibid., 15.

72. Ibid., 16.

Notes to Chapter 5

1. Francisco Severo Maldonado, *Nuevo Pacto Social propuesto a la Nación Española para su discusión en las próximas cortes de 1822–1823* (Guadalajara: Oficina de Doña Petra Manjarrés, 1821), 18.

2. Ibid., 30.

3. Ibid., 66.

4. Ibid., 67.

5. Ibid., 26–27, 60, 67.

6. Ibid., 92.

7. Ibid., 1.

8. Traditionalists would also eventually publish pamphlets anonymously, as will be seen in the following chapters.

9. Francisco Severo Maldonado, *Contrato de asociación para la República de los Estados Unidos del Anáhuac por un ciudadano del Estado de Xalisco* (Guadalajara: Imprenta de la viuda de D. José Fruto Romero, 1823), unpaginated. This pamphlet was reprinted by the government of Jalisco in 1973.

10. *Sentimientos de un Polar* (Guadalajara: Oficina de don Ignacio Bramblia, 1823), 2. We will primarily be citing the original publications of the man who became known as "El Polar." A collection of his writings has been published: *La Estrella Polar, polémica federalista* (Guadalajara: Poderes de Jalisco, 1977). The writer's real name was Anastasio Cañedo.

11. Ibid., 2–3.

12. Prisciliano Sánches [sic], *El Pacto Federal de Anáhuac* (Guadalajara: Oficina del C. Mariano Rodríguez, ca. 1823), 1–2. This work was reprinted by the Jalisco government in a volume titled *Memoria sobre el estado actual de la administración política del Estado de Jalisco* (Guadalajara: Poderes de Jalisco, 1974).

13. To get a fuller idea of the discourse on these themes, see – in addition to the pamphlets quoted directly – the following: J.M.G., *Proyecto de ley sobre contribuciones* (Guadalajara: Imprenta de D. Mariano Rodríguez, 1821); Diego Solís, *Específico y único remedio de la pobreza del Imperio Mexicano. Primera Parte* (Guadalajara: Oficina de D. Urbano Sanromán, 1822); F.M.M. *República Federada le conviene al Anáhuac* (Guadalajara: Imprenta libre del C. Ignacio Brambila, 1823); *Dictamen presentado al Congreso de Jalisco* (Guadalajara: Imprenta del C. Urbano Sanromán, 1824); El Josué de Xalisco, *Josué deteniendo El Sol o sea eclipse político del periódico de este nombre visible el martes 13 del corriente* (Guadalajara: Imprenta del C. Mariano Rodríguez, 1824); *Oiga el pueblo* (Mexico City: Oficina del C. J.M. Benavente y Socios, 1824); *Dictamen de la Comisión de Sistema de Hacienda* (Mexico City: Imprenta del Supremo Gobierno, 1824); *Proyecto de ley adicional a la orgánica de Hacienda* (Guadalajara: Imprenta del C. Urbano Sanromán, 1828); *Representación de la sociedad de artesanos y comerciantes dirigida al Soberano Congreso de la Unión* (Guadalajara: Imprenta de Gobierno en Palacio, 1828); *Si los cristianos se van tantos hereges que harán* (Guadalajara, reprinted in Mexico City: Oficina del C. Núnez, 1828); *Dictamen presentado por la Comisión de Hacienda* (Guadalajara: Imprenta del Supremo Gobierno, a cargo del C. Juan María Brambila, 1829); *Colección de acuerdos, órdenes y decretos* (Guadalajara: Imprenta del gobierno del Estado, a cargo de J. Santos Orosco, 1849).

14. Mora, *Obras sueltas*, xcix–c.

15. On the role of the state in the Bourbon Reforms and its later presence in the liberal era, see Herr, *The Eighteenth Century Revolution in Spain*; Sarrailh, *La España ilustrada*; Miranda, "El liberalismo español"; Miranda, "El liberalismo mexicano"; and Hale, *Mexican Liberalism*.

16. *Sentimientos de un Polar*, 7.

17. William Blake, *Jerusalem*, quoted in Hill, *Reformation to Industrial Revolution*, 275.

18. Groethuysen, *La formación de la conciencia burguesa*, 2.

19. J.J.C., *La docilidad y gratitud de los mexicanos, ¿cómo ha sido correspondida por Iturbide?* (Guadalajara: Oficina de D. Urbano Sanromán, 1823), 16.

20. Ibid., 2–3.

21. El Cuerpo de liberales, *Establecimiento de la República en Guadalajara. O sea Manifiesto de los liberales de dicha ciudad a sus conciudadanos* (Guadalajara, reprinted in Mexico City: Oficina de D. José Mariano Fernández de Lara, 1823). The document was originally dated 6 April 1823 and has no page numbers.

22. Ibid. Note the use of the term "healthy portion" and the contrasting "crowd." Liberal radicalism about the effective exercise of popular sovereignty had its class limits, already evident here.

23. El Pensador Mexicano, *La Victoria del Perico* (Guadalajara: reprint by Oficina del C. Brambila, 1823), 2–3.

24. Luis Quintanar, *Manifiesto del Capitán General a los Habitantes del Estado Libre de Xalisco* (Guadalajara: Imprenta del C. Mariano Rodríguez, ca. 1823), 7. The real extent given to this last concept in the everyday exercise of political rights and the vote remains to be established. Carlos San Juan Victoria and Salvador Velázquez Ramírez suggest that the struggle for popular sovereignty was translated into a "compromise between regional oligarchies, the clerical and military upper ranks, along with the still powerful remains of the colonial oligarchy." They do not deny that there was an attempt at alliance between local oligarchies and the middle sectors of the population in the 1820s, but they

consider that the expulsion of the Spaniards and the failed military seizure of authority by Guerrero destroyed that possibility. The fear of the masses and the fiscal crisis from the end of the decade were important parts of this process. They assert that "unless allied with the forces of regional oligarchies," the middle sectors "did not represent a crucial social power." San Juan Victoria and Velázquez Ramírez, "La formación del Estado y las políticas económicas (1821–1880)," in Ciro Cardoso (ed.), *México en el siglo XIX (1821–1910, Historia Económica y de la estructura social* (Mexico City: Editorial Nueva Imagen, 1980), 62.

25. Quintanar, *Manifiesto,* 9.
26. R.P. *Peor me la esperaba yo* (Guadalajara: Imprenta de Sanromán, ca. 1823), 8.
27. Ibid., 8, 10.
28. Sánches [*sic*], *El Pacto Federal de Anáhuac,* 5.
29. José Joaquín Fernández de Lizardi, *Concluye el sueño del pensador mexicano. Perora la verdad ante S.M.I. y el Soberano Congreso* (Guadalajara: reprint by Oficina de D. Urbano Sanromán, 1822), 28. Italics in original.
30. Ibid., 24–25. Italics in original.
31. Ibid., 29. Italics in original.
32. Ibid., 31.
33. A.R.F., *El despertador* (Mexico City: Impreso en Guadalajara y por su original en la oficina liberal a cargo del C. Juan Cabrera, 1823), 7. See also the position against popular sovereignty taken by the bishop of Sonora and published in Guadalajara in 1824: Bernardo del Espíritu Santo, *La soberanía del Altísimo* (Guadalajara: Imprenta de la viuda de Romero, 1824).
34. For example, see Fernández de Lizardi, *Carta segunda [tercera y cuarta]del pensador al papista* (Guadalajara: reprint by Oficina de D. Urbano Sanromán, 1822) and *Campos Santos* (Guadalajara: Imprenta de D. Mariano Rodríguez, 1823).
35. El Enemigo de las cosas a medias, *La voz de la libertad pronunciada en Jalisco* (Guadalajara, reprinted in Mexico City: Oficina del finado Ontiveros, 1825), 2–3. Italics in original. Note the appearance here of an inclination that is equally statist and liberal.
36. Ibid., 5.
37. Ibid., 6–7.
38. Ibid., 11.
39. *Conjuración del Polar contra los abusos de la Iglesia* (Guadalajara: Imprenta del C. Urbano Sanromán, 1825), reprinted in *La Estrella Polar,* 85–86. One might reasonably doubt whether El Polar had personally been subjected to the hard work he speaks of. On matters of rhetoric about the people and sovereignty, a certain skepticism – placing doubt before certainty – is called for.
40. Ibid., 86–93.
41. *Constitución Federal de los Estados Unidos Mexicanos sancionada por el Congreso General Constituyente el 4 de octubre de 1824 y Constitución Política del Estado Libre de Jalisco sancionada por su Congreso Constituyente en 18 de noviembre de 1824* (Guadalajara: Poderes de Jalisco, 1973). On Article 7, also see Chapter Six.
42. El Eclesiástico despreocupado, *No hay peor cuña que la del propio palo* (Guadalajara: Imprenta del C. Urbano Sanromán, 1825), 7.
43. Ibid., 6.
44. El Eclesiástico despreocupado, *Ultima contestación de la Cuña al Tepehuaje* (Guadalajara: Imprenta del C. Urbano Sanromán, 1825). This pamphlet undoubtedly did show real concern for the living conditions of the common people. It is not surprising that it was purportedly a cleric who expressed these concerns,

given the connection of certain sectors of the clergy with popular lives, but the reform of the lower clergy had no certainty of counting on general support. See Powell, "Priests and Peasants."

45. *Ultraje a las Autoridades por los Canónigos de Guadalajara.* (Guadalajara, reprinted in Mexico City: Oficina de Mariano Ontiveros, ca. 1825), 2–3.

46. Ibid., 4–7.

47. The Church's response to such suggestions will be analyzed in the following chapters. The number and tenor of ecclesiastical pamphlets dedicated to refuting these ideas give an idea of their general acceptance and the clear danger they represented for the Church.

48. Norberto Pérez Cuyado, *Disertación sobre la naturaleza y límites de la autoridad eclesiástica* (Mexico City, reprinted in Guadalajara: Oficina del C. Urbano Sanromán, 1825), 1. Costeloe attributes this work to Bernardo Couto, a priest who would take part in decisions relating to the Church in 1833 and 1845. See Costeloe, *Church and state*, 93, 132, 166.

49. Pérez Cuyado, *Disertación*, 4–5.

50. Ibid., 16, 21–22, 25.

51. Ibid., 27, 31–33, 34, 40, 40–48.

52. Ibid., 69.

53. Ibid., 71–72.

54. Ibid., 74, 75–78.

55. Spes in Livo, *Llegó de Roma la bula más escandalosa y nula* (Mexico City, reprinted in Guadalajara: Oficina del C. Urbano Sanromán, 1826), 1, 3. On the first page of the reprinting, the author reaffirmed his agreement with what he had written.

56. Ibid., 4. The "author of the Ruins" probably refers to Constantin–François Volney, who wrote *Las ruinas, o meditación sobre las revoluciones de los imperios,* Madrid: Rosa, 1821.

57. Ibid., 6–7.

58. José Miguel Gordoa, et al., *Dictamen de la Junta de Censura Eclesiástica,* included in *La Estrella Polar,* 189.

59. "Conjuración," *La Estrella Polar,* 91–92.

60. "Concordatos del Polar con el Estado de Jalisco," *La Estrella Polar,* 167–73.

61. *El Polar convertido,* (Guadalajara; reprinted in Mexico: Oficina del finado Ontiveros, 1825), 2–3.

62. Ibid., 7–8.

63. Ibid., 8.

64. Otro Polar. *Una ráfaga de luz a un abismo de tinieblas* (Guadalajara: Imprenta del C. Urbano Sanromán, 1825). See also the defense of Lizardi by Rafael Dávila, *Justo castigo y destierro del Pensador Mexicano* (Guadalajara: Imprenta de Don Mariano Rodríguez, 1822 [reprint]), and a fierce attack on the canons in Preguntas Sueltas, *Las pascuas a los canónigos* (Guadalajara, reprinted in Mexico City: Oficina del finado Ontiveros, 1826).

65. Ibid., 3–4, 6.

66. Ibid., 8.

67. *Fuego del cielo ha de caer si se ahorcan a los traidores. Diálogo entre una vieja y su hijo* (Mexico City, reprinted in Guadalajara: Oficina del C. Urbano Sanromán, ca. 1827). Unpaginated.

68. Ibid.

Notes to Chapter 6

1. Of course, there are those who believe the Church had been on the defensive since long before this time. In his book *Iglesia y Estado en Nueva Viscaya (1562–1821)* (Pamplona: Universidad de Navarra, 1966), Guillermo Porras Muñoz argues that the state had tried for excessive control over the Church since the fifteenth century. The state's goal was to use the Church as a simple pillar of its power. According to Porras Muñoz, the state conveniently blurred religious obligation with the defense of its own interests. Porras Muñoz always sees the state in terms of interest and power, and the Church in terms of its ideals. His reading is distorted by an anachronistic approach born out of a disillusionment with the ups and downs of the Church since the Bourbon Reforms.

2. This process will be treated in more detail below. The sermons of 1821–22 have already been seen to represent a first attempt at reconciliation.

3. "Article 7: The state Religion is the Apostolic Roman Catholic without tolerance of any other. The state will set and pay all the expenses necessary to promote worship." *Constitución Federal … y Constitución Política.*

4. Pablo de la Llave, *Ministerio de Justicia y Negocios Eclesiásticos*, "El Excm. Sr, Presidente de los Estados Unidos Mexicanos se ha servido dirigirme el decreto que sigue*," unpaginated.

5. Green, *The Mexican Republic*, 94–98, 203–5. "For Independent Mexico the printing press became a symbol of intellectual sovereignty, and for the provinces a symbol of statehood." Ibid., 94. Laws were directed to controlling certain abuses by writers, but "it was difficult to obtain a conviction. Juries tended to sympathize more with writers than prosecutors. In an indulgent era, governments were not yet inclined to narrow one of those freedoms felt to be the fruit of independence." Ibid., 98. After 1830, the atmosphere would change significantly, but for the most part, this meant a more rigorous application of legislation already on the books. Ibid., 203–5.

6. It is risky to write off more traditional thinking as absolutely opposed to liberal republican thought. Hale insists that the consolidation of a conservative project based on a genuine alternative to the republic only took place slowly. He holds that it only crystallized in the 1840s, above all after losing the war with the United States. Hale, *Mexican Liberalism*, 27–33, 144–47. Noriega seems to offer more evidence for this perspective from a legal standpoint in his *El pensamiento conservador*. Even Reyes Heroles admits "how tenuous the border between Enlightened liberalism and the ideas of supporters of oligarchical constitutionalism turns out to be at certain times." In this case, he is speaking of the thinking expressed in the 1836 Constitution of Seven Laws. Reyes Heroles, *El liberalismo mexicano*, 256. For the example of Estevan de Antuñano, a man of traditionalist leanings who in 1846 turned towards greater liberalism, see Hale, *Mexican Liberalism*, 286–89.

7. On the porousness of traditionalist or conservative thought to reformist and liberal ideas, see Romero, *Pensamiento conservador*, 24. Noriega makes the same point, especially about the 1836 Constitution of Seven Laws. Noriega, *El pensamiento conservador*, I: 115–53. Costeloe presents evidence for the shifting nature of alliances in the years immediately following Independence. It was already apparent that those leading different political groups would run into sharp internal contradictions. Costeloe asserts that "Federalists and American

Creole generals ended up resenting the influence and power centralists and the upper classes had over the Executive. In August or early September 1825, some of their principal politicians decided they needed to establish a stronger and more organized base for federalist and popular support, and to achieve it, they founded a new society, known as the Yorkinos [for the York Rite, a Freemason group], which from then on would be the core of the popular federalist party." From early on, "the Yorkinos were made up of diverse groups, and the political designs of some of their leaders contrasted with the more personal aspirations of the majority of the rank-and-file." By contrast, the Escoceses (for the Scottish Rite, another Freemason group) "had the majority of prominent politicians in the early years among their members, and provided a forum for the spread of liberal ideas, both to republicans and constitutional monarchists." When Iturbide fell, the Escoceses were associated with centralism and "some monarchists were members or at least kept close ties to the society. The result was that the Escoceses, in political terms, ended up identified more with centralism and Bourbonism than with the liberal ideas some of their members still professed." They were seen "as a more-or-less exclusive club dominated by European Creoles and Spaniards who represented and attempted to maintain the dominant position of the privileged classes of the country." Costeloe, *La primera república*, 49, 58–59. If the Escoseses were torn apart by an internal split between more conservative and more liberal members, the Yorkinos felt a similar tension between provincial elites and ambitious members of more humble social origins. See Green, *The Mexican Republic*, 89–90; San Juan Victoria and Velázquez Ramírez, "La formación del Estado."

8. Mora, *Obras sueltas*, cxi–cxii.
9. Ibid., cxiii.
10. Dale Baum, "Retórica y Realidad en el México Decimonónico – Ensayo de Interpretación de su Historia Política," *Historia Mexicana* 27 , no. 1 (1977):79–102.
11. The origins of this process are in the Bourbon Reforms and the critical reflections on established society formulated since the writings of Father Feijóo. See Chapter One of this study and the eighteenth-century essay by Joseph del Campillo y Cosío, *Nuevo sistema de gobierno económico para la América* (Mérida, Venezuela: Universidad de los Andes, 1971).
12. This is in line with the perspective developed in Chapters Two and Three. For example, note the complexity of the outlooks of Juan José Moreno and Gaspar González de Cándamo.
13. He writes that "gradualism is the criterion and method of the moderate liberals and that line of conduct, in its logical inexorability, leads them at times to agree with the conservatives who deceptively use the slogan 'not time yet.' Without knowing a person's affiliations, it is difficult to determine if his 'not time yet' is due to quietism, the delaying measure of those who at root are secretly opposed to the measure, or if it is the result of the gradualism which guides moderates .... In addition, in between the 'not time yet' approach, quietism and gradualism, there is a whole range of responses producing the most complicated and unsettling personal outcomes." Reyes Heroles, *El liberalismo mexicano*, 425. In his chapters on the political thought and action of conservatives, he does not develop a similar interpretation, but they can be read from this perspective, with some effort. Ibid., II, 215–43, 315–53. He himself has confessed "how tenuous the border between Enlightened liberalism and the ideas of supporters of oligarchical constitutionalism turns out to be at certain times." Ibid., II, 256.

14. On Lucas Alamán, see Moisés González Navarro, *El pensamiento político de Lucas Alamán* (Mexico City: El Colegio de México, 1952); José C. Valadés, *Alamán, Estadista e Historiador* (Mexico City: UNAM, 1977). Reyes Heroles believed that "Alamán, the political brain of conservative forces, knows that it is impossible to maintain the colonial framework unchanged; he knows that it is not possible for society to remain immobile. His conservatism is complex and guided ... by English traditionalism, and above all, by the powerfully pragmatic political school of Edmund Burke, rich in historical perspectives. Under these conditions, Alamán anticipates the formation of a new class which he does not want to see destroying, as in France, the traditional classes of nobility and the clergy, but rather taking its place among them as a privileged class. The privileged classes of our country were the clergy and the Army. It was necessary to form a new class in order to strengthen traditions by broadening them. At root, this is Edmund Burke's idea of integrating the new class in the set of the ancient ones." But Reyes Heroles pays too much attention to Alamán's industrial project and its exceptional foresight. Reyes Heroles, *El liberalismo mexicano*, II, 168–69. In the present study we see that people of traditionalist outlooks recognized more than is commonly believed that Mexico and the world were in the midst of an unavoidable change with a broad historical and social base.

15. Hale summarizes the many similarities he found between liberal and conservative thought prior to the war with the United States: see *Mexican Liberalism*, 290–305. He emphasizes the cases of José María Luis Mora and Lucas Alamán. The matter of the role of the Church, he stresses, and not the form of government, caused the greatest disagreements between them. Hale suggests that even liberals themselves had varying opinions about the colonial past: "Mora ... was more sympathetic to the Colony than was Zavala, though less so than Alamán." Ibid., 24. This surely opened the door for post-Independence reformism on the part of persons of more traditionalist leanings. From a certain standpoint, the growing polarization between liberals and conservatives reflected a difference of emphasis with respect to changes undertaken since the Bourbon Reforms. These changes were, on the one hand, anti-clerical and anti-corporatist, and tended to promote greater participation by royal subjects in matters of state. On the other hand, they never specified a level of popular participation in matters of government, nor ceased to constantly update the historical legacy of the Hapsburg regime. Thus even the most enthusiastic liberal might have doubts about what course of action to take; Mora doubted more than once. Hale mentions his attitude towards religious tolerance – Mora fought for secularization, but "caught between his instinctive attachment to Hispanic values and his utilitarian and liberal aspirations, he counseled moderation, implying that tolerance was a matter that must be left to education." That is to say, he deferred the question to some point in the future. Ibid., 166.

16. See earlier chapters about the tendency of a more traditional reformism, favorable to Church participation, to support matters of practical renewal and interweave their arguments first with regionalism, and later with nationalism. In both cases, they moved away from absolute principles of reform and employed a notion of social collectivity opposed to the individualist premises of ultra-liberal reformers.

17. Texts cited below will give examples of this approach. Perhaps there is a greater analogy here than one would expect with the workings of the Inquisition in Spain and America. "Unlike the Papal Index, the Spanish Index noted the corrections and suppressions that needed to be done for a book to be offered

to the public once more." This avoided "total condemnation of the work and its definitive separation from the Spanish public." Of course, this porosity towards new ideas depended on the uncertain efficiency of the Inquisition bureaucracy. See Connaughton, *España y Nueva España*, 276 and following.

18. In *Dos etapas ideológicas*, Pérez Marchand observed that already in eighteenth-century Mexico even the Inquisition had found itself obliged to adopt a growing laxity towards new ideas. The emphasis on renewal was unavoidable. Nevertheless, this does not indicate a lack of worry or concern about the changes, just a limit of venom such worries could take on.

19. Naturally, the Church did not wish to allow much opportunity for such misconduct within Mexico. Its actions in the case of El Polar give an idea of the limits of its patience: see Chapter Seven.

20. The clergy's discursive calls were increasingly directed towards the broad public. The change from a monarchy to a republic demanded a crucial shift in the social discourse of the clergy. The pressures themselves, however, were not entirely new. For the origins of state antagonism toward the Church, see William B. Taylor, *Entre el proceso global y el conocimiento local: ensayos sobre el estado, la sociedad y la cultura en el México del siglo XVIII* (Mexico City: UAM-Iztapalapa and Miguel Ángel Porrúa, forthcoming).

21. The precedents for this process can be found in the cases of Bishops Alcalde and Cabañas. Documents from after Independence will be cited below. See also Dennis Paul Ricker, "The Lower Secular Clergy of Central Mexico" (Ph.D. diss., University of Texas, 1982). Ricker offers evidence of the broadening and modernizing of seminary studies in this period, providing interesting material on the Guadalajara Diocese. In addition to reinforcing their ecclesiastical studies properly speaking, seminaries tried to include scientific and general literary matters. By 1856, the Guadalajara Seminary would offer courses in Mathematics, Physics, French and English, as well as an impressive range of courses about ecclesiastical discipline, the Holy Scriptures, dogma, canon law, Greek and Latin. Ibid., 79–148. See also Daniel Loweree, *El seminario conciliar de Guadalajara ... Apéndice* (Guadalajara: self-published, 1964).

22. Hale and Reyes Heroles repeatedly show the failure of the loftiest versions of liberalism to prevail.

23. As will be shown throughout this study, such an insinuation would be an important part of the reconstitution of clerical discourse in Guadalajara.

24. Here the contrast would be with the seventeenth century. At that time, critical thinking [*arbitrismo*] promoted various changes to attack Spanish "decadence," without coming together in an overall critique – based on general principles – of the socio-economic structure of the whole. See J. H. Elliot, "The Spanish Peninsula 1598–1648" in J. P. Cooper (ed.), *The Decline of Spain and the Thirty Years War 1609–48/49, The New Cambridge Modern History Vol IV* (Cambridge: Cambridge University Press, 1970). Nevertheless, the activity of these critics deserves more attention than it has received, including its possible influence on Mexico. Elliot notes: "the years 1598 to 1621 were pre-eminently years of national introspection, the first of those recurrent moments in modern Spanish history when the country turns inward upon itself in an agony of self-appraisal." Ibid., 435.

25. For the French case, see Groethuysen. For the Mexican case, see Chapter Four and the remainder of this study.

26. A separate study would be needed to more adequately specify each one of these points. What is least addressed in this study is the direct participation of outstanding members of the clergy in government committees and the exercise of elected office, but several Guadalajara Church figures, such as José de Jesús Huerta, Miguel Gordoa, José Miguel Ramírez and Diego Aranda, had important political careers in this sense. Except for the first, they all contributed to the political renewal of Mexico without straying from the dominant positions of the Guadalajara Church. On Huerta, see Juan B. Iguíniz, "El Doctor Don José de Jesús Huerta," in *Anuario de la Comisión Diocesana de Historia del Arzobispado de Guadalajara,* Mexico City: Editorial Jus, 1968. To see lists of priests who participated in national congresses, see Ricker, "The Lower Secular Clergy," 231–34. See also the footnotes about several prominent clergymen in Chapters Four, Seven and Eight of this study.

27. I have dealt with this problem in Connaughton, *Dimensiones.*

28. El obispo auxiliar de Madrid, *Artículo interesante que se insertó en el noticioso de México* (Guadalajara: D. Mariano Rodríguez, 1822), 1.

29. Ibid., 2.

30. Ibid., 2, 5.

31. Ibid., 5, 6.

32. Ibid., 6.

33. El Católico, *Legítimo punto de vista en la causa de los fracmasones.* (Guadalajara: Oficina del C. Mariano Rodríguez, 1824), unpaginated.

34. Ibid.

35. Ibid.

36. Count Muzzarelli, *Opúsculo V. Indiferencia de la religión* (Guadalajara: Oficina de la viuda de Romero, 1824 [reprint]).

37. Ibid., 47–48.

38. Count Muzzarelli, *Opúsculo XI. De las riquezas del clero.* (Guadalajara: Oficina de la viuda de Romero, 1824 [reprint]).

39. Ibid., 44.

40. Count Muzzarelli, *Opúsculo XVIII. Inmunidad Eclesiástica personal, carta única* (Guadalajara: Oficina de la viuda de Romero, 1824 [reprint]), 24.

41. Ibid., 30–31.

42. Count Muzzarelli, *Opúsculo de la excomunión* (Guadalajara: Oficina de la viuda de Romero, 1824 [reprint]), 4–5.

43. Ibid., 11, 13.

44. Ibid., 15, 21, 15, 22.

45. See Chapters Two, Three, and Four above. By contrast, Joaquín Antonio de Villalobos, in giving his approval in 1723 to the publication of a sermon, expressed an interesting judgment on its merits: "because reading it has given me … much to admire, and much to applaud. Admiration is the legitimate product of novelty; due applause is a sign of worthiness, and since there is so much worthiness in the preacher and so many novelties in the sermon, both the sermon and the preacher deserve admiration, and applause. Well it is, that since the feast, in this Court of Guadalajara, is new; new is [its] fame in this new world; new, very new is the matter of panegyrics; new, even extremely new, although so solid and so discrete, are the theses, propositions, proofs, nuances, rhetorical sweep; only one thing is not new: the wisdom with which the whole course of the sermon is perfected by its eloquent author; the majesty with which the argument enters into confrontation with difficulty; the skill with which he frees himself from such tangled circumstances; the clarity with which he makes

evident such obscure enigmas; the perspicacity with which he penetrates the deepest and most arcane matters; the valor with which he dares to venture down such untraveled paths; the gravity with which he handles matters of the Holy Scriptures; the genuine intelligence with which he expounds on the authority of the Holy Fathers; the mastery with which he treats the most obscure points of theology; the transparency, the diaphanous propriety of the words with which he explains such emphatic subtleties; the eloquence with which he extends across such thorny materials." Diego de Estrada Carbajal y Galindo, *Excesos del Amor del Eterno Padre* (Mexico City: Los Herederos de la Viuda de Francisco Rodríguez Lupercio, 1724), unpaginated.

46. Fray Veremundo, Archbishop of Valencia, *Representación del Arzobispo de Valencia a las Cortes* (Valencia, reprinted in Guadalajara: Oficina del C. Mariano Rodríguez, 1824).

47. Ibid., 6, 8.

48. Ibid., 9.

49. Ricker, "Lower Secular Clergy," 330–31. For a point of comparison, see discussion of the dynamics of the French clergy in the eighteenth century in Norman Ravitch, *Sword and Mitre: Government and Episcopate in France and England in the Age of Aristocracy* (The Hague: Mouton, 1966). Various aspects of the situation in Mexico are treated in Costeloe, *Church and State*.

50. For the precedents for this change, see Connaughton, *España y Nueva España.*

51. Fray Veremundo, *Representación*, 9–16. Along with monasticism, the archbishop defended, in general, the religious orders.

52. Ibid., 19–21.

53. Ibid., 23.

54. Ibid., 24–25.

55. Ibid., 27. Italics in original; indicate citation of Book V of Charlemagne's *Capitularies.*

56. Ibid., 29–32, 33, 34.

57. Ibid., 34.

58. *Pronta y oportuna respuesta al papel titulado "Hereje a la tapatía porque no fía"* (Guadalajara: Imprenta del C. Mariano Rodríguez, 1824), 7, 12. This reproduces *Alcance al número 86 del Caduceo de Puebla* and *Alcance al número 7 del Caduceo de Puebla.*

59. *Otra zurra a la tapatía por retobada y por impía* (Guadalajara: Imprenta del C. Mariano Rodríguez, 1824), 1–3, 6–7.

60. Ibid., 2.

61. F.M.M., *Preservativo contra la irreligión* (Guadalajara: Imprenta del C. Mariano Rodríguez, 1824), 23–25.

62. Ibid., 26, 28–35.

63. Ibid., 35–41. Pedro Lissaute was a French mathematician later named the first director of the Institute of Sciences which was created to replace the University by the liberal government. Lissaute was a liberal with a clear anti-clerical stance. See Iguíniz, *La antigua Universidad*, and Muriá, *Historia de Jalisco*, II: 522–23.

64. F.M.M., *Preservativo*, 42–43, 44, 46, 48–50,

65. Ibid., 51, 58–59, 66.

66. Ibid., 67.

67. *Conversación familiar entre un sacristán y su compadre contra el papel titulado Hereje a la tapatía* (Guadalajara: Imprenta del C. Mariano Rodríguez, 1824), 1.

68. Ibid., 2.

69. Ibid., 6–8.

70. Ibid., 8–9. Voltaire (1694–1778), Jean le Rond d'Alembert (1717–1783) and Denis Diderot (1713–1784) were frequently singled out by religious spokesmen for sharp criticism.

71. Ibid., 10.

72. Ibid., 11.

73. Antonio, Obispo de Puebla, *Contestación del Señor Obispo de Puebla al Honorable Congreso de Veracruz* (Puebla, reprinted in Guadalajara: Imprenta del C. Mariano Rodríguez, 1824), 2–3.

74. Ibid., 3–4.

75. Ibid., 7.

76. *Artículo 7o de la Constitución de Jalisco, "El estado fijará y costeará todos los gastos necesarios para la conservación del culto"* (Guadalajara: Imprenta del C. Mariano Rodríguez, 1824), 3–4

77. Ibid., 5–8.

78. *Contestación al Defensor del Artículo 7o* (Guadalajara: Imprenta del C. Mariano Rodríguez, 1824), 6, 8–9.

79. Ibid., 9–10.

80. Ibid., 11–12.

81. C.A., *También los callados suelen hablar* (Guadalajara: Imprenta del C. Mariano Rodríguez, 1824), unpaginated.

82. Ibid.

83. Ibid.

84. El sacristán, *La mala fe descubierta, y herida con sus propias armas* (Guadalajara: Imprenta del C. Mariano Rodríguez, 1824), 3.

85. Ibid., 7–10.

86. Ibid., 12–13.

87. Ibid., 13.

88. Ibid., 13–14.

89. *Sobre la cuestión del día* (Guadalajara: Imprenta de la viuda de Romero, 1824), 1–3.

90. Ibid., 3.

91. Ibid., 5.

92. Ibid., 6–11.

93. Ibid., 12.

94. Ibid., 12–15.

95. *El error despojado de los adornos y aliños de la virtud y presentado bajo su propia forma* (Guadalajara: Imprenta del C. Mariano Rodríguez, 1824), 1, 3, 15, 16, 17.

96. Ibid., 17.

97. Ibid., 18.

98. Ibid., 33–34.

99. Ibid., 36.

100. Ibid., 37.

101. Ibid., 37–38.

102. Ibid., 47.

103. Ibid., 49, 54, 58.

104. *La Cruz* (Guadalajara: Imprenta de la viuda de Romero, 1824), 1: 3–4.

105. Ibid., 2: 6.

106. Ibid., 2: 8.

107. Ibid., 3: 10–12, 5: 20, 7: 26.

108. Ibid., 7: 28.

Notes to Chapter 7

1. On the tumultuous course of events in Spain, see Callahan, *Church, Politics and Society*. For the situation in Mexico, see Pérez Memen, *El episcopado*, 146–252. This covers the response of the Mexican ecclesiastical hierarchy to the complex period between 1820 and 1824.

2. Costeloe recognizes the importance of the new parameters of freedom of the press and the proliferation of newspapers and pamphlets for the intellectual life of the Mexican clergy. Costeloe, *Church and state*, 176–81.

3. Original titles: *También los callados suelen hablar, Sobre la cuestión del día, La mala fe descubierta y herida por sus propias armas, Artículo 7 de la Constitución de Jalisco, Otra zurra a la tapatía por retobada y por impía.*

4. Original titles: *El error despojado de los adornos y aliños de la virtud ... y presentado bajo su propia forma* and *Preservativo contra la irreligión.*

5. See Chapters Five and Six. Some of the authors of anonymous pamphlets treated here are identified by Iguíniz, *Catálogo biobibliográfico*. Costeloe agrees that the Church questioned the privileges of the state but did not stop demanding that it comply with its duties towards the Church. His study extensively examines matters related to the *patronato* and the main clerical postures towards it. Costeloe, *Church and State*, 177. This process is also addressed by Paul Murray and Fernando Pérez Memen. Murray treats the period summarily. He emphasizes the difficulty of dispassionately establishing what happened, and he reviews some primary documents and secondary sources to demonstrate this. He stresses that a substantial change of values had already taken place in the country, coloring visions of events with marked partisanship. Yet his commentaries frequently assume an apologetic tone, favoring the Church. See Murray, *The Catholic Church in Mexico: Historical Essays for the General Reader* (Mexico City: Editorial E.P.M., 1964) and Pérez Memen, *El episcopado.*

6. *El Amante de la Religión, Una palabra al Polar convertido* (Guadalajara: Imprenta de la viuda de Romero, 1825), unpaginated.

7. Ibid.

8. *El Amante de la Religión, A los Editores del Nivel* (Guadalajara: Imprenta de la viuda de Romero, 1825), unpaginated.

9. "Article 171. The articles of this Constitution and the Constitutive Act establishing the freedom and independence of the Mexican nation, its religion, its form of government, the freedom of the press and the division of supreme powers between the federation and the states can never be modified." After 1830, modifications to the Constitution were addressed in Articles 166–69. *Constitución Federal*, 44–45.

10. *El verdadero defensor de nuestra constitución, ¡Atención! Que los apóstatas quieren variar nuestra religión* (Mexico City, reprinted in Guadalajara: Oficinas de los CC. Alejandro Valdés y Mariano Rodríguez, 1825), 2–3.

11. Ibid., 4–6.

12. Ibid., 7.

13. "Article 3. The religion of the Mexican nation is and perpetually will be the Apostolic Roman Catholic Church. The nation will protect it by means of wise and just laws, and prohibit the exercise of any other." *Constitución Federal*, 13.

14. Ibid., 7–8.

15. Ibid., 8.

16. *Verdades amargas para los Editores del Nivel* (Guadalajara: Imprenta de la viuda de Romero, 1825), unpaginated.
17. Ibid.
18. El Inválido, *Por más que hable el Pensador, No hemos de ser tolerantes, sino cristianos como antes* (Mexico City, reprinted in Guadalajara: Oficina del C. Mariano Rodríguez, 1825).
19. Ibid.
20. Ibid.
21. Another pamphlet which refers to freedom of the press, and which incidentally suggests the difficulty of controlling it, is *La Verdad desfigurada* (Guadalajara: Imprenta del C. Mariano Rodríguez, 1825).
22. Pamphlets also argued that religion was not only good for Mexico, but also for its government. One asserted that "whoever snipes at God, as is commonly said, will just as well snipe at the government." El amigo del mexicano, *Ya Jalisco perdió su Nivel* (Mexico City: Imprenta del C. Alejandro Valdés, 1825), 7. In another pamphlet, the magistrate of a town concedes "so you see how the priests are usually the most important voice in towns and they don't pay taxes, [but] exhort everyone else to pay, and that is why there hasn't been too much opposition." Later on, the priest managed to say that "I hadn't heard the clergy called a corporation until now, and you don't call the laborers or tailors of a place that." *Tertulia en una aldea de Jalisco entre el cura, que lleva la voz, el Alcalde, D. Blas y D. Diego.* Mexico City:Imprenta del Aguila, 1826), 2, 7. Another pamphlet insisted on religion's usefulness for society and demanded that Article 3 of the Constitution be kept intact, as Article 171 required. El amigo del otro amigo, *Por aquí rapa el Nivel: por allí lo rapan a él* (Mexico City: Imprenta del C. Alejandro Valdés, 1826).
23. La Maceta de Tepeguage, *A cuña de palo dulce mazeta [sic] de tepeguage* (Guadalajara: Imprenta del C. Mariano Rodríguez, 1825), 2. Iguíniz attributes this publication to José Manuel Covarrubias y Sierra, a doctor in theology from the University of Guadalajara and prominent cleric in the diocese. Iguíniz, *Catálogo biobibliográfico*, 132–33.
24. Ibid., 2–3.
25. Ibid., 3.
26. Ibid., 3–5.
27. Ibid., 5.
28. Ibid., 7.
29. Tepehuage, *Respuesta de Tepehuage al Sr. de la media palabra* (Guadalajara: Imprenta del C. Mariano Rodríguez, 1825), 2–5.
30. Ibid., 5–6.
31. Ibid.
32. Ibid., 6–14.
33. José María Covarrubias, *Comunicado que dio el C. Dr. José María Covarrubias y corre en el Sol núm. 875.* (Guadalajara: Oficina del C. Mariano Rodríguez, 1825 [reprint]). Another pamphlet on the question of clerical abuses is Tepehuage, *Quien mal pleito tiene a boruca lo mete* (Guadalajara: Oficina del C. Mariano Rodríguez, 1825), which, as already mentioned, Iguíniz attributes to Covarrubias. The reform of the clergy was addressed from an orthodox perspective – invoking the work of Father Ceballos quoted in Chapter Two – in *Advertencia a los del Nivel y todo el pueblo de Jalisco* (Guadalajara: Imprenta del C. Mariano Rodríguez, 1825).

34. *Polar embarazada, o visita de Leonor a Madama Polar* (Guadalajara: Oficina del C.Mariano Rodríguez, 1825), unpaginated.
35. Ibid.
36. Ibid.
37. Ibid.
38. Ibid.
39. Casimiro Bienpica, *El Canónigo Bien-pica* [*sic*], *a su Prelado El Polar* (Guadalajara: Oficina del C. Mariano Rodríguez, 1825), unpaginated.
40. Ibid.
41. El Fanático, supersticioso y devoto, *Un geringazo al Polar* (Guadalajara: Imprenta del C. Mariano Rodríguez, 1825), unpaginated.
42. Ibid.
43. Ibid. I.e., that even the doctrine of the Trinity was only grasped through rumor at best, not through solid reasoning, and that tolerance would thus imperil the fledgling faith of the populace.
44. *Ignorancia descubierta y temeridad confundida* (Guadalajara: Imprenta del C. Mariano Rodríguez, 1825), 22. In addition to its argumentative content, this pamphlet reproduced Article 3 and parts of Articles 2 and 6 of the Constitution in order to suggest that its opponents were violating the Constitution in matters of the freedom of the press and protection for religion guaranteed by the national state.
45. Ibid., 2.
46. Ibid., 4.
47. Ibid., 4–5.
48. Ibid., 5–6.
49. Ibid., 6. The cathedral chapter publication referred to is *Colección de documentos …* (Guadalajara: Imprenta del C. Mariano Rodríguez, 1825).
50. Perhaps in Jalisco, the process had not been completed by which, beginning in the eighteenth century, a "secular priesthood" of "inspired writers" became the intellectual class in the West, displacing clerics as the spiritual guides of society. Paul Bénichou, *La coronación del escritor 1750–1830. Ensayo sobre el advenimiento de un poder espiritual laico en la Francia moderna* (Mexico City: Fondo de Cultura Económica, 1981), 11–73, 150, 254.
51. For more information, see Chapter Four.
52. In this sense, the sources of Mexican ecclesiastical thought are worthy of greater study. Such research could be quite fruitful. For the eighteenth century, we can cite Benito Jerónimo Feijóo, especially his *Teatro crítico*. Yet one author repeatedly cited in the nineteenth century is Jacques Bénigne Bossuet, the Bishop of Meaux in France. Referring to his *Discourse on Universal History* in particular, Robert Nisbet states that "there is simply no question but that for Bossuet *progress* characterizes the whole of universal history." Further along, Nisbet adds that "[Bossuet] leaves no doubt in our minds that the very heart of the progress of mankind through the ages has been religious in character and that Jesus Christ and the founding of Christianity have all the majesty in the Age of Louis XIV that they had earlier." But this is more complicated still. Nisbet asserts that "the striking aspect of [the] … third and final part of the *Discourse* is its remarkably secular character. We are never in any doubt that the first and final cause of everything is Providence; but, this accepted, we are presented with a sequence of social, economic, cultural, and political insights into the rise and fall of empires." Robert Nisbet, *History of the Idea of Progress* (New York: Basic

Books, 1980), 140–45. Paul Hazard devoted an entire chapter of his book *The European Mind* to the life and works of Bossuet. He reached this conclusion: "No imperturbable, untroubled builder, he, of some splendid cathedral in the sumptuous Louis XIV style; no, not that, but much rather a harassed workman, hurrying away, without a moment to lose, to patch up cracks in the edifice that every day grow more and more alarming. He sees deep down into the underlying principles of things. He was not deceived about the extent, the power, the diversity of what the sceptics had done, and were doing, to undermine and destroy the very foundations of the Church of God." Further on Hazard added: "Living in an age that was intoxicated with Cartesianism, and up to a point a Cartesian himself, Bossuet meditates, draws distinctions, and defends his own position." Hazard, *The European Mind*, 211, 213.

In fact, it may be in the writings of men like Bossuet that many Mexican clerics in the first republic nourished their conviction that there was in fact an Enlightenment which was just as progressive as it was Catholic. Even the style of writing of the most refined clerical thinkers may have been influenced by authors like Bossuet. Research along different lines than this book could determine this with greater precision.

53. *Ladridos del perro al lobo-pastor* (Guadalajara: Oficina de D.Mariano Rodríguez, 1826).

54. El Caballero del Verde Gabán, *El Polar Reformador o el Quijote de estos tiempos* (Guadalajara: Imprenta del C. Mariano Rodríguez, 1826), unpaginated.

55. El Amigo del Orden, *Tiene razón el General Rayón, o sea respuesta al comunicado inserto en la Gaceta núm. 29* (Guadalajara: Imprenta de la viuda de Romero, 1826), unpaginated.

56. El Apestado, *El coco de los impíos, o La Escolta de Dragones. Respuesta a un comunicado de la Gaceta* (Guadalajara: Imprenta del C. Mariano Rodríguez, 1826), unpaginated.

57. Ibid.

58. Ibid.

59. Maceta. *Para esos huesos la maceta* (Mexico City, reprinted in Guadalajara: las Oficinas de los CC. Alejandro Valdés y Mariano Rodríguez, 1826), 8–18. This pamphlet adopts a particularly virulent and defiant attitude. It asks the opposing pamphleteer: "Were priests so wise and skillful in the arts of deception that not even one of them took one false step that would reveal the mess, nor even one of those deceived came to realize their delusion, until this de-stupidyfing [*sic*] gentleman came along to the peoples to bring them out of their *stupidity*? To be sure, whoever has such an idea of priests' aptness … in maintaining such arrogance is not such an enemy of the clergy, nor is it reasonable to hold one … who supposes men to be so foolish and cowardly to be their friend." Iguíniz, *Catálogo biobibliográfico*, 33, attributes this to José María Covarrubias y Sierra..

60. *Contestaciones a los EE. del Nivel, y una palabra al polar* (Guadalajara: Imprenta de la viuda de Romero, 1826), unpaginated.

61. Ibid.

62. Pufendorf had been nothing less that the man who "by drawing a distinction between Natural Law and Divine Law, had completely laicized the character of juridical studies." Hazard, *European Mind*, 172–73.

63. *Otro palo, a los Editores del Nivel* (Guadalajara: Imprenta de la viuda de Romero, 1826), unpaginated. Iguíniz attributes it to Pedro Espinoza y Dávalos, who received a doctorate in theology from the University of Guadalajara in 1821 and was a very prominent cleric in the diocese and Bishop of Guadalajara after 1854.

64. Ibid., 6.
65. Ibid., 6–7.
66. Ibid., 8.
67. *Colección de documentos* ... *(Guadalajara: Imprenta del C. Mariano Rodríguez, 1825).*
68. First Toribio González, and then José Miguel Ramírez held the Mitre of Guadalajara – making them the highest Church official, in the absence of a bishop. Governor Sánchez of Jalisco went so far as to complain to Ramírez that he was not following the agreement made with the previous authority, Toribio González. According to Governor Sánchez, González had agreed that direct contributions (from the Church to the state) would be paid in thirds as loans, until their constitutionality was determined. The first third had not been completely paid, Sánchez claimed, and the second third had almost not been paid at all. In the eyes of Sánchez, this was simply a case of "how certain churches, monasteries and ecclesiastical persons gain capital in lucrative negotiations under the auspices of the state just like lay people, and therefore accidentally find themselves included in taxes which should extend to all capitalists in business." But Canon Ramírez did not see things this way, and defended the Church's prerogatives. Before paying the second third, he demanded that they await the resolution of the "Supreme Government of the Federation." This produced great annoyance, but Ramírez defended his own patriotism and that of the clergy, while Sánchez insisted that the "support of society" benefitted all and therefore all had to care for it. Ramírez and the cathedral chapter relented, but the former underscored the good name and intentions of the clergy and categorically affirmed: "I have a right to my political and public reputation." *Contestaciones habidas entre el Supremo Gobierno del Estado de Jalisco y el Gobernador de la Mitra sobre contribución directa* (Guadalajara: Imprenta del C. Urbano Sanromán, 1825), 4–9, 10–12, 19, 21–30. The distinguished ecclesiastical career of Ramírez is summarized in Iguíniz, *Catálogo biobibliográfico*, 237–38.
69. Francisco Semería, *Contra Palanca, Palanca, Haber* [*sic*] *cual levanta más, o sea adición a la Palanca núm. 15* (Guadalajara: Imprenta de la viuda de Romero, 1826), unpaginated.
70. Mariano Carrasco, et al., *Representación que el Ayuntamiento Constitucional de Guadalajara dirige al Excelentísimo Señor Presidente de la República* (Mexico City: Oficina de la Testamentaría de Ontiveros, 1826), 1–4.
71. Ibid., 4–8.
72. *Exposición del Sr. Gobernador de la Mitra sobre la exclusiva concedida al Gobierno* (Guadalajara: Imprenta del C. Urbano Sanromán, 1826). On Prisciliano Sánchez, see Luis Pérez Verdía, *Biografías: Fray Antonio Alcalde y Prisciliano Sánchez* (Guadalajara: Ediciones ITG, 1952) and Costeloe, *Church and State*, 76–78, 82, 104. Staples states that the Interdiocesan Conference in Mexico in 1822 refused to accept that the *patronato* was inherent to the nation. "Yet the Interdiocesan Conference did accept that the traditional rights of the government on matters of ecclesiastical appointments should be maintained in order to preserve harmony between temporal and spiritual powers." Staples, *La iglesia*, 38–39. According to Pérez Memen, this should have obviated the 1826 dispute in Jalisco about the governor's right to exclude undesireable clerics from the names proposed by the ecclesiastical authorities for new appointments. But he admits that "in Guadalajara the state's assertion of its exclusive privilege was very controversial. In the legislature itself two groups formed, one in

favor of state exercise of that right, and the other opposed." Pérez Memen, *El episcopado y la Independencia*, 265–66. On José Miguel Gordoa, see Iguíniz, *Catálogo biobibliográfico*, 168–71. After being Governor of the Mitre, Gordoa was named Bishop of Guadalajara in 1831, but he was one of many Guadalajara clerics with an impressive political trajectory, in addition to his ecclesiastical career. He was a deputy for Zacatecas in the Spanish Cortes in 1810, 1812, and 1813, playing an active role. In 1820, he was named deputy for Guadalajara to the Cortes, and he was president of the mining section of the Patriotic Society of Guadalajara in 1821. During 1823 and 1824 he was a representative for Zacatecas to the General Constitutional Congress of Mexico, and he signed the Constitution in 1824.

73. *Exposición*, 5.
74. Ibid., 6.
75. Ibid., 7.
76. Ibid., 7–9.
77. Ibid., 9.
78. Ibid., 9–10.
79. Ibid., 10.
80. Ibid., 12, 15, 16.
81. Ibid., 18–19.
82. Ibid., 19.
83. Ibid., 19–21.
84. Ibid., 22.
85. Ibid., 22–23.
86. Ibid., 23.
87. Ibid., 23–27.
88. Ibid., 27–28.
89. Ibid., 28.
90. Ibid., 28–29.
91. Ibid., 29–30.
92. Ibid., 32.
93. Ibid., 32–35. The resolution of the Congress is reprinted on page 36.

Notes to Chapter 8

1. The origins of the Mexican fiscal crisis are debated in Hamnett, *Revolución*, 79–117, and San Juan Victoria and Velázquez Ramírez, "La formación del Estado," 65–96.
2. See Chapter Seven and Jaime Olveda, *El sistema fiscal de Jalisco* (Guadalajara: Gobierno del Estado de Jalisco, 1983), 32–34. In 1829 income would be taxed, not wealth. The Church was still included among the list of taxpayers, as can be seen in the *Dictamen presentado por la Comisión de Hacienda* ... (Guadalajara: Imprenta del Supremo Gobierno, a cargo del C. Juan María Brambilia, 1829).
3. Pérez Memen, *El episcopado*, 252; San Juan Victoria and Velázquez Ramírez, "La formación del Estado," 69.
4. Costeloe, *Church and State*, 105. The Church ultimately won the dispute, but only in 1831. Pérez Memen, *El episcopado*, 257.
5. The background for this has been treated in depth in Chapters Five to Seven.
6. Costeloe, *Church and state*, 68–112; Staples, *La iglesia*, 35–58; Chapters Six and Seven above.

7. Pedro Lissaute, *Discurso prounciado en la solemnidad* ... (Guadalajara: Imprenta del
    Supremo Gobierno, 1830). For more information on Lissaute, see the biographi-
    cal footnote in Chapter Six. He taught at the Institute, which had replaced the
    University of Guadalajara, taking over its facilities. It was legally established on 20
    March 1826 and inaugurated on 14 February 1827. "Established on a markedly
    liberal basis, its plan of studies included matters of positive interest which were
    taught in Guadalajara for the first time and without any doubt fit the needs
    of the era." See Iguíniz, *Catálogo biobibliográfico*, 33–34, and Iguíniz, *La antigua
    universidad*. Incidentally, Iguíniz argues against the appropriation of the property
    of the university and against the anti-religious radicalism of its teaching.
8. Lissaute, *Discurso*, xii–xv, 22, 31–32, 35–41.
9. Ibid., 23. Italics mine.
10. Ibid., 21–26.
11. Ibid., 38.
12. Ibid., 2–24, 40–41. Lissaute also mentioned the education of women as a means
    of freeing them, along with the "masses," from the "deplorable vestiges of
    peninsular barbarism and fanaticism." Ibid., 43–44.
13. Prisciliano Sánchez, *Memoria sobre el estado actual de la administración pública del
    Estado de Jalisco en todos los ramos de su comprensión* (Guadalajara: Imprenta del C.
    Urbano Sanromán, ca. 1826), 23–27.
14. Ibid., 4–5.
15. See Chapters Six and Seven. According to Costeloe, "In the years immediately
    following Independence ... the Church, despite reduced numbers of clergy,
    much diminished legal powers and privileges and the effects of the strong
    secularist influences from Europe, retained, and in various ways controlled, the
    respect, obedience, and even fanatical devotion of the majority of Mexicans of
    all social classes. Mexico remained a nation in which both the spiritual and
    the temporal power of the Church pervaded all aspects of life. This social and
    economic power inevitably generated political influence. Although certain pro-
    clerical authors have denied that clerics actively participated in politics, there
    are many indications to the contrary. Lizardi persistently denounced them for
    campaigning in elections. He wrote that in the 1826 national and state congres-
    sional elections, local priests had used their influence to get themselves or their
    cohorts elected so successfully that some congresses were more like ecclesiastical
    councils than political assemblies.... Priests were often denounced for using their
    sermons to preach on political affairs of the day." Costeloe, *Church and State*, 41.
16. Ibid., 15.
17. Ibid., 4.
18. Juan Nepomuceno Cumplido, *Memoria sobre el estado actual de la administración
    pública del Estado de Jalisco (*Guadalajara: Oficina del C. Urbano Sanromán, ca.
    1827), 6, 11–13. Prisciliano Sánchez died on 30 December 1826 and Vice-
    Governor Cumplido took power from 19 January 1827 to 23 September 1828.
    See Ramiro Villaseñor y Villaseñor, *Los primeros federalistas de Jalisco 1821–1834*
    (Guadalajara: Gobierno de Jalisco, 1981), 48, 103. Apologetic writings about
    Prisciliano Sánchez appeared quickly, and joining the political personality of the
    deceased Governor with the crisis of the state and a critique of the Church,
    pointed towards the solution Lissaute would offer in 1830. See *Dictamen sobre
    las exequias, luto y honores fúnebres que deben decretarse al difunto Gobernador del
    Estado de Jalisco* (Guadalajara: Imprenta del C. Urbano Sanromán, 1826); Luis
    de la Rosa, *Elogio fúnebre dedicado a la memoria del ciudadano Prisciliano Sánchez*
    (Mexico City: Imprenta del Aguila, 1827); Antonio Pacheco Leal, *Discurso que el*

ciudadano … socio de la junta patriótica , pronunció ante las autoridades de la Capital el 18 de noviembre de 827 [sic] (Guadalajara: Imprenta del C. Brambila, 1827); Antonio Pacheco Leal, *Elogio fúnebre que pronunció el C. …, individuo de la Junta de Artesanos de la Capital de Jalisco, en la conmemoración que la misma junta dedicó a la memoria póstuma del Exmo. Gobernador benemérito del Estado, C. Prisciliano Sánchez* (Guadalajara: Imprenta del C. Urbano Sanromán, 1828).

19. Juan Nepomuceno Cumplido, *Informe sobre el estado actual de la administración pública del Estado de Jalisco* (Guadalajara: Imprenta del Gobierno a cargo del C. Juan María Brambila, 1828), 5. The economic crisis the Vice-Governor spoke of was also discussed in *Representación de la sociedad de artesanos y comerciantes dirigida al Soberano Congreso de la Unión* (Guadalajara: Imprenta de Gobierno en Palacio, 1828) and *Si los cristianos se van tantos hereges* [sic] *qué harán. O sea ligera manifestación de los insufribles males que aflige a la nación mexicana como preciso resultado de la libertad y franquicia de comercio concedido a los estranjeros* (Guadalajara, reprinted in Mexico City: Oficina del C. Núñez, 1828). Interestingly, this last publication tied the economic crisis to a threat to "religion and independence" and condemned the "tolerance in fact permitted in violation of … constitutional laws." *Si los cristianos se van*, 3–4, 6.

20. Cumplido, *Informe*, 6–8, 11–13. According to the Vice-Governor, virtually every municipality in the state had sent a professor to Guadalajara to learn the Lancaster Method, and the government was trying to ensure that the remaining municipalities would also do so. Fifty-one professors had attended and were later examined and certified by the Board of Directors of Studies. Three hundred and eighty-five children attended the Lancaster school in Guadalajara. The state provided the necessary supplies and the vice governor was trying to do the same for the other schools of the same kind across Jalisco. Ibid., 12–13.

21. José Ignacio Herrera, *Memoria sobre el estado actual de la administración pública del Estado de Jalisco en todos los ramos de su comprensión* (Guadalajara: No publisher, ca. 1831), 15. His allusion to the "half of what it earns from such hard work" being taken away is in reference to the clumsiness and excesses of the tax system and monopolies. Ibid, 14–15. Vice-Governor since 1829, Herrera would serve as Governor from 1830 until February 1833. See Villaseñor y Villaseñor, *Los primeros federalistas*, 67. Herrera took office in the middle of a national civil war, when Vicente Guerrero was overthrown by Anastasio Bustamante and Lucas Alamán. The military commander in Jalisco in 1830, General Miguel Barragán, had asked the Federal Congress to call a "conciliatory junta" to solve the problem: "The august National Congress, the Supreme Government, the Honorable Legislatures of the states, the respectable magistrates entrusted with the administration of justice, the venerable Clergy, the Generals of the Army, the landowners, the merchants, the simple citizens, all will see their reciprocal and individual interests advanced with this step, since for the stability of all the peace of society and concord among all its individuals are radically necessary, so that we may join in unison to make … [this great nation] respectable, and to mock the insidious gazes of those who are pleased by our ruin." *Exposición del General Barragán al Soberano Congreso Nacional* (Guadalajara: Imprenta del C. Ignacio Brambila, 1830), unpaginated. See also Costeloe, *La primera república*, 259–60, 310–12.

22. Herrera, *Memoria*, 7–9, 16–20, 26–28. Olveda discusses the economic and fiscal disorganization of Jalisco during the First Republic and the state's inability to carry out adequate public works of any kind or to even cover its annual mandatory contribution to the Treasury of the Federal Government. Some order

had barely been introduced into public coffers in 1831–32 when the ensuing conflicts threw everything into disorder once again. He adds that "at the end of the first republican period (1835) the poverty of the government of Jalisco was such that even the committee entrusted with drafting the Civil Code had to interrupt its efforts for lack of funds. Olveda, *El sistema fiscal*, 27–50. Problems with money and coinage are discussed in Muriá, *Historia de Jalisco*, II: 482–485.

23. Costeloe, *Church and State*, 29–31, 88, 116; Staples, *La iglesia*, 21–31, 59–64.

24. *Reflecciones* [*sic*] *sobre el dictamen de las comisiones eclesiástica y de relaciones, acerca de las instrucciones al enviado a Roma* (Mexico City, reprinted in Guadalajara: Oficina del C. Mariano Rodríguez, 1826). The debate about the patronage in 1827 included the publication of many newspaper pieces and pamphlets like *Contestación del Obispo y Cabildo de la Santa Iglesia Catedral de Oaxaca al oficio del Exmo. Señor Ministro de Justicia y Negocios Eclesiásticos* (Guadalajara: Oficina de la viuda de Romero, 1827 [reprint]) and *Contestación sobre patronato, dada por los presbíteros Fernando Antonio Dávila, Dr. Angel María Candina y Dr. Antonio González* (Guatemala: Imprenta de Beteta, 1824; reprinted in Guadalajara: Imprenta del C. Mariano Rodríguez, 1827).

25. *Reflecciones*, 28–29.

26. Ibid., 33.

27. *El Defensor de la Religión* (Guadalajara: Imprenta a cargo de José Orosio Santos Plazuela, 1827–1830), 3 vols. The first issue was published on 26 January 1827, although the "Prospectus" is marked 19 December 1826. Iguíniz points to Pedro and Francisco Espinosa and Pedro Barajas as the major authors. All three had doctorates from the university. Pedro Espinosa would become Bishop of Guadalajara in 1854; his brother Franscisco would function as the rector of the Seminary; Pedro Barajas would be named Bishop of San Luis Potosí in 1855. See Iguíniz, *El periodismo*, 47–50 and P. Eucario López, "El Cabildo de Guadalajara. 1 de mayo 1552 – 1 de febrero 1968. Elenco," in *Anuario de la Comisión Diocesana de Historia del Arzobispado de Guadalajara* (Mexico City: Editorial Jus, 1968), 175–218. More information is provided in Iguíniz, *Cátalogo biobibliográfico*, 80–84, 142–58. Pedro Barajas was a representative for Guadalajara to the National Congress in the years of the Constitution of the Seven Laws, "having enjoyed great influence which he employed in public service and ecclesiastical affairs." Francisco Espinosa was also involved in conservative politics after 1834, first in the reaction against the government of Valentín Gómez Farías (1833–34) and later in the return of Antonio López de Santa Anna to the presidency in 1853. Ibid., 142. His brother Pedro had a similar political career. He was a representative in the General Congress from 1834 to 1836, during the reaction against Gómez Farías. In addition, he was a counselor of state to Santa Anna, who presented his name to the Holy See as a candidate for the bishopric of Guadalajara in 1853. Ibid., 145.

28. Iguíniz writes that the issues of *El Defensor* "are written in a quite elevated form and an overly severe style, as the gravity of the matter was thought to demand, which is why they seem to be directed to persons well versed in theological and canonical matters." Iguíniz, *El periodismo*, I: 48.

29. For instance, the newspaper said of John Toland, author of *Christianity not Mysterious* (London, 1696), that "he was vain, bizarre and unique up to the point of rejecting an opinion simply because it had a great man as a patron. Tenacious in debate, he argued with the shamelessness and vulgarity of a cynic." *El Defensor* 2, no. 1(18 January 1828), 4.

30. In an attack on José Guadalupe Gómez Huerta's ideas about the patronage, the paper's writers argued, "The clergy is not an enemy of national liberty, and its efforts were of great aid in shaking off the ignominious chains of oppression; but it is an implacable enemy of licentiousness decked out in the cape of liberty, of reforms by incompetent authorities, and of everything which means not recognizing and respecting the authority of the Church, of the Vicar of Christ and of other things along these lines …." *El Defensor* 1, no. 45 (19 June 1827): 188. Of José Francisco Arroyo's *Apuntamientos sobre concordato y patronato, para servir la historia de México,* the writers asserted, "one can be very free, very independent, very republican, just as Germans, Swiss, and North Americans are; at the same time one can be Catholic and subjects of the Pope in spiritual matters, just as all of them are, and they are many." *El Defensor* 1, no. 66 (31 August 1827): 273.

31. The articles continued from one issue to the next, but see for example *El Defensor* 1, no. 53 (13 July 1827): 218, and *El Defensor* 1, no. 63 supplement (24 August 1827): 263.

32. The article about the immortality of the soul continued until *El Defensor* 2, no. 22 (1 April 1828): 22. The articles about revelation went on, and one was not yet finished in *El Defensor* 2, no. 104 (18 January 1829): 413–14.

33. While the article about oral confession ended in *El Defensor* 2, no. 17 (14 March 1828): 65–66, the "Discurso sobre prohibición de libros" (book banning,) which had already begun, went on until *El Defensor* 2, no. 41 (6 June 1828): 162. "Los principios de fe sobre el gobierno de la Iglesia" began before the previous article had concluded, and later continued. Thus the articles were presented in a sequential but staggered fashion. An important article about the "Revolución contra el clero de Francia" began in *El Defensor* 2, no. 95 (12 December 1828): 380.

34. "And when their lives [of the pontiffs] were not befitting the holiness of their character, the inviolable rights of the Apostolic See were respected by detesting the disorders of those who dishonored it …. Despite the barbarity of the age, Christians had enough equanimity not to confuse the holy power of the ministry with the indignity of the minister, and … even the ignorant knew to honor pontifical power which comes from Jesus Christ in hands stained by sin." *El Defensor* 2, no. 4 (29 January 1828): 15.

35. On continuities between Bourbon Absolutism and liberalism, as well as the problems inherent to this continuity, see Miranda, "El liberalismo español" and "El liberalismo mexicano." Hale categorically stated that "Mora found inspiration in the Hispanic enlightened despot, Charles III." Later on he adds: "It is undeniable that liberalism in Mexico has been conditioned by a traditionalist Hispanic ethos, and that as a system of values its strength has been diluted. Yet seen as a part of the continuity of Bourbon policies, the legacy of liberalism has been significant." Hale, *Mexican Liberalism,* 160, 304–5.

36. José Miguel Gordoa, *Reflexiones que se hicieron por su autor* (Mexico City: Imprenta del Águila, 1827). The author closed his reflections with a date and location: Guadalajara, March 2, 1827. It should be noted that at this time Gordoa still held the office of Governor of the Mitre in the bishopric of Guadalajara. Prisciliano Sánchez wrote of him that he was "an ecclesiastic of well-known enlightenment and virtue, who possesses practical knowledge of politics, who has taken part in popular affairs, and has manifested on many occasions the desire animating him to cooperate for the good of the state." Sánchez, *Memoria sobre el estado actual,* 19. For more information about Gordoa, see the footnote with biographical information in Chapter Seven.

37. Gordoa, *Reflexiones*, 1–5.
38. Ibid., 6.
39. Ibid., 11–14.
40. Ibid., 14.
41. Ibid., 15.
42. Ibid., 16. Costeloe indicates that opinions on patronage had become very con-
    fused after 1823. The basic Church premises, as expressed by the high clergy, were
    "the patronage was no more than the right of appointment or presentation to
    vacant benefices; the former regal patronage conceded by the Holy See to the
    kings of Spain had terminated with independence; it could only be renewed,
    or a new patronage granted, by recourse to Rome; in the meantime, the right
    of appointment to lesser benefices devolved upon the bishops; some form of
    allowing the civil authority to exclude candidates could be permitted." The
    regalist perspective held that "the patronage subsisted by automatic transfer to
    the new government or nation; or the formerly Spanish patronage had ended,
    but since patronal powers were part of sovereignty, the new sovereign authority
    automatically possessed them; radical opinion insisted that there was no need
    to go to Rome to ask for the patronage which the nation should proceed to
    exercise; moderate opinion argued that, although Mexico possessed the patronage,
    its use or exercise should be confirmed by Rome; the patronage was principally
    the right of appointment but it was implied ... that it also included the authority
    to implement other reforms, for example, territorial changes in dioceses, reform
    of the regular orders, abolition of ecclesiastical taxes, changes in the tithes, admis-
    sion of papal documents, legal jurisdiction over patronal cases." After 1825, the
    issue of patronage was argued with new force in the national congress. "During
    1826 and 1827, state after state enacted laws affecting a variety of Church activi-
    ties in an attempt either to by-pass the patronage issue or more likely, to pressure
    the national congress into action." Costeloe, *Church and State*, 66, 93, 99.
43. See Staples, *La iglesia*, 105–14, 127–36, and Pérez Memen, *El episcopado*, 252–58,
    418 and following.
44. *Decretos espedidos por la Legislatura de Jalisco, suprimiendo el Tribunal de Haceduría
    de la Santa Iglesia de Guadalajara* (Mexico City: Imprenta de Galván a cargo de
    Mariano Arévalo, 1827), 1–4. Decree 78 issued regulations for the new situation
    in the wake of Decree 77.
45. *Representación elevada al Honorable Congreso del Estado de Jalisco por el Cabildo
    Eclesiástico con el fin de hacer revocar el Decreto número 77, y Dictamen que abrió su
    Comisión Especial sobre este asunto.* (Guadalajara: Imprenta del C. Sanromán, 1827).
46. Ibid., 3–12.
47. *Decretos espedidos por la Legislatura de Jalisco*, 7, 13.
48. Ibid., 15.
49. Ibid., 19.
50. Mariano Primo de Rivera, *Defensa del Venerable Cabildo Eclesiástico de Guadalajara,
    contra el informe que ha hecho en ofensa suya la junta directiva de diezmos y el gobierno
    civil de Jalisco* (Mexico City: Imprenta del Águila, 1827), 6–11. The statement
    contained the word "degradan" (they degrade), later clarified as "desagradan"
    (they displease), in reference to the civil authorities. Despite its name, *Decretos
    espedidos por la Legislatura de Jalisco* presents the official Church version of the
    document in question. The relevant sentence appears on page 20. The key phrase
    is "we are very ready, whenever you judge it necessary to end these official
    responses which 'displease' Your Excellency and mortify the Cathedral Chapter,
    to renounce our income and turn to the contributions of the faithful which we

administer, in which case, excluded from all participation in decimal tithes, by the same measure our obligations and rights will also cease." As can be seen, interpretations of this phrase vary considerably according to whether one word or the other is included. This same pamphlet also includes other writings on this dispute. Interestingly enough, it begins with the following gloss of Thomas Paine: "it would be a despotic and arbitrary act to prohibit investigating the good or bad principles which serve as the foundation for the law itself, or for anything else. If a law is bad, it is one thing to oppose its passage, and something very different to point out its errors, reason through its defects, and make clear the reason why it should be overruled, or another substituted in its place." *Rights of Man*, Chapter 4. (See Thomas Paine, *Rights of Man*, with an introduction by George Jacob Holyoake, London & Toronto, J. M. Dent & Sons, n.d.) In an observation at the end of the pamphlet, it was pointed out that Jalisco's actions against the Church's tithe offices were usurping the rights of the federation and the other states included within the Guadalajara diocese. The critic demanded the "rights of property and security" under the 1824 Constitution to defend the Church's administration of tithes. On this point, he cited Jeremy Bentham in the sense that "the public interest … is nothing more than an abstract term which only represents the mass of individual interests." Yet "individual interests are the only real interests: take care of … individuals, do not bother them, do not ever allow anyone to bother them, and you will have done enough for the public interest." *Decretos espedidos por la Legislatura de Jalisco*, 50–54.

51. Primo de Rivera, *Defensa*, 11–41.
52. Ibid., 12.
53. Ibid., 13.
54. Ibid., 14.
55. Ibid., 14–15. On Huerta, see Iguíniz, "El doctor don José de Jesús Huerta" in *Anuario de la Comisión Diocesana de Historia del arzobispado del Guadalajara* (Mexico City: Jus, 1968), 155–66.
56. Primo de Rivera, *Defensa*, 16–17.
57. Ibid., 17.
58. Ibid., 17–18.
59. Ibid., 18–19. Italics mine.
60. Ibid., 23–24. Italics mine.
61. Ibid., 24–27.
62. Ibid., 27.
63. Ibid., 29–30.
64. Ibid., 30, 34–35.
65. Ibid., 35–39.
66. Ibid., 39–40.
67. In this context, it is worth recalling that Costeloe states that "every attempt by the civil authorities to confiscate Church owned property … was met with the response that all ecclesiastical wealth was sacred and inalienable." Costeloe, *Church and State*, 8. Although the response of the Jalisco clergy is more complex than what this statement might suggest, as has been seen, still Costeloe's observation underscores the theocratic tendencies which until this point have been evident especially in Chapter Four.
68. Ibid., 40.
69. José Francisco Arroyo, *Discurso que el Sr. Don D … pronunció en la H. Asamblea del Estado de Nuevo León* (Guadalajara: Imprenta de la viuda de Romero, 1827),

unpaginated. José Francisco Arroyo y Villagómez had a doctorate in theology from the University of Guadalajara and was very active there, teaching in the Conciliar Seminary and the University, as well as directing the Clerical College as Rector from 1805 to 1815. He was a deputy for Guadalajara in the Spanish Cortes in 1820–21, and later went on to a political career in the Legislature of Nuevo León and an ecclesiastical career in the Cathedral Chapter of Monterrey. He returned to Guadalajara in 1831, holding important ecclesiastical offices. He was a profuse writer. José Guadalupe Gómez Huerta had a doctorate in canon law from the University of Guadalajara. He taught canon law at the Conciliar Seminary of Guadalajara and was a parish priest in Zacatecas. In 1823, he was elected to the Constitutional Congress and later to the Legislature of Zacatecas. According to Iguíniz, he "belonged to the caste of priests ... who based on the achievement of independence accepted and defended liberalism, and within the Congress [of Zacatecas] he stood out for his radicalism." Iguíniz, *Catálogo biobibliográfico*, 76–79, 162–63.

70. Arroyo, *Discurso*, unpaginated.
71. Ibid.
72. Ibid.
73. Iguíniz, *Catálogo biobibliográfico*, 78, credits Arroyo with writing articles for *El Defensor*.
74. José Miguel Ramírez y Torres, *Contestación al discurso del Señor Huerta. Pronunciado (según se dice en Guadalajara) en la sesión secreta del 15 de mayo del presente año de 1827* (Guadalajara: Imprenta del C. Mariano Rodríguez, ca. 1827). This is the same Ramírez y Torres whose *Elogio fúnebre* was quoted in Chapter Three. Iguíniz attributes the 1827 publication to Ramírez; see Iguíniz, *Catálogo biobibliográfico*, 237–38. Ramírez had a doctorate in theology from the University of Guadalajara (1808) and was a lawyer from the Royal Audiencia of Nueva Galicia (1818). He was a canon of the cathedral chapter of Guadalajara and represented Guadalajara in the Spanish Cortes in 1820–21. He was a representative for Guadalajara to the Constitutional Congress of 1823–24, in which he was on the committee entrusted with addressing patronage. Huerta also had a doctorate in theology from the University of Guadalajara. See Iguíniz, "El doctor don José de Jesús Huerta," 192–94. He combined a markedly liberal political career with an ecclesiastical career. He was the president of the same patronage committee Ramírez served on in 1823–24.
75. Ramírez, *Contestación*, 17.
76. Ibid., 23–40, 47, 50–51.
77. Ibid., 51–56.
78. José Miguel Ramírez y Torres, *Voto particular que sobre el punto de Patronato Eclesiástico presentó al Soberano Congreso Constituyente de la Federación Mexicana el Señor Diputado D. ...* (Mexico City: Imprenta del Supremo Congreso en Palacio, 1824; reprinted in Guadalajara: Oficina del C. Mariano Rodríguez, 1827), 12. Reyes Heroles concedes that this document is "erudite and interesting": Reyes Heroles, *El liberalismo mexicano*, I: 301.
79. Ibid.
80. Ibid., 11.
81. Ibid., 13, 25, 27, 51. It is worth recalling that Hale suggested that "a thoroughgoing study of Bentham in Spain and Spanish America, which attempts to explain his impact, should be made." Hale, *Mexican Liberalism*, 156, note 21. Hale noted the "nonpolitical nature of utilitarian doctrine" in Jeremy Bentham and the

fact that he accepted that laws were not perfectly egalitarian. The less radical
Mora of the 1820s based himself firmly on Bentham in establishing a theoretical
balance between the rights of individuals and the rights of the state in defending
the rights of the collectivity. Ibid., 155–57. "During his lifetime, Bentham's
greatest influence was not in England, but in Spain ... and in Spanish America,"
Frederick Artz has noted. "Before his death in 1832, forty thousand copies of
his works in French had been sold in Spanish America alone." Artz, *Reaction
and Revolution*, 84, note 3. Artz does not ignore Bentham's anti-clericalism,
but sees him as a pragmatic. He points to the recognition Bentham gave
to nationality – a common set of cultural traditions and goals – as the appropriate basis for state and government. Ibid., 88, 99, 106. He also adds that
"[t]hrough Bentham's writings may be traced the process by which much of
the epoch-making theorizing of eighteenth-century liberalism was reduced to
terms a businessman of the nineteenth-century could understand." Ibid., 84.
In *Radicalism not Dangerous* (1820), Bentham clearly argued that "changes in
the existing political and social order could be made without violence and
even without serious disturbance." Ibid., 216. The mentions of the writings of
Bentham and others by traditionalist thinkers suggest greater cultivation and
flexibility on their part than is often thought. Tracing conservative tastes on this
point is a task still awaiting the efforts of a scholar.

82.   Reyes Heroles reproaches Ramírez for justifying state exercise of patronage
solely on the basis of the protection the state provides religion, and for his
demand for a Concordat so that the state could present candidates for ecclesiastical benefices. Reyes Heroles seems to accept the liberal conviction, very
common at the time, that the exercise of patronage was inherent to the sovereignty assumed by the independent Mexican state. He realizes that subordination
of the Church was indispensable for the state to be able to categorically assert
authority based on popular sovereignty. He states that the new "demoliberal state
... admitted no power other than state power." Reyes Heroles, *El liberalismo
mexicano*, I: 301–14, esp. 305–7.

83.   The article began in *El Defensor* 2, no. 95 (12 December 1828): 380.

84.   *El Defensor* 2, no. 97 (19 December 1828): 388.

85.   *El Defensor* 2, no. 98 (23 December 1828): 392.

86.   *El Defensor* 2, no. 99 (26 December 1828): 396; *El Defensor* 2, no. 100 (30
December 1828): 400; *El Defensor* 2, no. 101 (2 January 1829): 404; *El Defensor*
2, no. 102 (6 January 1829): 408; *El Defensor* 2, no. 103 (9 January 1829): 412;
El Defensor 2, no. 104 (13 January 1829): 416; *El Defensor* 2, no. 105 (16 January
1829): 420.

87.   *El Defensor* 2, no. 105 (16 January 1829): Supplement. Unpaginated.

88.   Ibid.

89.   Ibid.

90.   Ibid. In this context of bewilderment, the reprinting of a Papal document is
worth noting: Pío VI. *Dos Breves de N S P El Señor ..., reprobando la herética
Constitución Civil del Clero de Francia ....* (Guadalajara: Imprenta a cargo del
C. José O. Santos, 1828). The volume containing this document in the Public
Library of the state of Jalisco belonged to Pedro Espinosa.

91.   Un Sacerdote Secular, *Observaciones*.

92.   See note 82 above.

93. Pedro Espinosa, *Contestación del Comisionado por el Venerable Cabildo de Guadalajara a las observaciones de los del Honorable Congreso de Zacatecas sobre administración de diezmos* (Guadalajara: Oficina del C. Dionisio Rodríguez, 1831), 2. On Espinosa, see note 27 above.

94. Ibid., 15–39.

95. Ibid., 39–43, 45, 49–50.

96. Ibid., 51.

97. Pedro Espinosa, *Informe que el Dr. D. ..., como individuo de la Comisión del Venerable Cabildo Eclesiástico de Guadalajara presentó en la primera conferencia con la del Honorable Congreso del Estado de Jalisco, nombrada para tratar con aquélla sobre reforma de aranceles* (Mexico City: Imprenta de Galván a cargo de Mariano Arévalo, 1831), 3–25, 28–29.

98. Ibid., 24–30.

99. *Cañón de a treinta y seis contra el rastrero buscapiés* (Guadalajara: Imprenta del c. Dionisio Rodríguez, 1831), 1–8.

100. *Después de uno, dos y tres no ha prendido el Buscapiés* (Guadalajara: Imprenta del C. Dionisio Rodríguez,1831), 3.

101. Ibid., 3–4.

102. *Es hablar contra razón atacar la religión* (Guadalajara: Imprenta del C. Dionisio Rodríguez, 1831), 1–3.

103. Ibid., 13.

104. Ibid., 6. The last page of his text read as follows:
CONSTITUTIONAL ARTICLES
The religion of the Mexican nation is and always will be Apostolic Roman Catholic, the nation will protect it with wise and just laws and prohibit the exercise of any other. Article 3, General Constitution.
Give instructions to reach agreements with the Apostolic See, approve them for ratification, and arrange the exercise of patronage in all of the Federation. Article 50, Faculty 12, of the same Constitution.
GENERAL DECREE, 18 DECEMBER 1824
As long as the General Congress, in virtue of the faculty of Article 50 of the Constitution, has not passed the laws arranging exercise of patronage there will be no changes in the states on points concerning ecclesiastical income, unless both authorities accept those changes with either of them able to propose to the General Congress the forms they esteem to be appropriate on the remaining points, as well as resort to the General Congress on issues related to income when they do not reach agreement between them.

105. Jacques Bénigne Bossuet had carefully balanced the rights of the French state and the Vatican within Catholic orthodoxy. He defended the social usefulness of French Absolutism no less than the "efficiency and propriety" of Catholic principles. Based on his *Exposition de la foi catolique* (1668) and his *Histoire de variations dans les églises protestantes* (1688), he has been seen as a utilitarian and Cartesian thinker. See Frederick L. Nussbaum, *The Triumph of Science and Reason 1660–1685* (New York: Harper & Row, 1962), 18, 63, 86, 184. However, his moderate Gallicanism was abandoned by the French Church after 1840. Once the state was secularized, the Church could no longer depend on it, and it drew closer to the Vatican. On this point, see Adrien Dansette, *Religious History of Modern France* (New York: Herder and Herder, 1961), I: 359–60. On Bossuet himself, see also discussion in note 52 in Chapter Seven.

Notes to Chapter 9

1. Costeloe, *Church and State*, 118–20; Staples, *La iglesia*, 76–85; Pérez Memen, *El episcopado*, 272–76.
2. Quoted in Muriá, *Historia de Jalisco*, II: 513.
3. José Miguel Gordoa, *Carta pastoral del Illmo. Sr. D. …, Obispo de Guadalajara, a sus diocesanos* (Mexico City: Imprenta de Galván a cargo de Mariano Arévalo, 1831), 1.
4. Ibid., 5.
5. Ibid., 6.
6. Ibid., 7.
7. Ibid., 8. Italics mine.
8. Ibid., 9. Italics mine.
9. Ibid., 10.
10. José Miguel Gordoa was consecrated bishop on 21 August 1831, after having been appointed on 28 February 1831. Iguíniz, *Catálogo biobibliográfico*, 169.
11. Pedro Barajas, *Elogio fúnebre del Illmo. Sr. Dr. D. José Miguel Gordoa* (Guadalajara: Imprenta de Rodríguez a cargo de Trinidad Buitrón, 1833), 4.
12. Ibid., 7, 11–12.
13. Ibid., 12. Italics mine.
14. Joaquín Lorenzo Villanueva was a well-known Spanish liberal cleric in the late eighteenth and early nineteenth century, influential in the 1810–1814 and 1820–1823 Cortes. See Callahan, *Church, Politics and Society*, 71, 93, 95, 102, 113, 119, 120. Domingo de la Rochefoucauld was the Cardinal of Rouen who took part in the French Estates General from 1789 to 1792, vigorously defending the rights of the clergy.
15. Ibid., 12–13.
16. Ibid, 13–14.
17. Ibid, 4.
18. Ibid., 15–16, 19–21.
19. Ibid., 22–23.
20. *Rentas eclesiásticas. Contestación a los números 88 y 89 del Fénix* (Guadalajara: Imprenta de Rodríguez, a cargo de Trinidad Buitrón, 1833), 1. One year later, still another pamphlet would be published on this same theme, this time attacking a dissertation by José Luis Mora the Zacatecas Congress had published in 1833. See Pedro Espinosa, *Rentas eclesiásticas o sea impugnación de la disertación que sobre la materia se ha publicado de orden del Honorable Congreso de Zacatecas* (Guadalajara: Imprenta a cargo de Teodosio Cruz Aedo, 1834). The pamphlet was published anonymously, but Iguíniz attributes it to Espinosa. Iguíniz, *Catálogo biobibliográfico*, 147.
21. Ibid., 1.
22. Ibid., 1.
23. Ibid., 1–2.
24. Ibid., 4. Italics mine.
25. Ibid., 4–6.
26. Ibid.
27. Liberal thinkers were persistently concerned with the wealth bequeathed by individuals to the Church, frequently on their deathbed, and wished to impede this.
28. Ibid.

29. *El Censor del Siglo XIX* (Guadalajara) 2 (15 May 1833): 2. The first issue of this paper had mocked the editors of El Siglo XIX for their attempt to disdain theologians' knowledge by associating it with a certain forum and a certain form of the printed word. It also called those editors ignorant and ill-disposed towards the Church. *El Censor del Siglo XIX* (Guadalajara) 1 (30 April 1833): 1–4.

30. *El Censor del Siglo XIX* (Guadalajara) 2 (15 May 1833): 7, 8, 10.

31. *Contestación a los EE. del Siglo 19* (Guadalajara: Imprenta de Dionisio Rodríguez, 1833), unpaginated. The pamphlet is dated 26 April 1833.

32. Ibid.

33. Ibid.

34. Ibid.

35. *Otra puya a los del Siglo XIX* (Guadalajara: Imprenta de Dionisio Rodríguez, 1833), unpaginated.

36. Ibid.

37. Ibid.

38. *Dogma y disciplina* (Guadalajara: Imprenta de Dionisio Rodríguez, ca. 1833), unpaginated.

39. *Día de amargos desengaños o sea triunfo de nuestra religión* (Guadalajara: Imprenta de Dionisio Rodríguez, 1833), unpaginated.

40. Ibid.

41. A.T. *Hablen los predicadores y confundan la impiedad* (Guadalajara: Imprenta de Dionisio Rodríguez, 1833), unpaginated. While this pamphlet was only dated by year, not day or month, it was directed against an article entitled "Sedición" from 25 January 1833.

42. Ibid.

43. *Contestación a los enemigos de los predicadores* (Guadalajara: Imprenta de Dionisio Rodríguez a cargo de Trinidad Buitrón, 1833), 1–2.

44. Ibid., 2–3.

45. Ibid., 3.

46. Ibid., 4.

47. Pedro Espinosa, *Patronato en la nación* (Guadalajara: Imprenta de Dionisio Rodríguez, 1833), 1. Italics mine. The pamphlet was published without the name of its author, but Iguíniz attributes a pamphlet with the same title, published in Mexico City in 1835, to Pedro Espinosa. Iguíniz, *Catálogo biobibliográfico*, 148. Costeloe attributes a pamphlet of the same title published in Mexico in 1833 to Francisco Espinosa. Costeloe, *Church and State*, 191.

48. Ibid., 1.

49. Ibid., 1.

50. Ibid., 2.

51. Ibid., 3–8.

52. Pedro Espinosa, *Patronato en la nación. Núm. 2 Contestación al dictamen de la comisión eclesiástica del Senado sobre que el patronato de la Iglesia mexicana reside radicalmente en la nación* (Guadalajara: Imprenta de Dionisio Rodríguez, 1833), 1–6.

53. Joaquín José Ladrón de Guevara et al., *Nos el Deán y Cabildo Gobernador de esta Santa Iglesia metropolitana de México. A nuestros amados diocesanos, salud y paz en Nuestro Señor Jesucristo* (Mexico City: Imprenta de Galván a cargo de Mariano Arévalo, 1833), 3, 7–8.

54. Ibid., 8–10.

55. Ibid., 10.

56. Ibid., 11.

57. *Representación del V. Cabildo de Guadalajara al Exmo. Sr. Presidente de los Estados Unidos Mexicanos.* (Guadalajara: Imprenta de Dionisio Rodríguez, 1833) and *Representación de los señores curas y venerable clero secular y regular residentes en Guadalajara, al E. Sr. Presidente de la República Mexicana D. José Antonio López de Santa Ana [sic]* (Guadalajara: Imprenta de Dionisio Rodríguez, 1833).

58. "Exposición del gobierno eclesiástico de Guadalajara, al supremo del estado, sobre la ley de fincas pertenecientes a manos muertas," *La Lima del Vulcano,* no. 25 (11 Jan. 1834) (Mexico City: José Uribe y Alcalde). Diego Aranda y Carpinteiro was born in the City of Puebla on 20 December 1776. He was brought to Guadalajara in 1796 by Bishop Cabañas as part of his retinue. By 1810 he had finished his studies and received his doctoral degree from the University of Guadalajara. In 1813 and 1814 he was a deputy to Cortes in Cádiz. Thereafter, he began a long career in the cathedral chapter of the Guadalajara Church, but this did not stop him from participating in the Congress of Jalisco of 1823–24 which drew up the 1824 state constitution, which he signed. He became Bishop of the Diocese of Guadalajara in November 1836. Iguíniz, *Catálogo biobibliográfico,* 67–73.

59. Ibid., 99.

60. Ibid., 99–100.

61. *Gobernador y peineta* (Guadalajara: Oficina de Dionisio Rodríguez, 1833), s/n. The reference is to a stiff comb women wore in public. The verse, which rhymes in Spanish:

> Sin mucho de fantasía
> Aun el más rudo lector
> Verá cierta analogia
> Entre un buen governador,
> Y una peineta del día.

62. Ibid.

63. *Segundo azote a los embusteros: sea reimpresión del grito de la verdad, corregido de las erratas que sacó en la primera edición (A pilón y fiado.)* (Guadalajara: Imprenta a cargo de Teodosio Cruz Aedo, 14 May 1834), unpaginated.

64. *Ahí va ese tiro sin puntería: si a alguno descalabra, no es culpa mía* (Guadalajara: Imprenta a cargo de Teodosio Cruz Aedo, 1834), unpaginated. The verse, which rhymes in Spanish:

> Aunque el gobernador no sea Polar,
> Tomar lo que es ajeno, es hurtar;
> Y si el dueño es Iglesia o colegio,
> Sobre ser robo es sacrilegio.
> Decir que esta raspa no es impía,
> Es robo, es sacrilegio, es herejía.

65. El Tirador, *Respuesta del Tirador a su chusco anotador. Carta segunda* (Guadalajara: Imprenta a cargo de Teodosio Cruz Aedo, 1834), unpaginated.

66. Ibid.

67. Villaseñor y Villaseñor, *Los primeros federalistas,* 113–14.

68. Ibid., 48, 98. According to Villaseñor, Vice-Governor Juan Nepomuceno Cumplido was in charge of the government between 23 June and 11 August, that is, during the period immediately prior to the dissolving of the federal government.

69. The Cuernavaca Plan, launched on 25 May 1834, became the rallying cry for all who demanded a change of government. The president, Antonio López de Santa Anna, was to step in and overturn the liberal legislation against the Church

which had been carried out under Vice-President Valentín Gómez Farías, and there was to be a complete renewal of government. See Costeloe, *La primera república*, 428–29. The pamphlet in question is *O muertos o federados quieren ser los arrancados. O sea impugnación al folleto titulado 'Pocos quieren centralismo y los más federalismo'* (Guadalajara: Imprenta de Dionisio Rodríguez, 1834), unpaginated. In his two-part pamphlet from the same year, José Ramón Pacheco upheld much of what *O muertos o federados* argued. He stated that "the chain of events … has led us to a position in which there is nothing legitimate; the nation has no leader and is almost in a state of nature, as just after overthrowing the Spanish government." He deplored the sad economic and fiscal outlook as much as the other pamphlet, but Pacheco took a more liberal attitutude towards the clergy, accusing it of now tending towards monarchism, and he insisted on the forceable reestablishment of federalism. He accepted that it would have to be a respectable federalism, not tyrannical or factious, but he maintained that religious reforms could go forward as long as they were moderate. To support his position, he appealed to the thinking of Francisco Severo Maldonado, which was "not … as paradoxical as many suppose." José Ramón Pacheco, *Cuestión del día o nuestros males y sus remedios* (Guadalajara: Ediciones del Instituto Tecnológico, 1953 [1834]), 33, 81–82, 85, 93–97.

70. *O muertos o federados*, unpaginated.
71. Ibid.
72. Ibid.
73. *Nos el Presidente y Cabildo de la Santa Iglesia Catedral de Guadalajara. Al venerable clero secular y regular, y a todos los fieles de la Diócesis, salud y paz en nuestro Señor Jesucristo* (Guadalajara: No publisher, 20 Aug 1834), unpaginated. This was not the first formal manifestation of the clergy's view, although the political importance of this one is undeniable. They had earlier appealed to the state government itself, for example, to try to overturn Decree 525 about the sale of Church lands. See *Segunda exposición del Gobierno Eclesiástico de Guadalajara, al Supremo del Estado, sobre la ley de fincas pertenecientes a manos muertas* (Guadalajara: Imprenta a cargo de Teodosio Cruz Aedo, 24 March 1834).
74. Ibid.
75. José Antonio González Plata, *Sermón predicado en la Santa Iglesia Catedral de Guadalajara el día de Nuestra Señora de Guadalupe*, 16–17. The theme of the hardly promising state of the economy and citizens' disillusionment with it appeared constantly. In addition to Pacheco, in his *Cuestión del día*, the Governor himself had referred to it in his annual report. As González Plata's sermon suggests, perhaps there was a convergence of groups who were protectionist, both ideologically and economically, and this would be worthy of investigation. The governor indicated that centralism was advisable in politics, and the promotion of the National Development Bank [Banco de Avío] was recommendable in economics. See José Antonio Romero, *Informe dirigido por el Gobierno del Estado de Jalisco al Exmo. Sr. Presidente, a consecuencia de la circular mandada por el Ministerio de Relaciones al mismo, en [sic] 20 de agosto del presente año* (Guadalajara: Imprenta del Gobierno a cargo de D. Nicolás España, 1834), unpaginated.
76. Ibid., 20.
77. Ibid., 22–23.
78. José Antonio Romero, *Informe sobre el estado actual de la administración pública del Estado de Jalisco, leído por el Exmo. Sr. Gobernador del mismo* (Guadalajara: Imprenta del Gobierno a cargo de D. Nicolás España, 1835), 3–4.

79. Ibid., 7–10.
80. Ibid., 11–20.
81. Ibid., 23.
82. *Iniciativa que el Congreso de Jalisco dirige a las augustas Cámaras de la Unión, contraída a variar el actual sistema en República Central* (Guadalajara: Imprenta del Supremo Gobierno, a cargo de D. Nicolás España, 1835), unpaginated.
83. Ibid.
84. Ibid.
85. Ibid.
86. Ibid.
87. See *Triunfo del sansculotismo, debido a los rastreros y viles medios con que intenta fascinar al caudillo de los mexicanos* (Guadalajara: Imprenta del Gobierno, 1835), unpaginated. This pamphlet applauded "the reigning harmony, especially among the privileged classes" and denounced the "ragged thieves, Moths of the Nation."
88. Francisco Espinosa, *Oración que en las solemnes exequias celebradas en la Santa Iglesia Catedral de Guadalajara por el descanso de la alma [sic] del Exmo. Sor. Don Miguel Barragán* ... (Guadalajara: Imprenta del Gobierno a cargo de D. Nicolás España, 1836), 10.
89. Ibid., 22–23, 26.
90. Cobieya, *Oración panegirica* (Guadalajara: Imprenta de M. Brambila, 1837); Francisco Espinosa, *Sermón predicado en el Convento de Santa María de Gracia de esta Ciudad* (Guadalajara: Imprenta de Dionisio Rodríguez, 1838).
91. *Breve impugnación de las ochenta y cinco proposiciones del Synodo de Pistoya, condenadas por el Sr. Pío VI en [sic] 28 de agosto de 1794. Preceden algunas reflexiones del Illmo. Sr. Obispo y Cabildo de Puebla, que prueban la necesidad en que estamos de admitir la Bula Auctorem fidei condenatoria de dichas proposicones*(Guadalajara: Imprenta del Gobierno, 1838). This same Bull had already been published in Latin in the midst of the change of government in 1835: *Bulla SMI. Domini Nostri PII VI. Quae incipit Auctorem Fidei* (Guadalajara: Tipografia a Nicolao España Directa, 1835).
92. Diego Aranda, *Nos el Dor. ... , por la gracia de Dios y de la Santa Sede Apostólica Obispo de Guadalajara* (Guadalajara: Imprenta del Gobierno, 2 Jan 1837), unpaginated. Italics mine.
93. Ibid. Italics mine.
94. Ibid.
95. Diego Aranda, *Instrucción pastoral sobre los cinco preceptos de Nuestra Sta. Madre Iglesia* (Guadalajara: Imprenta de Brambila, 1 Feb 1840), 1.
96. Ibid., 3.
97. Ibid., 5, 10–11.
98. Ibid., 13–14.
99. Ibid., 14–16.
100. See, for example, Pedro L. de la Cueva, et al., *Manifestación dirigida al Exmo. Sr. Presidente, por varios ciudadanos de Zapotlán el Grande, sobre el actual estado de la República* (Guadalajara: Imprenta de Sanromán, 1837) and Muriá, *Historia de Jalisco*, III: 40–44.
101. Mariano Paredes y Arrillaga, *Exposición que el General D. ... hace a sus conciudadanos, en manifestación de su conducta política, militar y económica en la presente revolución* (Mexico City: Impreso por I. Cumplido, 1841), 10–12.
102. Ibid., 12.
103. Ibid., 8, 13.

104. Mariano Otero, *Discurso que en la solemnidad del 16 de septiembre de 1841 pronunció en la Ciudad de Guadalajara el Licenciado C.* .... (Guadalajara: Imprenta del Gobierno, no date), 11, 17–18, 22–23. Other indications of the persistence of liberal idealism can be seen in Anastasio Cañedo, *Discurso cívico que pronunció en esta capital el Licenciado ... el día 16 de septiembre de 1843 en el aniversario del glorioso grito de independencia* (Guadalajara: Oficina de Manuel Brambila, 1843). Cañedo had published under the pseudonym "El Polar" in the 1820s, and his influence was explored in Chapter Five. Another important liberal spokesman in the mid-1840s was Sabás Sánchez Hidalgo, *Oración cívica, en la celebración del aniversario del 16 de septiembre, leída por el ciudadano ... en la plaza principal de Guadalajara* (Guadalajara: Imprenta del Gobierno, 1846). As a point of contrast, see *Discurso pronunciado el día 27 de septiembre de 1839 en el salón principal de la Universidad Nacional de Guadalajara, por J. D. S.Y C., Síndico menos antiguo del M. I. Ayuntamiento de esta Capital, en celebridad del aniversario de nuestra independencia el año de 1821* (Guadalajara: Imprenta del Gobierno, 1839). Note that the independence the last speaker is celebrating only dates from 1821, under the establisment-oriented General Agustín de Iturbide.
105. Ibid., 24.
106. Ibid., 25.
107. Ibid., 30.
108. Juan Rodríguez de San Miguel, *Discurso pronunciado en* [*sic*] *14 de noviembre de 1842 por el Sr. Diputado ... contra el proyecto de Constitución en su discusión general. Tomado del Siglo Diez y Nueve Num. 410* (Guadalajara: Imprenta del Gobierno, 1842), 4–5.
109. Ibid., 5–9,11.
110. Ibid., 15.
111. Ibid., 16–17.
112. *Observaciones que hace el Venerable Cabildo de Guadalajara al Soberano Congreso Constituyente, sobre el proyecto de Constitución* (Guadalajara: Imprenta del Gobierno, 1842), 3.
113. Ibid., 6.
114. Ibid., 8–9, 17.
115. Ibid., 9.
116. Ibid., 11–18.
117. Manuel de San Juan Crisóstomo, *Sermón que el día 26 de diciembre de 1842 predicó en la Santa Iglesia Catedral de Guadalajara,* (Guadalajara: Imprenta del Gobierno, ca. 1842), 19–20.
118. Muriá, Historia de Jalisco, III: 47. Considering these events, it is worth stressing that as late as 6 February the Church demonstrated its resolve on constitutional matters by authorizing the publication of the *Cartas del Conde Muzzarelli, sobre el juramento de la Constitución Cispadana, Traducidas del italiano por Fr. José María Guzmán* (Guadalajara: Imprenta del Gobiero, 1843 [reprint]). After making very similar arguments to those the Guadalajara clergy offered against the 1842 constitutional project, Muzzarelli stated: "We therefore conclude, saying that the form of the oath is everywhere illicit, and no Catholic clergy can take that oath in good conscience." *Cartas,* 65. In terms of the possibility of reconciling the changes of nineteenth-century Mexico with Catholic orthodoxy, the reprints of Spanish (Catalan) theologian Jaime Balmes are interesting. Without accepting ascendant liberalism, Balmes sought to build connections between new knowledge and the new opinions and needs of society and ancient Catholic

truths. See, for example, his *Observaciones sociales, políticas y económicas sobre los bienes del clero* (Guadalajara: Oficina de Manuel Brambila, 1842 [reprint]) and *Suma de civilización mayor posible* [!] *en el mundo, en un estado, en un individuo* (Guadalajara: Imprenta del Gobierno, 1843 [reprint]). The title of the later document is particularly relevant (and noteworthy).

119. *Observaciones que sobre el proyecto de Bases Orgánicas hacen a la H. Junta Legislativa el Obispo y Cabildo de Guadalajara* (Guadalajara: Imprenta del Gobierno, 1843), 3–6. Of course, the Guadalajara Church had approved of the dissolving of the Federal Congress by Antonio López de Santa Anna on 31 May 31 1834, and was therefore implicated in preparing the ensuing constitutions.

120. Ibid., 7–11.

121. Ibid.

122. Ibid., 11–12, 14.

123. Ibid., 15.

124. Ibid., 15–16. Italics mine.

125. Jan Bazant, *Alienation of Church Wealth in Mexico: Social and Economic Aspects of the Liberal Revolution 1856–1875* (Cambridge: Cambridge University Press, 1971), 26.

126. *Observaciones sobre el dictamen del Señor Licenciado don Manuel de la Peña y Peña relativo al decreto de 31 de agosto de 1843* (Guadalajara: Imprenta del Gobierno, 1843). Iguíniz attributes this pamphlet to Pedro Espinosa. Iguíniz, *Catálogo biobibliográfico*, 148.

127. Noriega, *El pensamiento conservador*, II: 336–38; Muriá, *Historia de Jalisco*, III: 48–49.

128. *Patriótica iniciativa que la Exma. Asamblea Departamental de Jalisco eleva a las Augustas Cámaras, y otros documentos de la misma importancia* (Guadalajara: Imprenta del Gobierno, 1844), 1–2.

129. Ibid., 4, 6–10.

130. Ibid., 10–11.

131. Ibid., 13–18, 19–39.

132. Ibid., 23.

133. Ibid., 31–34. See also Antonio López de Santa Anna, *Manifiesto del Exmo. Sr. Benemérito de la patria y Presidente Constitucional de la República D.* ... (Mexico City: Impreso por Vicente García Torres, 1844) and *Exposición que dirige la Exma. Asamblea Departamental de Jalisco, a las Augustas Cámaras* (Guadalajara: Imprenta del Gobierno, 1844).

134. See *Iniciativa que la Asamblea del Departamento de Jalisco, elevó al Soberano Congreso Nacional, sobre las reformas que, en su sentir, deben hacerse en las Bases Orgánicas de la República* (Guadalajara: Imprenta del Gobierno, 1845) and *Ultimas comunicaciones habidas entre los electores del Departamento de Jalisco* (Guadalajara: Imprenta de Manuel Brambila, 1845). Muriá insists on the similarity between the new Bases Orgánicas and the Constitution of the Seven Laws of 1836. He notes these significant changes: the Moderating Council (*Poder Moderador*) was suppressed, the presidential term was reduced to five years, and the Departmental Juntas became Assemblies with a larger number of members. Muriá, *Historia de Jalisco*, III: 47. But Noriega and Reyes Heroles insist on the fragile nature of the new arrangement, as long as a solid alliance was not achieved within the wealthy sectors and between them and the designs of Antonio López de Santa Anna, as suggested in this study. Noriega, *El pensamiento conservador*, II: 331, 336–37; Reyes Heroles, *El liberalismo*, II: 311–20.

135. Muriá, *Historia de Jalisco*, III: 49, 53–56. The powerful of Jalisco would go along with these results. See, for example, *Voto del M.I. Ayuntamiento de Guadalajara,*

sobre la forma de gobierno que debe adoptar la nación (Guadalajara: Imprenta del Gobierno, 7 Sep 1846). For national dynamics at this moment, see Miguel Soto, *La conspiración monárquica en México, 1845–1846* (Mexico: Eosa, 1988).

136. *Protesta del Illmo. Sr. Obispo y Venerable Cabildo de la Santa Iglesia de Guadalajara, sobre el decreto de ocupación de bienes eclesiásticos publicado en México el día 13 de enero del presente año de 1847* (Guadalajara: Imprenta de Brambila, 1847); Luis de la Rosa, Ministerio de Justicia y Negocios Eclesiásticos, "Excitativa a que el clero de la República ayude con los gastos de la guerra con los Estados Unidos" (No publisher, 19 May 1847); *Juicio imparcial sobre la circular del Sr. Rosa* (Guadalajara: Imprenta de Rodríguez, 1847); *Algunas observaciones sobre la circular del Señor Rosa* (Guadalajara: Imprenta de Rodríguez, 1847); *Cuestión sobre los bienes de manos muertas. Edicto del Sr. Obispo de Puebla* (Mexico City: Imprenta de Torres, 1847); *Bienes de la Iglesia o sea Impugnación del 'Discurso sobre bienes eclesiásticos' inserto en el Diario del Gobierno* (Guadalajara: Imprenta de Dionisio Rodríguez, 1847); *Contestación del Illmo. Sr. Vicario Capitular del Arzobispado a la circular de 19 de mayo del Ministerio de Justicia, suscrita por el Señor Don Luis de la Rosa* (Mexico City, reprinted in Guadalajara: Oficina de Rodríguez, 1847); *Protestas de los Illmos. Señores Obispos de Durango y Oaxaca* (Guadalajara: Oficina de Dionisio Rodríguez, 1847 [reprint]); *Préstamos, contribuciones y exacciones de la Iglesia de Guadalajara* (Guadalajara: Imprenta de Manuel Brambila, 1847); and *Protesta del Illmo Señor Obispo de Guadalajara, contra la que con el mismo nombre hizo el Supremo Gobierno de la nación* (Guadalajara: Imprenta de Rodríguez, 1848). It is worth noting that the Church was not the only opponent of special tax assessments due to war with the United States. See *Representación que hacen los vecinos de la Ciudad de Guadalajara, al Supremo Gobierno de la Unión por medio de una junta nombrada por el Gobierno del Estado* (Guadalajara: Imprenta del Gobierno del Estado, a cargo de J. Santos Orosco, 1847).

137. La Voluntad Nacional, *¡Viva la Religión! Compendio crítico histórico de la llamada ley de ocupación de bienes eclesiásticos* (Guadalajara: Imprenta de Minerva a cargo de M. R. Toledo, ca. 1847 [reprint]), unpaginated.

138. Ibid.

139. "Article 112, III. The President cannot occupy the property of any individual owner or corporation, nor disturb their possession, use or employment of it, and if in some case it were necessary to take the property of an individual owner or corporation for an object of known public utility, [this should be done] by the Senate, or during recesses, the Council of Government, always indemnifying the interested party, according to the judgment of good men chosen by the party and the government. Article 101. The President and Vice-President newly elected every four years must be present on 1 April in the place where the supreme powers of the Federation reside, and must swear before the combined chambers to fulfill their duties according to the following oath: "I, named President (or Vice-President) of the United Mexican States, swear by God and the Holy Gospels that I will faithfully exercise the office these united states have entrusted to me, and that I will follow and enforce the Constitution and the general laws of the Federation." *Constitución Federal*, 30–33, 34.

140. Voluntad Nacional, *¡Viva la Religión!*, unpaginated.

141. Diego Aranda, *Nos el Doctor D. ..., por la gracia de Dios y de la Santa Sede Apostólica Obispo de Guadalajara. Al Venerable Clero Secular, salud, paz y gracia en nuestro Señor Jesucristo* (Guadalajara: Imprenta de Rodríguez, 12 May 1845), 4. On this same theme, see also Pedro Espinosa, *Nos el Dr. D. ..., Dignidad Maestrescuelas de esta*

Santa Iglesia Catedral, y Gobernador de la Mitra por el Illmo. Señor Dr. D. Diego Aranda Dignísimo Obispo de esta Diócesis (Guadalajara: Imprenta de Rodríguez, 4 Dec. 1847).

142. Diego Aranda, *Carta pastoral del Illmo. Sr. Dr. D. … Obispo de Guadalajara, al Venerable Clero Secular y Regular, y a todos los fieles de sus Diócesis* (Guadalajara: Oficina de Rodríguez, 3 Mar. 1845). Also recall what the late Bishop Gordoa had said on this point years before.

143. Diego Aranda, *Nos el Doctor D. …, por la gracia de Dios y de la Santa Sede Apostólica, Obispo de Guadalajara, al Venerable Clero Secular y Regular y a todos los fieles de nuestra Diócesis salud, paz y gracia en nuestro Señor Jesucristo* (Guadalajara: Imprenta de Dionisio Rodríguez, 15 May 1847), 1–3. In this letter, the Bishop reproduced an encyclical from Pope Pius IX, dated 9 November 1846, in which the Holy Father, after portraying a sad panorama for the universal Church, called for "safeguarding the conservative execution of the laws of the Church." Ibid., 22.

144. *Pastoral del Illmo. Sr. Dr. D. …, Dignísimo Obispo de Guadalajara a sus Diocesanos, contra la introducción de las falsas religiones en el país* (Guadalajara: Imprenta de Rodríguez, 14 Sep 1848), 1–3.

145. Ibid., 5–20.

146. Diego Aranda, *Nos el Dr. D. …, por la gracia de Dios y de la Santa Sede Apostólica Obispo de Guadalajara, Al Venerable Clero Secular y Regular, y a los fieles de esta Diócesis, salud y bendición* (Guadalajara: No publisher, 13 May 1848), 2.

147. Diego Aranda, *Carta pastoral sobre lectura de libros y escritos prohibidos o que contienen doctrinas antirreligiosas e inmorales* (Guadalajara: Imprenta de Dionisio Rodríguez, 1848), 2. Italics mine.

148. Ibid., 3.

149. Ibid., 7–8. See also Diego Aranda, *Segunda carta pastoral sobre lectura de libros y escritos prohibidos o que contienen doctrinas irreligiosas e inmorales* (Guadalajara: Imprenta de Dionisio Rodríguez, 9 Feb. 1849). In another 1849 ecclesiastical document, another cleric lamented the "spirit of novelty that dominates our age … the religious spirit has let down its guard … the frenzy of fashion has replaced it, and the spirit of vertigo which does not respect the barriers of the piety and the holy religion we profess." José María Cayetano Orozco, *Sermón de Honras de los Venerables Sacerdotes* (Mexico City: Imprenta de J. M. Lara, 1849), unpaginated. In such circumstances, ensuring respect for Catholic orthodoxy in a prudent and effective manner was a delicate task. The tastes of the age burst into Mexico, and building a simple dike to hold them back was impossible. Total acceptance of new tendencies was equally unacceptable. The writings of Spanish (Catalan) theologian Jaime Balmes are interesting on this point, and they were published in Guadalajara throughout the 1840s, surely with the approval of Bishop Aranda. See note 118 above.

150. Diego Aranda, *Carta pastoral del Illmo. S. Obispo de esta Diócesis sobre el jubileo del presente año* (Guadalajara: Tipografía de Rodríguez, 7 May 1852), 7–8.

151. Ibid., 21–35.

152. Diego Aranda, *Pastoral del Obispo … comentando la persecución que sufría en esos momentos el jefe de los católicos, el Papa Pío IX* (Guadalajara: No publisher, 19 Feb 1849), unpaginated. See Dorantes, et al., *Inventario*, I, No. 193-14. Also see Aranda, *Nos el Dr. D. …, por la gracia de Dios y de la Santa Sede Apostólica Obispo de esta Diócesis, Prelado doméstico de su Santidad y Asistente al Sacro Solio Pontificio….* (Guadalajara: Tipografía de Dionisio Rodríguez, 21 June 1850); *Artículo de La España, periódico político, mercantil, industrial y literario, México, febrero 24 de 1849*

(Guadalajara: Imprenta de Dionisio Rodríguez, 1849 [reprint]); Jaime Balmes, *Pío IX. Por Don …, Presbítero* (Madrid, reprinted in Guadalajara: Oficina de Gobierno a cargo de J. Santos Oroso, 1848). The advance of radical liberalism and a new morality also altered Balmes' thinking. This is evident in *Pío IX* and also in *"Un cristianismo extraño," Opúsculo tomado de los escritos selectos del presbítero D. …, reimpreso en Guadalajara para instrucción del pueblo* (Guadalajara: Tipografía de Rodríguez, 1855 [reprint]).

153. Ortiz, *Sermón que predicó en el Santuario de Guadalupe de esta Ciudad*, 28, 32. Marianism seemed to intensify in those years at the same time that the Church faced a liberal (and statist) uprising against its economic and cultural hegemony. See some of the following examples: Orozco, *Sermón que en la solemne festividad de la Concepción de María*; the sermons of Román y Bugarín dedicated to Our Lady of Refuge and Our Lady of Guadalupe which were published in 1852; Rafael S. Camacho, *Sermón que predicó el Dr. D. … Catedrático del Seminario Conciliar de esta Ciudad en la Iglesia de Santa Mónica* (Guadalajara: Tipografía de Rodríguez, 1855); Ignacio de Jesús Cabrera, *Oración panegírica que para solemnizar el Convento de Franciscanos de esta Ciudad de Guadalajara la declaración dogmática de la Concepción Inmaculada de María* (Guadalajara: Tipografía del Gobierno, a cargo de J. Santos Orosco, 1855); Pedro Cobieya, *Descripción breve de la solemnidad con que el V. Orden Tercero de N.S.P.S. Francisco de Guadalajara celebró la declaración dogmática de María Santísima* (Guadalajara: Tipografía de Rodríguez, 1855); José María Cayetano Orozco, *Sermón que para celebrar el misterio de la Concepción en gracia de María* (San Juan de los Lagos, Tipografía de R. Martín, 1856); Jesús Ortiz, *Sermón que predicó en el Santuario de Guadalupe de esta Ciudad, el Señor Cura del Sagrario Lic. D. … el día 14 de diciembre de 1856* (Guadalajara: Tipografía de Rodríguez, 1856). There was also some cultivation of a specifically Jaliscan Marianism, as can bee seen in the earlier publications *Tierna despedida y acción de gracias del devoto jalisciense a María Santísima de Zapopan al volverse a su Santuario* (Guadalajara: Imprenta de Dionisio Rodríguez, 1833) and *Tierno recibimiento del pueblo de Guadalajara a su amorosa Madre María Santísima de Zapopan, en el feliz día de su llegada a esta capital* (Guadalajara: Imprenta de Rodríguez, 1839). Just as the Church had never denied the intrinsic value of monasticism and the regular orders, however much it accepted the need for that life to provide more social services to the community, so one can clearly sense it was now placing renewed emphasis on the spiritual devotions of the flock. This has as much or more to do with reverential practices of the faith as with matters of religious dogma. Since this tendency also came from Rome, and was not exclusive to the Mexican clergy, it can also be considered part of the Church's global response to the liberal offensive of the nineteenth century.

154. See the Plan of Ayutla, 1 March 1854, and the Plan of Ayutla with modifications made in Acapulco, 11 March 1854, in Álvaro Matute, *México en el siglo XIX, antología de fuentes e interpretaciones históricas* (Mexico City: UNAM, 1981): 287–95. The Plans sought to reestablish the republic, to restore territorial integrity − recently violated by the sale of the Mesilla − and to promote a stable, supposedly non-partisan, government as well as a robust economy, by means of a less taxing fiscal regime and greater freedoms for commerce. This would be the liberal response to Santa Anna conservatism in 1853. It is worth emphasizing that the orientation of Santa Anna's 1853 government was under dispute from the beginning. See the conservative efforts to orient Santa Anna in the letter from Lucas Alamán dated 23 March 1853, reproduced in Matute, *México*, 284–86.

The opposite tendency can be sensed in *Exposición dirigida al Exmo. Sr. General Presidente D. Antonio López de Santa Anna, por una comisión del Partido Progresista Democrático de la Ciudad de México* (Guadalajara: Tipografía de Brambila, 1853). Dated 18 March 1853, the pamphlet carried the following final note when it was reprinted on 2 May: "Since the Progressive Democratic Party of the entire state of Jalisco sees its own feelings, its own ideas, and its own principles in this exposition, it has not vacillated one instant in making this exposition its own." *Exposición*, 22. A moderate posture can be seen in *Carta dirigida a Santa Anna por el Ayuntamiento de Guadalajara felicitándolo por haber vuelto al poder* (Guadalajara: No publisher, 2 April 1853). See Dorantes, et al., *Inventario*, I, No. 199–8. For a general historical overview of events in Jalisco in this period, see Muriá, *Historia de Jalisco*, III: 79–96, 153–56.

Notes to Conclusion

1. See Chapters Four and Nine.
2. See Chapters Six, Seven, and Eight.
3. See Chapter Nine. Noriega, *El pensamiento conservador*, I; Reyes Heroles, *El liberalismo mexicano*, II: 215–43, 331–53; Ricker, "Lower Secular Clergy," 147–48.
4. See Green, *The Mexican Republic*, 140–209; Costeloe, *La primera república*, 115–272; Hale, *Mexican Liberalism*, 98–214.
5. In addition to Chapter Nine of this study, see *Colección de las leyes, decretos, circulares y providencias relativas a la desamortización eclesiástica, a la nacionalización de los bienes de corporaciones y a la reforma de la legislación civil que tenía relación con el culto y con la iglesia*, 2 vols. (Mexico City: Secretaría de Hacienda y Crédito Público, 1979). Volume 1 includes projected laws about public debt and the Church in 1833. On liberal education, see Abraham Talavera, *Liberalismo y educación*, 2 vols. (Mexico City: Colección SepSetentas, 1973), especially volume 1.
6. Even liberal spokesmen would later have to acknowledge clerical complaints against the 1833–34 liberal government. See, for example, José Ramón Pacheco, *Cuestión del día o nuestros males y sus remedios* and Mariano Otero, *Discurso que en la solemnidad del 16 de septiembre de 1841 pronunció* ....
7. Noriega, *El pensamiento conservador*, I; Reyes Heroles, *El liberalismo mexicano*, II: 243, 331–53.
8. For the French case, see Gérard Mairet, "El liberalismo" and "Pueblo y nación."
9. See Mariano Otero, *Consideraciones sobre la situación política* ... and *Ensayo sobre el verdadero estado* ..., both reproduced in Jesús Reyes Heroles (ed.), *Mariano Otero, obras* (Mexico City: Porrúa, 1967), 2 vols. See also Luis de la Rosa, *La política de los Editores del Tiempo*.
10. See the pastoral letters of Bishops Gordoa and Aranda on this point.
11. In this context, recall the necessary distinction between the bureaucratic and economic strength of the Church on the one hand, and its relative lack of moral force and internal cohesion due to its long-standing association with the state. On this point, see the introduction and Chapter One of this study.
12. In addition to what was discussed in this study, see Brading, *Los orígenes*, and Lafaye, *Quetzalcóatl*.

Bibliography

1. Archival Sources

Archivo General de la Nación: Ramo de Obispos y Arzobispos, vols. 5 and 17.
Archivo Histórico de Jalisco: Legajos G-4-802, JAL/3163; G-4-808, JAL/3159;
G-4-719, GUA/4.

2. Printed Primary Sources

A.R.F. *El despertador.* Mexico City, reprinted in Guadalajara: Oficina liberal a
cargo del C. Juan Cabrera, 1823.
A.T. *Hablen los predicadores y confundan la impiedad.* Guadalajara: Imprenta de
Dionisio Rodríguez, 1833.
Abad y Queipo, Manuel. *Representación sobre la inmunidad personal del clero reducida
por las leyes del nuevo código en la cual se propuso al rey el asunto de diferentes leyes
que establecidas harían la base principal de un gobierno liberal y benéfico para las
Américas y para su metrópoli.* Pamphlet reproduced in Mora, *Obras sueltas.*
Abascal y Sousa, José Fernando. "Provincia de Guadalajara. Estado que demuestra
los frutos y efectos de agricultura, industria y comercio ... en el año de
1803 ...." In Florescano y Gil Sánchez, *Descripciones económicas regionales de
Nueva España, Provincias del Centro, Sureste y Sur, 1766–1827.* Mexico City:
INAH, 1976.
Advertencia a los del Nivel y todo el pueblo de Jalisco. Guadalajara: Imprenta del C.
Mariano Rodríguez, 1825.
Aguirre, Juan de. *Panegírico que en honor del glorioso San Ladislao Rey predicó en la
Iglesia del convento de Religiosas Dominicas de Jesús María de esta ciudad el día
28 de junio de 1829 el R.P. Lector Fr. ... Religioso Mercedario de este Convento
de Nuestra Señora de la Merced.* Guadalajara: Oficina a cargo del C. Dionisio
Rodríguez, ca. 1829.
Ahí va ese tiro sin puntería: si a alguno descalabra, no es culpa mía. Guadalajara:
Imprenta a cargo de Teodosio Cruz Aedo, 1834.

Algunas observaciones sobre la circular del Señor Rosa. Guadalajara: Imprenta de Rodríguez, 1847.

El Amante de la Religión. *Una palabra al Polar convertido.* Guadalajara: Imprenta de la viuda de Romero, 1825.

———. *A los Editores del Nivel.* Guadalajara: Imprenta de la viuda de Romero, 1825.

El Amigo del mexicano. *Ya Jalisco perdió su Nivel.* Mexico City: Imprenta del C. Alejandro Valdés, 1825.

El Amigo del orden. *Tiene razón el General Rayón, o sea respuesta al comunicado inserto en la Gaceta núm. 29.* Guadalajara: Imprenta de la viuda de Romero, 1826.

El Amigo del otro amigo. *Por aquí rapa el Nivel: por allí lo rapan a él.* Mexico City: Imprenta del C. Alejandro Valdés, 1826.

El Apestado. *El coco de los impíos, o La Escolta de Dragones. Respuesta a un comunicado de la Gaceta.* Guadalajara: Imprenta del C. Mariano Rodríguez, 1826.

Aranda, Diego. *Carta pastoral del Illmo. Sr. Dr. D. ... Obispo de Guadalajara, al Venerable Clero Secular y Regular, y a todos los fieles de sus Diócesis.* Guadalajara: Oficina de Rodríguez, 3 Mar 1845.

———. *Carta pastoral del Illmo. S. Obispo de esta Diócesis sobre el jubileo del presente año.* Guadalajara: Tipografía de Rodríguez, 7 May 1852.

———. *Carta pastoral sobre lectura de libros y escritos prohibidos o que contienen doctrinas antirreligiosas e inmorales.* Guadalajara: Imprenta de Dionisio Rodríguez, 1848.

———. *Instrucción pastoral sobre los cinco preceptos de Nuestra Sta. Madre Iglesia, dirigida por el Ilustrísimo Señor Dr. D. ..., Obispo de Guadalajara, a sus diocesanos.* Guadalajara: Imprenta de Brambila, 1 Feb. 1840.

———. *Nos el Doctor D. ..., por la gracia de Dios y de la Santa Sede Apostólica Obispo de Guadalajara. Al Venerable Clero Secular, salud, paz y gracia en nuestro Señor Jesucristo.* Guadalajara: Imprenta de Rodríguez, 12 May 1845.

———. *Nos el Doctor D. ..., por la gracia de Dios y de la Santa Sede Apostólica, Obispo de Guadalajara, al Venerable Clero Secular y Regular y a todos los fieles de nuestra Diócesis salud, paz y gracia en nuestro Señor Jesucristo.* Guadalajara: Imprenta de Dionisio Rodríguez, 15 May 1847. Letter reproduces an encyclical from Pius IX dated 9 Nov. 1846.

———. *Nos el Dor. ..., por la gracia de Dios y de la Santa Sede Apostólica Obispo de Guadalajara.* Guadalajara: Imprenta del Gobierno, 2 Jan. 1837.

———. *Nos el Dr. D. ..., por la gracia de Dios y de la Santa Sede Apostólica Obispo de esta Diócesis, Prelado doméstico de su Santidad y Asistente al Sacro Solio Pontificio....* Guadalajara: Tipografía de Dionisio Rodríguez, 21 June 1850.

———. *Nos el Dr. D. ..., por la gracia de Dios y de la Santa Sede Apostólica Obispo de Guadalajara, Al Venerable Clero Secular y Regular, y a los fieles de esta Diócesis, salud y bendición.* Guadalajara: No publisher, 13 May 1848.

———. *Pastoral del Obispo ... comentando la persecución que sufría en esos momentos el jefe de los católicos, el Papa Pío IX.* Guadalajara: No publisher, 19 Feb. 1849.

———. *Protesta del Illmo Señor Obispo de Guadalajara, contra la que con el mismo nombre hizo el Supremo Gobierno de la nación en [sic] 3 de diciembre pasado, contestación a una nota del referido Gobierno en que pide un préstamo de 400,000 pesos, así como a la exención que concedió a la Diócesis de Guadalajara para que pudiera exigir la redención de capitales de plazo cumplido.* Guadalajara: Imprenta de Rodríguez, 1848.

————. *Pastoral del Illmo. Sr. Dr. D. ..., Dignísimo Obispo de Guadalajara a sus Diocesanos, contra la introducción de las falsas religiones en el país.* Guadalajara: Imprenta de Rodríguez, 14 Sep. 1848.

————. *Protesta del Illmo. Sr. Obispo y Venerable Cabildo de la Santa Iglesia de Guadalajara, sobre el decreto de ocupación de bienes eclesiásticos publicado en México el día 13 de enero del presente año de 1847.* Guadalajara: Imprenta de Brambila, 1847.

————. *Segunda carta pastoral sobre lectura de libros y escritos prohibidos o que contienen doctrinas irreligiosas e inmorales.* Guadalajara: Imprenta de Dionisio Rodríguez, 9 Feb. 1849.

Arroyo, José Francisco. *Discurso que el Sr. Don D... pronunció en la H. Asamblea del Estado de Nuevo León de que es diputado, al discutirse en ella el proyecto presentado al H. Congreso de Zacatecas por su diputado el Sr. Gómez Huerta.* Guadalajara: Imprenta de la viuda de Romero, 1827.

Artículo de La España, periódico político, mercantil, industrial y literario, México, febrero 24 de 1849. Guadalajara: Imprenta de Dionisio Rodríguez, 1849 (reprint).

Artículo 7o de la Constitución de Jalisco, "El estado fijará y costeará todos los gastos necesarios para la conservación del culto." Guadalajara: Imprenta del C. Mariano Rodríguez, 1824.

Balmes, Jaime. *Observaciones sociales, políticas y económicas sobre los bienes del clero, por el Dr. D. ..., presbítero.* Guadalajara: Oficina de Manuel Brambila, 1842 (reprint).

————. *Pío IX. Por Don ..., Presbítero.* Madrid; reprinted in Guadalajara: Oficina de Gobierno a cargo de J. Santos Orosco, 1848.

————. *Suma de civilización mayor posible en el mundo, en un estado, en un individuo. Por Don ...* Guadalajara: Imprenta del Gobierno, 1843 [reprint].

————. *"Un cristianismo extraño," Opúsculo tomado de los escritos selectos del presbítero D. ..., reimpreso en Guadalajara para instrucción del pueblo.* Guadalajara: Tipografía de Rodríguez, 1855 [reprint].

Barajas, Pedro. *Elogio fúnebre del Illmo. Sr. Dr. D. José Miguel Gordoa Dignísimo Obispo de esta diócesis que en sus solemnes exequias celebradas en el Seminario Conciliar de esta ciudad pronunció el Lic. D. ... prebendado de esta Santa Iglesia Catedral, el día 26 de enero de 1833.* Guadalajara:Imprenta de Rodríguez a cargo de Trinidad Buitrón, 1833.

————. *Sermón que en la solemne profesión de Sor María Loreto de Sr. S. José Gómez Navarrete, predicó en el Convento de la Encarnación de México el día 25 de julio de 1841, el Sr. Dr. D. ..., Canónigo de la Santa Iglesia de Guadalajara y Diputado en el Congreso General de la República Mexicana.* Mexico City: Imprenta del Aguila, 1841.

————. *Sermón predicado por el Sr. Canónigo de esta Santa Iglesia Catedral de Guadalajara Dr. D. ... el día 7 de mayo de 1848, en la función que anualmente se hace en la Iglesia del Convento de Santa Mónica, en honor de Jesús, María y José.* Guadalajara: Imprenta de Dionisio Rodríguez, ca. 1848.

Bienes de la Iglesia o sea Impugnación del 'Discurso sobre bienes eclesiásticos' inserto en el Diario del Gobierno. Guadalajara: Imprenta de Dionisio Rodríguez, 1847.

Bienpica, Casimiro. *El Canónigo Bien-pica [sic], a su Prelado El Polar.* Guadalajara: Oficina del C. Mariano Rodríguez, 1825.

Blasco y Navarro, Tomás. *Canción elegíaca sobre los desastres que ha causado en el Reino de Nueva Galicia, señaladamente en su capital Guadalajara, la rebelión del apóstata Bachiller Miguel Hidalgo y Costilla, Capataz de la Gavilla de Insurgentes,*

*cura que fue del pueblo de la Congregación de Dolores en la Diócesis de Michoacán.
Compuesta por el R.P.F. ..., del Orden de Predicadores, Presentado en Sagrada
Teología, Doctor de la Real Universidad de Guadalajara, Catedrático en ella del
Angélico Doctor Santo Tomás, y Examinador Sinodal de este obispado.* Guadalajara:
No publisher, 1811.

————. *Sermón gratulatorio que en la función celebrada en la Santa Iglesia Catedral
de Guadalajara para dar gracias al Altísimo por la feliz y triunfante entrada de
nuestro inmortal héroe Don Agustín de Iturbide en la corte del nuevo M.R.P. Fr.
..., Maestro en Sagrada Teología, Doctor en ella por la universidad de esta ciudad,
catedrático del Angélico Dr. Santo Tomás, y examinador sinodal de este obispado.*
Guadalajara: Imprenta de D. Urbano Sanromán, 1821.

*Breve impugnación de las ochenta y cinco proposiciones del Synodo de Pistoya, condenadas
por el Sr. Pío VI en [sic] 28 de agosto de 1794. Preceden algunas reflexiones del
Illmo. Sr. Obispo y Cabildo de Puebla, que prueban la necesidad en que estamos
de admitir la Bula Auctorem fidei condenatoria de dichas proposicones.* Guadalajara:
Imprenta del Gobierno, 1838.

Bulla SMI. Domini Nostri PII VI. Quae incipit Auctorem Fidei. Guadalajara:
Tipografía a Nicolao España Directa, 1835

C.A. *También los callados suelen hablar.* Guadalajara: Imprenta del C. Mariano
Rodríguez, 1824.

El Caballero del verde Gabán. El Polar Reformador o el Quijote de estos tiempos.
Guadalajara: Imprenta del C. Mariano Rodríguez, 1826.

Cabañas, Juan Cruz Ruiz de. "Excitativa a todos los fieles y clero regular y secular
para que envíen su donativo para ayudar a la expulsión de los franceses del
terrritorio español: 10 de septiembre, 1810." See Dorantes, et al., *Inventario,*
III, No. 774-2.

————. *Nos el Doctor D. ... por la gracia de Dios y de la Santa Sede Apostólica obispo
de Guadalajara en el Nuevo Reino de Galicia, del Consejo de S. M..* Guadalajara:
No publisher, 4 Apr. 1812.

————. *Nos el Dr. D. ... por la gracia de Dios, y de la Santa Sede Apostólica obispo
de Guadalajara. A todo el venerable clero secular, y regular, y a todos nuestros muy
amados fieles: salud, paz y gracia en nuestro señor Jesucristo.* Guadalajara: No
publisher, 30 Apr. 1810.

————. *Nos el Dr. ..., por la gracia de Dios y de la Santa Sede Apostólica obispo de
Guadalajara, Nuevo Reino de Galicia del Consejo de su Majestad.* Guadalajara:
No publisher, 3 Sep. 1815.

Cabrera, Ignacio de Jesús. *Oración panegírica que para solemnizar el Convento
de Franciscanos de esta Ciudad de Guadalajara la declaración dogmática de la
Concepción Inmaculada de María, pronunció el Reverendo Padre Lector de Sagrada
Teología, Fr. ..., el día 14 de abril de 1855.* Guadalajara: Tipografía del
Gobierno, a cargo de J. Santos Orosco, 1855.

Camacho, Juan Nepomuceno. *Sermón predicado por el Sr. Magistral de esta Santa
Iglesia Catedral de Guadalajara Dr. D. ..., el día 25 de abril de 1841, en la
función que anualmente se hace en la Iglesia del Convento de Santa Mónica, en
honor de Jesús, María y José.* Guadalajara: La Oficina de Dionisio Rodríguez,
ca. 1841.

————. *Sermón predicado por el Sr. Magistral de esta Santa Iglesia Catedral Dr. D. ...,
en la Iglesia de Capuchinas de esta ciudad, con motivo de la profesión religiosa de
su sobrina Sor María Concepción Josefa en el siglo D.ª Apolonia Camacho, el 10 de
diciembre de 1845.* Guadalajara: Imprenta de M. Brambila, 1845.

Camacho, Rafael S. *Sermón que predicó el Dr. D. ... Catedrático del Seminario Conciliar de esta Ciudad en la Iglesia de Santa Mónica el día 20 de mayo de 1855 en la solemne función que el comercio de Guadalajara hizo para celebrar el grandioso acontecimiento de la definición dogmática sobre la concepción inmaculada de la Sma. Virgen María verificada en Roma el 8 de diciembre de 1854*. Guadalajara: Tipografía de Rodríguez, 1855.

Campillo y Cosío, Joseph del. *Nuevo sistema de gobierno económico para la América*. Mérida, Venezuela: Universidad de los Andes, 1971.

Campos Santos. Guadalajara: Imprenta de D. Mariano Rodríguez, 1823.

Cañedo, Anastasio. *Discurso cívico que pronunció en esta capital el Licenciado ... el día 16 de septiembre de 1843 en el aniversario del glorioso grito de independencia*. Guadalajara: Oficina de Manuel Brambila, 1843.

[———.] *Concordatos del Polar con el Estado de Jalisco*, reproduced in *La Estrella Polar. Polémica Federalista*. Reprinted in Guadalajara: Poderes de Jalisco, 1977: 167–73.

[———.] *Conjuración del Polar contra los abusos de la Iglesia* Guadalajara: Imprenta del C. Urbano Sanromán, 1825, reprinted in *La Estrella Polar:* 83–93.

[———.] *El Polar convertido*. Guadalajara, reprinted in Mexico City: Oficina del finado Ontiveros, 1825.

[———.] *La Estrella Polar. Polémica Federalista*. Reprinted in Guadalajara: Poderes de Jalisco, 1977.

Cañón de a treinta y seis contra el rastrero buscapiés. Guadalajara: Imprenta del c. Dionisio Rodríguez, 1831.

Carrasco, Mariano, et al. *Representación que el Ayuntamiento Constitucional de Guadalajara dirige al Excelentísimo Señor Presidente de la República*. Mexico City: Oficina de la Testamentaría de Ontiveros, 1826.

Carta dirigida a Santa Anna por el Ayuntamiento de Guadalajara felicitándolo por haber vuelto al poder. Guadalajara: No publisher, 2 Apr. 1853.

El Católico. *Legítimo punto de vista en la causa de los fracmasones*. Reprinted in Guadalajara: Oficina del C. Mariano Rodríguez, 1824.

El Censor del Siglo XIX. Guadalajara, 1833.

Cevallos, Fernando. *Observaciones sobre reforma eclesiástica. Obra póstuma del P. Fr. ..., Aumentada*. Coruña: Oficina del Exacto Correo, 1812; reprinted in Puebla: Oficina del Gobierno, 1820.

"Circular a todos los curas párrocos de las ciudades y villas del Obispado de Guadalajara, sobre el establecimiento de cementerios fuera de los poblados. Año de 1814." See Dorantes, et al., *Inventario*, III, No. 774-4.

Cobieya, Pedro. *Descripción breve de la solemnidad con que el V. Orden Tercero de N.S.P.S. Francisco de Guadalajara celebró la declaración dogmática del Misterio de la Concepción Inmaculada de María Santísima, y Oración panegírica que en la misma Solemnidad fue pronunciada por S. R. P. Comisario Visitador Dr. Fray ..., el día 17 de mayo de 1855*. Guadalajara: Tipografía de Rodríguez, 1855.

———. *Oración panegírica, que sobre las excelencias de la vida religiosa, pronunció el P. Fr. ..., en la solemne profesión de la madre María Guadalupe del Santo Rosario, en el Convento de Religiosas Dominicas de Santa María de Gracia, de la Ciudad de Guadalajara, el día 23 de abril de 1837*. Guadalajara: Imprenta de M. Brambila, ca. 1837.

Colección de acuerdos, órdenes y decretos, sobre tierras, casas y solares, de los indígenas, bienes de sus comunidades y fundos legales de los pueblos del Estado de Jalisco. Guadalajara: Imprenta del gobierno del Estado, a cargo de J. Santos Orosco, 1849.

Colección de documentos relativos a la conducta del Cabildo Eclesiástico de Guadalajara y del clero secular y regular de la misma, en cuanto a rehusar el juramento de la segunda parte del Artículo Séptimo de la Constitución del Estado Libre de Jalisco. Guadalajara: Imprenta del C. Mariano Rodríguez, 1825.

Colección de las leyes, decretos, circulares y providencias relativas a la desamortización eclesiástica, a la nacionalización de los bienes de corporaciones y a la reforma de la legislación civil que tenía relación con el culto y con la iglesia. Edición facsimilar en 2 vols. Mexico City: Secretaría de Hacienda y Crédito Público, 1979.

Constitución Federal de los Estados Unidos Mexicanos sancionada por el Congreso General Constituyente el 4 de octubre de 1824 y Constitución Política del Estado Libre de Jalisco sancionada por su Congreso Constituyente en 18 de noviembre de 1824. Guadalajara: Poderes de Jalisco, 1973.

Contestación a los EE. del Siglo 19. Guadalajara: Imprenta de Dionisio Rodríguez, 26 April 1833.

Contestación a los enemigos de los predicadores. Guadalajara: Imprenta de Dionisio Rodríguez a cargo de Trinidad Buitrón, 1833.

Contestación al Defensor del Artículo 7o. Guadalajara: Imprenta del C. Mariano Rodríguez, 1824.

Contestación del Illmo. Sr. Vicario Capitular del Arzobispado a la circular de 19 de mayo del Ministerio de Justicia, suscrita por el Señor Don Luis de la Rosa. Mexico City, reprinted in Guadalajara: Oficina de Rodríguez, 1847.

Contestación del Obispo y Cabildo de la Santa Iglesia Catedral de Oaxaca al oficio del Exmo. Señor Ministro de Justicia y Negocios Eclesiásticos fecha 26 de marzo del presente año de 1826 con que a nombre del Exmo. Señor Presidente de la Federación Mexicana les remitió el Dictamen de los Señores de las Comisiones unidas de Relaciones y Eclesiástica de 28 de febrero del mismo año sobre instrucciones al Enviado a Roma cerca de S.S. la Suprema Cabeza de la Iglesia. Guadalajara: Oficina de la viuda de Romero, 1827 (reprint).

Contestación sobre patronato, dada por los presbíteros Fernando Antonio Dávila, Dr. Angel María Candina y Dr. Antonio González a la advertencia patriótica del Doctor José Simeón Cañas, diputado del Congreso de San Salvador en la República de Guatemala. Guatemala: Imprenta de Beteta, 1824; reprinted in Guadalajara: Imprenta del C. Mariano Rodríguez, 1827.

Contestaciones a los EE. del Nivel, y una palabra al Polar. Guadalajara: Imprenta de la viuda de Romero, 1826.

Contestaciones habidas entre el Supremo Gobierno del Estado de Jalisco y el Gobernador de la Mitra sobre contribución directa. Guadalajara: Imprenta del C. Urbano Sanromán, 1825.

Conversación familiar entre un sacristán y su compadre contra el papel titulado Hereje a la tapatía. Guadalajara: Imprenta del C. Mariano Rodríguez, 1824

Covarrubias, José María. *Comunicado que dio el C. Dr. José María Covarrubias y corre en el Sol núm. 875.* Guadalajara: Oficina del C. Mariano Rodríguez, 1825 (reprint).

La Cruz. Guadalajara: Imprenta de la viuda de Romero, 1824.

El Cuerpo de liberales. *Establecimiento de la República en Guadalajara. O sea Manifiesto de los liberales de dicha ciudad a sus conciudadanos.* Mexico City: Oficina de D. José Mariano Fernández de Lara, 1823 (reprint).

Cuestión sobre los bienes de manos muertas. Edicto del Sr. Obispo de Puebla. El Obispo de Puebla, el Gobernador del mismo Estado y el Ministro de Justicia y Negocios Eclesiásticos. Protesta del Sr. Obispo de Guadalajara y Contestación del Supremo Gobierno. Exposición del Sr. Obispo de Oaxaca y contestación del Supremo Gobierno. Protesta hecha por los señores curas de esta capital al Sr. Vicario Capitular. Mexico City: Imprenta de Torres, 1847.

Cueva, Pedro L. de la, et al. *Manifestación dirigida al Exmo. Sr. Presidente, por varios ciudadanos de Zapotlán el Grande, sobre el actual estado de la República.* Guadalajara: Imprenta de Sanromán, 1837.

Cumplido, Juan Nepomuceno. *Informe sobre el estado actual de la administración pública del Estado de Jalisco. Leído por el vice-gobernador del mismo, ante la Honorable Asamblea Legislativa en la apertura de sus sesiones ordinarias el día 1 de septiembre de 1828.* Guadalajara: Imprenta del Gobierno a cargo del C. Juan María Brambila, 1828.

————. *Memoria sobre el estado actual de la administración pública del Estado de Jalisco. Leída por el c. Vice-gobernador del mismo ante la Honorable Asamblea Legislativa en la apertura de sus sesiones ordinarias el día 1 de febrero de 1827.* Guadalajara: Oficina del C. Urbano Sanromán, ca. 1827.

Dávila, Rafael. *Justo castigo y destierro del Pensador Mexicano.* Guadalajara: Imprenta de Don Mariano Rodríguez, 1822 (reprint).

Decretos expedidos por la Legislatura de Jalisco, suprimiendo el Tribunal de Haceduría de la Santa Iglesia de Guadalajara, representaciones que sobre esto se ha hecho el V. Cabildo, y contestaciones que han mediado entre esta corporación y el gobierno de aquel estado, con algunas observaciones sobre las cuestiones que merecen examinarse. Mexico City: Imprenta de Galván a cargo de Mariano Arévalo, 1827.

El Defensor de la Religión, que se publica en la Ciudad de Guadalajara Capital del Estado de Jalisco para impugnar los errores de los últimos siglos. Por algunos ciudadanos amantes de su Patria y Religión, 3 vols. Guadalajara: Imprenta a cargo de José Orosio Santos Plazuela, 1827–30.

El Despertador Americano. Reprinted in Mexico City: INAH, 1964.

Después de uno, dos y tres no ha prendido el Buscapiés. Guadalajara: Imprenta del C. Dionisio Rodríguez, 1831.

Día de amargos desengaños o sea triunfo de nuestra religión. Guadalajara: Imprenta de Dionisio Rodríguez, 1833.

Dictamen de la Comisión de Sistema de Hacienda, del Congreso de la Federación Mexicana, sobre las observaciones que hizo una comisión del Congreso de Jalisco acerca del proyecto de clasificación de rentas. Mexico City: Imprenta del Supremo Gobierno, 1824.

Dictamen presentado al Congreso de Jalisco por su Comisión de Hacienda sobre el que dio al Congreso General, su comisión del mismo ramo acerca de clasificación de rentas generales y particulares de la Federación Mexicana. Guadalajara: Imprenta del C. Urbano Sanromán, 1824.

Dictamen presentado por la Comisión de Hacienda al Honorable Congreso del Estado, sobre la ley expedida por las cámaras de la Unión, imponiendo a los individuos de los Estados un cinco por ciento sobre sus rentas, y aprobado por el propio Congreso por unanimidad de los votos presentes en [sic] 4 de julio del año corriente. Guadalajara: Imprenta del Supremo Gobierno, a cargo del C. Juan María Brambila, 1829.

Dictamen sobre las exequias, luto y honores fúnebres que deben decretarse al difunto Gobernador del Estado de Jalisco, Excelentísimo Ciudadano Prisciliano Sánchez, formado por una comisión especial del Honorable Congreso, aprobado por el mismo, y mandado imprimir de su orden. Guadalajara: Imprenta del C. Urbano Sanromán, 1826.

*Discurso pronunciado el día 27 de septiembre de 1839 en el salón principal de la
Universidad Nacional de Guadalajara, por J. D. S. y C., Síndico menos antiguo
del M. I. Ayuntamiento de esta Capital, en celebridad del aniversario de nuestra
independencia el año de 1821.* Guadalajara: Imprenta del Gobierno, 1839.

"Disposiciones que da el obispo de Guadalajara a los señores curas para prevenirse de la peste que asoló en 1813." See Dorantes, et al., *Inventario*, I,
No. 95-6.

Dogma y disciplina. Guadalajara: Imprenta de Dionisio Rodríguez, ca. 1833.

El Eclesiástico despreocupado. No hay peor cuña que la del propio palo. Guadalajara:
Imprenta del C. Urbano Sanromán, 1825.

————. *Ultima contestación de la Cuña al Tepehuaje.* Guadalajara: Imprenta del C.
Urbano Sanromán, 1825.

El Enemigo de las cosas a medias. La voz de la libertad pronunciada en Jalisco.
Guadalajara, reprinted in Mexico City: Oficina del finado Ontiveros, 1825.

El error despojado de los adornos y aliños de la virtud y presentado bajo su propia forma.
Guadalajara: Imprenta del C. Mariano Rodríguez, 1824. Three parts.

Es hablar contra razón atacar la religión. Guadalajara: Imprenta del C. Dionisio
Rodríguez, 1831.

Esparza, José María. *Sermón predicado el día 1° de marzo de 1825 en la solemne
profesión de religiosas de coro que con el nombre de Sor Mariana y Sor María
Guadalupe de Jesús María y José hicieron Doña Mariana y Doña Guadalupe
Romero en el Monasterio de Religiosas Dominicas de Santa María de Gracia de
la Ciudad de Guadalajara. Por el Presbítero D. ....* Guadalajara: Oficina de C.
Mariano Rodríguez, ca. 1825.

Espinosa, Casiano. *Sermón predicado por el Br. Presb. D. ..., catedrático de Teología
Escolástica del Seminario Conciliar, en la profesión religiosa de Sor María del
Refugio del Divino Salvador, en el Convento de Religiosas Dominicas de Santa
María de Gracia de esta capital, el día 26 del mes de enero del año del Señor de
1840.* Guadalajara: Imprenta de Manuel Brambila, ca. 1840.

Espinosa, Francisco. *Elogio fúnebre del Illmo. Sr. Dr. D. Diego Aranda y Carpinteiro,
Digmo. Obispo de la Diócesis de Guadalajara, que en sus solemnes exequias
celebradas en la Santa Iglesia Catedral pronunció el Sr. Dr. D. ..., Dignidad
Maestrescuelas de la misma, el día 28 de julio de 1853, publicado en Honras
fúnebres celebradas en la Sta. Iglesia Catedral de Guadalajara en los días 27 y 28
de julio en memoria del Illmo. Sr. Dr. Don Diego Aranda y Carpinteiro, Prelado
doméstico de Su Santidad, Asistente al Sacro Solio Pontificio, Presidente Protector del
Instituto de Africa y Dignísimo Obispo de la misma Diócesis de Guadalajara. Año
de 1853.* Guadalajara: Tipografía de Dionisio Rodríguez, ca. 1853.

————. *Oración que en las solemnes exequias celebradas en la Santa Iglesia Catedral de
Guadalajara por el descanso de la alma [sic] del Exmo. Sor. Don Miguel Barragán,
General de División en los Ejércitos Mexicanos y Presidente Interino de la República
dijo el Dr. D. ..., prebendado de la misma Santa Iglesia el día 11 de abril de 1836.*
Guadalajara: Imprenta del Gobierno a cargo de D. Nicolás España, 1836.

————. *Sermón predicado en el Convento de Santa María de Gracia de esta Ciudad.
Por el Sr. Dr. Don ... Canónigo de esta Santa Iglesia Catedral, y Diputado del
Congreso General. En la Profesión de Sor María Encarnación del Espíritu Santo.*
Guadalajara: Imprenta de Dionisio Rodríguez, 1838.

————. *Sermón predicado por el Lic. Don ... el 26 de diciembre de 1831 en la solemne
función de gracias al Todo Poderoso, que, estando su divina majestad manifiesto,
celebró en su capilla el venerable orden tercero de penitencia de NSPS Francisco de*

Guadalajara, por el beneficio de haber dado pastores a la Iglesia mexicana nuestro Santísimo Padre Señor Gregorio XVI. Guadalajara: Imprenta de la Casa de Misericordia, a cargo del C. Jesús Portillo, 1832.

Espinosa, Pedro. *Contestación del Comisionado por el Venerable Cabildo de Guadalajara a las observaciones de los del Honorable Congreso de Zacatecas sobre administración de diezmos.* Guadalajara: Oficina del C. Dionisio Rodríguez, 1831.

———. *Informe que el Dr. D. …, como individuo de la Comisión del Venerable Cabildo Eclesiástico de Guadalajara presentó en la primera conferencia con la del Honorable Congreso del Estado de Jalisco, nombrada para tratar con aquélla sobre reforma de aranceles.* Mexico City: Imprenta de Galván a cargo de Mariano Arévalo, 1831.

———. *Nos el Dr. D. …, Dignidad Maestrescuelas de esta Santa Iglesia Catedral, y Gobernador de la Mitra por el Illmo. Señor Dr. D. Diego Aranda Dignísimo Obispo de esta Diócesis.* Guadalajara: Imprenta de Rodríguez, 4 Dec. 1847.

———. *Observaciones sobre el dictamen del Señor Licenciado don Manuel de la Peña y Peña relativo al decreto de 31 de agosto de 1843.* Guadalajara: Imprenta del Gobierno, 1843.

———. *Patronato en la nación.* Guadalajara: Imprenta de Dionisio Rodríguez, 1833.

———. *Patronato en la nación. Núm. 2 Contestación al dictamen de la comisión eclesiástica del Senado sobre que el patronato de la Iglesia mexicana reside radicalmente en la nación* Guadalajara: Imprenta de Dionisio Rodríguez, 1833.

———. *Rentas eclesiásticas o sea impugnación de la disertación que sobre la materia se ha publicado de orden del Honorable Congreso de Zacatecas.* Guadalajara: Imprenta a cargo de Teodosio Cruz Aedo, 1834.

Espíritu Santo, Bernardo del. *La soberanía del Altísimo, defendida por el Illmo. Sr. D. Fr. … acusado como reo a la Superioridad.* Guadalajara: Imprenta de la viuda de Romero, 1824.

Estrada Carabajal y Galindo, Diego de. *Excesos del Amor del Eterno Padre discurridos por el Señor Doctor D. …, Marqués de Uluapa, Consultor del Santo Oficio, Dean de la Santa Iglesia Catedral de Guadalajara, Juez Provisor, y Vicario General del Obispado de la Nueva Galicia, en dicha Santa Iglesia, en la Dominica Quinta Post Pascham. Dálos a la luz pública D. Diego de Arcaraz, Presbítero, Secretario de Gobierno en Sede Vacante. Y los dedica al Muy Ilustre Señor Venerable Dean, y Cabildo de Dicha Santa Iglesia Catedral de Guadalajara.* Mexico City: Los Herederos de la Viuda de Francisco Rodríguez Lupercio, 1724.

Exposición del General Barragán al Soberano Congreso Nacional. Guadalajara: Imprenta del C. Ignacio Brambila, 1830.

"Exposición del gobierno eclesiástico de Guadalajara, al supremo del estado, sobre la ley de fincas pertenecientes a manos muertas." *La Lima del Vulcano* Núm. 25 (11 January, 1834) Mexico City: José Uribe y Alcalde.

Exposición del Sr. Gobernador de la Mitra sobre la exclusiva concedida al Gobierno. Guadalajara: Imprenta del C. Urbano Sanromán, 1826.

Exposición dirigida al Exmo. Sr. General Presidente D. Antonio López de Santa Anna, por una comisión del Partido Progresista Democrático de la Ciudad de México. Guadalajara: Tipografía de Brambila, 18 Mar 1853; reprinted 2 May 1853.

Exposición que dirige la Exma. Asamblea Departamental de Jalisco, a las Augustas Cámaras. Guadalajara: Imprenta del Gobierno, 1844.

F.M.M. *Preservativo contra la irreligión, en la manifestación de los errores contenidos en diferentes números del periódico titulado La Fantasma. Dedicado al pueblo de Jalisco. F.M.M. Con licencia del ordinario.* Guadalajara: Imprenta del C. Mariano Rodríguez, 1824.

———. *República Federada le conviene al Anáhuac*. Guadalajara: Imprenta libre del C. Ignacio Brambila, 1823.

El Fanático, supersticioso y devoto. Un geringazo al Polar. Guadalajara: Imprenta del C. Mariano Rodríguez, 1825.

Feijóo, Benito Jerónimo. *Teatro Crítico Universal*. 3 vols. Madrid: Espasa-Calpe, 1975.

Fernández de Lizardi, José Joaquín. *Carta segunda, tercera y cuarta del pensador al papista*. Guadalajara: Oficina de D. Urbano Sanromán, 1822 [reprint].

[Fernández de Lizardi, José Joaquín]. *Concluye el sueño del Pensador Mexicano. Perora la verdad ante S.M.I. y el Soberano Congreso*. Guadalajara: Oficina de D. Urbano Sanromán, 1822 [reprint].

[Fernández de Lizardi, José Joaquín]. *La Victoria del Perico. Por el Pensador Mexicano*. Guadalajara: Oficina del C. Brambila, 1823 (reprint).

Fuego del cielo ha de caer si se ahorcan a los traidores. Diálogo entre una vieja y su hijo. Guadalajara: Oficina del C. Urbano Sanromán, ca. 1827.

García Diego, Francisco. *Sermón, que en la solemnísima función que hizo este colegio de N.S. de Guadalupe de Zacatecas en acción de gracias por la feliz conclusión de la Independencia del Imperio Mexicano, dijo el P. Fr. …, Por. Apostólico y Lector de Artes en su mismo colegio, el día 11 de noviembre de 1821*. Guadalajara: Imprenta de D. Mariano Rodríguez, 1822.

Gobernador y peineta. Guadalajara: Oficina de Dionisio Rodríguez, 1833.

González de Cándamo, Gaspar. *Sermón de honras del rey nuestro señor D. Carlos Tercero, que de Dios goce, predicado en la Santa Iglesia Catedral de la Ciudad de Guadalajara en la Nueva Galicia, el día 28 de julio de 1789*. No publisher, no date.

———. *Sermón de honras, predicado en las solemnes que celebró la Santa Iglesia Metropolitana de México, el día 24 de noviembre del año de 1800 a la buena memoria de su difunto arzobispo el Excelentísimo e Ilustrísimo Señor D. Alonso Nuñez de Haro y Peralta, del Consejo de S.M. Virrey, Gobernador y Capitán General que fue de esta Nueva España, el Caballero Gran Cruz Prelado de la Real y Distinguida Orden Española de Carlos III, por el Sr. Dr. D. …, Canónigo Magistral·de la misma Santa Iglesia*. No publisher, no date.

González Plata, José Antonio. *Sermón predicado en la Santa Iglesia Catedral de Guadalajara el día de Nuestra Señora de Guadalupe, por el M.R.P.L.J. y Comendador Fr. …. En el año de 1834*. Guadalajara: Imprenta del Supremo Gobierno a cargo de D. Nicolás España, 1834.

Gordoa, José Miguel. *Carta pastoral del Illmo. Sr. D. …, Obispo de Guadalajara, a sus diocesanos*. Mexico City: Imprenta de Galván a cargo de Mariano Arévalo, 1831.

———, et al. *Dictamen de la Junta de Censura Eclesiástica*. Reprinted in *La Estrella Polar*: 177–203.

———. *Reflexiones que se hicieron por su autor a consulta del Honorable Congreso de Zacatecas que según parece se han reservado, y un amante de la justicia que ha podido conseguirlas, las da a luz para que el público califique su mérito*. Mexico City: Imprenta del Águila, 1827.

Gutiérrez de Estada, J.M. *Méjico en 1840 y en 1847 por Don …*. Paris: Imprenta de Lacrampe Hijo Y[sic], Calle Damiette, No. 2, 1848.

Herrera, José Ignacio. *Memoria sobre el estado actual de la administración pública del Estado de Jalisco en todos los ramos de su comprensión. Leída por el C. Gobernador del mismo ante la Honorable Asamblea Legislativa en la apertura de sus sesiones ordinarias el día 1 de febrero de 1831*. Guadalajara: No publisher, ca. 1831.

Hidalgo y Badillo, José María. *Sermón eucarístico que en la solemne función celebrada en la Santa Iglesia Catedral de Guadalajara, el día 29 de agosto de 1811 por el singular beneficio recibido del cielo, en haberse descubierto e impedido la conspiración tramada en México contra el primero y más digno jefe del reino, y contra todos los buenos ciudadanos. Dijo el Doctor D. ..., Canónigo Magistral de la misma Iglesia por encargo de el M.I. Señor Brigadier D. José de la Cruz, Comandante General del Ejército de Reserva, Gobernador Intendente de esta Provincia, y Presidente de la Real Audiencia.* Guadalajara: No publisher, ca. 1811.

———. *Sermón panegírico de la Natividad de María Santísima que en la solemne función celebrada por el cuerpo de abogados de la Ciudad de Guadalajara, en la Iglesia de Santo Tomás de la Real Universidad el día 8 de septiembre de 1815. Dijo el Señor Dr. Don ..., Canónigo Magisterial de la Santa Iglesia Catedral de dicha Ciudad. Lo publican a sus expensas los mismos abogados deseosos de promover el culto y devoción de su ilustre Patrona.* Guadalajara: Oficina de José Fructo Romero, 1816.

———. *Sermón predicado en la solemne Acción de Gracias, que por el cumplimiento de un siglo de su fundación celebró el Convento de Religiosas Agustinas Recolectas de Santa Mónica de la Ciudad de Guadalajara Capital de la Nueva Galicia el día 19 de febrero de 1820, por el Señor Doctor Don ..., Canónigo Magistral de la Santa Iglesia Catedral de dicha Ciudad.* Guadalajara: Oficina de D. Mariano Rodríguez, ca.1820.

Huerta, José de Jesús. *Sermón que en la solemne bendición de las banderas del Regimiento de Infantería de la Milicia Nacional Local de Guadalajara, predicó el Dr. D. ..., cura de Atotonilco El Alto, y Diputado Provincial, en 25 de marzo de 1822. Dedicado al excelentísimo Señor D. Pedro Celestino Negrete, Libertador y Capitán General de esta provincia.* Guadalajara: Imprenta de Urbano Sanromán, 1822.

Ignorancia descubierta y temeridad confundida. Guadalajara: Imprenta del C. Mariano Rodríguez, 1825.

Iniciativa que el Congreso de Jalisco dirige a las augustas Cámaras de la Unión, contraída a variar el actual sistema en República Central. Guadalajara: Imprenta del Supremo Gobierno, a cargo de D. Nicolás España, 1835.

Iniciativa que la Asamblea del Departamento de Jalisco, elevó al Soberano Congreso Nacional, sobre las reformas que, en su sentir, deben hacerse en las Bases Orgánicas de la República. Guadalajara: Imprenta del Gobierno, 1845.

El Inválido. *Por más que hable el Pensador, no hemos de ser tolerantes, sino cristianos como antes.* Mexico City, reprinted in Guadalajara: Oficina del C. Mariano Rodríguez, 1825.

J.J.C. *La docilidad y gratitud de los mexicanos, ¿cómo ha sido correspondida por Iturbide?* Guadalajara: Oficina de D. Urbano Sanromán, 1823 (reprint).

J.M.G. *Proyecto de ley sobre contribuciones.* Guadalajara: Imprenta de D. Mariano Rodríguez, 1821.

El Josué de Xalisco. *Josué deteniendo El Sol o sea eclipse político del periódico de este nombre visible el martes 13 del corriente.* Guadalajara: Imprenta del C. Mariano Rodríguez, 1824.

Juicio imparcial sobre la circular del Sr. Rosa. Guadalajara: Imprenta de Rodríguez, 1847.

Ladridos del perro al lobo-pastor. Guadalajara: Oficina de D.Mariano Rodríguez, 1826.

Ladrón de Guevara, Joaquín José, et al. *Nos el Deán y Cabildo Gobernador de esta Santa Iglesia metropolitana de México. A nuestros amados diocesanos, salud y paz en Nuestro Señor Jesucristo.* Mexico City: Imprenta de Galván a cargo de Mariano Arévalo, 1833.

Lissaute, Pedro. *Discurso pronunciado en la solemnidad del tercer aniversario de la apertura del Instituto de Jalisco, por el ciudadano ..., Profesor de la Primera Sección en el mismo establecimiento.* Guadalajara: Imprenta del Supremo Gobierno, 1830.

Llave, Pablo de la, Ministerio de Justicia y Negocios Eclesiásticos. "El Exmo. Sr. Presidente de los Estados Unidos Mexicanos se ha servido dirigirme el decreto que sigue." (Decree of the General Constituent Congress, December 2, 1824, saying that Article 7 of the Constitution of the State of Jalisco should be understood as not affecting Faculty 12 of Article 50 of the National Constitution, for which reason the Cathedral Chapter should take the oath to the Constitution of the State of Jalisco.)

López de Santa Anna, Antonio. *Manifiesto del Exmo. Sr. Benemérito de la patria y Presidente Constitucional de la República D. ...* Mexico City: Impreso por Vicente García Torres, 1844.

Maceta. *Para esos huesos la maceta.* Mexico, Guadalajara: las Oficinas de los CC. Alejandro Valdés y Mariano Rodríguez, 1826.

La Maceta de Tepeguage. *A cuña de palo dulce mazeta [sic] de tepeguage.* Guadalajara: Imprenta del C. Mariano Rodríguez, 1825.

Maldonado, Francisco Severo (ed.). *El Telégrafo de Guadalajara.* Guadalajara: 27 May 1811–15 Feb. 1813.

———. *Contrato de asociación para la República de los Estados Unidos del Anáhuac por un ciudadano del Estado de Xalisco.* Guadalajara: Imprenta de la viuda de D. José Fruto Romero, 1823.

———. *Nuevo Pacto Social propuesto a la Nación Española para su discusión en las próximas cortes de 1822–1823.* Guadalajara: Oficina de Doña Petra Manjarrés, 1821.

Memoria sobre el estado actual de la administración pública del estado de Jalisco leída por el C. Gobernador del mismo Prisciliano Sánchez ante la Honorable Asamblea Legislativa en la apertura de sus sesiones ordinarias el día 1 de febrero de 1826 seguida del Pacto Federal de Anáhuac. Guadalajara: Poderes de Jalisco, 1974.

Menéndez Valdés, José. *Descripción y Censo General de la Intendencia de Guadalajara 1789–1793.* Estudio preliminar de Ramón Ma. Serrera. Guadalajara: Gobierno de Jalisco, 1980.

Mora, José María Luis. *Méjico y sus Revoluciones.* 3 vols. Mexico City: EUFESA, 1981 [1836].

———. *Obras sueltas de José María Luis Mora, ciudadano mexicano.* 2 vols. París: Librería de Rosa, 1837.

Moreno, Juan Joseph. *Sermón predicado el día 10 de noviembre de 1792. En las solemnes exequias que la Santa Iglesia Catedral de Guadalajara celebró a su pastor el Illmo. y Rmo. Señor Ntro. D. Fr. Antonio Alcalde por el Lic. D. ..., tesorero dignidad de dicha Santa Iglesia.* No publisher, no date.

———. *Sermón predicado en la solemne acción de gracias que expuesto el augusto sacramento de la eucaristía, celebró por el cumplimiento de dos siglos de su fundación, el convento de religiosas dominicas, de Santa María de Gracia en la Ciudad de Guadalajara, corte de la Nueva Galicia. Por el Lic. D. ... Canónigo Magistral de la Santa Iglesia Catedral, de dicha Ciudad, el día 17 de agosto de 1788.* Mexico City: Imprenta Nueva Madrileña de los Herederos del Lic. D. Joseph de Jáuregui, 1789.

Muzzarelli, Count. *Cartas del Conde Muzzarelli, sobre el juramento de la Constitución Cispadana, Traducidas del italiano por Fr. José María Guzmán.* Guadalajara: Imprenta del Gobiero, 1843 [reprint].

————. *Opúsculo de la excomunión escrita por el conde Muzzarelli en la obra titulada: El buen uso de la lógica en materia de religión. Con licencia del Ordinario.* Guadalajara: Oficina de la viuda de Romero, 1824 (reprint).

————. *Opúsculo V. Indiferencia de la religión. Escrito por el conde Muzzarelli en su obra titulada: El buen uso de la lógica en materia de religión. Con licencia del ordinario.* Guadalajara: Oficina de la viuda de Romero, 1824 (reprint).

————. *Opúsculo XI. De las riquezas del clero. Escrito por el conde Muzzarelli en su obra titulada: El buen uso de la lógica en materia de religión. Con licencia del Ordinario.* Guadalajara: Oficina de la viuda de Romero, 1824 (reprint).

————. *Opúsculo XVIII. Inmunidad Eclesiástica personal, carta única. Escrita por el conde Muzzarelli en su obra titulada: El buen uso de la lógica en materia de religión. Con licencia del Ordinario.* Guadalajara: Oficina de la viuda de Romero, 1824 (reprint).

Nava, José Ignacio María de. *Sermón de la Purísima Concepción que en el día ocho de diciembre del año de 1804, y primero del solemne Triduo, que se celebró en este Convento de la Purísima Concepción de la Ciudad de Zacatecas, a devoción y expensas de los Señores Mineros de Rondanera, en obsequio y culto de este Misterio Dulcísimo predicó el R.P.Fr. …. Sácanlo a luz los mismos muy nobles mineros de la expresada Negociación, en testimonio de su cordial devoción, y con el más vivo deseo de que ésta se propague todo lo posible entre los fieles.* Guadalajara: Oficina de D. Mariano Valdés Téllez Girón, 1806.

Niño Jesús, Pablo Antonio del. *Sermón predicado en la Santa Iglesia Catedral de Guadalajara, el día 29 de abril de 1853, con motivo del regreso a la República y de la Presidencia del Exmo. Sr. General, Benemérito de la Patria, D. Antonio L. de Santa-Anna, por Fr. …, Prior del Carmen.* Guadalajara: Tipografía del Gobierno, a cargo de J. Santos Orosco, 1853.

Nos el Presidente y Cabildo de la Santa Iglesia Catedral de Guadalajara. Al venerable clero secular y regular, y a todos los fieles de la Diócesis, salud y paz en nuestro Señor Jesucristo. Guadalajara: No publisher, 20 Aug. 1834.

O muertos o federados quieren ser los arrancados. O sea impugnación al folleto titulado 'Pocos quieren centralismo y los más federalismo.' Guadalajara: Imprenta de Dionisio Rodríguez, 1834.

El Obispo auxiliar de Madrid. Artículo interesante que se insertó en el noticioso de México del viernes 29 de marzo de 1822, y que se va reimpreso a expensas de un amante de nuestra Santa Religión. Guadalajara: D. Mariano Rodríguez, 1822.

El Obispo Cimarrón de Jalisco: o sea diálogo entre el hacendado de Jalisco D. Juan y el mexicano D. Manuel. Mexico City, reprinted in Guadalajara: Oficina del C. Mariano Rodríguez, 1826.

Obispo de Puebla, Antonio. *Contestación del Señor Obispo de Puebla al Honorable Congreso de Veracruz.* Guadalajara: Imprenta del C. Mariano Rodríguez, 1824 (reprint).

Observaciones que hace el Venerable Cabildo de Guadalajara al Soberano Congreso Constituyente, sobre el proyecto de Constitución. Guadalajara: Imprenta del Gobierno, 1842.

Observaciones que sobre el proyecto de Bases Orgánicas hacen a la H. Junta Legislativa el Obispo y Cabildo de Guadalajara. Guadalajara: Imprenta del Gobierno, 1843.

Oiga el pueblo mexicano lo que dicen en Xalisco de los europeos empleados. Segunda conversación con el pueblo. Mexico City: Oficina del C. J.M. Benavente y Socios, 1824.

Orosco y Albares [*sic*], Manuel Tiburcio. *Oración eucarístico moral que en la solemne acción de gracias tributadas debidamente al Todopoderoso, por la rendición de los fuertes de Mescala y Cuiristarán, conocido por el de San Miguel, indulto de sus respectivas guarniciones, y juramento de obediencia y fidelidad a nuestro augusto soberano el Señor D. Fernando VII (Q.D.G.) Dijo en la Iglesia de los Reyes el 29 de diciembre de 1816 el B.D. …, Presbítero del Obispado de Valladolid. Dáse a luz a instancias y a expensas de D. José María Bargas, D. José Trinidad Salgado y D. Manuel de la Parra.* Guadalajara: Oficina de José Fructo Romero, 1817.

Orozco, José María Cayetano. *Sermón de Honras de los Venerables Sacerdotes, predicado el día 26 de enero de 1849 en la Catedral Metropolitana de México, por el Dr. D. …, catedrático de Elocuencia y de Historia en el Seminario de Guadalajara, Examinador Sinodal del Arzobispado de México, y Diputado al Soberano Congreso General.* Mexico City: Imprenta de J. M. Lara, 1849.

———. *Sermón que en la solemne festividad de la Concepción de María dijo en la Iglesia de San Felipe Neri de esta capital, el 8 de diciembre de 1850, el Dr. D. …, Cura de Analco, suburbio de Guadalajara.* Guadalajara: Tipografía de Rodríguez, 1851.

———. *Sermón que para celebrar el misterio de la Concepción en gracia de María, predicó en el Santuario de S. Juan de los Lagos, el día 8 de diciembre de 1855, El Dr. D. …, prebendado de la Santa Iglesia Catedral de Guadalajara.* San Juan de los Lagos: Tipografía de R. Martín, 1856.

Orozco y Jiménez, Francisco, Coordinador. *Colección de documentos históricos inéditos o muy raros referentes al Arzobispado de Guadalajara*, IV, Núm. 4 (Guadalajara, 1 Oct. 1925).

Ortiz, Jesús. *Sermón que predicó en el Santuario de Guadalupe de esta Ciudad, el Señor Cura del Sagrario Lic. D. … el día 14 de diciembre de 1856, en la solemnísima función que se hace todos los años a María Sma. de Guadalupe.* Guadalajara: Tipografía de Rodríguez, 1856.

———. *Historia, progreso y estado actual en que se encuentra la Hermandad del Sagrado Viático, con el sermón predicado por el Sr. Lic. D. Jesús Ortiz Cura del Sagrario de Guadalajara el 17 de noviembre de 1850.* Guadalajara: Tipografía de Rodríguez, 1851.

Otero, Mariano. *Consideraciones sobre la situación política y social de la República Mexicana en el año 1847.* Mexico City: 1848.

———. *Discurso que en la solemnidad del 16 de septiembre de 1841 pronunció en la Ciudad de Guadalajara el Licenciado C. ….* Guadalajara: Imprenta del Gobierno, no date.

———. *Ensayo sobre el verdadero estado de la cuestión social y política que se agita en la República Mexicana.* Mexico City: No publisher, 1842.

Otra puya a los del Siglo XIX. Guadalajara: Imprenta de Dionisio Rodríguez, 1833.

Otra zurra a la tapatía por retobada y por impía. Guadalajara: Imprenta del C. Mariano Rodríguez, 1824.

Otro palo, a los Editores del Nivel. Guadalajara: Imprenta de la viuda de Romero, 1826.

Otro Polar. Una ráfaga de luz a un abismo de tinieblas. O sea, algunas observaciones sobre la junta eclesiática celebrada el 19 del corriente. Guadalajara: Imprenta del C. Urbano Sanromán, 1825.

Pacheco, José Ramón. *Cuestión del día o nuestros males y sus remedios.* Guadalajara: Ediciones del Instituto Tecnológico, 1953 (1834).

Pacheco Leal, Antonio. *Discurso que el ciudadano ... socio de la junta patriótica , pronunció ante las autoridades de la Capital el 18 de noviembre de 827* [sic]. Guadalajara: Imprenta del C. Brambila, 1827.

————. *Elogio fúnebre que pronunció el C. ..., individuo de la Junta de Artesanos de la Capital de Jalisco, en la conmemoración que la misma junta dedicó a la memoria póstuma del Exmo. Gobernador benemérito del Estado, C. Prisciliano Sánchez.* Guadalajara: Imprenta del C. Urbano Sanromán, 1828.

Paredes y Arrillaga, Mariano. *Exposición que el General D. ... hace a sus conciudadanos, en manifestación de su conducta política, militar y económica en la presente revolución.* Mexico City: Impreso por I. Cumplido, 1841.

Patriótica iniciativa que la Exma. Asamblea Departamental de Jalisco eleva a las Augustas Cámaras, y otros documentos de la misma importancia. Guadalajara: Imprenta del Gobierno, 1844.

Pérez Cuyado, Norberto. *Disertación sobre la naturaleza y límites de la autoridad eclesiástica: que llevó el premio ofrecido por el Congreso Constituyente del Estado de Méjico en decreto de 27 de julio del presente año. Escrita por ....* Mexico City, reprinted in Guadalajara: Oficina del C. Urbano Sanromán, 1825.

Pío VI. *Dos Breves de N S P El Señor ..., reprobando la herética Constitución Civil del Clero de Francia....* Guadalajara: Imprenta a cargo del C. José O. Santos, 1828.

La Polar embarazada, o visita de Leonor a Madama Polar. Guadalajara: Oficina del C. Mariano Rodríguez, 1825.

Preguntas Sueltas, *Las pascuas a los canónigos.* Guadalajara, reprinted in Mexico City: Oficina del finado Ontiveros, 1826.

Préstamos, contribuciones y exacciones de la Iglesia de Guadalajara, Conducta que ha observado el Illmo. Sr. Obispo, Venerable Cabildo y Clero de la Diócesis sobre estos puntos, consignada en las contestaciones habidas entre el Superior Gobierno de la Nación y del Estado, y el Eclesiástico de la misma Diócesis. Guadalajara: Imprenta de Manuel Brambila, 1847.

Primo de Rivera, Mariano. *Defensa del Venerable Cabildo Eclesiástico de Guadalajara, contra el informe que ha hecho en ofensa suya la junta directiva de diezmos y el gobierno civil de Jalisco.* Mexico City: Imprenta del Águila, 1827.

Pronta y oportuna respuesta al papel titulado "Hereje a la tapatía porque no fía." Guadalajara: Imprenta del C. Mariano Rodríguez, 1824.

Protestas de los Illmos. Señores Obispos de Durango y Oaxaca. Guadalajara: Oficina de Dionisio Rodríguez, 1847 (reprint).

Proyecto de ley adicional a la orgánica de Hacienda, presentada por la Comisión del mismo ramo al Congreso Constitucional del Estado Libre de Jalisco. De cuya orden se imprime. Guadalajara: Imprenta del C. Urbano Sanromán, 1828.

Quintanar, Luis. *Manifiesto del Capitán General a los Habitantes del Estado Libre de Xalisco.* Guadalajara: Imprenta del C. Mariano Rodríguez, ca. 1823.

R.P. *Peor me la esperaba yo.* Guadalajara: Imprenta de Sanromán, ca. 1823.

Ramírez y Torres, José Miguel. *Contestación al discurso del Señor Huerta. Pronunciado (según se dice en Guadalajara) en la sesión secreta del 15 de mayo del presente año de 1827.* Guadalajara: Imprenta del C. Mariano Rodríguez, ca. 1827.

————. *Elogio fúnebre que en las solemnes exequias celebradas de orden de S.M. El Señor Don Fernando VII, Rey de España y de las Indias por el alma de su augusta madre, la Señora Doña María Luisa de Borbón dijo en la Santa Iglesia Catedral de Guadalajara en la Nueva Galicia el día 14 de enero de 1820. El Doctor Don ..., Racionero de la misma Iglesia.* Guadalajara: Imprenta de la Viuda y Herederos de Don José Romero, ca. 1820.

————. *Voto particular que sobre el punto de Patronato Eclesiástico presentó al Soberano Congreso Constituyente de la Federación Mexicana el Señor Diputado D. ...,* individuo de la comisión encargada de aquel asunto. Mexico City, by order of the Sovereign Congress: Imprenta del Supremo Congreso en Palacio, 1824; reprinted in Guadalajara: Oficina del C. Mariano Rodríguez, 1827.

Reflecciones [sic] sobre el dictamen de las comisiones eclesiástica y de relaciones, acerca de las instrucciones al enviado a Roma. Mexico City, reprinted in Guadalajara: Oficina del C. Mariano Rodríguez, 1826.

Rentas eclesiásticas. Contestación a los números 88 y 89 del Fénix. Guadalajara: Imprenta de Rodríguez, a cargo de Trinidad Buitrón, 1833.

Representación de la sociedad de artesanos y comerciantes dirigida al Soberano Congreso de la Unión. Guadalajara: Imprenta de Gobierno en Palacio, 1828.

Representación de la sociedad de artesanos y comerciantes, dirigida al Soberano Congreso de la Unión y otra de la misma sociedad al Honorable Congreso del Estado. Guadalajara: Imprenta de Gobierno, ca. 1828.

Representación de los señores curas y venerable clero secular y regular residentes en Guadalajara, al E. Sr. Sr. Presidente de la República Mexicana D. José Antonio López de Santa Ana [sic]. Guadalajara: Imprenta de Dionisio Rodríguez, 1833.

Representación del V. Cabildo de Guadalajara al Exmo. Sr. Presidente de los Estados Unidos Mexicanos. Guadalajara: Imprenta de Dionisio Rodríguez, 1833.

Representación elevada al Honorable Congreso del Estado de Jalisco por el Cabildo Eclesiástico con el fin de hacer revocar el Decreto número 77, y Dictamen que abrió su Comisión Especial sobre este asunto. Se publica de orden del mismo Congreso. Guadalajara: Imprenta del C. Sanromán, 1827.

Representación que hacen los vecinos de la Ciudad de Guadalajara, al Supremo Gobierno de la Unión por medio de una junta nombrada por el Gobierno del Estado, para la designación de cuotas, pidiendo se le disminuya a éste una parte considerable de los 123,450 pesos que se fue impuesta por el decreto de 19 de junio del corriente año. Guadalajara: Imprenta del Gobierno del Estado, a cargo de J. Santos Orosco, 1847.

Reseña de la solemne fiesta en la cual renovó el comercio de Guadalajara, a 24 de abril de 1898 la Jura del Patronato especial de Nuestra Señora de Guadalupe, que había hecho el mismo comercio en 11 de diciembre de 1758; y sermón predicado por el Sr. Canónigo Magistral Dr. Don Luis Silva, con motivo de esta renovación. Guadalajara, 1898.

Respuestas de un jalisciense al preguntón zacatecano. Guadalajara: Imprenta del C. Manuel Brambila, 1831.

Río de la Loza, Agustín Joseph Mariano. *Continuo espiritual holocausto latreútico, propiciatorio, eucarístico e impetratorio, cuya oblación, consagración y sumpción desde la mañana del 19 de octubre de 1796 celebra Sor María Francisca de Señor San Joseph, en el siglo Pérez y Leal, en el Convento de Religiosas Dominicas de Santa María de Gracia, con la vocación, entrada y solemne profesión, en que es hostia y juntamente ministro, al modo del incruento sacrificio del altar. Discurso del Doctor Don ..., Canónigo Magistral de la Santa Iglesia Matriz de Guadalajara, Nuevo Reino de Galicia, cuyos pensamientos estampa el padre natural de dicha niña D. Joseph Narciso Pérez Calleros, Notario del Santo Oficio y mayor del Gobierno de este Obispado, en obsequio del Patriarca Señor San Joseph, su antiguo Patrono y Protector.* Guadalajara: Oficina de Don Mariano Valdéz Téllez Girón, 1798.

————. *La más clara idea del más obscuro misterio, la sagrada eucaristía.* *Sermón panegírico que el domingo 14 de junio de 1789, dentro de la octava de corpus, predicó en la Santa Iglesia Catedral de la Ciudad de Guadalajara, Nuevo Reino de Galicia, El Sr. Dr. D. … a expensas del Lic. Don Gerónimo Miguel Pulgar y Segura, Abogado de las Reales Audiencias de estos Reinos, Agente Fiscal Interino de lo Civil en esta Cancillería, Defensor del Juzgado General de Bienes de Difuntos y de Temporalidades, que fue, Regidor perpetuo de esta Nobilísima Ciudad, quien lo dedica a la nación de los americanos.* Mexico City: Don Felipe Zúñiga y Ontiveros, 1789.

Rodríguez de San Miguel, Juan. *Discurso pronunciado en [sic] 14 de noviembre de 1842 por el Sr. Diputado … contra el proyecto de Constitución en su discusión general. Tomado del Siglo Diez y Nueve Núm. 410.* Guadalajara: Imprenta del Gobierno, 1842.

Román y Bugarín, Juan Bautista José. *Oración panegírica de Nuestra Señora de Guadalupe, que en desempeño de la orden que le impuso el Illmo. Sr. Dr. D. Juan Cruz Ruiz de Cabañas, dignísimo Obispo de esta Diócesis de Guadalajara, predicó en su Santuario el día 12 de diciembre del año de 1806, el Doctor ….* Guadalajara: Tipografía de Rodríguez, 1852.

————. *Oración panegírica de Nuestra Señora del Refugio, que en desempeño de la orden que le impuso el Illmo. Sr. Dr. D. Juan Cruz Ruiz de Cabañas, dignísimo Obispo de esta Diócesis de Guadalajara, predicó en la Iglesia del Seminario Clerical, en el día cuatro de julio del año de 1807, el Doctor ….* Guadalajara: Tipografía de Rodríguez, 1852.

Romero, José Antonio. *Informe dirigido por el Gobierno del Estado de Jalisco al Exmo. Sr. Presidente, a consecuencia de la circular mandada por el Ministerio de Relaciones al mismo, en [sic] 20 de agosto del presente año.* Guadalajara: Imprenta del Gobierno a cargo de D. Nicolás España, 1834.

————. *Informe sobre el estado actual de la administración pública del Estado de Jalisco, leído por el Exmo. Sr. Gobernador del mismo, D. …, ante la Honorable Asamblea Legislativa en la apertura de sus sesiones ordinarias el día 1º de febrero de 1835.* Guadalajara: Imprenta del Gobierno a cargo de D. Nicolás España, 1835.

Rosa, Luis de la. *Elogio fúnebre dedicado a la memoria del ciudadano Prisciliano Sánchez, pronunciado la noche del 8 del [sic] enero en la Sociedad Patriótica de Aguascalientes, por el Vice-presidente de ella c. Lic. ….* Mexico City: Imprenta del Aguila, 1827.

————. Ministerio de Justicia y Negocios Eclesiásticos, "Excitativa a que el clero de la República ayude con los gastos de la guerra con los Estados Unidos." No publisher, 19 May 1847.

————. *La política de los Editores del Tiempo analizada ante la nación.* Guadalajara: J. Manuel Brambila, 1846.

Un Sacerdote secular. *Observaciones sobre la Bula de su Santidad el Señor Gregorio XVI, relativa a reformas de regulares en México.* Mexico City: Imprenta de Galván a cargo de Mariano Arévalo, 1831.

El Sacristán. *La mala fe descubierta, y herida con sus propias armas.* Guadalajara: Imprenta del C. Mariano Rodríguez, 1824.

San Juan Crisóstomo, Manuel de. *Sermón que el día 26 de diciembre de 1842 predicó en la Santa Iglesia Catedral de Guadalajara, en la función de Acción de Gracias con que el Gobierno del Departamento celebró los últimos sucesos de la Capital de la República, Fr. …. Publícase de orden del Exmo. Sr. Don Mariano Paredes y Arrillaga.* Guadalajara: Imprenta del Gobierno, ca. 1842.

San Martín, José de, *Sermón que en la Santa Iglesia Catedral de Guadalajara predicó el Ciudadano Doctor Don ... el día 23 de junio de 1821, en que se solemnizó el juramento de la gloriosa Independencia americana bajo los auspicios del Ejército de las Tres Garantías.* Guadalajara: Oficina de Don Mariano Rodríguez, 1821.

Sánchez [Sanches], Prisciliano. *Memoria sobre el estado actual de la administración pública del Estado de Jalisco en todos los ramos de su comprensión. Leída por el Exmo. Gobernador del mismo ante la Honorable Asamblea Legislativa en la apertura de sus sesiones ordinarias el día 1 de febrero de 1826.* Guadalajara: Imprenta del C. Urbano Sanromán, ca. 1826.

———. *El Pacto Federal de Anáhuac.* Guadalajara: Oficina del C. Mariano Rodríguez, ca. 1823 (reprint).

Sánchez Hidalgo, Sabás. *Oración cívica, en la celebración del aniversario del 16 de septiembre, leída por el ciudadano ... en la plaza principal de Guadalajara.* Guadalajara: Imprenta del Gobierno, 1846.

Sánchez Reza, José Domingo. *Elogio fúnebre del Exmo. e Illmo. Sr. Doctor D. Juan Cruz Ruiz de Cabañas y Crespo. Dignísimo Obispo de esta diócesis que en sus solemnes exéquias celebradas en esta Santa Iglesia Catedral pronunció el Doctor D. ..., Prebendado de la misma, el día 20 de mayo de 1825, en Exequias que por muerte del Excmo. e Ilmo. Señor Dr. D. Juan Cruz Ruiz de Cabañas y Crespo se celebraron en la Santa Iglesia Catedral de Guadalajara y Elogios Fúnebres que se dijeron en ellas.* Guadalajara: Imprenta del C. Mariano Rodríguez, 1825.

———. *Elogio fúnebre del muy excelso y poderoso Señor Don Carlos IIII [sic] Rey de España y de las Américas que en sus solemnes exequias celebradas en la Santa Iglesia Catedral de Guadalajara pronunció el Doctor Don ..., prebendado de la misma el día 15 de enero de 1820.* Guadalajara: Imprenta de la Viuda y Herederos de Don José Romero, ca. 1820.

Santa María, Nicolás de. *Sermón que predicaba en la Santa Iglesia Catedral el Padre Carmelita Fr. .... Guadalajara, mayo 16 de 1822.* Guadalajara: Imprenta de D. Urbano Sanromán, ca. 1822.

Segunda exposición del Gobierno Eclesiástico de Guadalajara, al Supremo del Estado, sobre la ley de fincas pertenecientes a manos muertas. Guadalajara: Imprenta a cargo de Teodosio Cruz Aedo, 24 March 1834.

Segundo azote a los embusteros: sea reimpresión del grito de la verdad, corregido de las erratas que sacó en la primera edición. (A pilón y fiado.). Guadalajara: Imprenta a cargo de Teodosio Cruz Aedo, 14 May 1834.

Semería, Francisco. *Contra Palanca, Palanca, Haber [sic] cual levanta más, o sea adición a la Palanca núm. 15.* Guadalajara: Imprenta de la viuda de Romero, 1826.

Sentimientos de un Polar. Guadalajara: Oficina de D. Ignacio Brambila, 1823.

Si los cristianos se van tantos hereges [sic] qué harán. O sea ligera manifestación de los insufribles males que aflige a la nación mexicana como preciso resultado de la libertad y franquicia de comercio concedido a los estranjeros. Guadalajara, reprinted in Mexico City: Oficina del C. Núñez, 1828.

Sobre la cuestión del día. Guadalajara: Imprenta de la viuda de Romero, 1824.

Solís, Diego. *Específico y único remedio de la pobreza del Imperio Mexicano. Primera Parte.* Guadalajara: Oficina de D. Urbano Sanromán, 1822.

Spes in Livo, *Llegó de Roma la bula más escandalosa y nula.* Mexico City, reprinted in Guadalajara: Oficina del C. Urbano Sanromán, 1826.

Tepehuage. *Quien mal pleito tiene a boruca lo mete.* Guadalajara: Oficina del C. Mariano Rodríguez, 1825.

———. *Respuesta de Tepehuage al Sr. de la media palabra.* Guadalajara: Imprenta del C. Mariano Rodríguez, 1825.

Tertulia en una aldea de Jalisco entre el cura, que lleva la voz, el Alcalde, D. Blas y D. Diego. Mexico City: Imprenta del Aguila, 1826.

Tierna despedida y acción de gracias del devoto jalisciense a María Santísima de Zapopan al volverse a su Santuario. Guadalajara: Imprenta de Dionisio Rodríguez, 1833.

Tierno recibimiento del pueblo de Guadalajara a su amorosa Madre María Santísima de Zapopan, en el feliz día de su llegada a esta capital. Guadalajara: Imprenta de Rodríguez, 1839.

El Tirador. *Respuesta del Tirador a su chusco anotador. Carta segunda.* Guadalajara: Imprenta a cargo de Teodosio Cruz Aedo, 1834.

Triunfo del sansculotismo, debido a los rastreros y viles medios con que intenta fascinar al caudillo de los mexicanos. Guadalajara: Imprenta del Gobierno, 1835.

Ultimas comunicaciones habidas entre los electores del Departamento de Jalisco. Guadalajara: Imprenta de Manuel Brambila, 1845.

Ultraje a las Autoridades por los Canónigos de Guadalajara. Segunda Edición. Guadalajara, reprinted in Mexico City: Oficina de Mariano Ontiveros, ca. 1825.

Uría, José Simeón de. *Oración fúnebre que en las solemnes exequias de la reina nuestra señora Doña María Isabel Francisca de Braganza y Borbón, dijo en la Santa Iglesia Catedral de Guadalajara de Indias el Dr. Don …, del Consejo de S.M., Canónigo Penitenciario de la misma Iglesia, e Inquisidor Honorario del Santo Tribunal de la Inquisición de México en 11 de octubre del año de 1819.* Guadalajara: Imprenta de la Viuda y Herederos de Don José Romero, ca. 1819.

El Verdadero defensor de nuestra constitución *¡Atención! Que los apóstatas quieren variar nuestra religión.* Mexico City, reprinted in Guadalajara: Oficinas de los CC. Alejandro Valdés y Mariano Rodríguez, 1825.

Verdades amargas para los Editores del Nivel. Guadalajara: Imprenta de la viuda de Romero, 1825.

La Verdad desfigurada. Guadalajara: Imprenta del C. Mariano Rodríguez, 1825.

Veremundo, Fr., Archbishop of Valencia. *Representación del Arzobispo de Valencia a las Cortes. En que se tratan los puntos siguientes. Primero: Que no se puede privar del derecho de recibir diezmos y primicias a los Eclesiásticos, y que éstos pueden tener cualesquiera bienes espiritualizados. Segundo: Que la inmunidad eclesiástica es de derecho divino. Tercero: Que la disciplina eclesiástica aún en lo exterior sólo la suprema Cabeza de la Iglesia la puede variar. Cuarto: Que las religiones monacales son útiles a la Iglesia y Sociedad.* Guadalajara: Oficina del C. Mariano Rodríguez, 1824 [reprint].

La Voluntad nacional. ¡Viva la Religión! Compendio crítico histórico de la llamada ley de ocupación de bienes eclesiásticos. Guadalajara: Imprenta de Minerva a cargo de M. R. Toledo, ca. 1847 [reprint].

Voto del M.I. Ayuntamiento de Guadalajara, sobre la forma de gobierno que debe adoptar la nación. Guadalajara: Imprenta del Gobierno, 7 Sep. 1846.

3. Printed Secondary Sources

Alamán, Lucas. *Historia de Méjico.* 5 vols. Mexico: Editorial Jus, 1942.

Anderson, Benedict. *Imagined Communities: Reflections on the Origin and Spread of Nationalism.* New York:Verso, 2000 (1991).

Annino,Antonio. "Soberanías en lucha." In Antonio Annino, L. Castro Leiva, and F.-X. Guerra (ed.), *De los imperios a las naciones: Iberoamérica.* Zaragoza: iberCaja, 1994, 229–53.

———. "Cádiz y la revolución territorial de los pueblos mexicanos 1812–1821." In Antonio Annino (ed.), *Historia de las elecciones en Iberoamérica, siglo XIX. De la formación del espacio político nacional.* Buenos Aires: Fondo de Cultura Económica, 1995, 177–226.

———. "Otras naciones: sincretismo político en el México decimonónico." In François-Xavier Guerra and Mónica Quijada (ed.), *Imaginar la Nación, Cuadernos de Historia Latinoamericana* (Münster: Lit) 2 (1994): 216–55.

———. "Ciudadanía 'versus' gobernabilidad republicana en México. Los orígenes de un dilema." In Hilda Sabato (ed.), *Ciudadanía política y formación de las naciones. Perspectivas históricas de América Latina.* Mexico City: El Colegio de México, Fideicomiso Historia de las Américas, and Fondo de Cultura Económica, 1999, 62–93.

Archer, Christon I. "Politicization of the Army of New Spain during the War of Independence, 1810–1821." In Jaime E. Rodríguez O. (ed.), *The Origins of Mexican National Politics, 1808–1847.* Wilmington, Delaware: Scholarly Resources, 1997, 11–37.

Artz, Frederick B. *Reaction and Revolution 1814–1832.* New York: Harper Torchbooks, 1963.

Assadourian, Carlos Sempat, et al. *Modos de producción en América Latina.* Mexico City: Cuadernos de Pasado y Presente, 1973.

Bailyn, Bernard (ed.). *Pamphlets of the American Revolution 1750–1776,* vol 1. Cambridge, Mass.: Harvard University Press, 1965.

Bakewell, Peter. *Silver Mining and Society in Colonial Mexico: Zacatecas, 1546–1700.* New York: Cambridge University Press, 1971.

Barcala Muñoz,Andrés. *Censuras Inquisitoriales a las obras de P.Tamburini y al Sínodo de Pistoya.* Madrid: Centro de Estudios Históricos, 1985.

Bauer,A. J. (ed.). *La Iglesia en la economía de América Latina, siglos XVI al XIX.* Mexico City: INAH, 1986.

Baum, Dale. "Retórica y realidad en el México decimonónico: ensayo de interpretación de su historia política." *Historia Mexicana* 27, no. 1 (1977): 79–102.

Baumer, Franklin L. *El pensamiento europeo moderno, continuidad y cambio en las ideas, 1600–1950.* Mexico City: Fondo de Cultura Económica, 1985.

Bazant, Jan. *Alienation of Church Wealth in Mexico: Social and Economic Aspects of the Liberal Revolution 1856–1875.* Cambridge: Cambridge University Press, 1971.

———. *A Concise History of Mexico.* New York: Cambridge University Press, 1977.

Beezley,William, Cheryl English Martin, and William French (ed.). *Rituals of Rule, Rituals of Resistance: Public Celebrations and Popular Culture in Mexico.* Wilmington, Del.: SR Books, 1994.

Bell,Aubrey F. G. *El Renacimiento español.* Zaragoza: Ebro, 1944.

Bénichou, Paul. *La coronación del escritor 1750–1830. Ensayo sobre el advenimiento de un poder espiritual laico en la Francia moderna.* Mexico City: Fondo de Cultura Económica, 1981.

Benson, Nettie Lee. *La diputación provincial y el federalismo mexicano.* Mexico City: El Colegio de México, 1955.

Berthe, Jean–Pierre. "Introducción a la historia de Guadalajara y su región." In Jean Piel, et al. *Regiones y ciudades en América Latina.* Mexico City: Colección SepSetentas, 1973, 130–47.

Bethell, Leslie (ed.). *The Cambridge History of Latin America.* 11 vols. Cambridge: Cambridge University Press, 1984–1995.

Bitar Letayf, Marcelo. *Los economistas españoles del siglo XVIII y sus ideas sobre el comercio con las Indias.* Mexico City: IMCE, 1975.

Borah, Woodrow Borah. "Discontinuity and Continuity in Mexican History." *Pacific Historical Review* 48, no. 1 (1979): 1–25.

Brading, David A. "El clero mexicano y el movimiento insurgente de 1810." *Relaciones* 2, no.5 (1981): 5–26.

———. *Los orígenes del nacionalismo mexicano.* Mexico City: Colección SepSetentas, 1973.

———. "Tridentine Catholicism and Enlightened Despotism in Bourbon Mexico." *Journal of Latin American Studies* 15 (1983): 1–22.

———. "El jansenismo español y la caída de la monarquía católica en México." In Josefina Zoraida Vázquez (ed.), *Interpretaciones del siglo XVIII mexicano. El impacto de las reformas borbónicas.* México: Nueva Imagen, 1992, 187–215.

———. *The First America, The Spanish Monarchy, Creole Patriots, and the Liberal State 1492–1867.* Cambridge: Cambridge University Press, 1993.

———. *Una Iglesia Asediada: el obispado de Michoacán, 1749–1810.* Mexico City: Fondo de Cultura Económica, 1994.

Bravo Ugarte, José. "El clero y la independencia." *Ábside* 5, no. 10 (1941): 612–30.

———. "El clero y la independencia. Factores económico e ideológico." *Ábside* 15, no. 2 (1951): 199–218.

Briseño Senosiain, Lillian (ed.). *La Independencia de México. Textos de su Historia.* 3 vols. Mexico City: SEP/Instituto de Investigaciones Dr. José María Luis Mora, 1985.

Burkholder, M. A. and D. S. Chandler. *De la impotencia a la autoridad. La corona española en América 1687–1808.* Mexico City: Fondo de Cultura Económica, 1984.

———. "Creole Appointments and the Sale of Audiencia Positions in the Spanish Empire under the Early Bourbons, 1701–1750." *Journal of Latin American Studies* 4, no. 2 (Nov. 1972): 187–206.

Burks, Richard V. "A Conception of Ideology for Historians." *Journal of the History of Ideas* 10, no. 2 (1949): 183–98.

Burns, E. Bradford. *The Poverty of Progress: Latin America in the Nineteenth Century.* Berkeley: University of California Press, 1980.

Bushnell, David and Neill Macaulay. *The Emergence of Latin America in the Nineteenth Century.* New York: Oxford University Press, 1988.

Calcott, Wilfrid Hardy. *Church and State in Mexico 1822–1857.* New York: Octagon Books, 1971.

Callahan, William J. *Church, Politics and Society in Spain 1750–1874.* Cambridge, Mass.: Harvard University Press, 1984.

———. "The Origins of the Conservative Church in Spain, 1793–1823." *European Studies Review* 1, no. 2 (April 1979): 199–223.

————. "Two Spains and Two Churches, 1760–1835." *Historical Reflections* 2, no. 2 (Winter 1976): 158–81.

Camelo, Rosa. "El cura y el alcalde mayor." In Woodrow Borah (coordinador), *El Gobierno Provincial en la Nueva España 1570–1787*. Mexico City: UNAM, 1985, 149–65.

Cardoso, Ciro (ed.). *México en el siglo XIX (1821–1910). Historia económica y de la estructura social*. Mexico City: Editorial Nueva Imagen, 1980.

Cardoso Galué, Germán. *Michoacán en el siglo de las luces*. Mexico City: El Colegio de México, 1973.

Carmagnani, Marcello. "Finanzas y Estado en México, 1820–1880." In Enrique Montalvo Ortega (ed.), *El águila bifronte. Poder y liberalismo en México*. Mexico City: INAH, 1995, 121–76.

————. "Del territorio a la región. Líneas de un proceso en la primera mitad del siglo XIX." In Alicia Hernández Chávez and Manuel Miño Grijalva (ed.), *Cincuenta Años de Historia de México*, vol. 2. Mexico City: El Colegio de México, 1991, 221–41.

Cassirer, Ernst. *La Filosofía de la Ilustración*. Mexico City: Fondo de Cultura Económica, 1972.

Castañeda García, Carmen. "La educación en Guadalajara durante la colonia, 1552–1821." Doctoral dissertation, El Colegio de México, 1974.

————. "La formación de la burguesía en Guadalajara colonial: Los licenciados, doctores y maestros graduados en la Universidad de Guadalajara entre 1792–1821." *Primer Encuentro de Investigación Jalisciense. Economía y Sociedad* (Conference Proceedings, 11–14 Aug. 1981): volume entitled Theme V. *La Cultura Regional*, Presiding Chair Manuel Rodriguez Lapuente, 1–32 [each paper paginated independently].

The Catholic Encyclopedia. New York: The Encyclopedia Press, 1913.

Chust, Manuel. *La cuestión nacional americana en las Cortes de Cádiz*. Valencia: Fundación Instituto Historia Social and IIH/Universidad Nacional Autónoma de México, 1999.

Connaughton, Brian. *España y Nueva España ante la crisis de la modernidad*. Mexico City: SEP/Fondo de Cultura Económica (Colección Sep/80), 1983.

————. "Ágape en disputa: fiesta cívica, cultura política regional y la frágil urdimbre nacional antes del Plan de Ayutla." *Historia Mexicana* 65, no. 2 (Oct.–Dec. 1995): 281–316.

————. "Conjuring the Body Politic from the 'Corpus Mysticum': The Post-independent Pursuit of Public Opinion in Mexico, 1821–1854." *The Americas* 55: 3 (1998), 459–79.

————. "A Most Delicate Balance: Representative Government, Public Opinion and Priests in Mexico, 1821–1834." *Mexican Studies/Estudios Mexicanos* 17: 1 (2001), 41–69.

————. *Dimensiones de la identidad patriótica. Religión, política y regiones en México, Siglo XIX*. Mexico City: UAM-Iztapalapa/Miguel Ángel Porrúa, 2001.

Cosío Villegas, Daniel (ed.). *Historia Moderna de México*. Mexico City: Editorial Hermes, 1955.

Costeloe, Michael P. *Church and State in Independent Mexico: A Study of the Patronage Debate 1821–1857*. London: Royal Historical Society, 1978.

————. *La primera república federal de México (1824–1835)*. Mexico City: Fondo de Cultura Económica, 1975.

————. *The Central Republic in Mexico, 1835–1846*. Cambridge: Cambridge University Press, 1993.

Crahan, Margaret E. "Spanish and American Counterpoint: Problems and Possibilities in Spanish Colonial Administrative History." In Richard Graham and Peter Smith (ed.), *New Approaches to Latin American History.* Austin: University of Texas Press, 1974, 36–70.

Cuenca Toribio, José Manuel. *Estudios sobre la iglesia española del XIX.* Madrid: Ediciones Rialp, 1973.

Churruca Peláez, Agustín, S. J. *El pensamiento insurgente de Morelos.* Mexico City: Editorial Porrúa, S.A., 1983.

Dansette, Adrien. *Religious History of Modern France.* 2 vols. New York: Herder and Herder, 1961.

Dávila Garibi, J. Ignacio. *Apuntes para la historia de la iglesia en Guadalajara,* vol. IV:1. Mexico City: Editorial Cultura, 1966.

———. *Biografía de un gran prelado,* Guadalajara: Tipografía C.M. Sainz, 1925.

Díaz y Díaz, Fernando. *Caudillos y caciques: Antonio López de Santa Anna y Juan Alvarez.* Mexico City: El Colegio de México, 1972.

Di Tella, Torcuato. "Las clases peligrosas a comienzos del siglo XIX en México." *Desarrollo Económico* 12, no. 48 (1972): 761–91.

Dorantes, Alma, et al, eds. *Inventario e índice de las Misceláneas de la Biblioteca Pública del Estado de Jalisco.* 3 vols. Guadalajara: INAH-CRO, 1978.

Duby, Georges. "Ideologies in Social History." In Jacques Le Goff and Pierre Nora (ed.), *Constructing the Past: Essays in Historical Methodology.* Cambridge: Cambridge University Press, 1985, 151–65.

Elliot, J. H. *Imperial Spain, 1469–1716.* Harmondsworth: Pelican Books, 1970.

———. "The Spanish Peninsula 1598–1648" In J. P. Cooper (ed.), *The New Cambridge Modern History,* vol. 4: *The Decline of Spain and the Thirty Years War 1609–48/49.* Cambridge: Cambridge University Press, 1970, 435–73.

Farriss, Nancy M. *Crown and Clergy in Colonial Mexico 1759–1821: The Crisis of Ecclesiastical Privilege.* London: The Athlone Press, 1968.

Feijóo, Benito Jerónimo. *Teatro crítico universal.* 3 vols. Madrid: Espasa-Calpe, 1975.

Florescano, Enrique. "El problema agrario en los últimos años del virreinato, 1820–1821." *Historia Mexicana* 20, no. 4 (1971): 477–510.

Florescano, Enrique and Isabel Gil Sánchez. "La época de las reformas borbónicas y el crecimiento económico, 1750–1808." In *Historia General de México,* vol. II. Mexico City: El Colegio de México, 1976, 183–301.

Florescano, Enrique and Isabel Gil Sánchez (ed.). *Descripciones económicas regionales de Nueva España. Provincias del Centro, Sureste y Sur, 1766–1827.* Mexico City: INAH, 1976.

Foucault, Michel. *El discurso del poder.* Oscar Terán, editor and compiler. Mexico City: Folios Ediciones, 1983.

———. *La arqueología del saber.* Mexico City: Siglo XXI, 1970.

Ganster, Paul. "Churchmen." In Louisa Schell Hoberman and Susan Migden Socolow (ed.), *Cities and Society in Colonial Latin America.* Albuquerque: University of New Mexico Press, 1986, 137–63.

García Cantú, Gastón. *El pensamiento de la reacción mexicana: Historia documental 1810–1962.* Mexico City: Empresas Editoriales, 1965.

García de Cortázar, Fernando. "La Nueva Historia de la Iglesia Contemporánea en España." In Manuel Tuñón de Lara (ed.), *Historiografía española contemporánea.* Madrid: Siglo XXI, 1980, 207–29.

Garner, Richard L. and William Taylor (ed.), *Iberian Colonies, New World Societies: Essays in Memory of Charles Gibson.* Self-published, 1986.

Gibson, Charles. *Spain in America.* New York: Harper Torchbooks, 1967.

Giménez, Gilberto. *Poder, estado y discurso: Perspectivas sociológicas y semiológicas del discurso político-jurídico.* Mexico City: UNAM, 1983.

Gómez Álvarez, Cristina. *El alto clero poblano y la revolución de Independencia, 1808–1821.* Mexico City: Facultad de Filosofía y Letras, UNAM and Benemérita Universidad Autónoma de Puebla, 1997.

Góngora, Mario. *Studies in the Colonial History of Spanish America.* London: Cambridge University Press, 1975.

González Casanova, Pablo. *El misoneísmo y la modernidad cristiana en el siglo XVIII.* Mexico City: El Colegio de México, 1948.

González y González, Luis. "El optimismo nacionalista como factor de la Independencia de México." In *Estudios de la historiografía americana.* Mexico City: El Colegio de México, 1948, 155–215.

González Navarro, Moisés. *El pensamiento político de Lucas Alamán.* Mexico City: El Colegio de México, 1952.

Green, Stanley C. *The Mexican Republic: The First Decade 1823–1832.* Pittsburgh: University of Pittsburgh Press, 1987.

Groethuysen, Bernhard. *La formación de la conciencia burguesa en Francia durante el siglo XVIII.* Mexico City: Fondo de Cultura Económica, 1981.

Guardino, Peter F. *Peasants, Politics and the Formation of Mexico's National State: Guerrero, 1800–1857.* Palo Alto: Stanford University Press, 1996.

Guedea, Virginia. *En busca de un gobierno alterno: los guadalupes de México.* Mexico City: UNAM, 1992.

Guerra, François-Xavier. *Modernidad e independencias. Ensayos sobre las revoluciones hispánicas.* Mexico City: Fondo de Cultura Económica, 1993.

———. "La independencia de México y las revoluciones hispánicas." In Antonio Annino and Raymond Buve (ed.), *El liberalismo en México, Cuadernos de Historia Latinoamericana* (Münster: Lit) 1 (1993): 15–48.

Guerra, François-Xavier and Annick Lempérière (ed.). *Los espacios públicos en Iberoamérica. Ambigüedades y problemas. Siglos XVIII y XIX.* Mexico City: Centro Francés de Estudios Mexicanos y Centroamericanos and Fondo de Cultura Económica, 1998.

Hale, Charles. *Mexican Liberalism in the Age of Mora, 1821–1853.* New Haven and London: Yale University Press, 1968.

———. "The Reconstruction of Nineteenth-Century Politics in Spanish America: A Case for the History of Ideas." *Latin American Research Review* 8, no. 2 (1973): 53–73.

———. "The War with the United States and the Crisis in Mexican Thought." *The Americas* 14, no. 2 (1957): 153–73.

———. *The Transformation of Liberalism in Late Nineteenth-Century Mexico.* Princeton: Princeton University Press, 1989.

Hamill, Hugh. *The Hidalgo Revolt: Prelude to Mexican Independence.* Westport, Connecticut: Greenwood Press Publishers, 1981.

———. "The Rector to the Rescue: Royalist Pamphleteers in the Defense of Mexico, 1808–1821." In Roderic A. Camp, Charles A. Hale and Josefina Zoraida Vázquez (ed.), *Los intelectuales y el poder en México / Intellectuals and Power in Mexico.* Mexico City: El Colegio de México and UCLA Latin American Center Publications, 1991, 49–61.

Hamnett, Brian R. "The Appropriation of Mexican Church Wealth by the Spanish Bourbon Government: The 'Consolidación de Vales Reales,' 1805–1808." *Journal of Latin American Studies* 1, no. 2 (Nov. 1969): 85–113.

————. "Obstáculos a la política agraria del despotismo ilustrado." *Historia Mexicana* 20, no. 1 (1970): 55–75.

————. *Revolución y contrarrevolución en México y el Perú. Liberalismo, realeza y separatismo 1800–1824.* Mexico City: Fondo de Cultura Económica, 1978.

————. *Roots of Insurgency: Mexican regions, 1750–1824.* Cambridge: Cambridge University Press, 1986.

Hardon, John A., S. J. *Modern Catholic Dictionary.* Garden City, New York: Doubleday, 1980.

Haring, Charles. *The Spanish Empire in America.* New York: Harbinger Books, 1963.

Hastings, Adrian. *The Construction of Nationhood: Ethnicity, Religion and Nationalism.* Cambridge: Cambridge University Press, 1997.

Hazard, Paul. *The European Mind, 1680–1715.* New York: World, 1963.

————. *European Thought in the Eighteenth Century.* Cleveland: Meridian Books, 1963.

Herr, Richard. *The Eighteenth Century Revolution in Spain.* Princeton: Princeton University Press, 1969.

Hill, Christopher. *Reformation to Industrial Revolution.* Harmondsworth: Pelican Books, 1969.

Ibarra, Ana Carolina. *El Cabildo Catedral de Antequera: Oaxaca y el movimiento insurgente.* Mexico City: El Colegio de Michoacán, 2000.

Iguíniz, Juan B. "Adiciones." *Boletín de la Biblioteca Nacional de México* 12, no. 8 (Oct. 1919–Jun. 1920): 57–76.

————. *La antigua universidad de Guadalajara.* Mexico City: UNAM, 1959.

————. "Apuntes biográficos del Dr. D. Francisco Severo Maldonado." *Anales del Museo Nacional de Arqueología, Historia y Etnología* 3, no. 11 (1911): 132–54.

————. *Catálogo Biobibliográfico de los Doctores, Licenciados y Maestros de la Antigua Universidad de Guadalajara.* Mexico City: UNAM, 1963.

————. "El Doctor Don José de Jesús Huerta." In *Anuario de la Comisión Diocesana de Historia del Arzobispado de Guadalajara.* Mexico City: Editorial Jus, 1968, 155–66.

————. "La imprenta en la Nueva Galicia 1793–1821. Apuntes Bibliográficos." *Anales del Museo Nacional de Arqueología, Historia, y Etnología* 3, no. 4 and 5 (1911): 249–336.

————. *El periodismo en Guadalajara 1809–1915.* 2 vols. Guadalajara: Universidad de Guadalajara, 1955.

Israel, Jonathan I. *Race, Class, and Politics in Colonial Mexico, 1610–1670.* London: Oxford University Press, 1975.

Jaramillo Magaña, Juvenal. *Hacia una Iglesia beligerante. La gestión episcopal de Fray Antonio de San Miguel en Michoacán, (1784–1804). Los proyectos ilustrados y las defensas canónicas* Mexico City: El Colegio de Michoacán, 1996.

Lafaye, Jacques. *Quetzalcóatl y Guadalupe: The Formation of Mexican National Consciousness 1531–1813.* Chicago: University of Chicago Press, 1976.

Laski, Harold J. *The Rise of Euopean Liberalism: An Essay in Interpretation.* London: George Allen & Unwin Ltd., 1958.

Le Goff, Jacques and Pierre Nora. *Faire de l'histoire.* 2 vols. Paris: Gallimard, 1974.

Lempérière, Annick. "¿Nación moderna o república barroca?" in François-Xavier Guerra and Mónica Quijada (ed.), *Imaginar la Nación. Cuadernos de Historia Latinoamericana* (Münster: Lit) 2 (1994): 135–77.

Lindley, Richard. *Haciendas and Economic Development: Guadalajara, México, at Independence.* Austin: University of Texas Press, 1983.

Lira, Andrés. *Comunidades indígenas frente a la Ciudad de México: Tenochtitlan y Tlatelolco, sus pueblos y barrios, 1812–1919.* Mexico City: El Colegio de Michoacán/Conacyt, 1983.

———— and Luis Muro. "El siglo de la integración," In *Historia General de México,* vol 2. Mexico City: El Colegio de México, 1976, 83–181.

Lomnitz, Claudio. *Deep Mexico, Silent Mexico: An Anthropology of Nationalism.* Minneapolis, MN: University of Minnesota Press, 2001.

López, P. Eucario. "El Cabildo de Guadalajara. 1 de mayo 1552–1 de febrero 1968. Elenco." In *Anuario de la Comisión Diocesana de Historia del Arzobispado de Guadalajara.* Mexico City: Editorial Jus, 1968, 175–218.

————. *Centenario de la Arquidiócesis de Guadalajara.* Guadalajara: Self-published, 1964.

Loweree, Daniel R. *El seminario conciliar de Guadalajara ... Apéndice.* Guadalajara: Self-published, 1964.

Lynch, John. *Spanish Colonial Administration 1782–1810.* New York: Greenwood Press, 1969.

McAlister, L. N. "Social Structure and Social Change in New Spain," *Hispanic American Historical Review* 43, no. 3 (1963): 349–70.

Mairet, Gérard. "El liberalismo: Presupuestos y Significaciones." In François Châtelet (ed.), *Historia de las Ideologías,* III. Mexico City: Premia Editora, 1981, 116–39.

————. "Pueblo y Nación." In Châtelet (ed.), *Historia,* 43–62.

Mallon, Florencia E. *Peasant and Nation: The Making of Postcolonial Mexico and Peru.* Berkeley and Los Angeles: University of California Press, 1995.

Mannheim, Karl. *Ideology and Utopia: An Introduction to the Sociology of Knowledge.* London: Routledge & Kegan Paul, 1979 [1936].

Marichal, Carlos. "La Iglesia y la crisis financiera del virreinato, 1780–1808: Apuntes sobre un tema viejo y nuevo." *Relaciones* no. 40 (1989): 103–29.

Marichal, Juan. *El secreto de España. Ensayos de historia intelectual y política.* Madrid: Santillana, S.A. Taurus, 1995.

Matute, Álvaro. *México en el siglo XIX: antología de fuentes e interpretaciones históricas.* Mexico City: UNAM, 1981.

Mayer, Arno J. *Dynamics of Counterrevolution in Europe, 1870–1956: An Analytical Framework.* New York: Harper Torchbooks, 1971.

Mazín Gómez, Oscar. *Entre dos majestades: El obispo y la iglesia del Gran Michoacán ante las reformas borbónicas, 1758–1772.* Zamora, Michoacán: El Colegio de Michoacán, 1987.

Miquel I Vergés, J. M. and Hugo Díaz-Thomé. *Escritos inéditos de Fray Servando Teresa de Mier.* Mexico: El Colegio de México, 1994.

Miranda, José. *Las ideas y las instituciones políticas mexicanas.* Mexico City: UNAM, 1978.

————. "El liberalismo español hasta mediados del siglo XIX." *Historia Mexicana* 6, no. 2 (1956): 161–99.

————. "El liberalismo mexicano y el liberalismo europeo." *Historia Mexicana* 8, no. 4 (1959): 512–23.

Morales, Francisco. *Clero y política en México (1767–1834). Algunas ideas sobre la autoridad, la independencia y la reforma eclesiástica.* Mexico City: Colección SepSetentas, 1975.

Morales, Humberto and William Fowler (ed.). *El conservadurismo mexicano en el siglo XIX (1810–1910)*. Puebla: Benemérita Universidad Autónoma de Puebla/Saint Andrews University/Secretaría de Cultura del Gobierno del Estado de Puebla, 1999.

Moreno Toscano, Alejandra, and Enrique Florescano. *El sector externo y la organización espacial y regional de México (1521–1910)*. Mexico City: Universidad Autónoma de Puebla, 1977.

Mörner, Magnus. *Estado razas y cambio social en la Hispanoamérica Colonial*. Mexico City: Colección SepSetentas, 1974.

Muriá, José María (ed.). *Historia de Jalisco*. 4 vols. Guadalajara: Gobierno de Jalisco, 1980–82.

———. *Historia de las divisiones territoriales de Jalisco*. Mexico City: INAH-CRO, 1976.

———, et al. *Lecturas Históricas de Jalisco. Antes de la Independencia*. 2 vols. Guadalajara: Gobierno de Jalisco, 1976.

Murray, Paul V. *The Catholic Church in Mexico: Historical Essays for the General Reader*. Mexico City: Editorial E.P.M., 1964.

Navarro García, Luis. *José de Gálvez y la Comandancia General de las Provincias Internas*. Sevilla: Escuela de Estudios Hispanoamericanos, 1964.

———. *Intendencias en Indias*. Sevilla: Escuela de Estudios Hispanoamericanos, 1959.

The New Catholic Encyclopedia. New York: McGraw-Hill, 1967.

Niblo Stephen R. and Laurens B. Perry. "Recent Additions to Nineteenth-Century Mexican Historiography." *Latin American Research Review* 13 (1978): 3–45.

Nisbet, Robert. *History of the Idea of Progress*. New York: Basic Books, 1980.

Noel, C. C. "Opposition to Enlightened Reform in Spain: Campomanes and the Clergy, 1765–1775." *Societas* 3, no. 1 (Winter 1973): 21–43.

———. "The Clerical Confrontation with the Enlightenment in Spain." *European Studies Review* 5, no. 2 (April 1975): 103–22.

Noriega, Alfonso. *El pensamiento conservador y el conservadurismo mexicano*. 2 vols. Mexico City: UNAM, 1972.

———. *Francisco Severo Maldonado. El precursor*. Mexico City: UNAM, 1980.

Nussbaum, Frederick L. *The Triumph of Science and Reason 1660–1685*. New York: Harper & Row, 1962.

O'Gorman, Edmundo. *Historia de las divisiones territoriales de México*. Mexico City: Editorial Porrúa, 1966.

Olveda, Jaime. *La política de Jalisco durante la primera época federal*. Guadalajara: Poderes de Jalisco, 1976.

———. *El sistema fiscal de Jalisco*. Guadalajara: Gobierno del Estado de Jalisco, 1983.

Ortiz Escamilla, Juan. *Guerra y Gobierno. Los pueblos y la independencia de México*. Seville, Spain: Universidad Internacional de Andalucía/Universidad de Sevilla/Colegio de México/Instituto Mora, 1997.

Paéz Brotchie, Luis. *Guadalajara, Jalisco, México. Su crecimiento, división y nomenclatura durante la época colonial 1542–1821*. Guadalajara: "Gráfica", 1951.

Pani, Erika. *Para mexicanizar el Segundo Imperio. El imaginario político de los imperialistas*. Mexico: El Colegio de México e Instituto Mora, 2001.

Pereyra, Carlos. *El sujeto de la historia*. Madrid: Alianza Editorial, 1984.

————. *Configuraciones: Teoría e historia*. Mexico City: Edicol, 1979.

Pérez Herrero, Pedro. "'Crecimiento' colonial vs. 'crisis' nacional en México, 1765–1854: Notas a un modelo económico explicativo." In Virginia Guedea and Jaime E. Rodríguez O. (ed.), *Cinco Siglos de Historia de México*, vol. 2. Mexico City: Instituto de Investigaciones Dr. José María Luis Mora and University of California, Irvine, 1992, 81–105.

Pérez Memen, Fernando. *El episcopado y la Independencia de México (1810–1836)*. Mexico City: Editorial Jus, 1977.

Pérez Verdía, Luis. *Biografías: Fray Antonio Alcalde y Prisciliano Sánchez*. Guadalajara: Ediciones ITG, 1952.

————. *Historia particular del estado de Jalisco*. Guadalajara, 1951.

Pérez-Marchand, Monalisa Lina. *Dos etapas ideológicas del siglo XVIII en México a través de los papeles de la Inquisición*. Mexico City: El Colegio de México, 1945.

Perry, Laurens Ballard. *Juárez and Díaz: Machine Politics in Mexico*. DeKalb: Northern Illinois University Press, 1978.

Pike, Frederick. "Spanish Origins of the Social-Political Ideology of the Catholic Church in Nineteenth-Century Spanish America." *The Americas* 29, no. 1 (1972): 1–16.

Porras Muñoz, Guillermo. *Iglesia y Estado en Nueva Viscaya (1562–1821)*. Pamplona: Universidad de Navarra, 1966.

Portantiero, Juan Carlos. *Los usos de Gramsci*. Mexico City: Folios Ediciones, 1981.

Portelli, Hughes. *Gramsci y el bloque histórico*. Mexico City: Siglo XIX, 1973.

————. *Gramsci y la cuestión religiosa: una sociología marxista de la religión*. Barcelona: Editorial Laia, 1977.

Potash, Robert A. "Historiography of Mexico since 1821." *Hispanic American Historical Review* 40, no. 3 (1960): 383–424.

Powell, T. G. "Priests and Peasants in Central Mexico: Social Conflict During La Reforma." *Hispanic American Historical Review* 57, no. 2 (1975): 296–313.

————. *El liberalismo y el campesinado en el centro de México (1850–1876)*. Mexico City: Colección SepSetentas, 1974.

Ramírez Flores, José. "El Real Consulado de Guadalajara. Notas Históricas." In R. Smith, et al. *Los consulados de comerciantes en Nueva España*. Mexico City: IMCE, 1976, 65–171.

Ravitch, Norman. *Sword and Mitre: Government and Espiscopate in France and England in the Age of Aristocracy*. La Haya: Mouton, 1966.

Rees Jones, Ricardo. *El despotismo ilustrado y los intendentes de la Nueva España*. Mexico City: UNAM, 1979.

Reyes Heroles, Jesús. *El liberalismo mexicano*. 3 vols. Mexico City: Fondo de Cultura Económica, 1974.

Ricker, Dennis Paul. "The Lower Secular Clergy of Central Mexico." Ph.D. dissertation, The University of Texas at Austin, 1982.

Rivière D'Arc, Hélène. *Guadalajara y su región*. Mexico City: Colección SepSetentas, 1973.

Robertson, William Spence. *Rise of the Spanish-American Republics as Told in the Lives of their Liberators*. New York: The Free Press, 1965.

Rodríguez Casado, Vicente. "Iglesia y Estado en el Reinado de Carlos III." *Estudios Americanos* 1, no. 1 (Sep. 1948): 5–57.

Rodríguez O., Jaime E. *The Independence of Spanish America*. Cambridge: Cambridge University Press, 1998.

Romero, José Luis. *Pensamiento Conservador (1815–1898)*. Caracas: Biblioteca Ayacucho, 1978.

San Juan Victoria, Carlos and Salvador Velázquez Ramírez. "La formación del Estado y las políticas económicas (1821–1880)." In Ciro Cardoso (ed.), *México en el siglo XIX (1821–1910). Historia Económica y de la estructura social.* Mexico City: Editorial Nueva Imagen, 1980, 65–96.

Santoscoy, Alberto. "Veinte años de beneficencia y sus efectos durante un siglo." In *Obras Completas*, I. Guadalajara: El Gobierno del Estado, 1983, 171–288.

Sarrailh, Jean. *La España ilustrada de la segunda mitad del siglo XVIII.* Madrid: Fondo de Cultura Económica, 1974.

Schmitt, Karl M. "The Clergy and the Independence of New Spain." *Hispanic American Historical Review* 34, no. 3 (1954): 289–312.

Serrano Ortega, José Antonio. "Liberalismo gaditano y milicias cívicas en Guanajuato, 1820–1836." In Brian Connaughton, Carlos Illades and Sonia Pérez Toledo (ed.), *Construcción de la legitimidad política en México en el siglo XIX,* Mexico City: El Colegio de Michoacán/Universidad Autónoma Metropolitana/Universidad Nacional Autónoma de México/El Colegio de México, 1999, 169–92.

Serrera Contreras, Ramón. "Estado económico de la Intendencia de Guadalajara a principios del siglo XIX: la Relación de José Fernando Abascal y Sousa de 1803." *Jahrbuch Für Geschichte von Staat, Wirtshaft und Gesellshaft* 11 (1974): 121–48.

———. "La región de Guadalajara en el Virreinato de la Nueva España (1760–1805): estudio de la actividad ganadera." Doctoral dissertation, Universidad de Sevilla, 1975.

Simpson, Lesley B. "México's Forgotten Century." *The Pacific Historical Review* 29 (1953): 113–21.

Sordo Cedeño, Reynaldo. *El Congreso en la primera república centralista.* Mexico City: El Colegio de México e Instituto Tecnológico Autónoma de México, 1993.

Soto, Miguel. *La conspiración monárquica en México, 1845–1846.* Mexico City: Eosa, 1988.

Staples, Ann. *La iglesia en la primera república federal mexicana (1824–1835).* Mexico City: Colección SepSetentas, 1976.

Stein, Stanley and Bárbara Stein. *La herencia colonial de América Latina.* Mexico City: Siglo XIX, 1971.

Stevens, Donald F. "Economic Fluctuations and Political Instability in Early Republican Mexico." *Journal of Interdisciplinary History* 16, no. 4 (1986): 645–65.

———. *Origins of Instability in Early Republican Mexico.* Durham: Duke University Press, 1991.

Talavera, Abraham. *Liberalismo y educación.* 2 vols. Mexico City: Colección SepSetentas, 1973.

Tanck de Estrada, Dorothy. *Pueblos de indios y educación en el México colonial, 1750–1821.* Mexico City: El Colegio de México, 1999.

Taylor, William. "Conflict and Balance in District Politics: Tecali and the Sierra Norte de Puebla in the Eighteenth Century." In Ronald Spores and Ross Hassig (ed.), *Five Centuries of Law and Politics in Central Mexico.* Nashville, Tennessee: Publications in Anthropology No. 30, 1984, 87–106.

———. "Indian Pueblos of Central Jalisco on the Eve of Independence." In Richard L. Garner and William Taylor (ed.), *Iberian Colonies, New World Societies: Essays in Memory of Charles Gibson.* Self-published, 1986, 161–83.

————. "Sacarse de pobre. El bandolerismo en la Nueva Galicia 1794–1821." *Revista Jalisco* 2, no. 1–2 (1981): 34–45.

————. "The Virgin of Guadalupe in New Spain: An Inquiry into the Social History of Marian Devotion." *American Ethnologist* 14, no. 1 (1987): 9–33.

————. *Magistrates of the Sacred: Priests and Parishioners in Eighteenth-Century Mexico.* Palo Alto: Stanford University Press, 1996.

————. *Entre el proceso global y el conocimiento local: ensayos sobre el estado, la sociedad y la cultura en el México del siglo XVIII.* Mexico City: UAM-Iztapalapa and Miguel Ángel Porrúa, forthcoming.

Thomson, Guy P. C. "Los indios y el servicio militar en el México decimonónico. ¿Leva o ciudadanía?" In Antonio Escobar (ed.), *Indio, Nación y Comunidad en el México del Siglo XIX.* Mexico City: CEMCA/CIESAS, 1993, 207–51.

———— with David G. Lafrance. *Patriotism, Politics and Popular Liberalism in Nineteenth-Century Mexico: Juan Francisco Lucas and the Puebla Sierra.* Wilmington, Delaware: Scholarly Resources, 1999.

Thurman, Michael E. *The Naval Department of San Blas: New Spain's Bastion for Alta California and Nootka, 1767 to 1798.* Glendale, California: Arthur H. Clark, 1967.

————. "The Establishment of the Naval Department of San Blas and its Initial Fleet: 1767–1770." *Hispanic American Historical Review* 43, no. 1 (1963): 65–77.

Torres Bautista, Mariano E. "De la fiesta monárquica a la fiesta cívica: el tránsito del poder en Puebla, 1821–1822." *Historia Mexicana* 65, no.2 (Oct.–Dec. 1995): 221–39.

Tutino, John. "Hacienda Social Relations in Mexico: The Chalco Region in the Era of Independence." *Hispanic American Historical Review* 15, no. 3 (1975): 496–528.

Urías, Margarita, et al. *Formación y desarrollo de la burguesía en México, Siglo XIX.* Mexico City: Siglo XXI, 1978.

Valadés, José C. *Alamán, estadista e historiador.* Mexico City: UNAM, 1977.

Vallier, Ivan. *Catholicism, Social Control and Modernization in Latin America.* Englewood Cliffs, N. J.: Prentice Hall, 1970.

Van Dijk, Teun A. *Estructuras y funciones del discurso.* Mexico City: Siglo XXI, 1980.

Van Young, Eric. "Conflict and Solidarity in Indian Village Life: The Guadalajara Region in the Late Colonial Period." *Hispanic American Historical Review* 64, no.1 (1984): 55–79.

————. *Hacienda and Market in Eighteenth-Century Mexico City: The Rural Economy of the Guadalajara Region, 1675–1820.* Berkeley: University of California Press, 1981.

————. "Recent Anglophone Scholarship on Mexico and Central America in the Age of Revolution (1750–1850)." *Hispanic American Historical Review* 65, no. 4 (1985): 725–43.

————. "Urban Markets and Hinterland: Guadalajara and Its Region in the Eighteenth Century." *Hispanic American Historical Review* 54, no. 4 (1979): 593–635.

————. *The Other Rebellion: Popular Violence, Ideology, and the Mexican Struggle for Independence, 1810–1821.* Palo Alto: Stanford University Press, 2001.

Vázquez, Josefina Zoraida (ed.). *Interpretaciones del siglo XVIII mexicano. El impacto de las reformas borbónicas.* Mexico City: Nueva Imagen, 1992.

————. *Interpretaciones de la Historia de México. La fundación del Estado mexicano, 1821–1855.* Mexico City: Nueva Imagen, 1994.

————. *Interpretaciones sobre la Independencia de México.* Mexico City: Nueva Imagen, 1997.

Velázquez, María del Carmen. "La comandancia general de las provincias internas." *Historia Mexicana* 27, no. 2 (1977): 163–76.

————. "La jurisdicción militar en la Nueva Galicia." *Historia Mexicana* 9, no. 1 (1959): 15–34.

Villaseñor Bordes, Rubén. *El mercantil consulado de Guadalajara.* Guadalajara, 1970.

Villaseñor y Villaseñor, Ramiro. *Los primeros federalistas de Jalisco 1821–1834.* Guadalajara: Gobierno de Jalisco, 1981.

Warren, Richard. "Elections and Popular Political Participation in Mexico, 1808–1836." In Vincent Peloso and Barbara A. Tenenbaum (ed.), *Liberals, Politics, and Power: State Formation in Nineteenth-Century Latin America.* Athens, GA: University of Georgia Press, 1996, 30–57.

Wiarda, Howard J. "Corporatist Theory and Ideology: A Latin American Development Paradigm." *Journal of Church and State* 20, no. 1 (1978): 29–56.

Zahino Peñafort, Luisa. *Iglesia y sociedad en México, 1755–1800. Tradición, reforma y reacciones.* Mexico City: UNAM, 1996.

Zárate Toscano, Verónica. "Tradición y modernidad: la Orden Imperial de Guadalupe. Su organización y sus rituales." *Historia Mexicana* 65, no. 2 (Oct–Dec 1995): 191–220.

Index